CLYMER®

KAWASAKI

KX250 · 1992-1998

The world's finest publisher of mechanical how-to manuals

INTERTEC PUBLISHING
P.O. Box 12901, Overland Park, Kansas 66282-2901

Copyright ©1999 Intertec Publishing

FIRST EDITION
First Printing October, 1999

Printed in U.S.A.

CLYMER and colophon are registered trademarks of Intertec Publishing.

ISBN: 0-89287-740-5

Library of Congress: 99-67422

Technical photography by Ron Wright.

Technical assistance by Clawson Motorsports, Fresno, California.

Technical illustrations by Steve Amos and Robert Caldwell.

COVER: Photographed by Mark Clifford, Mark Clifford Photography, Los Angeles, California.

Intertec Book Division

President Raymond E. Maloney
Vice President, Book Division Ted Marcus

The following books and guides are published by Intertec Publishing.

CLYMER SHOP MANUALS
Boat Motors and Drives
Motorcycles and ATVs
Snowmobiles
Personal Watercraft

ABOS/INTERTEC/CLYMER BLUE BOOKS AND TRADE-IN GUIDES
Recreational Vehicles
Outdoor Power Equipment
Agricultural Tractors
Lawn and Garden Tractors
Motorcycles and ATVs
Snowmobiles and Personal Watercraft
Boats and Motors

AIRCRAFT BLUEBOOK-PRICE DIGEST
Airplanes
Helicopters

AC-U-KWIK DIRECTORIES
The Corporate Pilot's Airport/FBO Directory
International Manager's Edition
Jet Book

I&T SHOP SERVICE MANUALS
Tractors

INTERTEC SERVICE MANUALS
Snowmobiles
Outdoor Power Equipment
Personal Watercraft
Gasoline and Diesel Engines
Recreational Vehicles
Boat Motors and Drives
Motorcycles
Lawn and Garden Tractors

CONTENTS

QUICK REFERENCE DATA

VEHICLE HISTORY

MODEL:_____ YEAR:_____

VIN NUMBER:_____

ENGINE SERIAL NUMBER:_____

CARBURETOR SERIAL NUMBER OR I.D. MARK:_____

Record the numbers here for your reference

TRANSMISSION OIL CHANGE

Transmission oil type	SE, SF or SG SAE 10W-30 or 10W-40 motor oil
Quantity	850 ml (28.7 U.S. oz., 23.9 Imp. oz.)
Drain bolt torque specification	20 N•m (14.5 ft.-lb.)

RECOMMENDED LUBRICANTS AND FUEL

Engine oil	Kawasaki 2-stroke racing oil or equivalent
Transmission oil	SE, SF or SG SAE 10W-30 or 10W-40 motor oil
Air filter	Foam air filter oil
Drive chain*	Non-tacky O-ring chain lubricant or SAE 30-50 weight engine motor oil
Brake fluid	DOT 3 or DOT 4
Steering and suspension lubricant	Multipurpose grease
Fuel	Pump gasoline with Octane rating of 90 or higher
Control cables**	Cable lube

* Use kerosene to clean O-ring drive chain.
** Do not use chain lube to clean and lubricate control cables.

FUEL/OIL PREMIX RATIO—32:1

Gasoline U.S. gal.	Oil ml	Oil U.S. oz.
1	118	4
2	237	8
3	355	12
4	473	16
5	591	20

FUEL TANK CAPACITY

	Liters	U.S. gal.	Imp. gal.
All models	8.5	2.2	1.9

SPARK PLUG TYPE AND GAP

Spark plug gap	
1992-1993	0.5-0.6 mm (0.019-0.024 in.)
1994-on	0.6-0.7 mm (0.024-0.028 in.)
Spark plug type	
1992-1993	
U.S. models	NGK R6254E-9
All other models	NGK R6252E-9
1994-1996	
U.S. models	NGK B8EVX
All other models	NGK BR8EVX
1995-on	NGK BR8EVX

CARBURETOR PILOT AIR SCREW ADJUSTMENT

Model	Initial adjustment* Turns out
1992-1993	1 1/2
1994-1997	2.0
1998	1 1/2

*See text for adjustment procedure.

COOLANT CAPACITY

Model	ml	U.S. qt.	Imp. qt.
All	1.18	1.25	1.04

DRIVE CHAIN SLACK

	mm	in.
1992-1993	50-60	2-2 3/8
1994-on	60-70	2 3/8-2 3/4

TIRE INFLATION PRESSURE

	psi (kPa)
Front and rear tire	11-14 (80-100)

CHAPTER ONE

GENERAL INFORMATION

This manual covers the Kawasaki KX250 models.

Troubleshooting, tune-up, maintenance and repair are not difficult, if you know what tools and equipment to use and what to do. Step-by-step instructions guide you through jobs ranging from simple maintenance to complete engine and suspension overhaul.

This manual can be used by anyone from a first time do-it-yourselfer to a professional mechanic. Detailed drawings and clear photographs give you all the information you need to do the work right.

Some of the procedures in this manual require the use of special tools. The resourceful mechanic can, in many cases, think of acceptable substitutes for special tools—there is always another way. This can be as simple as using a few pieces of threaded rod, washers and nuts to remove or install a bearing or fabricating a tool from scrap material. However, using a substitute for a special tool is not recommended, as it can be dangerous to you and may damage the part.

Table 1 lists model coverage with frame serial numbers.

Table 2 lists general vehicle dimensions.

Table 3 lists weight specifications.

Table 4 lists decimal and metric equivalents.

Table 5 lists conversion tables.

Table 6 lists general torque specifications.

Table 7 lists technical abbreviations.

Table 8 lists metric tap drill sizes.

Tables 1-8 are at the end of this chapter.

MANUAL ORGANIZATION

This chapter provides general information and discusses equipment and tools useful both for preventive maintenance and troubleshooting.

Chapter Two provides methods and suggestions for quick and accurate diagnosis and repair of problems. Troubleshooting procedures discuss typical symptoms and logical methods to pinpoint the trouble.

Chapter Three explains all periodic lubrication and routine maintenance necessary to keep your Kawasaki operating well. Chapter Three also includes recommended tune-up procedures, eliminating the need to constantly consult other chapters.

Subsequent chapters describe specific systems such as the engine and transmission, clutch, fuel, exhaust, electrical, cooling system, suspension, drive train, steering, brakes and body panels. Each chapter provides disassembly, repair, and assembly procedures in simple step-by-step form. If a repair is impractical for a home mechanic, it is so indicated. It is usually faster and less expensive to take such repairs to a Kawasaki dealer or competent repair shop. Specifications concerning a particular system are included at the end of the appropriate chapter.

NOTES, CAUTIONS AND WARNINGS

The terms NOTE, CAUTION and WARNING have specific meanings in this manual. A NOTE provides additional information to make a step or procedure easier or clearer. Disregarding a NOTE could cause inconvenience, but would not cause damage or personal injury.

A CAUTION emphasizes an area where equipment damage could occur. Disregarding a CAUTION could cause permanent mechanical damage; however, personal injury is unlikely.

A WARNING emphasizes an area where personal injury or even death could result from negligence. Mechanical damage may also occur. WARNINGS *are to be taken seriously*. In some cases, serious injury and death resulted from disregarding similar warnings.

SAFETY FIRST

Professional mechanics can work for years and never sustain a serious injury. If you observe a few rules of common sense and safety, you can enjoy many safe hours servicing your motorcycle. Ignoring these rules can cause you to hurt yourself or someone working nearby, or cause damage to the motorcycle.

1. *Never* use gasoline or any type of low flash point solvent to clean parts. See *Cleaning Parts* and *Handling Gasoline Safely* in this chapter for additional information on parts cleaning, gasoline use, and safety.

NOTE
Flash point is the lowest temperature at which the vapors from a combustible liquid will ignite when contacting an open flame. A low flash point solvent will ignite at a lower temperature than a high flash point solvent.

2. *Never* smoke or use a torch in the vicinity of flammable liquids, such as gasoline or cleaning solvent, in open containers.

3. If welding or brazing is required on the machine, remove the fuel tank, carburetor and rear shocks to a safe distance, at least 50 feet (15 m) away.

4. Use the proper sized wrenches to avoid damage to fasteners and injury to yourself.

5. When loosening a tight or stuck nut, be guided by what would happen if the wrench slips.

6. When replacing a fastener, make sure you use one with the same measurements and strength as the old one. Incorrect or mismatched fasteners can result in damage to the vehicle and possible personal injury. Beware of fastener kits that are filled with cheap and poorly made nuts, bolts, washers and cotter pins. Refer to *Fasteners* in this chapter for additional information.

7. Keep all hand and power tools in good condition. Wipe greasy and oily tools after using them. They are difficult to hold and can cause injury. Replace or repair worn or damaged tools.

8. Keep your work area clean and uncluttered.

9. Wear safety goggles during all operations involving drilling, grinding, using a cold chisel, using chemicals, cleaning parts, using compressed air or *anytime* you feel unsure about the safety of your eyes.

10. Make sure you are wearing the correct type of clothes for the job. Long hair should be tied up or covered by a cap so that it can't accidentally fall out where it could be quickly grabbed by a piece of moving equipment or a tool.

11. Keep an approved fire extinguisher nearby. Be sure it is rated for gasoline (Class B) and electrical (Class C) fires.

12. When drying bearings or other rotating parts with compressed air, never allow the air jet to rotate the bearing or part. The air jet is capable of rotating them at speeds far in excess of those for which they were designed. The bearing or rotating part is very likely to disintegrate and cause serious injury and damage. To prevent bearing damage when using compressed air, hold the inner bearing race by hand.

WARNING
The improper use of compressed air is very dangerous. Using compressed air to dust off your clothes, bike or workbench can propel flying particles into your eyes or skin. Never direct or blow compressed air into your skin or through any body opening (including cuts) as this can cause severe injury or death. Use compressed air carefully. Never allow children to use or play with compressed air.

13. Never work on the upper part of the bike while someone is working underneath it.

14. When putting the bike on a stand, make sure the bike is secure before walking away from it.

15. Never carry sharp tools in your pockets.

16. There is always a right and wrong way to use tools. Learn to use them the right way.

17. Do not start and run the motorcycle in a closed area. The exhaust gases contain carbon monoxide, a colorless, tasteless, poisonous gas. Carbon monoxide levels build quickly in a small closed area and can cause unconsciousness and death in a short time. When you run the motorcycle during a service procedure, always do so outside or in a service area equipped with a ventilating system.

CLEANING PARTS

Cleaning parts is one of the more tedious and difficult service jobs performed in the home garage. While there are a number of chemical cleaners and solvents available for home and shop use, most are poisonous and extremely flammable. To prevent chemical overexposure, vapor buildup, fire and serious injury, observe all manufacturer's directions and warnings while noting the following.

1. Read the entire product label before using the chemical. Observe the precautions and warnings on the label. Always know what type of chemical you are using.

2. If the chemical product must be mixed, measure the proper amount according to the directions.

3. When a warning label specifies that the product should only be used with adequate ventilation, care must be taken to prevent chemical vapors from collecting in the shop. Always work in a well-ventilated area. Use a fan or ventilation system in the work area until the vapors are gone. If you are working in a small room or garage, simply opening a door or window may not provide adequate ventilation. Remember, when you can smell the chemical, there is some vapor in the air. The stronger the smell, the stronger the vapor concentration.

4. When a product is listed as combustible, flammable or an extremely flammable liquid, the danger of fire increases as the vapor collects and builds up in the shop.

5. When a product is listed as a poison, the vapor is poisonous as well as the liquid.

6. To prevent skin exposure, wear protective gloves when cleaning parts. Select a pair of chemical resistant gloves suitable for the type of chemicals you

will be working with. Replace the gloves when they become thin, damaged, change color or start to swell.

7. Wear safety goggles when using chemicals and cleaning parts.

8. Do not use more than one type of cleaning solvent at a time.

9. If a part must be heated to remove a bearing, clean it thoroughly to remove all oil, grease and cleaner residue. Wash with soapy water and rinse with clear water.

10. Wear a respirator, if the instruction label says to do so.

11. Keep chemical products out of reach of children and pets.

12. To prevent sparks, use a nylon bristle brush when cleaning parts.

13. When using a commercial parts washer, read and follow the manufacturer's instructions for selecting the type of solvent to use. Parts washers must be equipped with a fusible link designed to melt and drop the cover in the event of fire.

14. Wash your hands and arms thoroughly after cleaning parts.

HANDLING GASOLINE SAFELY

Gasoline, a volatile flammable liquid, is one of the most dangerous items in the shop. However, because gasoline is used so often, many people forget that it is a dangerous product. Gasoline should be used only as fuel for internal-combustion engines. Never use gasoline to clean parts, tools or to wash your hands. When working on a motorcycle or any other type of gasoline engine, gasoline will always be present in the fuel tank, fuel line and carburetor. To avoid a disastrous accident when working around gasoline or on the fuel system, carefully observe the following cautions:

1. *Never* use gasoline to clean parts. See *Cleaning Parts* in this chapter for additional information on parts cleaning and safety.

2. When working on the fuel system, work outside or in a well-ventilated area.

3. Do not add fuel to the fuel tank or service the fuel system while the motorcycle is in the vicinity of open flames, sparks or where someone is smoking. Gasoline vapors are actually more dangerous than liquid gasoline. Because these vapors are heavier than air, they collect in low areas and may be ignited

by floor-height ignition sources, such as a furnace or water heater.

4. Allow the engine to cool completely before working on any fuel system component.

5. When draining the carburetor, catch the gasoline in a plastic container. Pour it into a safety approved gas can.

6. Do not store gasoline in any type of glass container. If the glass should break, a serious explosion or fire could occur.

7. Wipe up spilled gasoline immediately with dry rags. Store the rags in a metal container with a lid until they can be properly disposed of or put them outside in a safe place to dry.

8. Do not pour water onto a gasoline fire. Water spreads the fire and makes it more difficult to put out. Use a class B, BC or ABC fire extinguisher to smother the flames and put the fire out.

8. Always turn the engine off before refueling. Use a wide mouth funnel to avoid spilling gasoline onto the engine, exhaust pipe or muffler. Do not overfill the fuel tank. Leave an air space at the top of the fuel tank to prevent fuel from spilling out when installing the cap.

9. Always refuel the motorcycle with it parked outside and away from all open flames and sparks.

10. When transporting the motorcycle in another vehicle, keep it upright and with the fuel valve turned off.

11. Do not perform a spark test (as described in Chapter Two) if there is any gasoline leaking from the fuel tank, fuel line or carburetor.

SERVICE HINTS

Most of the service procedures covered are straightforward and can be performed by anyone reasonably handy with tools. It is suggested, however, that you consider your own capabilities carefully before attempting any operation involving major disassembly of the engine assembly.

Take your time and do the job right. Don't forget that a newly rebuilt engine must be broken in the same way as a new one. Refer to the *Engine Break-In* procedure listed in Chapter Four.

1. Front, as used in this manual, refers to the front of the vehicle. The front of any component is the end closest to the front of the vehicle. The left and right sides refer to the position of the parts as viewed by a rider sitting on the seat facing forward. For example, the throttle control is on the right side. These rules are simple, but confusion can cause a major inconvenience during service. See **Figure 1**.

2. Whenever servicing an engine or suspension component, secure the vehicle in a safe manner.

3. Tag all similar internal parts for location and mark all mating parts for position. Record number and thickness of any shims as they are removed. Small parts such as bolts can be identified by placing them in plastic sandwich bags. Seal and label them with masking tape.

4. Tag disconnected wires and connectors with masking tape and a marking pen.

5. Protect finished surfaces from physical damage or corrosion. Keep gasoline and other chemicals off painted surfaces.

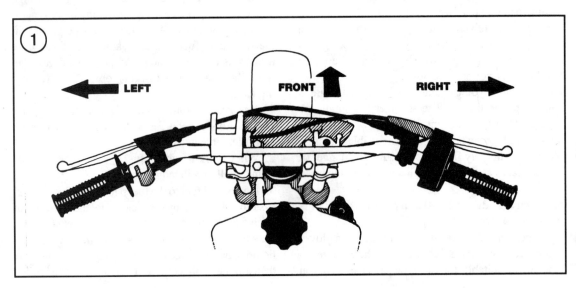

6. Use penetrating oil on frozen or tight bolts, then strike the bolt head a few times with a hammer and punch (use a screwdriver on screws). Avoid the use of heat where possible, as it can warp, melt or affect the temper of parts. Heat also ruins finishes, especially paint and plastics.

7. When a part is a press fit or requires a special tool to remove it, the necessary information or type of tool will be called out in the text. Otherwise, if a part is difficult to remove or install, find out why before proceeding.

8. To prevent small objects and abrasive dust from falling into the engine, cover all openings after exposing them.

9. Read each procedure completely while looking at the actual parts before starting a job. Make sure you thoroughly understand the procedural steps, then follow the procedure, step by step.

10. Recommendations are occasionally made to refer service or maintenance to a Kawasaki dealer or a specialist in a particular field. In these cases, the work will be done more quickly and economically than if you performed the job yourself.

11. In procedural steps, the term *replace* means to discard a defective part and replace it with a new or exchange unit. *Overhaul* means to remove, disassemble, inspect, measure, repair or replace parts as required to recondition an assembly.

12. Some operations require the use of a hydraulic press. If you do not own, or know how to operate a press, it is wiser to have these operations performed by a shop equipped for such work, rather than to try to do the job yourself with makeshift equipment that may damage your machine.

13. Repairs go much faster and easier if the motorcycle is clean before you begin work. There are many special cleaners on the market, like Bel-Ray Degreaser, for washing the engine and related parts. Follow the manufacturer's directions on the container for the best results. Clean all oily or greasy parts with cleaning solvent as you remove them.

CAUTION
Do not spray a chemical degreaser or other chemicals (except kerosene) on an O-ring drive chain. These chemicals will cause the O-rings to swell, permanently damaging the drive chain. Remove the drive chain (Chapter Eleven) before cleaning the bike.

WARNING
__Never__ use gasoline to clean parts or tools. It presents an extreme fire hazard. Be sure to work in a well-ventilated area when using cleaning solvent. Keep a fire extinguisher, rated for gasoline fires, handy in any case.

CAUTION
If you use a car wash to clean your motorcycle, don't direct the high pressure water hose at steering bearings, carburetor hoses, suspension components, wheel bearings, electrical components or the drive chain. The water will flush grease out of the bearings or damage the seals.

14. Much of the labor charge for repairs made at a dealership are for the time involved during in the removal, disassembly, assembly and reinstallation of other parts in order to reach the defective part. When possible, perform the preliminary operations yourself, then take the defective unit to the dealer for repair at considerable savings.

15. When special tools are required, make arrangements to get them before you start. It is frustrating and time-consuming to get partly into a job and then be unable to complete it. When special tools are required, they will be described (including part number) at the beginning of a procedure.

16. Make diagrams wherever similar-appearing parts are found. For instance, crankcase bolts are often not the same length. You may think you can remember where everything came from, but mistakes are costly. There is also the possibility that you may be sidetracked and not return to work for days or even weeks in which the time carefully laid out parts may become disturbed.

17. When assembling parts, be sure all shims and washers are reinstalled exactly as they came out.

18. Whenever a rotating part butts against a stationary part, look for a shim or washer. Use new gaskets if there is any doubt about the condition of the old ones. A thin coat of oil on non-pressure type gaskets may help them seal more effectively.

19. Use cold heavy grease to hold small parts in place if they tend to fall out during assembly. However, keep grease and oil away from electrical and brake components.

SERIAL NUMBERS

Kawasaki motorcycles can be identified by serial numbers stamped onto the frame and engine. Always write these numbers down and take them with you when ordering parts from a Kawasaki dealer. If a question should arise about a part number or production change with your motorcycle, these numbers will be required before the part in question can be ordered. These numbers are also useful when trying to identify a motorcycle that may have been repainted or modified in some way.

The frame number (VIN) is stamped on the right side of the front frame tube (**Figure 2**). Use this number to identify and register your Kawasaki.

The engine number is stamped on a raised pad on the right crankcase (**Figure 3**).

The frame numbers for all of the KX250 models covered in this manual are listed in **Table 1**.

WARNING LABELS

A number of warning labels have been attached to the Kawasaki motorcycles covered in this manual. These labels contain information that is important to the riders safety. Refer to the Owner's Manual for a description and location of each label. If a label is missing, order a replacement label from a Kawasaki dealership.

TORQUE SPECIFICATIONS

The materials used in the manufacturer of your Kawasaki can be subjected to uneven torque stresses if the fasteners used to hold the sub-assemblies are not installed and tightened correctly. Improper bolt tightening can cause cylinder head warpage, crankcase leaks, premature bearing and seal failure and suspension failure from loose or missing fasteners. An accurate torque wrench (described in this chapter) must be used with the torque specifications listed at the end of most chapters.

Torque specifications throughout this manual are given in Newton-meters (N•m), foot-pounds (ft.-lb.) and inch-pounds (in.-lb.).

Existing torque wrenches calibrated in meter kilograms (mkg) can be used by performing a simple conversion. All you have to do is move the decimal point one place to the right; for example, 3.5 mkg = 35 N•m. This conversion is accurate enough for mechanical work, even though the exact mathematical conversion is 3.5 mkg = 34.3 N•m.

Refer to **Table 6** for standard torque specifications for various size screws, bolts and nuts that may not be listed in the respective chapters.

FASTENERS

Fasteners (screws, bolts, nuts, studs, pins and clips) are used to secure various pieces of the engine, frame and suspension together. Proper selection and installation of fasteners are important to ensure that the motorcycle operates satisfactorily and can be serviced efficiently. Stripped, broken and missing fasteners cause excessive vibration, oil leaks and other performance and service related problems. For example, a loose or missing engine mount fastener can increase engine vibration that will eventually lead to a cracked frame tube or damaged crankcase.

Threaded Fasteners

Most of the components on your Kawasaki are held together by threaded fasteners—screws, bolts,

nuts, and studs. Most fasteners are tightened by turning clockwise (right-hand threads), although some fasteners may have left-hand threads if rotating parts can cause loosening.

Two dimensions are needed to match threaded fasteners: the number of threads in a given distance and the nominal outside diameter of the threads. Two standards are currently used in the United States to specify the dimensions of threaded fasteners, the U.S. common system and the metric system (**Figure 4**). Pay particular attention when working with un-identified fasteners; mismatching thread types can damage threads.

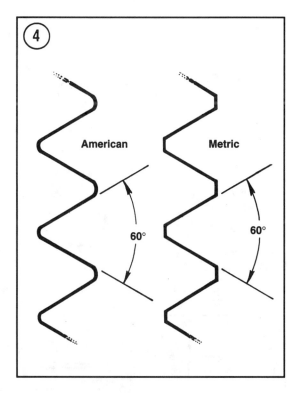

NOTE
During reassembly, start all fasteners by hand. This will help you make sure that the fastener threads are not mismatched or cross-threaded. If a fastener is hard to start or turn, stop and determine the cause before tightening with a wrench.

Metric screws and bolts are classified by length (L, **Figure 5**), nominal diameter (D) and distance between thread crests (T). A typical bolt might be identified by the numbers 8-1.25 × 130, which indicates that the bolt has a nominal diameter of 8 mm, the distance between threads crests is 1.25 mm and bolt length is 130 mm.

The strength of metric screws and bolts is indicated by numbers located on top of the screw or bolt as shown in **Figure 5**. The higher the number, the stronger the screw or bolt. Unnumbered screws and bolts are the weakest.

CAUTION
***Do not** install screws or bolts with a lower strength grade classification than installed originally by the manufacturer. Doing so may cause vehicle failure and possible injury.*

Tightening a screw or bolt increases the clamping force it exerts. The stronger the screw or bolt, the greater the clamping force. Critical torque specifications are listed in a table at the end of appropriate chapter. If not, use the torque specifications listed in **Table 6**. The Kawasaki torque specifications listed in the manual are for clean, dry threads (unless specified differently in text).

Screws and bolts are manufactured with a variety of head shapes to fit specific design requirements. Your Kawasaki is equipped with the common hex, Phillips and Allen head types.

The most common nut used is the hex nut (**Figure 6**). The hex nut is often used with a lockwasher. Self-locking nuts have a nylon insert that prevents loosening; no lockwasher is required. Wing nuts, designed for fast removal by hand, are used for convenience in non-critical locations. Nuts are sized using the same system as screws and bolts. On hex-type nuts, the distance between two opposing flats indicates the proper wrench size to use.

Self-locking screws, bolts and nuts may use a locking mechanism that uses an interference fit be-

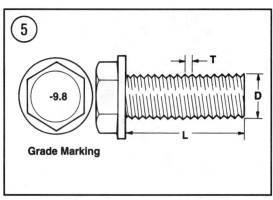

tween mating threads. Manufacturers achieve interference in various ways: by distorting threads, coating treads with dry adhesive or nylon, distorting the top of an all-metal nut, using a nylon insert in the center or at the top of a nut, etc. Self-locking fasteners offer greater holding strength and better vibration resistance than standard fasteners. For greatest safety, install new self-locking fasteners during reassembly.

Washers

There are two basic types of washers used on your Kawasaki: flat washers and lockwashers. Flat washers are simple discs with a hole to fit a screw or bolt. Lockwashers are designed to prevent a fastener from working loose. **Figure 7** shows several types of washers. Washers can be used to perform following functions:

   a. As spacers.
   b. To prevent galling or damage of the equipment by the fastener.
   c. To help distribute fastener load when tightening the fastener.
   d. As fluid seals (copper or laminated washers).

Cotter Pins

Cotter pins (**Figure 8**) secure fasteners in special locations. The threaded stud, bolt or axle must have a hole in it. Its nut or nut lock piece has castellations

around its upper edge into which the cotter pin fits to keep it from loosening.

Before installing a cotter pin, tighten the nut to the recommended torque specification. If the castellations in the nut do not align with the hole in the bolt or axle, tighten the nut until the slot and hole align. Do not loosen the nut to make alignment. Insert a *new* cotter pin through the nut and hole, then tap the head lightly to seat it. Bend one arm over the flat on the nut and the other against the top of the axle or bolt (**Figure 8**). Always carry extra cotter pins in your parts box.

Do not reuse cotter pins.

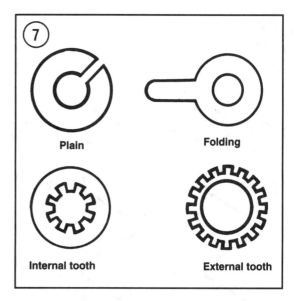

7

Plain   Folding

Internal tooth   External tooth

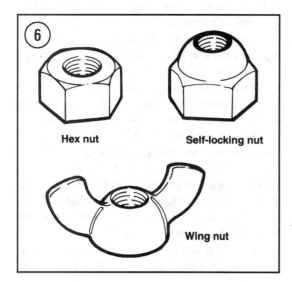

6

Hex nut   Self-locking nut

Wing nut

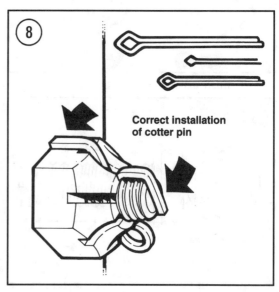

8

Correct installation
of cotter pin

Circlips (Snap Rings)

Circlips can be internal or external design (**Figure 9**). Circlips retain items on shafts (external type) or within tubes (internal type). In some applications, circlips of varying thickness are used to control the end play of assembled parts. These are often called selective circlips. Replace circlips during reassembly and installation as removal weakens and deforms them. Two other types of clips used on your Kawasaki are the plain snap ring and E-clip (**Figure 9**).

Two basic styles of circlips are available: machined and stamped circlips. Machined circlips (**Figure 10**) can be installed in either direction (shaft or housing) because both faces are machined, thus creating two sharp edges. Stamped circlips (**Figure 11**) are manufactured with one sharp edge and one

rounded edge. When installing stamped circlips in a thrust situation, the sharp edge must face away from the part producing the thrust. When installing circlips, observe the following:

    a. Remove and install circlips with circlip pliers. See *Circlip Pliers* in this chapter.

    b. Compress or expand circlips only enough to install them.

    c. After installing a circlip, make sure it seats in its groove completely.

Transmission circlips become worn with use and increase side play. For this reason, always use new circlips whenever a transmission is reassembled.

E-Clips

E-clips (**Figure 9**) are used when it is impractical or impossible to use a circlip. There are many different shapes and types of E-clips available.

Remove E-clips with a flat-blade screwdriver—pry between the shaft and E-clip. To install an E-clip, center it into its shaft groove, then tap or push it into place. Replace E-clips if they are easy to install.

Plain Snap Ring

The plain snap ring (**Figure 9**) is used to secure the piston pin in the piston. These are called piston pin clips. See *Piston* in Chapter Four. Plain clips are sometimes used to secure bearings in suspension components.

LUBRICANTS

Periodic lubrication assures long life for any type of equipment. The *type* of lubricant used is just as

⑨ RETAINING RINGS

Truarc internal snap ring

Plain snap ring

Truarc external snap ring

E-ring

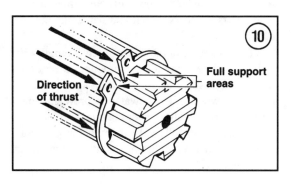

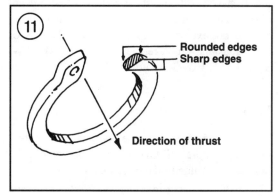

important as the lubrication service itself, although in an emergency the wrong type of lubricant is better than none at all. The following paragraphs describe the types of lubricants used most often when servicing motorcycles. Be sure to follow the manufacturer's recommendations for lubricant types.

Generally, all liquid lubricants are called oil. They may be mineral-based (including petroleum bases), natural-based (vegetable and animal bases), synthetic-based or emulsions (mixtures). Grease is an oil to which a thickening base has been added so that the end product is semi-solid. Grease is often classified by the type of thickener added; lithium soap is commonly used.

Two-Stroke Engine Oil

Two-stroke engine oil must have several special qualities to work well in your Kawasaki's engine. The oil must flow freely in cold temperatures, lubricate the engine sufficiently and burn easily during combustion. It must not leave behind excessive deposits and it must be appropriate for the high operating temperatures associated with two-stroke engines. Refer to *Engine Lubrication* in Chapter Three.

Transmission Oil

Kawasaki recommends the use of the following four-cycle engine oils that meet these oil classifications: API Service SE, SF, SG or their equivalent:

   a. SAE 10W30.
   b. SAE 10W40.

Another type of oil to consider is a two-cycle motorcycle transmission oil. These oils have the same lubricating qualities as an API SE, SF or SG oil but have additional shear additives that prevent oil break down and foaming from transmission operation. For example, the Bel-Ray Gear Saver SAE 80W transmission oil replaces SAE 30, SAE 10W-30 and SAE 10W-40 motor oils.

Grease

Greases are graded by the National Lubricating Grease Institute (NLGI). Greases are graded by number according to the consistency of the grease; these range from No. 000 to No. 6, with No. 6 being

the most solid. A typical multipurpose grease is NLGI No. 2. For specific applications, equipment manufacturers may require grease with an additive such as molybdenum disulfide (MOS2).

Antiseize Lubricant

An antiseize lubricant may be specified in some assembly applications. The antiseize lubricant prevents the formation of corrosion that may lock parts together.

SEALANT, CEMENTS AND CLEANERS

Sealants and Adhesives

Many mating surfaces of an engine require a gasket or seal between them to prevent fluids and gases from passing through the joint. At times, the gasket or seal is installed as is. However, some times a sealer is applied to enhance the sealing capability of the gasket or seal. Note, however, that a sealing compound may be added to the gasket or seal during manufacturing and adding a sealant may cause premature failure of the gasket or seal. Recommended sealants will be called out in the service procedures.

NOTE
If a new gasket leaks, check the two mating surfaces for warpage, old gasket residue or cracks. Also check to see if the new gasket was properly installed and if the assembly was tightened correctly.

RTV Sealants

One of the most common sealants is RTV (room temperature vulcanizing) sealant. This sealant hardens (cures) at room temperature over a period of several hours, which allows sufficient time to reposition parts if necessary without damaging the gaskets.

RTV sealant is available in different strengths. For example, while many RTV compounds offer excellent chemical resistance in bonding and sealing applications where oil and water is prevalent, most RTV compounds offers poor chemical resistance to gasoline. Always follow the manufacturer's recommendations when purchasing and using a particular compound.

Cements and Adhesives

A variety of cements and adhesives is available, their use is dependent on the type of materials to be sealed, and to some extent, the personal preference of the mechanic. Automotive parts stores offer cements and adhesives in a wide selection. Some points to consider when selecting cements or adhesives: the type of material being sealed (metal, rubber, plastic, etc.), the type of fluid contacting the seal (gasoline, oil, water, etc.) and whether the seal is permanent or must be broken periodically, in which case a pliable sealant might be desirable. Unless you are experienced in the selection of cements and adhesives, follow the recommendation if the text specifies a particular sealant.

Cleaners and Solvents

Cleaners and solvents are helpful in removing oil, grease and other residue when maintaining and overhauling your motorcycle. Before purchasing cleaners and solvents, consider how they will be used and disposed of, particularly if they are not water soluble. Local ordinances may require special procedures for the disposal of certain cleaners and solvents.

WARNING
Some cleaners and solvents are harmful and may be flammable. Follow any safety precautions noted on the container or in the manufacturer's literature. Use petroleum-resistant gloves to protect hands and arms from the harmful effect of cleaners and solvents.

Figure 12 shows a variety of cleaners and solvents. Cleaners designed for ignition contact cleaning are excellent for removing light oil from a part without leaving a residue. Cleaners designed to remove heavy oil and grease residues, called degreasers, contain a solvent that usually must "work" awhile. Some degreasers will wash off with water.

One of the more powerful cleaning solutions is carburetor cleaner. It is designed to dissolve the varnish that may build up in carburetor jets and orifices. A good carburetor cleaner is usually expensive and requires special disposal. Carefully read directions before purchase; do not immerse nonmetallic parts in a carburetor cleaner.

When using a degreaser, follow the manufacturer's instructions for proper cleanup and disposal.

Refer to *Cleaning Parts* in this chapter for more information.

Gasket Remover

Stubborn gaskets can present a problem during engine service as they can take a long time to remove. Consequently, there is the added problem of secondary damage occurring to the gasket mating surfaces from the incorrect use of gasket scraping tools. To remove stubborn gaskets, use a spray gasket remover. Spray gasket remover can be purchased through automotive parts houses. Follow the manufacturer's directions for use.

THREADLOCKING COMPOUND

A threadlocking compound is a fluid applied to fastener threads. After tightening the fastener, the fluid dries to a solid filler between the mating threads, thereby locking the threads in position and preventing loosening due to vibration. They are also used on threaded parts to help seal against leaks.

Before applying a threadlocking compound, clean the contacting threads with an aerosol electrical contact cleaner. Use only as much threadlocking compound as necessary, depending on the size of the fastener. Excess fluid can work its way into adjoining parts.

Thread locking compound is available in different strengths, so make sure you follow the manufacturer's recommendations when using their particular compound. Two manufacturers of threadlocking compound are ThreeBond of America and the Loctite Corporation. The following threadlocking compounds are recommended for many threadlocking requirements described in this manual:

    a. ThreeBond 1342: low strength, frequent repair for small screws and bolts.

    b. ThreeBond 1360: medium strength, high temperature.

    c. ThreeBond 1333B: medium strength, bearing and stud lock.

    d. ThreeBond 1303: high strength, frequent repair.

    e. Loctite 242 (blue): low strength, frequent repair.

    f. Loctite 271 (red): high strength, frequent repair.

There are other quality threadlock brands on the market.

BASIC HAND TOOLS

Many of the procedures in this manual can be carried out with simple hand tools and test equipment familiar to the average home mechanic. Keep your tools clean and in a tool box. Keep them organized with related tools stored together. After using a tool, wipe off dirt and grease with a clean cloth and return the tool to its correct place.

Top quality tools are essential; they are also more economical in the long run. If you are now starting to build your tool collection, avoid the advertised specials featured at some parts houses, discount stores and chain drug stores. These are usually a poor grade tool that can be sold cheaply and that is exactly what they are—*cheap*. They are usually made of inferior material, and are thick, heavy and clumsy. Their rough finish makes them difficult to clean and they usually do not last very long. If it is ever your misfortune to use such tools, you will probably find out that the wrenches do not fit the heads of bolts and nuts correctly and can round-off and damage the fastener heads.

Quality tools are made of alloy steel and are heat treated for greater strength. They are lighter and better balanced than cheap ones. Their surface is smooth, making them a pleasure to work with and easy to clean. The initial cost of good quality tools may be more, but they are cheaper in the long run. Do not try to buy everything in all sizes in the beginning; purchase a little at a time, until you have the necessary tools.

Screwdrivers

The screwdriver is a very basic tool, but if used improperly it will do more damage than good. The slot on a screw has a definite dimension and shape. A screwdriver must be selected to conform with that shape. Use a small screwdriver for small screws and a large one for large screws or the screw head will be damaged.

Two basic types of screwdriver are required: common (flat-blade) screwdrivers (**Figure 13**) and Phillips screwdrivers (**Figure 14**).

Screwdrivers are available in sets which often include an assortment of common and Phillips blades. If you buy them individually, buy at least the following:

    a. Slotted screwdriver—5/16 X 6 in. blade.

    b. Slotted screwdriver—3/8 X 12 in. blade.

    c. Phillips screwdriver—size 2 tip, 6 in. blade.

    d. Phillips screwdriver—size 3 tip, 6 and 10 in. blade.

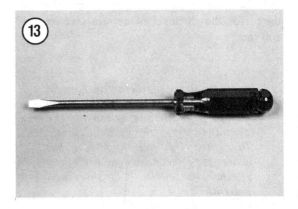

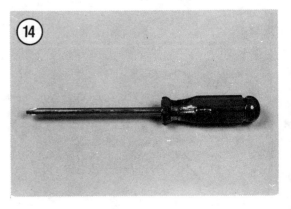

Use screwdrivers only for driving screws. Never use a screwdriver for prying or chiseling metal. Do not try to remove a Phillips or Allen head screw with a common screwdriver (unless the screw has a combination head that will accept either type); you can damage the head so that even the proper tool will be unable to remove it.

Keep screwdrivers in the proper condition and they will last longer and perform better. Always keep the tip of a common screwdriver in good condition. **Figure 15** shows how to grind the tip to the proper shape if it becomes damaged. Note the symmetrical sides of the tip.

Pliers

Pliers come in a wide range of types and sizes. Pliers are useful for cutting, bending and crimping. Do not use them to cut hardened objects or to turn bolts or nuts. **Figure 16** shows several pliers useful in motorcycle repair.

Each type of pliers has a specialized function. Slip-joint pliers are general purpose pliers and are used mainly for holding things and for bending.

Needlenose pliers are used to hold or bend small objects. Groove-joint pliers can be adjusted to hold various sizes of objects; the jaws remain parallel to grip around objects such as pipe or tubing. There are many more types of pliers. The ones described here are most suitable for vehicle repairs.

Locking Pliers

Locking pliers (**Figure 17**) are used to hold objects very tightly like a vise. Because their sharp jaws can permanently scar the objects they hold, select and use them carefully. Locking pliers are available in many types for more specific tasks.

Circlip Pliers

Circlip pliers (**Figure 18**) are special in that they are only used to remove and install circlips. When purchasing circlip pliers, there are two kinds from

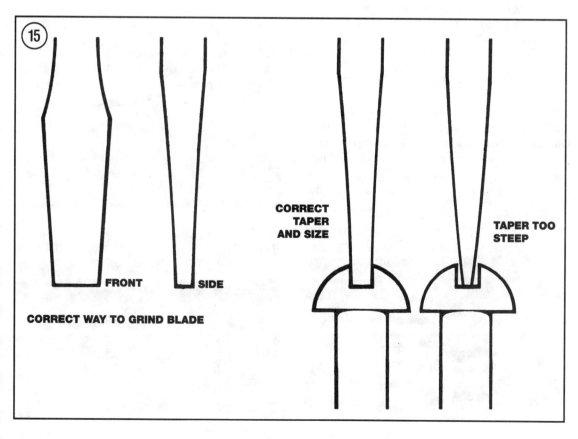

(15)

FRONT   SIDE

CORRECT WAY TO GRIND BLADE

CORRECT TAPER AND SIZE

TAPER TOO STEEP

which to distinguish. External pliers (spreading) are used to remove circlips that fit on the outside of a shaft. Internal pliers (squeezing) are used to remove circlips, which fit inside a gear or housing bore.

Circlip pliers are available where their action is fixed (either internal or external) or convertible (one tool works on both internal and external circlips).

An important part to consider when purchasing circlip pliers is the shape and length of the tips and how they are mounted on the tool. Generally fixed tip circlip pliers are available with straight and 90° tips. Pliers with replacement tips are available that include a number of tip sizes and shapes to fit a wide range of circlip sizes and applications. Pliers with both tip shapes will be required to service your Kawasaki. The straight tips work well for most engine jobs. Pliers with 90° tips will be required to remove and install the circlips used in the front and rear master cylinder bores.

For general use, select a convertible circlip plier equipped with different types of replacement tips.

WARNING
Because circlips can slip and "fly off" when removing and installing them, and broken tips can fly off, always wear safety glasses when using circlip pliers.

Box-end, Open-end and Combination Wrenches

Box-end, open-end and combination wrenches are available in sets or separately in a variety of sizes. On open and box end wrenches, the number stamped near the end refers to the distance between two parallel flats on the hex head bolt or nut. On combination wrenches, the number is stamped near the center.

Open-end wrenches (A, **Figure 19**) are speedy and work best in areas with limited overhead access. Their wide flat jaws make them unstable for situations where the bolt or nut is sunken in a well or close to the edge of a casting. These wrenches grip only two flats of a fastener, so if either the fastener head or the wrench jaws are worn, the wrench may slip off. While there are many instances where an open-end wrench can be used, use a box-end wrench or socket whenever possible, especially when loosening or tightening the fastener.

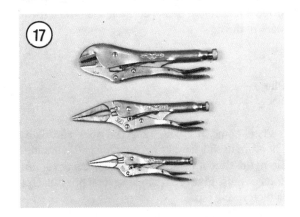

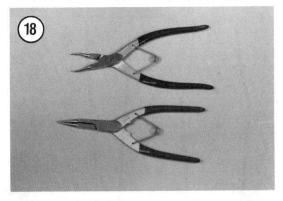

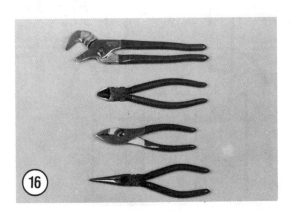

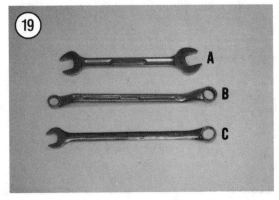

Box-end wrenches (B, **Figure 19**) require clear overhead access to the fastener but can work well in situations where the fastener head is close to another part. Box-end wrenches are available in either 6-point or 12-point openings. The 6-point gives superior holding power by gripping the fastener across all six edges for a very secure grip. However, a 6-point wrench does requires a greater swinging radius. The 12-point grips six points of a fastener and works better in situations with a limited swinging radius. While the 12-point design works well for many applications, it can slip if the fastener head is really tight, made of a weak material or has already started to round off. A 12-point wrench can also engage square fastener heads where a 6-point cannot. If you use a 12-point and it starts to slip, stop and use a 6-point wrench or socket (if possible).

Combination wrenches (C, **Figure 19**) have an open-end on one side and a box-end (either 6- or 12-point) on the other with both ends being the same size. These wrenches are favored by professionals because of their versatility.

Adjustable Wrenches

An adjustable wrench can be adjusted to fit nearly any nut or bolt head which has clear access around its entire perimeter. Adjustable wrenches (**Figure 20**) are best used as a backup wrench to keep a large nut or bolt from turning while the other end is being loosened or tightened with a proper wrench.

Adjustable wrenches have only two gripping surfaces which make them more subject to slipping off the fastener and damaging the part, also possibly injuring your hand. The fact that one jaw is adjustable only aggravates this shortcoming.

These wrenches are directional; the solid jaw must be the one transmitting the force. If you use the adjustable jaw to transmit the force, it can loosen and possibly slip off.

Adjustable wrenches come in all sizes but something in the 10 to 12 in. range is recommended as an all-purpose wrench.

Socket Wrenches

This type is undoubtedly the fastest, safest and most convenient to use. Sockets which attach to a ratchet handle (**Figure 21**) are available with 6-point or 12-point openings and different size drive openings. The drive size indicates the size of the square hole which mates with the ratchet handle (**Figure 22**).

When purchasing and using sockets, note the following:

    a. When working on your Kawasaki, use metric sockets. Individual sockets can be identified by the bolt-head sizes stamped on the side of the socket.

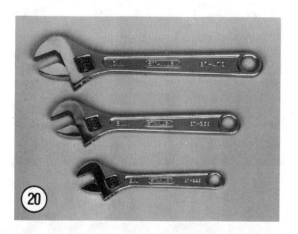

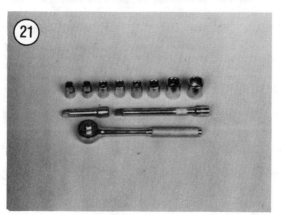

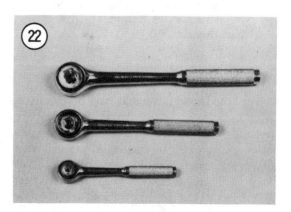

b. While you will be using metric sockets, the drive hole in the bottom of all sockets is always measured in inches: 1/4, 3/8 and 1/2 inch drive (larger drive sizes are available for industrial use). Socket adapters are available where you can use a 3/8 in. drive socket on a 1/2 in. drive ratchet (and vise versa).

c. Sockets are available with either 6- or 12-points (**Figure 23**). Point size refers to the number of points between the grooves cut inside the socket walls.

d. The 6-point socket (A, **Figure 23**) provides greater holding power and durability but requires a longer swinging radius than the 12-point socket.

e. The 12-point socket (B, **Figure 23**) needs to be moved only half as far as a 6-point socket before it is repositioned on the fastener. However, because of the larger number of points (and a smaller holding area between the points), the 12-point socket provides less holding power than a 6-point socket.

f. Sockets are available in hand sockets and impact sockets. Hand sockets can be chrome plated or have a black finish. Impact sockets generally have a black finish. Use hand sockets with ratchets and torque wrenches (hand use only). Use impact sockets when loosening or tightening fasteners with air tools and hand impact drivers. Impact sockets are made of ticker material for more durability. Compare the size and wall thickness of the regular 19 mm hand socket (A) with the corresponding 19 mm impact socket (B) in **Figure 24**.

WARNING
Do not use hand sockets with air tools and hand impact drivers as they may shatter and cause injury. Always wear eye protection when using any type of impact or air tool.

Impact Driver

The hand impact driver may have been designed with the motorcycle rider in mind. This tool makes removal of fasteners easy and eliminates damage to bolts and screw slots. Impact drivers and interchangeable bits (**Figure 25**) are available at most large hardware, motorcycle or auto parts stores. While sockets can also be used with a hand impact

driver, they must be designed for impact use. Use only impact sockets with impact drivers and air tools; see *Socket Wrenches* in this section.

WARNING
Do not use hand sockets with hand impact drivers as they may shatter and cause injury. Always wear eye protection when using any type of impact or air tool.

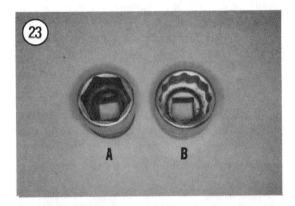

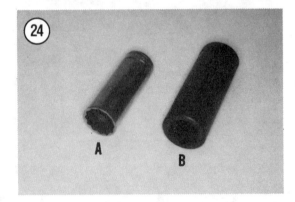

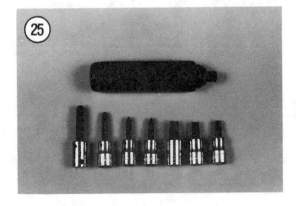

Allen Wrenches

Allen wrenches are available in sets or separately in a variety of sizes. These sets come in SAE and metric size, so be sure to buy a metric set (**Figure 26**). Allen bolts are sometimes called socket bolts.

Hammers

The correct hammer (**Figure 27**) is necessary for certain repairs. Use only a hammer with a face (or

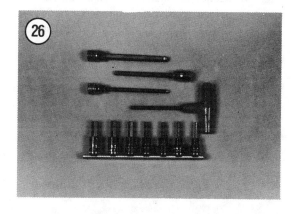

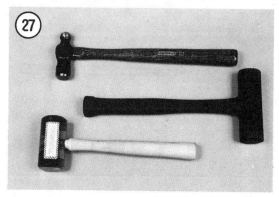

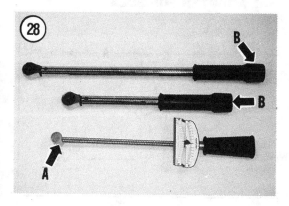

head) of rubber, plastic or the soft-faced type that is filled with buckshot. These are sometimes necessary during engine disassembly. *Never* use a metal-faced hammer on engine or suspension parts, as excessive damage will result in most cases. Ball-peen or machinist's hammers are required when striking another tool, such as a punch or impact driver. When it is necessary to strike hard against a steel part without damaging it, use a brass or lead hammer.

When using a hammer, note the following:

a. *Always* wear safety glasses.

b. Inspect hammers for a damaged or broken handle. Do *not* use a hammer with a cracked handle. Repair or replace the hammer if required.

c. The head of the hammer should always strike the object squarely. Do not use the side of the hammer or handle to strike an object.

d. Always wipe oil or grease off the hammer *before* using it.

e. Always use the correct hammer for the job.

Torque Wrench

A torque wrench is used with a socket, torque adapter or similar extension to measure how tightly a nut, bolt or other fastener is installed. They come in a wide price range and with either 1/4, 3/8 or 1/2 in. square drive. The drive size indicates the size of the square drive which mates with the socket, torque adapter or extension. Popular types are the deflecting beam (A, **Figure 28**), the dial indicator and the audible click (B, **Figure 28**) torque wrenches. As with any tools, there are advantages and disadvantages with each type of torque wrench. When choosing a torque wrench, consider its torque range, accuracy rating and price. The torque specifications listed at the end of most chapters in this manual will give you an idea on the range of torque wrench needed to service your Kawasaki.

Because the torque wrench is a precision tool, do not throw it in with other tools and expect it to remain accurate. Always store a torque wrench in its carrying case or in a padded tool box drawer. All torque wrenches require periodic recalibration. To find out more about this, read the information provided with the torque wrench or write to the manufacturer.

Torque Wrench Adapters

Torque adapters and extensions allow you to extend or reduce the reach of your torque wrench. For example, the torque adapter wrench shown in **Figure 29** can be used to extend the length of the torque wrench to tighten fasteners that cannot be reached with a torque wrench and socket. When a torque adapter lengthens or shortens the torque wrench (**Figure 29**), the torque reading on the torque wrench will not be the same amount of torque that is applied to the fastener. It is then necessary to recalibrate the torque specification to compensate for the effect of the added or reduced torque adapter length. When a torque adapter is set at a right angle on the torque wrench, relcalibration is not required (see information and figure below).

To recalculate a torque reading when using a torque adapter, it is first necessary to know the lever length of the torque wrench, the length of the adapter from the center of square drive to the center of the nut or bolt, and the actual amount of torque desired at the nut or bolt (**Figure 30**). The formula can be expressed as:

$$TW = \frac{TA \times L}{L + A}$$

TW = This is the torque setting or dial reading to set on the torque wrench when tightening the fastener.

TA = Actual torque setting. This is the torque specification listed in the service manual and will be the actual amount of torque applied to the fastener.

A = This is the lever length of the adapter from the centerline of the square drive (at the torque wrench) to the centerline of the nut or bolt. If the torque adapter extends straight from the end of the torque wrench (**Figure 31**), the center line of the torque adapter and torque wrench are the same.

However, when the centerlines of the torque adapter and torque wrench do not line up, the distance must be measured as shown in **Figure 31**. Also note in **Figure 31** that when the torque adapter is set at a right-angle to the torque wrench, no calculation is needed (the lever length of the torque wrench did not change).

L = This the lever length of your torque wrench. This specification is usually listed in the instruction manual provided with your torque wrench, or you can determine its length by measuring the distance from the center of the square drive on the torque wrench to the center of the torque wrench handle (**Figure 30**).

Example:

What should the torque wrench preset reading or dial reading be when :

TA = 20 ft.-lb.

A = 3 in.

L = 14 in.

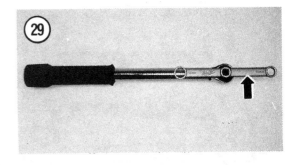

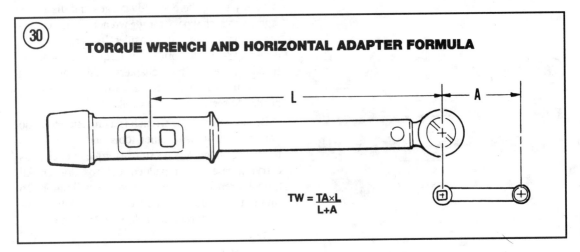

TORQUE WRENCH AND HORIZONTAL ADAPTER FORMULA

L   A

$$TW = \frac{TA \times L}{L + A}$$

$$TW = \frac{20 \times 14}{14 + 3} = \frac{280}{17} = 16.5 \text{ ft.-lb.}$$

In this example, the recalculated torque value of 16.5 ft.-lb. would be the amount of torque to set on the torque wrench. When using a dial or beam-type torque wrench, torque would be applied until the pointer aligns with the 16.5 ft.-lb. dial reading. When using a click type torque wrench, the micrometer dial would be pre-set to 16.5 ft.-lb. In all cases, even though the torque wrench dial or preset reading is

16.5 ft.-lb., the fastener will actually be tightened to 20 ft.-lb.

PRECISION MEASURING TOOLS

Measurement is an important part of motorcycle service. When performing many of the service procedures in this manual, you will be required to make a number of measurements. These include basic checks such as engine compression and spark plug

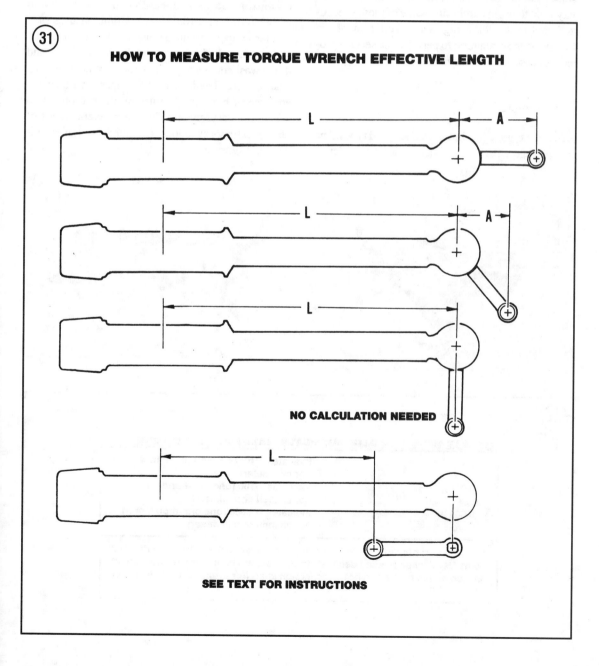

HOW TO MEASURE TORQUE WRENCH EFFECTIVE LENGTH

NO CALCULATION NEEDED

SEE TEXT FOR INSTRUCTIONS

gap. As you become more involved with engine work, measurements will be required to determine the size and condition of the piston and cylinder bore, crankshaft runout and so on. When making these measurements, the degree of accuracy dictates which tool is required. Precision measuring tools are expensive. If this is your first experience at engine or suspension service, it may be worthwhile to have the checks made at a Kawasaki dealership or machine shop. However, as your skills and enthusiasm for doing your own service work increase, you may want to begin purchasing some of these specialized tools. The following is a description of the measuring tools required to perform the service procedures described in this manual.

Feeler Gauge

Feeler gauges come in assorted sets and types. The feeler gauge is made of either a piece of a flat or round hardened steel of a specified thickness. Wire gauges (A, **Figure 32**) are used to measure spark plug gap. Flat gauges (B, **Figure 32**) are used for most other measurements.

Vernier Caliper

This tool (**Figure 33**) is invaluable when reading inside, outside and depth measurements. Although this tool is not as precise as a micrometer, it allows reasonably accurate measurements, typically to within 0.025 mm (0.001 in.). Common uses of a vernier caliper are measuring the length of clutch springs, the thickness of clutch plates, shims and thrust washers, brake pad thickness or the depth of a bearing bore. The jaws of the caliper must be clean and free of burrs at all times in order to obtain an accurate measurement. There are several types of vernier calipers available. The standard vernier caliper (A, **Figure 33**) has a highly accurate graduated

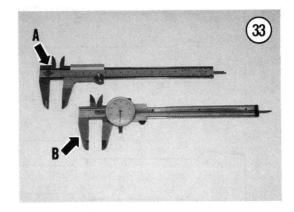

34

DECIMAL PLACE VALUES*

0.1	Indicates 1/10 (one tenth of an inch or millimeter)
0.01	Indicates 1/100 (one one-hundredth of an inch or millimeter)
0.001	Indicates 1/1,000 (one one-thousandth of an inch or millimeter)

* This chart represents the values of figures placed to the right of the decimal point. Use it when reading decimals from one-tenth to one one-thousandth of an inch or millimeter. It is not a conversion chart (for example: 0.001 in. is not equal to 0.001 mm).

scale on the handle in which the measurements must be calculated. The dial indicator caliper (B, **Figure 33**) is equipped with a small dial and needle that indicates the measurement reading, and the digital electronic type with an LCD display that shows the measurement on the small display screen. Some vernier calipers must be calibrated prior to making a measurement to ensure an accurate measurement. Refer to the manufacturer's instructions for this procedure.

Outside Micrometers

An outside micrometer is a precision tool used to accurately measure parts using the decimal divisions of the inch or meter (**Figure 34**). While there are many types and styles of micrometers, this section will describe steps on how to use the outside micrometer. The outside micrometer is the most common type of micrometer used when servicing motorcycles. It is useful in accurately measuring the outside diameter, length and thickness of parts. These parts include the piston, piston pin, crankshaft, piston rings and shims. The outside micrometer is also used to measure the dimension taken by a small hole gauge or a telescoping gauge described later in this section. After the small hole gauge or telescoping gauge has been carefully expanded to a limit within the bore of the component being meas-

ured, carefully remove the gauge and measure the distance across its arms with the outside micrometer.

Other types of micrometers include the depth micrometer and screw thread micrometer. **Figure 35** illustrates the various parts of an outside micrometer with its part names and markings identified.

Micrometer Range

A micrometer's size indicates the minimum and maximum size of a part that it can measure. The usual sizes are: 0-1 in. (0-25 mm), 1-2 in. (25-50 mm), 2-3 in. (50-75 mm) and 3-4 in (75-100 mm). These micrometers use fixed anvils.

Some micrometers use the same frame with interchangeable anvils of different lengths. This allows you to install the correct length anvil for a particular job. For example, a 0-4 in. interchangeable micrometer is equipped with four different length anvils. While purchasing one or two micrometers to cover a range from 0-4 or 0-6 inches is less expensive, its overall frame size makes it less convenient to use.

How to Read a Micrometer

When reading a micrometer, numbers are taken from different scales and then added together. The following sections describe how to read the standard inch micrometer, the vernier inch micrometer, the

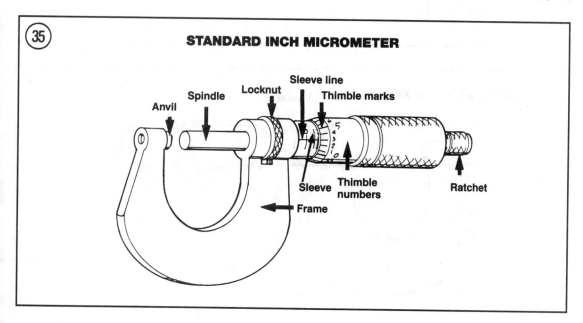

standard metric micrometer and the metric vernier micrometer.

Standard inch micrometer

The standard inch type micrometer is accurate to one-thousandth of an inch (0.001 in.). The heart of the micrometer is its spindle screw with 40 threads per inch. Every turn of the thimble will move the spindle 1/40 of an inch or 0.025 in. (to change 1/40 of an inch to a decimal: 1/40 = 0.025 in.).

Before you learn how to read a micrometer, study the markings and part names in **Figure 35**. Take your micrometer and turn the thimble until its zero mark aligns with the zero mark on the sleeve line. Now turn the thimble counterclockwise and align the next thimble mark with the sleeve line. The micrometer now reads 0.001 in. (one one-thousandth) of an inch. Each thimble mark is equal to 0.001 in. Every fifth

thimble mark is numbered to help with reading: 0, 5, 10, 15 and 20.

Reset the micrometer so that the thimble and sleeve line zero marks align. Turn the thimble counterclockwise one complete revolution and align the thimble zero mark with the first line in the sleeve line. The micrometer now reads 0.025 in. (twenty-five thousandths) of an inch. Each sleeve line represents 0.025 in.

Now turn the thimble counterclockwise while counting the sleeve line marks. Every fourth mark on the sleeve line is marked with a number ranging from 1 through 9. The last digit on the sleeve line is usually a zero (0) mark. The zero mark indicates that you have reached the end of the micrometer's measuring range. Each sleeve number represents 0.100 in. For example, the number 1 represents 0.100 in. and the number 9 represents 0.900 in.

When reading a standard inch micrometer, take the three measurements described and add them

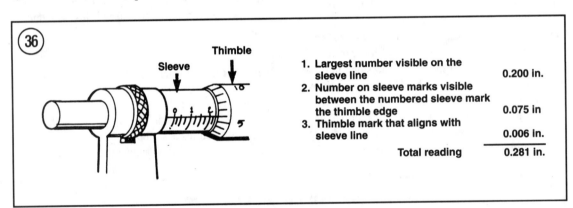

1. Largest number visible on the sleeve line		0.200 in.
2. Number on sleeve marks visible between the numbered sleeve mark the thimble edge		0.075 in
3. Thimble mark that aligns with sleeve line		0.006 in.
	Total reading	0.281 in.

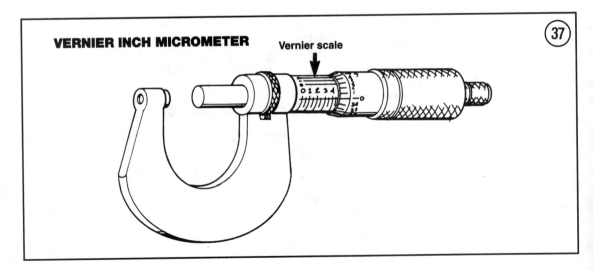

VERNIER INCH MICROMETER   Vernier scale

together. The first two readings are taken from the sleeve. The last reading is taken from the thimble. The sum of the three readings will give you the measurement in thousandths of an inch (0.001 in.).

To read a standard inch micrometer, perform the following steps while referring to the example in **Figure 36**.

1. Read the sleeve line to find the largest number visible—each sleeve number mark equals 0.100 in.

2. Count the number of sleeve marks visible between the numbered sleeve mark and the thimble edge—each sleeve mark equals 0.025 in. If there is no visible sleeve marks, continue with Step 3.

3. Read the thimble mark that aligns with the sleeve line—each thimble mark equals 0.001 in.

NOTE
If a thimble mark does not align exactly with the sleeve line but falls between two lines, estimate the decimal amount between the lines. For a more accurate reading, you must use a vernier inch micrometer.

4. Add the micrometer readings in Steps 1-3 to obtain the actual measurement.

Vernier inch micrometers

A vernier inch micrometer can accurately measure in ten-thousandths of an inch (0.0001 in.) increments. While it has the same markings as a standard micrometer, a vernier scale scribed on the sleeve (**Figure 37**) makes it unique. The vernier scale consists of eleven equally spaced lines marked 1-9 with a 0 on each end. These lines run parallel on the top of the sleeve where each line is equal to 0.0001 in. Thus the vernier scale divides a thousandth of an inch (0.001 in.) into ten-thousandths of an inch (0.0001 in.).

To read a vernier inch micrometer, perform the following steps while referring to the example in **Figure 38**.

1. Read the micrometer in the same way as the standard inch micrometer. This is your initial reading.

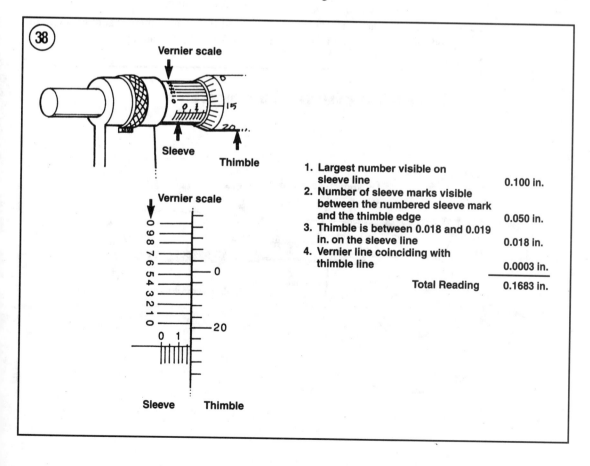

1. Largest number visible on sleeve line	0.100 in.
2. Number of sleeve marks visible between the numbered sleeve mark and the thimble edge	0.050 in.
3. Thimble is between 0.018 and 0.019 in. on the sleeve line	0.018 in.
4. Vernier line coinciding with thimble line	0.0003 in.
Total Reading	0.1683 in.

2. If a thimble mark aligns exactly with the sleeve line, reading the vernier scale is not necessary. If a thimble mark does not align exactly with the sleeve line, read the vernier scale in Step 3.

3. Read the vernier scale to find which vernier mark align with one thimble mark. The number of that vernier mark is the number of ten-thousandths of an inch to add to the initial reading taken in Step 1.

Metric micrometers

The metric micrometer is very similar to the standard inch type. The differences are the graduations on the thimble and sleeve as shown in **Figure 39**.

The standard metric micrometer is accurate of measuring one one-hundredth of a millimeter (0.01 mm). On the metric micrometer, the spindle screw is ground with a thread pitch of one-half millimeter (0.5 mm). Thus every turn of the thimble will move the spindle 0.5 mm.

The sleeve line is graduated in millimeters and half millimeters. The marks on the upper side of the sleeve line are equal to 1.00 mm. Every fifth mark above the sleeve line is marked with a number. The actual numbers will depend on the size of the mi-

crometer. For example, on a 0-25 mm micrometer, the sleeve marks are numbered 0, 5, 10, 15, 20 and 25. On a 25-50 mm micrometer, the sleeve marks are numbered 25, 30, 35, 40, 45 and 50. This numbering sequence continues with larger micrometers (50-75 and 75-100). Each mark on the lower side of the sleeve line is equal to 0.50 mm.

The thimble scale is divided into fifty graduations where one graduation is equal to 0.01 mm. Every fifth thimble graduation is numbered 0-45 to help with reading. The thimble edge is used to indicate which sleeve markings to read.

To read a metric micrometer, add the number of millimeters and half-millimeters on the sleeve line to the number of one one-hundredth millimeters on the thimble. To do so, perform the following steps while referring to the example in **Figure 40**.

1. Take the first reading by counting the number of marks visible on the upper sleeve line. Record the reading.

2. Look below the sleeve line to see if a lower mark is visible directly past the upper line mark. If so, add 0.50 to the first reading.

3. Now read the thimble mark that aligns with the sleeve line. Record this reading.

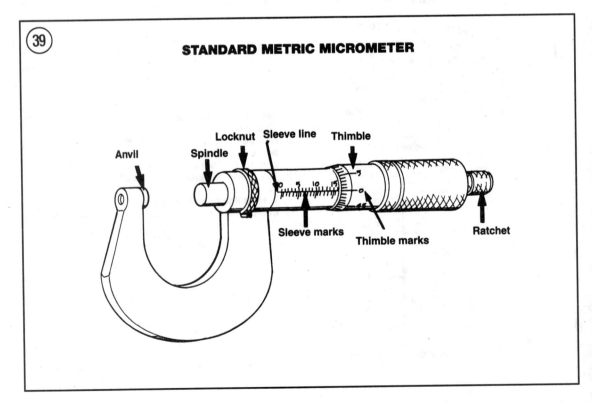

(39)

STANDARD METRIC MICROMETER

NOTE

If a thimble mark does not align exactly with the sleeve line but falls between two lines, estimate the decimal amount between the lines. For a more accurate reading, you must use a metric vernier micrometer.

4. Add the micrometer readings in Steps 1-3 to obtain the actual measurement.

Metric vernier micrometers

A metric vernier micrometer is accurate to two thousandths of a millimeter (0.002 mm). While it has the same markings as a standard metric micrometer, a vernier scale scribed on the sleeve (**Figure 41**) makes it unique. The vernier scale consists of five equally spaced lines marked 0, 2, 4, 6 and 8. These lines run parallel on the top of the sleeve where each line is equal to 0.002 mm.

To read a metric vernier micrometer, perform the following steps while referring to the example in **Figure 42**:

1. Read the micrometer in the same way as the standard metric micrometer. This is the initial reading.

2. If a thimble mark aligns exactly with the sleeve line, reading the vernier scale is not necessary. If a thimble mark does not align exactly with the sleeve line, read the vernier scale in Step 3.

3. Read the vernier scale to find which vernier mark aligns with one thimble mark. The number of that vernier mark is the number of thousandths of a millimeter to add to the initial reading taken in Step 1.

Micrometer Accuracy Check

Before using a micrometer, check its accuracy as follows:

1. Make sure the anvil and spindle faces (**Figure 35**) are clean and dry.

2. To check a 0-1 in. or 0-25 mm micrometer, perform the following:

   a. Turn the thimble until the spindle contacts the anvil. If the micrometer has a ratchet stop, use it to ensure that the proper amount of pressure is applied against the contact surfaces.

   b. Read the micrometer. If the adjustment is correct, the 0 mark on the thimble will align exactly with the 0 mark on the sleeve line. If the 0 marks do not align, the micrometer is out of adjustment

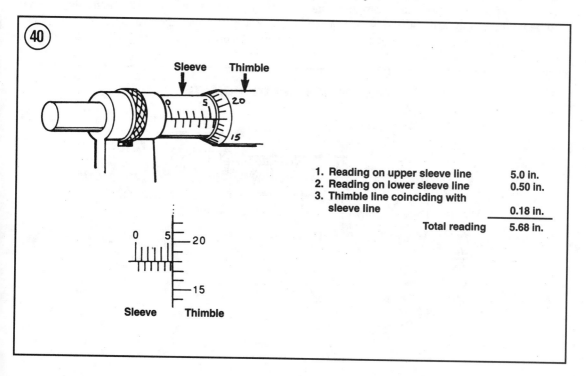

1. Reading on upper sleeve line	5.0 in.
2. Reading on lower sleeve line	0.50 in.
3. Thimble line coinciding with sleeve line	0.18 in.
Total reading	**5.68 in.**

c. To adjust the micrometer, follow the manufacturer's instructions provided with the micrometer.

3. To check the accuracy of micrometers above the 1 in. or 25 mm size, perform the following:

a. Manufacturer's usually supply a standard gauge with these micrometers. A standard is a steel block, disc or rod that is ground to an exact size to check the accuracy of the micrometer. For example, a 1-2 in. micrometer is equipped with a 1 inch standard gauge. A 25-50 mm micrometer is equipped with a 25 mm standard gauge (**Figure 43**).

b. Place the standard gauge between the micrometer's spindle and anvil (**Figure 43**) and measure its outside diameter or length. If the adjustment is correct, the 0 mark on the thimble will align exactly with the 0 mark on the sleeve line. If the 0 marks do not align, the micrometer is out of adjustment.

c. To adjust the micrometer, follow the manufacturer's instructions provided with the micrometer.

Proper Care of the Micrometer

The micrometer is a precision instrument and must be used correctly and with great care. When handling a micrometer, note the following:

1. Store a micrometer in its box or in a protected place where dust, oil and other debris cannot come in contact with it. Do not store micrometers in a drawer with other tools or hang them on a tool board.

2. When storing a 0-1 in. (0-25 mm) micrometer, turn the thimble so that the spindle and anvil faces do not contact each other. If they do, rust may form on the contact ends or the spindle can be damaged from temperature changes.

3. Do not clean a micrometer with compressed air. Dirt forced into the tool can cause premature wear.

4. Occasionally lubricate the micrometer with a light weight oil to prevent rust and corrosion.

5. Before using a micrometer, check its accuracy. Refer to *Micrometer Accuracy Check* in this section.

Dial Indicator

Dial indicators (A, **Figure 44**) are precision tools used to check dimension variations on machined parts such as transmission shafts and axles and to check crankshaft and axle shaft end play. Dial indicators are available with various dial types; for motorcycle repair, select an indicator with a continuous dial face (**Figure 45**).

When using a dial indicator, it must be mounted rigidly to a magnetic stand (B, **Figure 44**) or other support so that only the dial indicator plunger can move. An error in the reading will occur if the dial

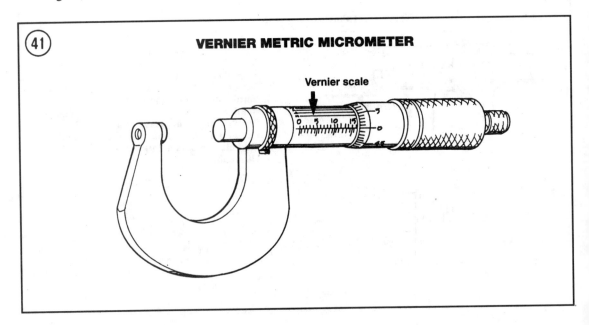

(41) **VERNIER METRIC MICROMETER**

Vernier scale

body or its mounting stand moves in relation to the plunger.

> *NOTE*
> *A dial indicator and spark plug adapter set is not required to check the ignition timing on the Kawasaki models covered in this manual. See* **Ignition Timing** *in Chapter Nine.*

V-Blocks

V-blocks are precision ground blocks used to hold a round object when checking its runout or condition. V-blocks can be used when checking the runout of such items as the transmission shafts and axles.

Cylinder Bore Gauge

The cylinder bore gauge is a very specialized precision tool. The gauge set shown in **Figure 46** is comprised of a dial indicator, handle and a number of length adapters to adapt the gauge to different bore sizes. The bore gauge can be used to make cylinder bore measurements such as bore size, taper and out-of-round. In some cases, an outside micrometer must be used to calibrate the bore gauge to a specific bore size.

Select the correct length adapter for the size of the bore to be measured. Zero the bore gauge according to its manufacturer's instructions, insert the bore gauge into the cylinder, carefully move it around in the bore to make sure it is centered and that the gauge foot is sitting correctly on the bore surface. This is necessary to obtain a correct reading. Refer to the manufacturer's instructions for reading the actual measurement obtained.

TEST EQUIPMENT

Spark Tester

A quick way to check the ignition system is to connect a spark tester to the end of the spark plug wire and operate the engine's kickstarter. A visible spark should jump the gap on the tester. A variety of

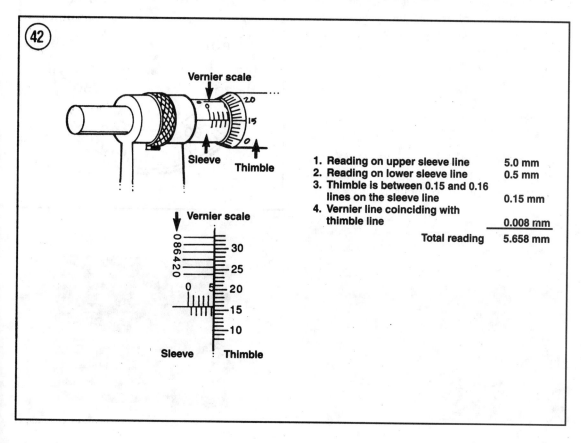

1. Reading on upper sleeve line		5.0 mm
2. Reading on lower sleeve line		0.5 mm
3. Thimble is between 0.15 and 0.16 lines on the sleeve line		0.15 mm
4. Vernier line coinciding with thimble line		0.008 mm
	Total reading	5.658 mm

spark testers are available from engine and aftermarket manufacturers. This tool and its use are described in Chapter Two.

Compression Gauge

An engine with low compression cannot be properly tuned and will not develop full power. A compression gauge (**Figure 47**) measures engine compression. The one shown has a flexible stem with an extension that can allow you to hold it while kicking the engine over. Open the throttle all the way when checking engine compression (Chapter Three).

Two-Stroke Leak Down Tester

A leak down tester check for air leaks in a two-stroke engine. You should perform this test when troubleshooting a two-stroke engine, after installing the reed valve assembly or after reassembling the engine's top end. Air leaks through the engine seals and/or gaskets can cause engine seizure, carburetor problems and power loss. Refer to Chapter Two for a full description of this test.

Multimeter or VOM

This instrument (**Figure 48**) is invaluable for electrical system troubleshooting. See *Electrical Troubleshooting* in Chapter Two for its use.

SPECIAL TOOLS

A few special tools will be required for engine and suspension service. These are described in the appropriate chapters and are available either from a

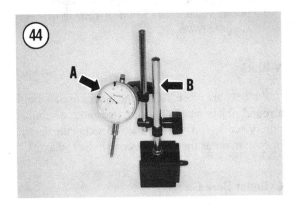

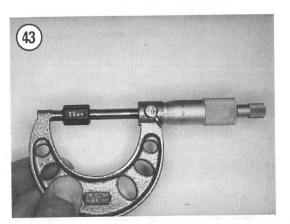

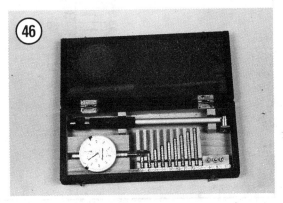

Kawasaki dealership or other manufacturers as indicated in the text.

MECHANIC'S TIPS

Removing Frozen Nuts and Screws

When a fastener rusts and cannot be removed, several methods may be used to loosen it. Apply penetrating oil such as Liquid Wrench or WD-40

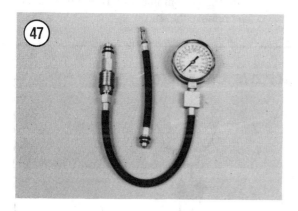

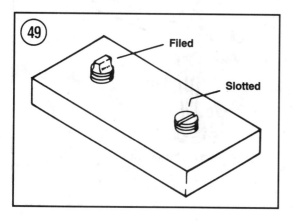

Filed

Slotted

(available at hardware or auto supply stores). Apply it liberally and let it penetrate for 10-15 minutes. Rap the fastener several times with a small hammer; do not hit it hard enough to cause damage. Reapply the penetrating oil, if necessary.

For frozen screws, apply penetrating oil as described. Insert a screwdriver in the slot and rap the top of the screwdriver with a hammer. This loosens the rust so the screw can be removed in the normal way. If the screw head is too chewed up to use this method, try to grip the fastener head with locking pliers and twist the screw out.

Avoid applying heat unless specifically instructed, as it may melt, warp or remove the temper from parts.

Removing Broken Screws or Bolts

When the head breaks off a screw or bolt, several methods are available for removing the remaining portion.

If a large portion of the remainder projects out, try gripping it with locking pliers. If the projecting portion is too small, file it to fit a wrench or cut a slot in it to fit a screwdriver tip (**Figure 49**). Loosen the fastener with a hand impact driver. See *Impact Driver* in this chapter.

If the head breaks off flush, use a screw extractor. To do this, centerpunch the exact center of the remaining portion of the screw or bolt. Drill a small hole in the screw and tap the extractor into the hole. Back the screw out with a wrench on the extractor (**Figure 50**).

Remedying Stripped Threads

Occasionally, threads are stripped through carelessness or impact damage. Often the threads can be cleaned by running a tap (for internal threads on nuts) or die (for external threads on bolts) through the threads (**Figure 51**). To clean or repair spark plug threads, use a spark plug tap.

If an internal thread is damaged, it may be necessary to install a thread insert. These are available for individual thread sizes and in large sets. Follow the manufacturer's instructions when installing their insert.

If it is necessary to drill and tap a hole, refer to **Table 8** for metric tap drill sizes.

Replacing Studs

1. Measure the height of the installed stud so that the new stud can be installed correctly.

> *NOTE*
> *When removing and installing studs in this section, check the shape of the new stud and compare it to the old one as the two stud ends may be different. For example, one end of the stud may use a different thread than the other or the threaded length of one end may be longer. Always check the studs for these differences so you can install them correctly.*

2A. If some threads of a stud are damaged, but some remain, you may be able to remove the stud as follows. If there are no usable threads, remove the stud as described in Step 2B.

   a. Thread two nuts onto the damaged stud (**Figure 52**), then tighten the nuts against each other so that they are locked together.

   b. Turn the bottom nut (**Figure 53**) to unscrew and remove the stud.

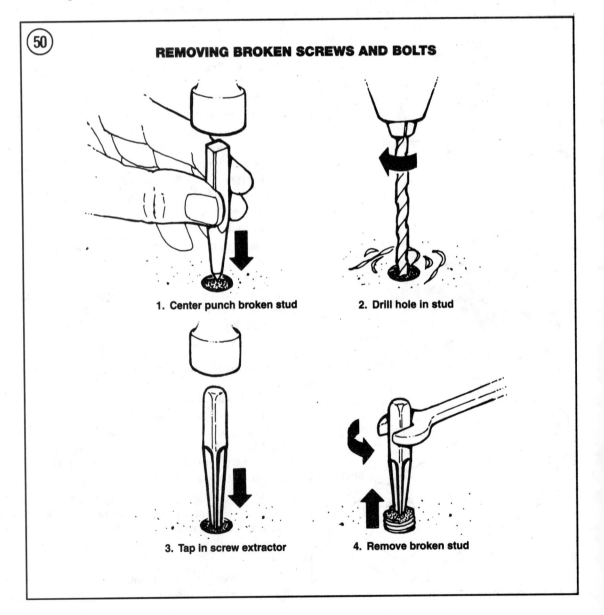

50

REMOVING BROKEN SCREWS AND BOLTS

1. Center punch broken stud

2. Drill hole in stud

3. Tap in screw extractor

4. Remove broken stud

NOTE
To avoid damaging the cylinder surface when replacing the cylinder studs, install the old head gasket over the cylinder.

2B. If the threads on the stud are damaged, remove the stud with a stud remover or, if possible, with a pair of locking pliers.

3. When reusing the stud, clean the threads with solvent or contact cleaner and allow to dry thoroughly.

4. Clean the threaded hole with contact cleaner or solvent and a wire brush (a rifle cleaning brush work well). Try to remove as much of the threadsealer residue from the hole as possible.

NOTE
After removing a stud, do not chase the mating hole threads hole with a tap (to

clean it) as the hole may have been threaded with a close class thread fit. The close class thread fit is often used in stud holes where no looseness is permitted between the stud and threaded hole. You can usually tell what type of thread tolerance is being used when threading the stud into the hole by hand. If the stud can be screwed into the hole by hand, a medium fit thread is used. If you cannot screw the stud in by hand, the hole uses close fit threads. Chasing a close fit hole with a standard (medium fit) tap will enlarge the hole and increase the looseness between the threads in the hole and stud. It will then be difficult to install the stud properly, and it will probably loosen later on. This can cause blown head and base gaskets and other damage. If the threaded hole is damaged and requires retapping, take the part to a motorcycle dealership or machine shop where the correct tap (thread fit) can be used.

5. Install two nuts on the top half of the new stud (**Figure 54**) as in Step 2A. Make sure they are locked securely.

6. Apply a high-strength threadlocking compound to the bottom threads on the new stud.

7. Turn the top nut and thread the new stud in (**Figure 55**). Install the stud to its correct height position (Step 1) or tighten it to its correct torque specification if one is listed (see appropriate chapter).

8. Remove the nuts and repeat for each stud as required.

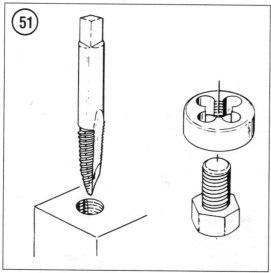

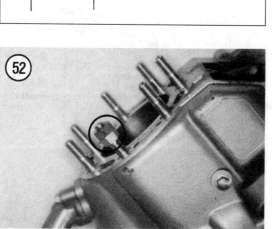

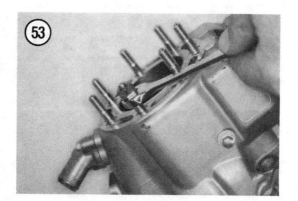

BALL BEARING REPLACEMENT

Ball bearings (**Figure 56**) are used throughout the engine and chassis to reduce power loss, heat and noise resulting from friction. Because ball bearings are precision-made parts, they must be maintained by proper lubrication and maintenance. If a bearing is damaged, replace it immediately. However, when installing a new bearing, use caution to prevent damage to the new bearing. While bearing replacement is covered in the individual chapters, the following should be used as a guideline.

NOTE

Unless otherwise specified, install bearings with their manufacturer's mark or number facing outward.

Purchasing New Bearings

Replacement bearings can be purchased through a Kawasaki dealership or from a local bearing supply house. When you purchase a bearing through your dealer, a part number recorded from the dealer's fiche card or computer will be used to order and identify the bearing. When using a local bearing supply house, the code number listed on the side of the bearing can be used to identify the bearing. When replacing a bearing, do not discard the old bearing until you are sure that the new bearing is an identical match.

Ball bearings are available in many types and series, for example, light, medium, heavy and max. They can be open on both sides, use one shield or two shields or use one or two seals. Principal bearing dimensions are width, outside diameter and inside diameter.

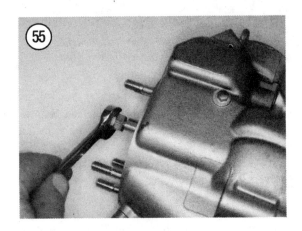

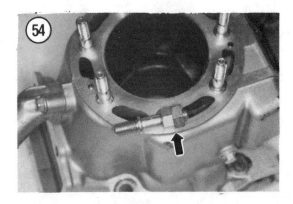

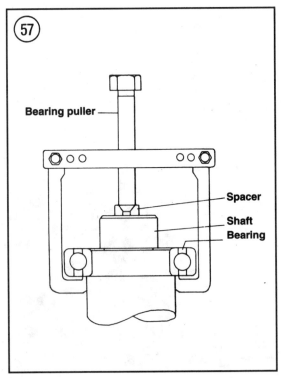

Bearing puller

Spacer

Shaft

Bearing

Bearing Removal

While bearings are normally removed only if damaged, there may be times when it is necessary to remove a bearing that is in good condition. However, improper bearing removal may damage the bearing, the mounting bore or shaft. Note the following when removing bearings.

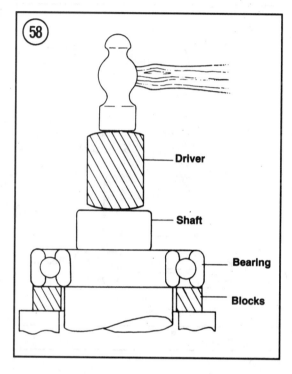

- **Driver**
- **Shaft**
- **Bearing**
- **Blocks**

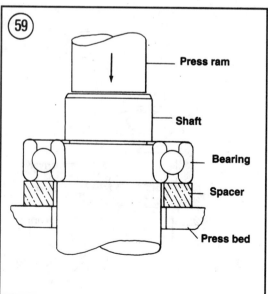

- **Press ram**
- **Shaft**
- **Bearing**
- **Spacer**
- **Press bed**

1. When using a puller to remove a bearing from a shaft, take care that the shaft is not damaged. Always place a piece of metal (**Figure 57**) between the end of the shaft and the puller screw. In addition, place the puller arms next to the bearing's inner bearing.

2. When using a hammer to drive a shaft off of a bearing, do not strike the shaft with the hammer. Doing so can crack or spread the end of the shaft, permanently damaging it. Instead, use a brass or aluminum driver between the hammer and shaft, making sure you support both bearing races with wooden blocks as shown in **Figure 58**.

3. The ideal method of bearing removal is with a hydraulic press. However, you must be follow certain procedures to prevent damage to the bearing, mounting bore or shaft. Note the following when using a press:

   a. Always support the inner and outer bearing races with a suitable size wood or aluminum spacer (**Figure 59**). If only the outer race is supported, the balls and/or the inner race will be damaged.

   b. Make sure the press ram (**Figure 59**) aligns with the center of the shaft. If the ram is not centered, it may damage the bearing and shaft.

   c. The moment the shaft is free of the bearing, it will drop to the floor. Secure or hold the shaft to prevent it from falling.

Bearing Installation

Refer to the following when installing bearings.

1. When installing a bearing in a housing, apply pressure to the *outer* bearing race (**Figure 60**). When

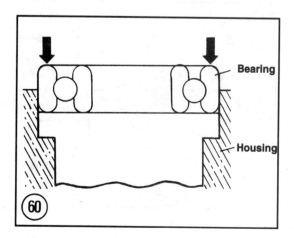

- **Bearing**
- **Housing**

installing a bearing on a shaft, apply pressure to the *inner* bearing race (**Figure 61**).

2. When installing a bearing as described in Step 1, some type of driver is required. Never strike the bearing directly with a hammer or you will damage the bearing. When installing a bearing, a bearing driver with an outside diameter that matches the bearing race is required. **Figure 62** shows the correct way to use a bearing driver and hammer when installing a bearing over a shaft.

3. Step 1 describes how to install a bearing in a housing and over a shaft. However, when installing a bearing over a shaft and into a housing at the same time, a snug fit is required for both outer and inner bearing races. In this situation, you must install a spacer underneath the driver tool to apply pressure evenly across *both* races (**Figure 63**). If the outer race is not supported, as shown in **Figure 63**, the balls will push against the outer bearing race and damage it.

Shrink Fit

1. *Installing a bearing over a shaft*: If a tight fit is required, the bearing inside diameter will be smaller than the shaft. In this case, driving the bearing on the shaft may cause bearing damage. Instead, heat the bearing before installation. Note the following:

   a. Secure the shaft so that it is ready for bearing installation.

   b. Clean the bearing surface on the shaft of all residue. Remove burrs with a file or sandpaper.

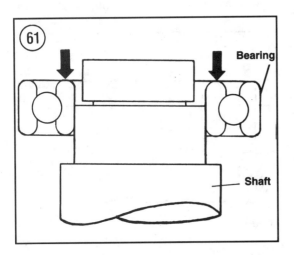

c. Fill a suitable pot or beaker with clean mineral oil. Place a thermometer (rated higher than 120°C [248° F]) in the oil. Support the thermometer so that it does not contact the bottom or side of the pot.

d. Secure the bearing with a piece of heavy wire bent to hold it in the pot. Hang the bearing in

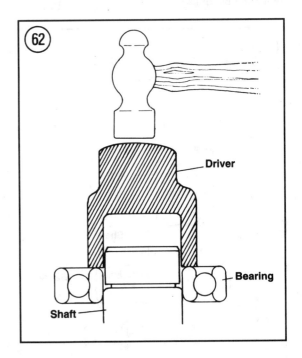

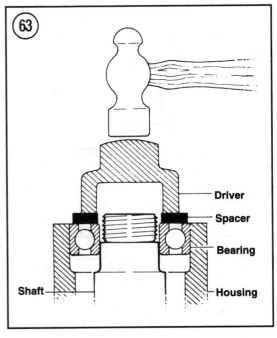

the pot so that it does not touch the bottom or sides of the pot.

e. Turn the heat on and monitor the thermometer. When the oil temperature rises to approximately 120° C (248° F), remove the bearing from the pot and quickly install it. If necessary, place a driver on the inner bearing race (**Figure 61**) and tap the bearing into place. As the bearing chills, it will begin to tighten on the shaft. To prevent the bearing from locking onto the shaft at the wrong spot, work quickly when installing it. Make sure the bearing is installed all the way.

2. *Installing a bearing in a housing*: Bearings are generally installed in a housing with a slight interference fit. Driving the bearing into the housing may damage the housing or cause bearing damage. Instead, heat the housing before the bearing is installed. Note the following.

CAUTION
Before heating the housing in this procedure to remove the bearings, wash the housing thoroughly with detergent and water. Rinse and rewash the housing as required to remove all traces of oil and other chemical deposits.

a. Heat the housing to a temperature of about 100° C (212° F) in a shop oven or on a hot plate. To monitor the temperature, place tiny drops of water on the housing as it starts to heat; when they start to sizzle and evaporate, the temperature is correct. Heat only one housing at a time.

CAUTION
Do not heat the housing with a torch (propane or acetylene)—never bring open flame into contact with the bearing or housing. The direct heat will destroy the case hardening of the bearing and will likely warp the housing.

b. Remove the housing from the oven or hot plate. Hold onto the housing with a kitchen pot holder, heavy gloves or heavy shop cloths—*it is hot.*

NOTE
A suitable size socket and extension work well for removing and installing bearings.

c. Hold the housing with the bearing side down and tap the bearing out. Repeat for all bearings in the housing.

d. If possible, before heating the housing, place the new bearings in a freezer. Chilling them will slightly reduce their overall diameter while the hot housing assembly is larger due to heat expansion. This will make installation much easier.

NOTE
Always install bearings with their manufacturer's mark or number facing outward unless the text directs otherwise.

e. While the housing is still hot, install the new bearing(s) into the housing. If possible install the bearings by hand. If necessary, lightly tap the bearing(s) into the housing with a socket placed on the outer bearing race. *Do not* install new bearings by driving on the inner bearing race. Install the bearing(s) until it seats completely.

SEALS

Seals (**Figure 64**) are used to prevent leakage of oil, grease or combustion gasses from between a housing and a shaft. The seal has a rubber or neoprene lip that rests against the shaft to form a seal.

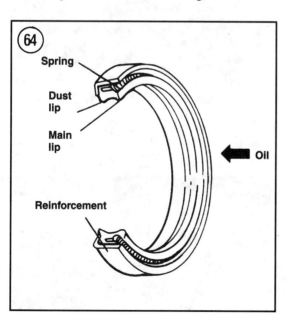

(64)
Spring

Dust lip

Main lip

Oil

Reinforcement

Depending on the application, the seal may have one or more lips, as well as a garter spring behind the lip to increase pressure on the seal lips. Improper procedures to remove a seal can damage the housing or shaft. Improper installation can damage the seal. Note the following:

a. Before removing a seal, note its installed position in its mounting bore. Is the seal flush with the top of the bore or is it installed down in the bore?

b. It is sometimes possible to remove a seal without damaging it. Prying is generally the easiest and most effective method of removing a seal from its mounting bore. Seals can usually be removed by prying with a suitable tool (**Figure 65**). A rag placed underneath the tool prevents the tool from damaging the housing bore. Seals will generally pop out, but when trying to remove a really tight seal , do not apply excessive pressure in one spot along the seal or you may damage the housing bore (and the seal if you are trying to save it). Instead, apply pressure in one spot, then stop and move the screwdriver around the seal and apply

pressure in a different spot. Continue to walk the screwdriver around the seal, applying small amounts of pressure, until the seal starts to move out of its mounting bore. If this technique does not work, use a hooked seal driver like the one shown in **Figure 66**. These tools work well but will damage the seal.

c. The lips of each seal should be packed with grease before installation. Some OEM seals are pre-packed with grease like the one shown in **Figure 67**. Otherwise, pack the seal lips with grease (**Figure 68**). If the procedure does

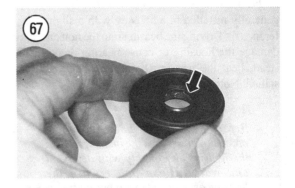

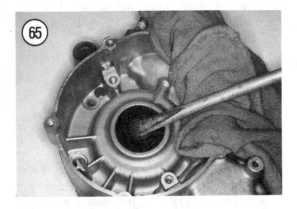

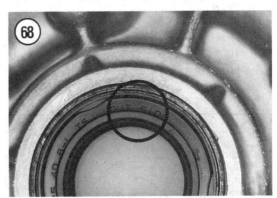

not specify a certain type of grease, use a waterproof grease.

d. Install seals with their manufacture's marks facing out, unless the text directs otherwise.

e. A socket of the correct size can often be used as a seal driver. Select a socket that fits the seal's outer diameter properly and clears any protruding shafts (**Figure 69**).

f. Some seals can be installed by pressing them into place with your fingers. When doing so, make sure the seal is positioned squarely in its bore.

g. Make sure the seal is driven squarely into the housing. Never install a seal by hitting directly against the top of the seal with a hammer.

Table 1 FRAME IDENTIFICATION NUMBERS

Model	Starting Frame Serial Number
1992 KX250-J1	KX250J-000001
1993 KX250-J2	KX250J-007501
1994 KX250-K1	KX250K-000001
1995 KX250-K2	KX250K-006001
1996 KX250-K3	KX250K-014001
1997 KX250-K4	KX250K-020001
1998 KX250-K5	KX250K-027001

Table 2 GENERAL DIMENSIONS

	mm	in.
Overall length		
1992-1993	2185	86.02
1994-1996	2155	84.84
1997	2170	85.43
1998		
U.S. models	2170	85.43
All other models	2175	85.62
Overall width	815	32.1
Overall height		
1992-1997	1215	47.8
1998	1210	47.6
Wheelbase		
1992-1993	1490	58.66
1994-1996	1460	57.48
1997	1475	58.07
1998		
U.S. models	1475	58.07
All other models	1480	58.26
Ground clearance		
1992-1997	385	15.15
1998	380	14.96
Seat height		
1992-1997	955	37.59
1998	950	34.40

Table 3 VEHICLE WEIGHT SPECIFICATIONS

	kg	lb.
Dry weight		
1992-1997	96.5	212.78
1998	97	213.88
Curb weight		
Front		
1992-1997	50	110.25
1998	51	112.45
Rear	52	114.66

Table 4 DECIMAL AND METRIC EQUIVALENTS

Fractions	Decimal in.	Metric mm	Fractions	Decimal in.	Metric mm
1/64	0.015625	0.39688	33/64	0.515625	13.09687
1/32	0.03125	0.79375	17/32	0.53125	13.49375
3/64	0.046875	1.19062	35/64	0.546875	13.89062
1/16	0.0625	1.58750	9/16	0.5625	14.28750
5/64	0.078125	1.98437	37/64	0.578125	14.68437
3/32	0.09375	2.38125	19/32	0.59375	15.08125
7/64	0.109375	2.77812	39/64	0.609375	15.47812
1/8	0.125	3.1750	5/8	0.625	15.87500
9/64	0.140625	3.57187	41/64	0.640625	16.27187
5/32	0.15625	3.96875	21/32	0.65625	16.66875
11/64	0.171875	4.36562	43/64	0.671875	17.06562
3/16	0.1875	4.76250	11/16	0.6875	17.46250
13/64	0.203125	5.15937	45/64	0.703125	17.85937
7/32	0.21875	5.55625	23/32	0.71875	18.25625
15/64	0.234375	5.95312	47/64	0.734375	18.65312
1/4	0.250	6.35000	3/4	0.750	19.05000
17/64	0.265625	6.74687	49/64	0.765625	19.44687
9/32	0.28125	7.14375	25/32	0.78125	19.84375
19/64	0.296875	7.54062	51/64	0.796875	20.24062
5/16	0.3125	7.93750	13/16	0.8125	20.63750
21/64	0.328125	8.33437	53/64	0.828125	21.03437
11/32	0.34375	8.73125	27/32	0.84375	21.43125
23/64	0.359375	9.12812	55/64	0.859375	22.82812
3/8	0.375	9.52500	7/8	0.875	22.22500
25/64	0.390625	9.92187	57/64	0.890625	22.62187
13/32	0.40625	10.31875	29/32	0.90625	23.01875
27/64	0.421875	10.71562	59/64	0.921875	23.41562
7/16	0.4375	11.11250	15/16	0.9375	23.81250
29/64	0.453125	11.50937	61/64	0.953125	24.20937
15/32	0.46875	11.90625	31/32	0.96875	24.60625
31/64	0.484375	12.30312	63/64	0.984375	25.00312
1/2	0.500	12.70000	1	1.00	25.40000

Table 5 CONVERSION TABLES

Multiply	By	To get equivalent of
Length		
Inches	25.4	Millimeter
Inches	2.54	Centimeter
Miles	1.609	Kilometer
Feet	0.3048	Meter
Millimeter	0.03937	Inches
Centimeter	0.3937	Inches
Kilometer	0.6214	Mile
Meter	3.281	Mile
Fluid volume		
U.S. quarts	0.9463	Liters
U.S. gallons	3.785	Liters
U.S. ounces	29.573529	Milliliters
Imperial gallons	4.54609	Liters
Imperial quarts	1.1365	Liters
Liters	0.2641721	U.S. gallons
Liters	1.0566882	U.S. quarts
Liters	33.814023	U.S. ounces
Liters	0.22	Imperial gallons
Liters	0.8799	Imperial quarts
Milliliters	0.033814	U.S. ounces
Milliliters	1.0	Cubic centimeters
Milliliters	0.001	Liters
Torque		
Foot-pounds	1.3558	Newton-meters
Foot-pounds	0.138255	Meters-kilograms
Inch-pounds	0.11299	Newton-meters
Newton-meters	0.7375622	Foot-pounds
Newton-meters	8.8507	Inch-pounds
Meters-kilograms	7.2330139	Foot-pounds
Volume		
Cubic inches	16.387064	Cubic centimeters
Cubic centimeters	0.0610237	Cubic inches
Temperature		
Fahrenheit	(F − 32) 0.556	Centigrade
Centigrade	(C × 1.8)	Fahrenheit
Weight		
Ounces	28.3495	Grams
Pounds	0.4535924	Kilograms
Grams	0.035274	Ounces
Kilograms	2.2046224	Pounds
Pressure		
Pounds per square inch	0.070307	Kilograms per square centimeter
Kilograms per square centimeter	14.223343	Pounds per square inch
Kilopascals	0.1450	Pounds per square inch
Pounds per square inch	6.895	Kilopascals
Speed		
Miles per hour	1.609344	Kilometers per hour
Kilometers per hour	0.6213712	Miles per hour 1-6

Table 6 KAWASAKI GENERAL TORQUE SPECIFICATIONS*

Thread diameter	N•m	in.-lb.	ft.-lb.
5	3.4-4.9	30-43	--
6	5.9-7.8	52-69	--
8	14-19	--	10-13.5
10	25-34	--	19-25
12	44-61	--	33-45
14	73-98	--	54-72
16	115-155	--	83-115
18	165-225	--	125-165
20	225-325	--	165-240

* This table lists general torque specifications for metric nuts and bolts. Use this table when a specific torque specification is not listed for a fastener at the end of the appropriate chapter. The torque specifications listed in this table are for use with clean, dry threads.

Table 7 TECHNICAL ABBREVIATIONS

ABDC	After bottom dead center
ATDC	After top dead center
BBDC	Before bottom dead center
BDC	Bottom dead center
BTDC	Before top dead center
C	Celsius (Centigrade)
cc	Cubic centimeter
CDI	Capacitor discharge ignition
cu. in.	Cubic inch
F	Fahrenheit
ft.-lb.	Foot-pound
gal.	Gallon
H/A	High altitude
hp	Horsepower
in.	Inch
kg	Kilogram
kg/cm2	Kilograms per square centimeter
kgm	Kilogram meter
km	Kilometer
L	Liter
m	Meter
MAG	Magneto
ml	Milliliter
mm	Millimeter
N•m	Newton-meters
psi	Pounds per square inch
PTO	Power take off
pt.	Pint
qt.	Quart
rpm	Revolutions per minute

Table 8 METRIC TAP DRILL SIZES

Metric (mm)	Drill size	Decimal equivalent	Nearest fraction
3 × 0.50	No. 39	0.0995	3/32
3 × 0.60	3/32	0.0937	3/32
4 × 0.70	No. 30	0.1285	1/8
4 × 0.75	1/8 0.125	1/8	
5 × 0.80	No. 19	0.166	11/64
5 × 0.90	No. 20	0.161	5/32
6 × 1.00	No. 9	0.196	13/64
7 × 1.00	16/64	0.234	15/64
8 × 1.00	J 0.277	9/32	
8 × 1.25	17/64	0.265	17/64
9 × 1.00	5/16	0.3125	5/16
9 × 1.25	5/16	0.3125	5/16
10 × 1.25	11/32	0.3437	11/32
10 × 1.50	R 0.339	11/32	
11 × 1.50	3/8 0.375	3/8	
12 × 1.50	13/32	0.406	13/32
12 × 1.75	13/32	0.406	13/32

1

CHAPTER TWO

TROUBLESHOOTING

Diagnosing mechanical problems is relatively simple, if you use orderly procedures and keep a few basic principles in mind. The first step in any troubleshooting procedure is to define the symptoms as closely as possible, then localize the problem. Subsequent steps involve testing and analyzing those areas which could cause the symptoms. A haphazard approach may eventually solve the problem, but it can be very costly in terms of wasted time and unnecessary parts replacement.

Proper lubrication, maintenance and periodic tune-ups, as described in Chapter Three, will reduce the necessity for troubleshooting. Even with the best of care, however, all motorcycles are prone to problems which will require troubleshooting.

Never assume anything. Do not overlook the obvious. If the engine will not start, is the engine stop switch shorted out? Is the engine flooded with fuel?

If the engine suddenly quits, what sound did it make? Consider this and check the easiest, most accessible problem first. If the engine sounded like it ran out of fuel, check to see if there is fuel in the tank. If there is fuel in the tank, is it reaching the carburetor? If not, the fuel tank vent hose may be plugged, preventing fuel from flowing from the fuel tank to the carburetor.

If nothing obvious turns up in a quick check, look a little further. Learning to recognize and describe symptoms will make repairs easier for you or a mechanic at the shop. Describe problems accurately and fully.

Gather as many symptoms as possible to aid in diagnosis. Note whether the engine lost power gradually or all at once, what color smoke (if any) came from the exhaust and so on.

After the symptoms are defined, areas which could cause problems can be tested and analyzed. Guessing at the cause of a problem may provide the solution; but, it usually leads to frustration, wasted time and a series of expensive, unnecessary parts replacements.

You do not need fancy equipment or complicated test gear to determine whether you should attempt repairs at home. A few simple checks could save a large repair bill and lost time while your bike sits in a dealer's service department. On the other hand, be realistic and *do not attempt repairs that are beyond your abilities*. Service departments tend to charge heavily for putting together an engine that someone else has disassembled or damaged. Some will not take on such a job, so use common sense and do not get in over your head.

OPERATING REQUIREMENTS

An engine needs three basics to run properly: correct fuel/air mixture, sufficient compression and a spark at the right time. If one basic requirement is missing, the engine will not run. If all of the basic requirements are present but one or more are not working or adjusted correctly, the engine may start and run but it will not run properly. Two-stroke engine operating principles are described in Chapter Four under *Engine Operating Principles*.

If the bike has been sitting for any length of time and refuses to start, check and clean the spark plug. If the plug is not fouled, then inspect the fuel delivery system. This includes the fuel tank, fuel shutoff valve, in-line fuel filter (if used) and fuel line. Gasoline deposits may have gummed up the carburetor's fuel valve and seat, jets and small air passages. Gasoline tends to lose its potency after standing for long periods. As gasoline evaporates, the fuel/oil mixture becomes richer. Condensation may also contaminate it with water. Drain the old gas and try starting with a fresh mixture.

STARTING THE ENGINE

If your engine refuses to start, frustration can cause you to forget basic starting principles. The following outline will guide you through basic starting procedures. In all cases, make sure that there is an adequate supply of properly mixed fuel in the tank.

Starting a Cold Engine

A rich air/fuel mixture is required when starting a cold engine. To accomplish this, a separate choke circuit is installed inside the carburetor. The choke circuit is controlled by a hand-operated choke knob mounted on the outside of the carburetor. To *open* the choke circuit for starting a cold engine, pull the choke knob up. To *close* the choke circuit after the engine is warm or when starting a warm or hot engine, push the choke knob down.

1. Shift the transmission into NEUTRAL.

2. Apply the front brake and rock the bike back and forth. This will help to mix the fuel in the tank.

3. Turn the fuel valve on (**Figure 1**).

4. Pull the choke knob up (**Figure 2**).

5. With the throttle completely *closed*, kick the engine over.

6. When the engine starts, work the throttle slightly to keep it running.

7. Idle the engine 1 to 2 minutes or until the throttle responds cleanly and the choke (**Figure 2**) can be closed. Warm the engine sufficiently to prevent cold seizure.

> *NOTE*
> *Cold seizure is a condition where the piston expands too fast, reducing the clearance between it and the cylinder before the engine is at normal operating temperature. Under normal operating conditions, the clearance between the piston and cylinder wall is filled with oil. Cold seizure can usually be identified by four visible contact or seizure points around the piston. Always make sure you warm the engine correctly.*

Starting a Warm or Hot Engine

1. Shift the transmission into NEUTRAL.

2. Turn the fuel valve on (**Figure 1**).

3. Make sure the choke is closed—push the choke knob (**Figure 2**) down.

4. Open the throttle slightly and kick the engine over.

Starting a Flooded Engine

If the engine is hard to start and there is a strong gasoline smell, the engine is probably flooded. Close the choke (**Figure 2**) and shift the transmission into NEUTRAL. Open the throttle all the way and kick the engine over until it starts. Depending on how badly the engine is flooded, it will generally start after a few hard kicks. If the engine is flooded badly, you may have to remove the spark plug and dry off its insulator, or install a new plug. When a flooded engine first starts to run, it will initially sputter and run slowly as it burns off the excess fuel. As this excess fuel is burned off, the engine will rev quickly and clear out. Release the throttle grip at this point and work it slowly to make sure the engine is running cleanly. Because a flooded engine smokes badly when it first starts to run, always start it outside and in a well-ventilated area with the bike's silencer pointing away from all objects. Do not start a flooded engine in a garage or other closed area.

> *NOTE*
> *If the engine refuses to start, check the carburetor overflow hose attached to the fitting at the bottom of the float bowl. If fuel is running out of the hose, the float valve is stuck open, allowing the carburetor to overfill. When this happens, try tapping the carburetor a few times to help dislodge the material holding the valve open. If this does not work and fuel continues to run out the end of the hose, turn the fuel valve off and service the carburetor, as described in Chapter Eight.*

STARTING DIFFICULTIES

If the engine cranks over but is difficult to start, or will not start at all, it does not help to wear out your leg on the kickstarter. Check for obvious problems even before getting out your tools. Go down the following list step-by-step. Do each one while remembering the three engine operating requirements that were described under *Operating Requirements* earlier in this chapter. If all of the three operating requirements are present, the engine should start and run. However, if one or more of the operating requirements are out of adjustment, or cannot operate properly because of worn or damaged parts, the engine may start and run, but it will not run well.

1. Is the choke (**Figure 2**) in the right position? Pull the choke knob *up* for a cold engine and push it *down* for a warm or hot engine.

2. Remove the spark plug and check to see if the insulator is wet. If the plug insulator is dry, fuel is not reaching the carburetor. Continue with Step 3.

3. Is there fuel in the tank? Remove the filler cap and rock the bike from side to side. Listen for fuel sloshing around. Is the fuel/oil mixture correct? Has the bike been sitting long enough for the fuel mixture to deteriorate? If in doubt, drain the fuel and fill with a fresh, correctly mixed fuel/oil mixture. Check that the fuel tank vent tube (**Figure 3**) is not clogged. Remove the tube from the filler cap, wipe off one end and blow through it. Remove the filler cap and check that its hose nozzle is not plugged.

> *NOTE*
> *Mix the fuel and oil in the correct ratio as listed in Chapter Three.*

> *WARNING*
> *Do not use an open flame to check in the tank. A serious explosion is certain to result.*

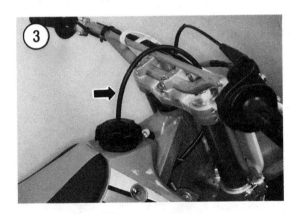

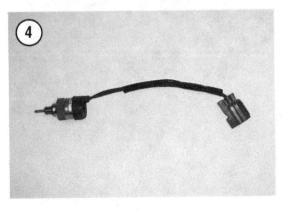

4. Pull off the fuel line at the carburetor and insert the end of the hose into a clear, plastic container. Turn the fuel valve on (**Figure 1**) and see if fuel flows freely. If fuel does not flow out and there is a fuel filter installed in the fuel line, remove the filter and turn the fuel valve on again. If the fuel now starts to flow, the filter is clogged and must be replaced. If no fuel comes out, the fuel valve may be shut off, blocked by foreign matter, or the fuel tank vent tube may be plugged.

5. If you suspect that the cylinder is flooded, or there is a strong smell of gasoline, open the throttle all the way and kick the engine over several times. If the cylinder is flooded (fouled or wet spark plug), remove the plug and dry the base and electrode thoroughly with a soft cloth. Reinstall the plug and attempt to start the engine. See *Starting A Flooded Engine* in this chapter.

6. Check the carburetor overflow hose on the bottom of the float bowl. If fuel is running out of the hose, the float is stuck open. Turn the fuel valve off and tap the carburetor a few times. Turn the fuel valve back on. If fuel continues to run out the end of the hose, remove and service the carburetor as de-

scribed in Chapter Eight. Check the carburetor vent hoses to make sure they are clear. Check the end of each hose for contamination.

7. On 1998 models, the fuel-cut valve (**Figure 4**) may be inoperative. Test the fuel-cut valve as described in Chapter Eight.

> *NOTE*
> *If fuel is reaching the carburetor, the fuel system could still be the problem. The jets (pilot and main) could be clogged or the air filter could be excessively restricted. However, before removing the carburetor, continue with Step 8 to make sure the bike has spark.*

8. Make sure the engine stop switch (**Figure 5**) is not stuck or working improperly. Disconnect the engine stop switch leads and try to restart the engine. If necessary, test the engine stop switch with a test light or ohmmeter as described in Chapter Nine.

> *NOTE*
> *If the engine stop switch was faulty, install a new switch as soon as possible. It is not safe to ride your bike with a missing or disconnected engine stop switch.*

9. Is the spark plug wire (**Figure 6**) on tight? Push it on and slightly rotate it to clean the electrical connection between the plug and the connector. Check also that the plug cap is installed tightly onto the coil wire.

> *NOTE*
> *If the engine will still not start, proceed with the following.*

10. Perform the *Spark Test* as described in this chapter. If there is a strong spark, perform Step 11. If there is no spark or if the spark is very weak, test the ignition system as described under *Ignition System* in this chapter.

> *NOTE*
> *If the fuel and ignition system are working properly, the one remaining area to check is the mechanical system. Unless the engine seized or there is some other type of mechanical problem, mechanical problems affecting the top end generally occur over a period of time. Isolate a mechanical problem to*

one of these areas: top end, exhaust valve and bottom end. The top and bottom end (as they relate to engine compression) are covered in Step 11.

11. Check cylinder compression as follows:

NOTE
You can usually tell the condition of your engine's compression by how easy or difficult it is to kick over. The following test shows how to check the compression when you are away from your shop. You may still have a compression problem even though it seems okay with the following test. Check engine compression with a compression gauge as described under **Tune-up** *in Chapter Three.*

   a. Turn the fuel valve off.

   b. Remove and ground the spark plug shell against the cylinder head and away from the plug hole.

   c. Put your finger tightly over the spark plug hole.

   d. Operate the kickstarter. As the piston comes up on the compression stroke, rising pressure in the cylinder will force your finger off of the spark plug hole. This indicates that the cylinder probably has sufficient cylinder compression to start the engine.

NOTE
If there is sufficient cylinder compression to start the engine, the engine may be suffering from a loss of crankcase pressure. During two-stroke operation, the air/fuel mixture is compressed twice, first in the crankcase, then in the combustion chamber. Crankcase pressure forces the air/fuel mixture to flow from the crankcase chamber through the transfer ports and into the combustion chamber. Before continuing, perform the **Leak Down Test** *in this chapter.*

Engine Fails To Start
Spark Test

Perform the following spark test to determine if the ignition system is operating properly.

CAUTION
Before removing the spark plug in Step 1, clean all dirt and debris away from the plug base. Dirt that falls into the cylinder will cause rapid piston, ring and cylinder wear.

1. Disconnect the plug wire (**Figure 6**) and remove the spark plug.

NOTE
A spark tester is a useful tool to check the ignition system. **Figure 7** *shows the Motion Pro Ignition System Tester (part No. 08-122). This tool is inserted in the spark plug cap and its base is set against the cylinder head for ground. The tool's air gap is adjustable, and it allows you to see and hear the spark while testing the intensity of the spark. This tool is available through most motorcycle dealerships.*

NOTE
If you are using a spark tester, set its air gap to 6 mm (1/4 in.).

2. Insert the spark plug (or spark tester) into the plug cap and ground the spark plug base against the cylinder head and away from the plug hole (**Figure 8**). Position the spark plug so you can see the electrodes.

NOTE
If the spark plug appears fouled, use a new spark plug.

CAUTION
Mount the spark plug or spark tester away from the plug hole in the cylinder head so the spark from the plug or tester

cannot ignite the gasoline vapor in the cylinder.

WARNING
Do not hold the spark plug, wire or connector, or a serious electrical shock may result.

3. Turn the engine over with the kickstarter. A fat blue spark should be evident across the spark plug electrodes or spark tester terminals. Note the following:

    a. If the spark is intermittent or weak (white or yellow in color), or if there is no spark, continue with Step 4.

    b. If the spark is good, go to Step 6.

4. Make sure the engine stop switch (**Figure 5**) is not stuck or working improperly or that a wire is broken and shorting out. Disconnect the engine stop switch leads and recheck the spark. Note the following:

    a. If there is now spark, the engine stop switch is damaged. Replace the switch and retest.

    b. If there is still no spark, test the engine stop switch with an ohmmeter (Chapter Nine) be-

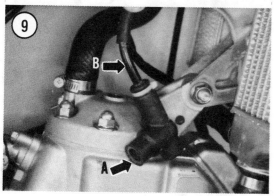

fore reconnecting it into the wiring harness to make sure it is not a secondary problem. If the switch tests okay, reconnect it back into the wiring harness and continue with Step 5.

NOTE
If the engine stop switch was faulty, install a new one as soon as possible. It is not safe to ride the motorcycle with a missing or disconnected engine stop switch.

5. A loose, corroded or damaged spark plug cap terminal (A, **Figure 9**) is a common source of ignition system problems, especially when the problem is intermittent. Perform the following:

    a. Disconnect the spark plug cap from the spark plug. Hold the plug wire and try to turn the cap. The cap must be a tight fit. If there is any looseness, the terminal inside the cap may have pulled away from the coil wire.

    b. Install the spark plug into the plug cap. The terminal ring inside the plug cap should snap tightly onto the spark plug when connecting the parts together.

    c. If there is a problem, remove the plug cap from the wire. If a plastic tie is used to help hold the plug cap in place, cut it before removing the plug cap.

    d. Check the metal terminal for corrosion or other damage. Remove any corrosion with a file or sandpaper. Check the terminal where it connects to the plug wire.

    e. Check the wire strands in the end plug wire for corrosion or other damage.

    f. Check the plug wire at the end of its outer rubber cover (B, **Figure 9**) for excessive looseness or play which may indicate a weak or broken plug wire. The plug wire can be damaged from vibration or mishandling.

    g. Hold the plug wire (without the spark plug cap and terminal) 6 mm (1/4 in.) from the cylinder head as shown in **Figure 10**. Have an assistant kick over the kickstarter. A fat blue spark should be evident. If there is a good spark, the spark plug cap terminal is faulty or its terminal was not making good contact with the plug wire.

    h. Cut the end of the plug wire (approximately 6 mm/1/4 in.) to provide fresh wire for the plug cap terminals to contact. If you cut the plug wire (rubber part only) to expose more of the wire core, do not cut into the wire core itself.

  i. Pack the plug cap or the wire end with dielectric grease to prevent moisture fromentering the plug cap and interrupting the spark.

  j. Install the plug cap securely, making sure to ensure good contact between the plug wire core and the plug cap terminal. Then repeat the spark test. If there is still no spark, continue with Step 6.

6. If the spark plug cap was not the problem, test the ignition system as described under *Ignition System* in this chapter.

7. If the spark is good, perform the *Engine is Difficult to Start* procedure in this chapter.

Engine is Difficult to Start

If the bike has spark, good compression and fuel is reaching the carburetor, but it is difficult to start, check for one or more of the following possible malfunctions:

1. Incorrect air/fuel mixture:
  a. Excessively dirty or blocked air filter element.
  b. Incorrect carburetor adjustment.
  c. Clogged pilot jet.
  d. Clogged pilot passage.
  e. Inoperative powerjet valve on 1998 models.

2. Engine flooded:
  a. Incorrect starting procedure.
  b. Incorrect fuel level (too high).
  c. Worn fuel valve and seat assembly.
  d. Fuel valve stuck open.
  e. Damaged float.

3. No fuel flow:
  a. Clogged fuel line.
  b. Clogged fuel filter (if used).
  c. Clogged fuel valve.
  d. Clogged or restricted fuel valve.
  e. Clogged fuel tank cap vent hose (**Figure 3**).
  f. Fuel valve turned off.
  g. No fuel.

4. Weak spark:
  a. Fouled or wet spark plug.
  b. Loose or damaged spark plug cap connection.
  c. Loose or damaged ignition coil plug wire-to-spark plug cap connection.
  d. Faulty ignition coil.
  e. Faulty igniter.

  f. Corroded stator coil and/or flywheel pickup surfaces (**Figure 11**). Remove corrosion with sandpaper.
  g. Damaged stator plate coils.
  h. Sheared flywheel key.
  i. Loose flywheel nut.
  j. Loose electrical connections.
  k. Dirty electrical connections.

5. Low engine compression:
  a. Loose spark plug or missing spark plug gasket.
  b. Stuck piston ring.
  c. Excessive piston ring wear.
  d. Excessively worn piston and/or cylinder.
  e. Loose cylinder head fasteners.
  f. Cylinder head incorrectly installed and/or torqued down.
  g. Warped cylinder head.
  h. Blown head gasket.
  i. Blown base gasket.
  j. Loose cylinder nuts.
  k. Excessively damaged reed valve assembly.

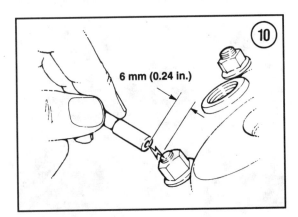

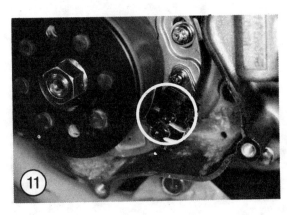

1. Carbon seized or damaged exhaust valve assembly.
6. Excessively worn, cracked or broken reed valves.

Engine Will Not Turn Over

If the engine will not turn over because of a mechanical problem, check for one or more of the following possible malfunctions:

NOTE
*After referring to the following list, refer to **Drive Train Noise** in this chapter for additional information.*

1. Defective kickstarter and/or gear.
2. Broken kickstarter return spring.
3. Damaged kickstarter ratchet gear.
4. Seized or damaged idler gear.
5. Seized piston.
6. Broken piston skirt (**Figure 12**).
7. Seized crankshaft bearings.

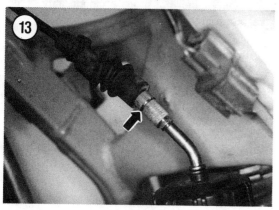

8. Seized connecting rod small end bearing.
9. Seized connecting rod big end bearing.
10. Broken connecting rod.
11. Seized primary drive gear/clutch assembly.
12. Seized transmission gear or bearing.

ENGINE PERFORMANCE

In the following check list, it is assumed that the engine runs, but is not operating at peak performance. This will serve as a starting point from which to isolate a performance malfunction.

Throttle Sticks

1. Damaged throttle cable.
2. Damaged throttle grip.
3. There is no operating clearance between the end of the throttle grip and handlebar.
4. Incorrect throttle cable routing.

NOTE
If you just installed the fuel tank, check that the throttle cable is routed next to the frame. Because the fuel tank drops down between the frame rails, it can catch and pull the throttle cable toward the center of the bike, causing the throttle valve to stick.

5. The throttle cable clip or adjuster (**Figure 13**), located on the carburetor cap, may have backed out, pulling the cable with it.
6. Dirt trapped between the carburetor throttle valve and bore.
7. Excessively worn throttle valve and/or bore.

Engine Will Not Idle

If you cannot get the engine to idle, as described in Chapter Three, check for one or more the following problem areas:
1. Incorrect carburetor adjustment.
2. Plugged pilot jet.

NOTE
If the engine starts with the choke on but cuts out when the choke is closed, or will not idle unless the choke is on, disassemble the carburetor (Chapter Eight) and check for a plugged pilot jet.

3. Obstructed fuel line or fuel shutoff valve.
4. Fouled or improperly gapped spark plug.
5. Leaking head gasket.

Poor Low Speed Performance

Check for one or more of the following possible malfunctions:
1. Incorrect air/fuel mixture:
   a. Clogged air filter element.
   b. Incorrect carburetor adjustment.
   c. Clogged pilot jet.
   d. Clogged air passage.
   e. Loose or cracked air box boot.
   f. Loose carburetor hose clamps.
   g. Clogged fuel tank cap vent hose.
   h. Carburetor choke stuck open.
   i. Incorrect fuel level (too high or too low).
2. Weak spark:
   a. Fouled or wet spark plug.
   b. Incorrect spark plug heat range.
   c. Loose or damaged spark plug cap connection.
   d. Loose or damaged secondary coil wire at coil or plug cap.
   e. Faulty ignition coil.
   f. Faulty igniter.
   g. Faulty stator coils.
   h. Loose electrical connections.
   i. Dirty electrical connections.
   j. Incorrect ignition timing.
3. Low engine compression:
   a. Loose spark plug or missing spark plug gasket.
   b. Stuck piston rings.
   c. Excessive piston ring wear.
   d. Excessively worn piston and/or cylinder.
   e. Loose cylinder head fasteners.
   f. Cylinder head incorrectly installed and/or torqued down.
   g. Warped cylinder head.
   h. Damaged cylinder head gasket.
   i. Blown base gasket.
   j. Loose cylinder nuts.
4. Exhaust valve stuck open:

NOTE
For proper exhaust valve operation, each part must be clean, within tolerance and able to move freely. Perform the exhaust valve cleaning and inspection procedures at the service intervals listed in Chapter Three. Exhaust valve service procedures are described in Chapter Four.

   a. Excessive carbon and oil deposits on exhaust valve and valve bore surfaces. Valve seizure.
   b. Excessive linkage play or linkage damage.
   c. Worn or damaged centrifugal advance governor assembly.
   d. Damaged exhaust advancer spring.
   e. Exhaust valve assembled incorrectly.
5. Excessively worn, cracked or broken reed valves.
6. Dragging brakes. Refer to *Brakes* in this chapter for additional information.

Poor High Speed Performance

Check for one or more of the following possible malfunctions:
1. Incorrect air/fuel mixture:
   a. Clogged air filter element.
   b. Clogged carburetor air vent tubes.
   c. Incorrect jet needle clip position.
   d. Incorrect main jet.
   e. Clogged main jet.
   f. Worn jet needle and/or needle jet.
   g. Clogged air jet or air passage.
   h. Loose or cracked air box boot.
   i. Loose carburetor holder clamps.
   j. Partially restricted fuel tank cap vent hose.
   k. Worn fuel valve and seat.
   l. Incorrect fuel level (too high or too low).
   m. Clogged fuel line.
   n. Clogged fuel filter.
   o. Clogged fuel valve.
   p. The fuel mixture is contaminated with water.
2. If the engine rpm drops off noticeably or decreases abruptly:
   a. Clogged air filter element.
   b. Restricted silencer.
   c. Damaged reed valves.
   d. Clutch slippage.
   e. Clogged main jet.
   f. Incorrect fuel level (too high or too low).
   g. Choke valve partially stuck.
   h. Throttle valve does not open all the way.
   i. Dragging brakes.
   j. Engine overheating.
   k. The fuel mixture is contaminated with water.

3. Low engine compression:
   a. Loose spark plug or missing spark plug gasket.
   b. Stuck piston ring.
   c. Excessive piston ring wear.
   d. Excessively worn piston and/or cylinder.
   e. Loose cylinder head fasteners.
   f. Cylinder head incorrectly installed and/or torqued down.
   g. Warped cylinder head.
   h. Damaged cylinder head gasket.
   i. Blown base gasket.
   j. Loose cylinder nuts.
   k. Cracked or broken reed valves.
4. Exhaust valve stuck closed:

> *NOTE*
> *The engine cannot make full power if the exhaust valve does not open fully. For proper exhaust valve operation, each part must be clean, within tolerance and able to move freely. Perform the exhaust valve cleaning and inspection at the service intervals listed in Chapter Three. Exhaust valve service is described in Chapter Four.*

   a. Excessive carbon and oil deposits on exhaust valve and valve bore surfaces.
   b. Excessive linkage play or linkage damage.
   c. Worn or damaged centrifugal advance governor assembly.
   d. Exhaust valve assembled incorrectly.

Engine Knocking

If the engine knocks under acceleration, check for the following:
1. Excessive carbon buildup in the combustion chamber (cylinder head and piston surfaces).
2. Too hot spark plug (see Chapter Three for the correct heat range spark plug).
3. Damaged igniter unit.
4. Incorrect ignition timing.

> *NOTE*
> *Steps 3 and 4 are related in the fact that a damaged igniter unit can change the ignition timing. If the engine accelerates to a higher rpm than before, the igniter unit is probably damaged. If the condition is allowed to continue,*

> *higher engine temperatures, resulting from overadvanced ignition timing, will burn a hole in the piston.*

5. Poor quality fuel.
6. Incorrect fuel type.

Engine Overheating

Check for one or more of the following possible malfunctions:
1. Low coolant level. This is probably due to a leak in the system. Visually check the system for leaks. If necessary, pressure test the cooling system as described in Chapter Three.
2. Coolant deterioration:
   a. Engine coolant contains additives to prevent cooling system corrosion. Because these anti-corrosion additives weaken in time, replace the coolant to prevent corrosion buildup. Replace the coolant at the intervals specified in Chapter Three.
   b. Coolant has a unique smell that does not change unless contaminated. When the engine is cold, drain some coolant into a clean, clear container (see Chapter Three). If the coolant gives off an abnormal smell, exhaust gas may be leaking into the engine water jacket.
3. Faulty cooling system:
   a. Faulty radiator cap.
   b. Defective water pump.
   c. Clogged radiator and engine coolant passages.
   d. Collapsed coolant hoses.
4. Other causes of engine overheating are:
   a. Excessive carbon buildup in the combustion chamber (cylinder head and piston).
   b. Incorrect air/fuel mixture.
   c. Clutch slippage.
   d. Brake drag.
   e. Transmission oil level too high.
   f. Too advanced ignition timing due to incorrect ignition timing or a defective ignition system component.

Black Exhaust and Engine Runs Roughly

1. Clogged air filter element.
2. Carburetor adjustment incorrect—mixture too rich.

3. Carburetor floats damaged or incorrectly adjusted.

4. Choke not operating correctly.

5. Water or other contaminants in fuel.

6. Excessive piston-to-cylinder clearance.

7. Restricted exhaust pipe and/or silencer.

Engine Loses Power

1. Incorrect carburetor adjustment.

2. Engine overheating.

3. Too advanced ignition timing due to incorrect ignition timing or a defective ignition system component.

4. Incorrectly gapped spark plug.

5. Cracked or broken reed valve.

6. Obstructed silencer.

7. Dragging brake.

Engine Lacks Acceleration

1. Incorrect carburetor adjustment.

2. Clogged fuel line.

3. Too advanced ignition timing due to incorrect ignition timing or a defective ignition system component.

4. Cracked or broken reed valve.

5. Dragging brake.

ENGINE

Engine problems are generally symptoms of something wrong in another system, such as ignition, fuel or starting.

Preignition

Preignition is the premature burning of fuel and is caused by hot spots in the combustion chamber. The fuel actually ignites before it should. Glowing deposits in the combustion chamber, inadequate cooling or an overheated spark plug can all cause preignition. This is first noticed in the form of a power loss but will eventually result in extended damage to the internal parts of the engine because of higher combustion chamber temperatures.

Detonation

Commonly called spark knock or fuel knock, detonation is the violent explosion of fuel in the combustion chamber instead of a controlled burn that occurs during normal combustion. Excessive damage can result. Use of low octane gasoline is a common cause of detonation.

Even when high octane gasoline is used, detonation can still occur if the engine is improperly timed. Other causes are a lean fuel mixture at or near full throttle, inadequate engine cooling, or the excessive accumulation of deposits on piston and combustion chamber.

Power Loss

Several factors can cause a lack of power and speed. Look for a clogged air filter or a fouled or damaged spark plug. A piston or cylinder that is galling, incorrect piston clearance or worn or sticky piston rings may be responsible. Look for loose bolts, defective gaskets or leaking machined mating surfaces on the cylinder head, cylinder or crankcase. Also check the crankshaft seals; refer to *Leak Down Test* in this chapter.

Piston Seizure

This is caused by incorrect bore clearance, piston rings with an improper end gap, compression leak, incorrect engine oil, spark plug of the wrong heat range, incorrect ignition timing or the use of an incorrect fuel/oil mixture. Overheating from any cause may result in piston seizure.

Piston Slap

Piston slap is an audible slapping or rattling noise resulting from excessive piston-to-cylinder clearance. When allowed to continue, piston slap will eventually cause the piston skirt to shatter. In some cases, a shattered piston (**Figure 12**) will cause some form of secondary engine damage. This type of damage can be prevented by measuring the cylinder bore and piston diameter at specified intervals (see Chapter Three), and by close visual inspection of all top end components, checking each part for scuff marks, scoring, cracks and other signs of abnormal wear. Replace parts that exceed service limits or show damage.

ENGINE NOISES

1. *Knocking or pinging during acceleration—* Caused by using a lower octane fuel than recommended. Pinging can also be caused by a spark plug of the wrong heat range and incorrect carburetor jetting (too lean). Refer to *Correct Spark Plug Heat Range* in Chapter Three. Also check for excessive carbon buildup in the combustion chamber or a faulty igniter.

2. *Slapping or rattling noises at low speed or during acceleration—* May be caused by piston slap, i.e., excessive piston-cylinder wall clearance. Also check for a bent connecting rod or worn piston pin and/or piston pin holes in the piston.

3. *Knocking or rapping while decelerating—* Usually caused by excessive rod bearing clearance.

4. *Persistent knocking and vibration or other noise—* Usually caused by worn main bearings. If these bearings are okay, consider the following:
   a. Loose engine mounts.
   b. Cracked frame.
   c. Leaking cylinder head gasket.
   d. Exhaust pipe leakage at cylinder head.
   e. Stuck piston ring.
   f. Broken piston ring.
   g. Partial engine seizure.
   h. Excessive small end connecting rod bearing clearance.
   i. Excessive big end connecting rod bearing clearance.
   j. Excessive crankshaft runout.
   k. Worn or damaged primary drive gear.

5. *Rapid on-off squeal—* Compression leak around cylinder head gasket or spark plug.

LEAK DOWN TEST

Many owners of two-stroke bikes are plagued by hard starting and generally poor running, for which there seems to be no cause. Carburetion and ignition may be good, and compression tests may show that all is well in the engine's upper end.

What a compression test does not show is lack of primary compression. The crankcase in a two-stroke engine must be alternately under pressure and vacuum. After the piston closes the intake port, further

downward movement of the piston causes the entrapped mixture to be pressurized so it can rush quickly into the cylinder when the scavenging ports are opened. Upward piston movement creates a slight vacuum in the crankcase, enabling the air/fuel mixture to be drawn in from the carburetor.

If the crankcase seals or cylinder gaskets leak, the crankcase cannot hold pressure or vacuum, and proper engine operation is impossible. Any other source of leakage such as a defective cylinder base gasket or porous or cracked crankcase castings will result in the same conditions (**Figure 14**).

It is possible, however, to test for and isolate primary engine pressure leaks. The test is simple but will require the use of a tool like the Motion Pro Leak Down Tester shown in **Figure 15**. Briefly, when you perform a leak down test, you seal off all normal engine openings, then apply air pressure into the engine. If the engine does not hold air, there are one or more air leaks. It is only necessary to locate and repair the leak(s).

The following procedure describes a typical leak down test.

1. If the engine is dirty, clean it before making this test.

2. Remove the flywheel and stator plate (Chapter Nine) to access the left side cranksfaft seal (**Figure 16**).

3. Remove the exhaust pipe (Chapter Four) and carburetor (Chapter Eight).

NOTE
Do not remove the intake manifold. The manifold must remain on the engine during this test as it can be the source of the leak.

NOTE
To get an air tight seal in the exhaust port, the port must be clean of all carbon and oil residue.

4. Plug the exhaust port with an expandable rubber plug (**Figure 17**). Tighten the plug securely.

5. Plug the intake manifold with a suitable adapter plug (A, **Figure 18**). Tighten the manifold's hose clamp.

6. Install the pressure gauge's hose adapter (B, **Figure 18**) into the intake manifold plug fitting.

7. Squeeze the pressure gauge lever or bulb until the gauge (**Figure 19**) indicates 5-6 psi (34-41 kPa).

CAUTION
Do not apply more than 8 psi (55 kPa)
or you can damage the crankcase seals.

8. Read the pressure gauge. If the engine is in good condition, the pressure will not drop more than 1 psi (6.9 kPa) in several minutes. A good rule of thumb is that an engine should hold 6 psi (41 kPa) for 5-6 minutes. Any immediate pressure loss or a pressure loss of 1 psi (6.9 kPa) in 1 minute indicates a serious leakage problem.

If leakage is noted, first make sure that there are no leaks in the test equipment or sealing plugs. Check the equipment sealing points by spraying them with soapy water (**Figure 20**). If all of the test equipment and its hose fittings are air tight, apply pressure to the engine again. If the pressure gauge shows a loss of pressure, spray all of the engine sealing points (**Figure 20**). When bubbles appear, you have found a leak. Some possible leakage points are listed below:

a. Left side crankshaft seal (**Figure 16**).

b. Right side crankshaft seal (**Figure 21**). To check this seal with the right crankcase cover installed on the engine, pour some of the soapy water into the transmission breather tube (**Figure 22**). If the tube bubbles, the right side crankshaft seal is leaking. A leaking right side crankshaft seal will allow oil to be drawn into the crankcase, causing excessive smoking and spark plug fouling. Before disassembling the engine, confirm the seal's condition by removing the right crankcase cover (Chapter Six)

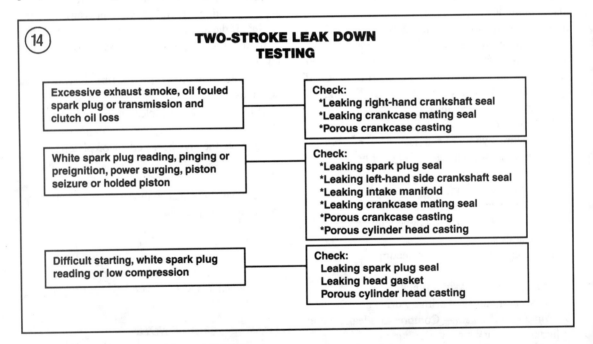

TWO-STROKE LEAK DOWN TESTING

Excessive exhaust smoke, oil fouled spark plug or transmission and clutch oil loss	Check: *Leaking right-hand crankshaft seal *Leaking crankcase mating seal *Porous crankcase casting
White spark plug reading, pinging or preignition, power surging, piston seizure or holed piston	Check: *Leaking spark plug seal *Leaking left-hand side crankshaft seal *Leaking intake manifold *Leaking crankcase mating seal *Porous crankcase casting *Porous cylinder head casting
Difficult starting, white spark plug reading or low compression	Check: Leaking spark plug seal Leaking head gasket Porous cylinder head casting

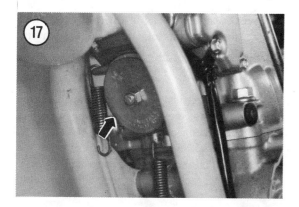

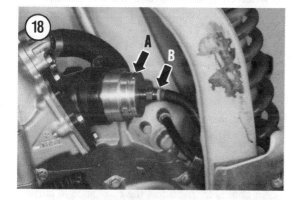

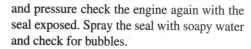

and pressure check the engine again with the seal exposed. Spray the seal with soapy water and check for bubbles.

c. Spark plug.

d. Cylinder head joint.

e. Intake manifold.

NOTE
The intake manifold mating surface is a common leakage point.

f. Cylinder base joint.

g. Crankcase joint.

h. Exhaust valve covers.

i. Porous crankcase, cylinder or cylinder head casting.

9. When a leak is detected, repair it or replace the damaged part. Repeat the test after replacing or repairing damaged parts and after reassembling the engine.

10. Remove the test equipment and reverse Steps 2 and 3 to complete engine assembly.

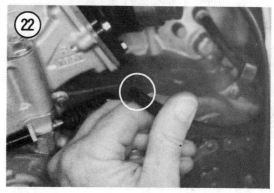

FUEL SYSTEM

Many riders automatically assume that the carburetor is at fault when the engine does not run properly. While fuel system problems are not uncommon, carburetor adjustment is seldom the answer. In many cases, adjusting the carburetor only compounds the problem by making the engine run worse.

When troubleshooting the fuel system, start at the gas tank and work through the system, reserving the carburetor as the final point. Most fuel system problems result from an empty fuel tank, a plugged fuel filter or fuel valve, or sour fuel. Fuel system troubleshooting is covered thoroughly under *Starting Difficulties, Engine Starting Troubles* and *Engine Performance* in this chapter.

A malfunctioning carburetor choke can also case engine starting and operating problems. Check the choke by opening and closing it at the carburetor (**Figure 2**). The choke must move between its OFF and ON positions without binding or sticking in one position. If necessary, remove the choke (Chapter Eight) and inspect its plunger and spring (**Figure 23**) for excessive wear or damage.

ELECTRICAL TROUBLESHOOTING

Electrical troubleshooting can be very time-consuming and frustrating without proper knowledge and a suitable plan. Refer to the wiring diagrams at the end of this book to help you determine how the circuit should work. Use them to trace the current paths from the power source through the circuit components to ground.

As with all troubleshooting procedures, analyze typical symptoms in a systematic procedure. Never assume anything and do not overlook the obvious like an electrical connector that has separated. Test the simplest and most obvious cause first and try to make tests at easily accessible points on the bike.

Preliminary Checks and Precautions

Prior to starting any electrical troubleshooting procedure perform the following:

1. Disconnect each electrical connector in the suspect circuit and check that there are no bent metal pins on the male side of the electrical connector (**Figure 24**). A bent pin will cause an open circuit.

2. Check each female end of the connector. Make sure that the metal connector on the end of each wire is pushed all the way into the plastic connector. To check, carefully push them in with a narrow blade screwdriver.

3. Check all electrical wires where they enter the individual metal connector in both the male and female plastic connector.

4. Make sure all electrical connectors within the connector are clean and free of corrosion. Clean, if necessary, then pack the connectors with a dielectric grease.

5. After all is checked out, push the connectors together and make sure they are fully engaged and locked together.

6. Never pull on the electrical wires when disconnecting an electrical connector—pull only on the connector plastic housing.

TEST EQUIPMENT

Ohmmeter

An ohmmeter measures the resistance to current flow within a circuit. When troubleshooting your Kawasaki, use an ohmmeter to check the following:

1. Wire continuity.

2. Engine stop switch operation.

3. Ignition coil resistance.

4. Stator coil resistance.

5. Voltage regulator/rectifier resistance on 1998 models.

When measuring resistance with an ohmmeter, low resistance means good continuity in a complete circuit. Before using an analog ohmmeter, calibrate

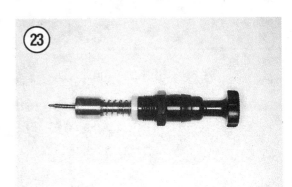

it by touching the leads together and turning the ohms calibration knob until the meter reads zero.

Continuity Test

A continuity test is made to determine if the circuit is complete with no opens in either the electrical wires or components within that circuit.

Unless otherwise specified, make all continuity tests with the electrical connector still connected. Insert the test leads into the backside of the connector and make sure the test lead touches the electrical wire or metal terminal within the connector.

Always check both sides of the connectors as one side may be loose or corroded thus preventing current flow through the connector. This type of test can be performed with a self-powered test light or an ohmmeter. An ohmmeter will give the best results.

1. Attach one test lead to one end of the part of the circuit to be tested.

2. Attach the other test lead to the other end of the part of the circuit to be tested.

3. Read the ohmmeter scale. The ohmmeter will indicate either a low or no resistance (means good continuity in a complete circuit) or infinite resistance (means an open circuit). When measuring the resistance of an electrical component, compare the actual reading to the service specification listed in the correct table (Chapter Nine).

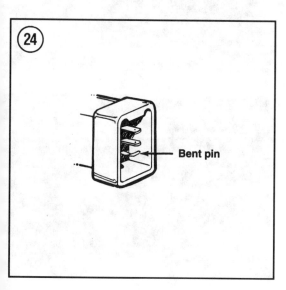

Bent pin

Voltmeter
(1998 Models)

A voltmeter is required to measure the voltage regulator/rectifier output voltage. Refer to Chapter Nine for voltage regulator/rectifier test procedures for 1998 models.

IGNITION SYSTEM

All models are equipped with a capacitor discharge ignition (CDI) system. This solid state system uses no contact breaker point or other moving parts. Because of the solid state design, problems with the capacitor discharge system are relatively few. However, if an ignition problem does occur, it generally causes weak or no spark. It is relatively easy to troubleshoot a CDI system that has weak or no spark. It is considerably more difficult to repair a system with an intermittent malfunction that only occurs when the system is hot or under load.

Ignition System Troubleshooting

If there is no spark or if the spark is intermittent, perform the following steps in order.

NOTE
If the problem is intermittent, perform the tests with the engine cold, then hot.

1. Remove the seat (Chapter Fifteen).
2. Remove the fuel tank (Chapter Eight).
3. Perform the spark test using a new spark plug or spark tester as described under *Engine Fails to Start (Spark Test)* in this chapter. If there is no spark, continue with Step 4.
4. Check the spark plug cap (A, **Figure 9**) as described under *Spark Test* in this chapter. Note the following:
   a. If there was a spark with the plug cap removed, replace the plug cap and retest.
   b. If there is no spark, continue with Step 5.
5. Check the spark plug wire connections at the ignition coil (**Figure 25**). Check the wires for cracks or brittle insulation. Check that the ignition coil's ground connection is tight and free of all corrosion. Visually check the ignition coil for cracks, carbon tracks or other damage indicating a problem. Check for a loose or damaged ignition coil mounting

bracket. If there is still no spark, continue with Step 6.

6. Make sure the engine stop switch (Figure 5) is not stuck or working improperly or that a wire is broken and shorting out. Disconnect the engine stop switch leads and recheck the spark. Note the following:

   a. If there is now spark, the engine stop switch is damaged. Replace the switch and retest.

   b. If there is still no spark, test the engine stop switch with an ohmmeter (Chapter Nine) before reconnecting it into the wiring harness to make sure it is not a secondary problem. If the switch operates correctly, reconnect it back into the wiring harness and continue with Step 7.

NOTE
If the engine stop switch is faulty, install a new one as soon as possible. It is not safe to ride the motorcycle with a missing or disconnected engine stop switch.

7. Remove the flywheel cover as described in Chapter Nine. Visually inspect the flywheel (A, **Figure 26**) for any cracks, loose rivets or other damage. If okay, grasp the flywheel by hand and try to move it up and down. If there is any excessive play, the crank main bearings may be worn, causing the flywheel to run out of true. This condition can cause ignition system problems.

NOTE
If you notice that there is dirt and water inside the flywheel cover, check the cover for warpage or other damage. Rust that forms on the flywheel, pickup coil and stator coil surfaces can cause ignition system problems. Dirt that enters past the flywheel cover can damage the left crankshaft oil seal and cause an air leak.

8. Remove the flywheel (Chapter Nine) and check that the Woodruff key is not sheared or damaged. If so, install a new key and the flywheel and start the engine.

9. Inspect the stator plate (B, **Figure 26**) for loose or missing mounting screws. If necessary, adjust the ignition timing and tighten the screws as described in Chapter Nine.

10. Inspect the stator coils (A, **Figure 27**) for discoloration or any type of damage caused by a wobbly or damaged flywheel or a loose flywheel rivet.

11. Check the pickup coil (B, **Figure 27**). If the screws have loosened, the pickup coil may have slipped down and become damaged from contact with the flywheel.

12. Check the stator coils, pickup coil and flywheel for rust. Carefully remove rust with sandpaper and clean with electric contact cleaner.

13. Test the stator plate coils (**Figure 27**) as described under *Stator Coil Testing* in Chapter Nine. Note the following:

   a. If all of the coils are good, perform Step 14.

   b. If one or both coils test incorrectly, replace the coil assembly and retest the ignition system.

14. Test the ignition coil (**Figure 25**) as described under *Ignition Coil* in Chapter Nine. Note the following:

   a. If the primary and secondary resistance is good, perform Step 15.

   b. If the primary and/or secondary resistance is out of specification, replace the ignition coil and retest.

15. If all of the previous checks fail find a problem or damaged part, take the igniter to a Kawasaki dealership and have it tested.

NOTE
The igniter cannot be tested effectively using conventional equipment. Because ignition system problems are most often caused by an open or short circuit or poor wiring connections, replace the igniter only if you are certain that all other ignition system components are in good condition. The igniter is expensive, and once purchased, generally cannot be returned. Therefore, repeat the preceding tests to verify the condition of the ignition system before replacing the igniter.

16. Install all parts previously removed.

CLUTCH

The two most common clutch problems are clutch slip (clutch does not engage fully) and clutch drag (clutch does not disengage fully). Problems associated with clutch noise will be discussed at the end of this section.

The main cause of clutch slip or drag is incorrect clutch adjustment or a rough operating clutch lever or clutch release lever at the engine. Before removing the clutch for inspection, perform the following checks:

1. Check the clutch cable routing from the handlebar to the engine. Make sure the cable is routed properly and both cable ends are mounted correctly.

2. With the engine turned off and the transmission in NEUTRAL, pull and release the clutch lever. If the clutch lever is hard to pull or its movement is rough, check for the following:
   a. Damaged clutch cable.
   b. Incorrect clutch cable routing (see Step 1).
   c. Dry clutch cable.
   d. Damaged clutch lever and perch assembly at the handlebar.
   f. Damaged clutch release lever assembly at the engine.

3. If the items in Step 1 and 2 are good, and the clutch lever moves without any excessive roughness or binding, check the clutch adjustment as described in Chapter Three. Note the following:
   a. If the clutch can not be adjusted within the limits specified in Chapter Three, check for a stretched or damaged clutch cable.
   b. If the clutch cable and its adjustment are good okay, the friction plates may be excessively worn.

4. If you have not found the problem, refer to the *Clutch Slipping* or *Clutch Dragging* procedure that follows in this section.

Clutch Slipping

When the clutch slips, the engine sounds like it is accelerating faster than what the actual forward speed indicates. The engine will act like you are feathering or slipping the clutch when you are not. When changing gears, the engine speed drops quickly, almost bogging down or stopping the engine. Because the clutch plates are spinning against each other and not engaging, an excessive amount of heat accummulates in the clutch. This heat causes rapid and excessive clutch plate wear and warpage and clutch spring fatigue.

If the clutch slips, check for one or more of the following possible malfunctions:
1. *Clutch wear or damage:*
   a. Incorrect clutch adjustment.
   b. Weak or damaged clutch springs.

NOTE
If the clutch springs are worn and the friction plates are within specifications, check the plates for a glaze buildup before reassembling the clutch. Deglaze the clutch plates as described in Chapter Six.

c. Loose clutch springs.

d. Worn friction plates.

e. Warped steel plates.

f. Incorrectly assembled clutch.

g. Clutch release mechanism wear or damage.

2. *Clutch/transmission oil*:

a. Low oil level.

b. Oil additives.

c. Low viscosity oil.

Clutch Dragging

Clutch drag occurs when the clutch does not slip enough. When in gear and releasing the clutch, the bike will creep or jump forward. Once underway, the transmission is difficult to shift. If this condition is not repaired, transmission gear and shift fork wear and damage will occur from the grinding of the transmission gears.

If the clutch drags, check for one or more of the following possible malfunctions:

1. *Clutch wear or damage:*

a. Incorrect clutch adjustment. The free play measurement at the clutch lever is excessive.

b. Clutch release mechanism wear or damage.

c. Incorrect push lever and pushrod engagement.

d. Warped steel plates.

e. Swollen friction plates.

f. Warped pressure plate.

g. Incorrect clutch spring tension.

h. Incorrectly assembled clutch.

i. Loose clutch nut.

j. Burnt primary driven gear bushing.

k. Notched clutch hub splines (A, **Figure 28**).

l. Notched clutch housing grooves (B, **Figure 28**).

NOTE
Wear as described in substeps k and l are a common cause of clutch drag on high-use engines.

m. Damaged clutch pushrod.

2. *Clutch/transmission oil*:

a. Oil level too high.

b. High viscosity oil.

Clutch Noise

Excessive clutch noise is usually caused by worn or damaged parts. If the clutch starts to exhibit more noise than normal, check for the following conditions:

1. A rattling noise in the right crankcase cover that is more noticeable at idle or low engine speeds is generally caused by excessive clutch needle bearing and collar wear (**Figure 29**). The noise is reduced or eliminated when the clutch housing is put under a load. Also inspect the clutch housing bore for excessive wear or damage.

2. Excessive friction disc to clutch housing clearance. Measure as described under *Clutch Inspection* in Chapter Six.

3. Excessive clutch housing-to-primary drive gear backlash. No specification given for backlash. Check both gears for excessive wear or damage.

4. Excessive pushrod holder and/or pushrod wear or damage.

EXTERNAL SHIFT MECHANISM AND TRANSMISSION

The KX250 engine is equipped with a five-speed constant mesh transmission. Some transmission symptoms are hard to distinguish from clutch symptoms. For example, if the gears grind during shifting, the problem may be caused by a dragging clutch. However, if the clutch drag problem is not repaired, transmission damaged will eventually occur. An incorrectly assembled or damaged external shift mechanism assembly will also cause shifting problems. Always investigate the easiest and most acces-

sible areas first. To prevent an incorrect diagnosis, perform the following inspection procedure to troubleshoot the external shift mechanism and transmission. At the same time, refer to the troubleshooting chart in **Figure 30** for a list of common transmission symptoms and possible causes.

The external shift mechanism assembly consists of the shift shaft (A, **Figure 31**), shift drum cam (B) and stopper lever (C) assembly.

NOTE
The following procedure will require you to shift the transmission by hand. When trying to shift a constant mesh transmission, one of the transmission shafts must be turning. An easy way to do this is to have an assistant turn the rear wheel (with the drive chain installed) while you shift the gearshift lever or turn the shift drum by hand.

1. First check that the clutch is properly adjusted. Eliminate any clutch drag or slipping problem. If the clutch adjustment is good, continue with Step 2.
2. Support the bike with the rear wheel off the ground.
3. Remove the clutch as described in Chapter Six.
4. Mount a small flat plate against the shift shaft (**Figure 32**) to prevent it from backing out when shifting the transmission.
5. Have an assistant slowly turn the rear wheel while you shift the transmission with the shift pedal. Note the following:
   a. Check that the shift shaft return spring is centered on the pin (D, **Figure 31**).
   b. If the transmission will not shift properly, remove the shift pedal and slide the shift shaft (A, **Figure 31**) out of the engine.

   c. Check the shift shaft for missing parts, incorrect assembly or damage (Chapter Six). If okay, continue with Step 6.

6. Have your assistant turn the rear wheel while you turn the shift drum (A, **Figure 33**) by hand. When doing so, watch the movement and operation of the stopper lever assembly (B, **Figure 33**). When turning the shift drum, the stopper lever roller should move in and out of the shift drum detents. Each detent position represents a different gear position. The raised detent position on the shift drum (C, **Figure 33**) is the NEUTRAL position. The stopper lever assembly is held under tight spring tension. When the shift drum turns and moves the stopper lever roller out of a detent, spring tension forces the stopper lever to stay in contact with the shift drum and to move into the next detent position. If this is not happening, try to pry the stopper lever out with a screwdriver (**Figure 34**). If the stopper lever will not move, it was installed incorrectly. Reinstall it and try the shifting again. If this was not the problem, remove the stopper lever assembly (Chapter Six) and check it for damage. If the stopper lever assembly is okay, continue with Step 7.

NOTE
If the transmission overshifts, check for a broken shift shaft arm spring or a weak or damaged stopper lever spring.

7. Check the shift drum as follows:
   a. Shift the transmission into NEUTRAL (if possible) and make a mark on the crankcase that aligns with the shift drum NEUTRAL detent position (C, **Figure 33**).
   b. While turning the rear wheel or the mainshaft, turn the shift drum to change gears. Each time the shift drum moves and a new detent position aligns with the mark made in sub-step a, the transmission should change gear.
   c. The transmission should shift into each gear. If the shift drum cannot be turned, or if it locks into a particular gear position, the transmission is damaged. A locked shift drum indicates a damaged shift fork, a seized transmission gear or bearing or damaged shift drum.

8. To service the transmission, disassemble the engine and remove the transmission as described in Chapter Five, then service the transmission as described in Chapter Seven.

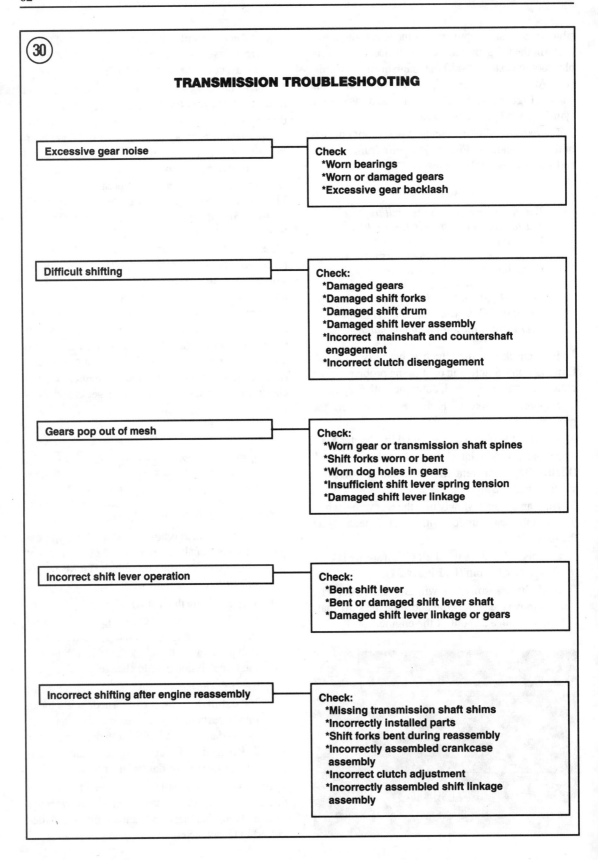

30

TRANSMISSION TROUBLESHOOTING

Excessive gear noise

Check
*Worn bearings
*Worn or damaged gears
*Excessive gear backlash

Difficult shifting

Check:
*Damaged gears
*Damaged shift forks
*Damaged shift drum
*Damaged shift lever assembly
*Incorrect mainshaft and countershaft
 engagement
*Incorrect clutch disengagement

Gears pop out of mesh

Check:
*Worn gear or transmission shaft spines
*Shift forks worn or bent
*Worn dog holes in gears
*Insufficient shift lever spring tension
*Damaged shift lever linkage

Incorrect shift lever operation

Check:
*Bent shift lever
*Bent or damaged shift lever shaft
*Damaged shift lever linkage or gears

Incorrect shifting after engine reassembly

Check:
*Missing transmission shaft shims
*Incorrectly installed parts
*Shift forks bent during reassembly
*Incorrectly assembled crankcase
 assembly
*Incorrect clutch adjustment
*Incorrectly assembled shift linkage
 assembly

9. Install all parts previously removed as described in the appropriate chapter.

KICKSTARTER

If the kickstarter lever sticks or slips at the bottom of its stroke, the problem is usually easy to find once the right crankcase cover is removed. The kickstarter assembly can be serviced with the engine mounted in the frame.

Refer to the following troubleshooting information for a list of common kickstarter symptoms and possible causes. To service the kickstarter assembly, refer to *Kickstarter* in Chapter Six.

> *NOTE*
> *A good way to inspect the kickstarter is to remove the clutch (Chapter Six), then reinstall the kick pedal (**Figure 35**) onto the kickstarter. Operate the kick pedal by hand while watching the movement of the ratchet gear when it engages the teeth on the kick gear.*

Kickstarter Lever or Shaft Slips

1. Excessively worn or damaged kickstarter shaft.
2. Excessively worn or damaged kick gear.
3. Excessively worn or damaged kick idle gear.
4. Kick ratchet gear not engaging.
5. Damaged kickstarter shaft circlip groove or circlip.

Kickstarter Does Not Return

1. Kickstarter incorrectly installed in crankcase.
2. Weak or damaged kickstarter return spring. Spring is not indexed properly in kickstarter shaft hole or in crankcase hole.
3. Kick gear seized on shaft.
4. Kickstarter return spring disengaged from one or both ends.
5. Incorrectly assembled kickstarter assembly.
6. Kickstarter ratchet guide loose or damaged.

Kickstarter is Hard to Operate

1. *Kickstarter axle*:
    a. Seized kickstarter gear.
    b. Seized kickstarter idler gear.
    c. Stripped kick pedal and/or kickstarter shaft splines.
    d. Kickstarter incorrectly installed in crankcase.
2. *Engine:*
    a. Seized piston and cylinder.
    b. Broken piston.
    c. Damaged crankcase assembly.
    d. Damaged right crankcase cover.
    e. Seized or broken crankshaft.
    f. Seized crankshaft main bearings.
3. *Transmission oil:*
    a. Low viscosity gear oil.
    b. Deteriorated gear oil.

DRIVE TRAIN NOISE

This section deals with noises that are restricted to the drive train assembly—drive chain, clutch and transmission. While some drive train noises have little meaning, abnormal noises are a good indicator of a developing problem. The problem is recognizing the difference between a normal and abnormal noise. A new noise, no matter how minor, must be investigated.

1. *Drive chain noise*— Normal drive chain noise can be considered a low-pitched, continuous whining sound. The noise will vary, depending on the speed of the bike and the terrain you are riding on, as well as proper lubrication, wear (both chain and sprocket) and alignment. When checking abnormal drive chain noise, consider the following:

    a. *Inadequate lubrication*—A dry chain will give off a loud whining sound. Clean and lubricate the drive chain at regular intervals (Chapter Three).

    b. *Incorrect chain adjustment*—Check and adjust the drive chain as described in Chapter Three.

    c. *Worn chain*—Check chain wear at regular intervals, and replace it when it's overall length exceeds the wear limit specified in Chapter Three.

    d. *Worn or damaged sprockets*—Worn or damaged sprockets accelerate chain wear. Inspect the sprockets carefully as described in Chapter Three.

    e. *Worn, damaged or missing drive chain sliders and rollers*—Chain sliders and rollers are in constant contact with the chain. Check them often for loose, damaged or missing parts. A missing chain slider or roller will increase chain slack and may cause rapid wear against the frame or swing arm.

2. *Clutch noise*— Investigate any noise that develops in the clutch. First, drain the transmission oil, checking for bits of metal or clutch plate material. If the oil looks and smells good, remove the clutch (Chapter Six) and check for the following:

    a. Worn or damaged clutch housing and primary drive gear teeth.

    b. Excessive clutch housing axial play.

    c. Excessive clutch housing-to-friction plate clearance.

    d. Excessive clutch housing gear-to-primary drive gear backlash.

    e. Excessive clutch needle bearing and collar wear.

3. *Transmission noise*— The transmission will exhibit more normal noises than the clutch, but like the clutch, a new noise in the transmission must be investigated. Drain the transmission oil into a clean container. Wipe a small amount of oil on your finger and rub the finger and thumb together. Check for the presence of metallic particles. Inspect the drain container for signs of water separation from the oil. Some transmission associated noises are caused by:

    a. Insufficient transmission oil level.

    b. Contaminated transmission oil.

c. Transmission oil viscosity too thin. A too thin oil viscosity will raise the transmission operating temperature.

d. Worn transmission gear(s).

e. Chipped or broken transmission gear(s).

f. Excessive gear side play.

g. Worn or damaged crankshaft-to-transmission bearing(s).

h. Worn or damaged kickstarter idle gear.

i. Kickstarter ratchet gear does not disengage from the kickstarter gear.

NOTE
If metallic particles are found in Step 2 or Step 3, remove and inspect the clutch, then if necessary, disassemble the engine and inspect the transmission.

FRONT SUSPENSION AND STEERING

Poor handling may be caused by improper front or rear tire pressure, a damaged or bent frame or front steering components, worn swing arm bushings, worn wheel bearings or dragging brakes.

1. Excessive handlebar vibration:
   a. Loose or damaged handlebar clamps.
   b. Incorrect handlebar clamp installation.
   c. Bent or cracked handlebar.
   d. Worn handlebar rubber dampers, if so equipped.
   e. Loose steering stem nut.
   f. Worn or damaged front wheel bearings.
   g. Bent axle.
   h. Damaged tire.
   i. Excessively worn front tire.
   j. Damaged rim.
   k. Loose, missing or broken engine mount bolts and mounts.
   l. Cracked frame, especially at the steering head.
   m. Incorrect tire pressure for prevailing riding conditions.
2. Difficult steering (handlebar is hard to turn):
   a. Front tire air pressure is too low.
   b. Incorrect throttle cable routing.
   c. Incorrect clutch cable routing.
   d. Steering stem adjustment is too tight.
   e. Bent steering stem.
   f. Improperly lubricated steering bearings.
   g. Damaged steering bearings and races.

REAR SUSPENSION

1. If the rear suspension is too soft, check for the following:
   a. Incorrect shock absorber adjustment.
   b. Leaking shock absorber.
2. If the rear suspension is too hard, check for the following:
   a. Incorrect shock absorber adjustment.
   b. Rear tire pressure too high.

FRAME NOISE

Noises that can be traced to the frame or suspension are usually caused by loose, worn or damaged parts. Various noises that are related to the frame are listed below:

1. *Disc brake noise*—A screeching sound during braking is the most common disc brake noise. Some other disc brake associated noises can be caused by:
   a. Glazed brake pad surface.
   b. Excessively worn brake pads.
   c. Warped brake disc.
   d. Loose brake disc mounting bolts.
   e. Loose or missing brake caliper mounting bolts.
   f. Damaged caliper.
   g. Cracked wheel hub where the brake disc mounts to the hub.
2. *Front fork noise:*
   a. Contaminated fork oil.
   b. Fork oil level too low.
   c. Broken fork spring.
   d. Worn or damaged front fork bushings.
3. *Rear shock absorber noise:*
   a. Loose shock absorber mounting bolts.
   b. Cracked or broken shock spring.
   c. Damaged shock absorber.
4. Some other frame associated noises are caused by:
   a. Broken frame.
   b. Broken swing arm.
   c. Loose engine mounting bolts.
   d. Dry or damaged steering bearings.
   e. Loose mounting bracket(s).

BRAKES

The disc brakes are critical to riding performance and safety. Inspect the front and rear brake fre-

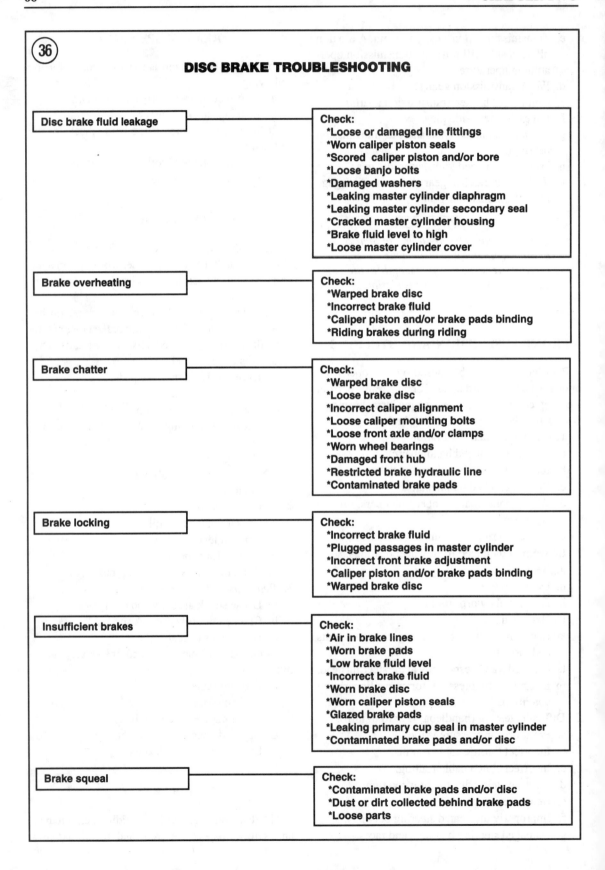

DISC BRAKE TROUBLESHOOTING

(36)

Disc brake fluid leakage

Check:
*Loose or damaged line fittings
*Worn caliper piston seals
*Scored caliper piston and/or bore
*Loose banjo bolts
*Damaged washers
*Leaking master cylinder diaphragm
*Leaking master cylinder secondary seal
*Cracked master cylinder housing
*Brake fluid level to high
*Loose master cylinder cover

Brake overheating

Check:
*Warped brake disc
*Incorrect brake fluid
*Caliper piston and/or brake pads binding
*Riding brakes during riding

Brake chatter

Check:
*Warped brake disc
*Loose brake disc
*Incorrect caliper alignment
*Loose caliper mounting bolts
*Loose front axle and/or clamps
*Worn wheel bearings
*Damaged front hub
*Restricted brake hydraulic line
*Contaminated brake pads

Brake locking

Check:
*Incorrect brake fluid
*Plugged passages in master cylinder
*Incorrect front brake adjustment
*Caliper piston and/or brake pads binding
*Warped brake disc

Insufficient brakes

Check:
*Air in brake lines
*Worn brake pads
*Low brake fluid level
*Incorrect brake fluid
*Worn brake disc
*Worn caliper piston seals
*Glazed brake pads
*Leaking primary cup seal in master cylinder
*Contaminated brake pads and/or disc

Brake squeal

Check:
*Contaminated brake pads and/or disc
*Dust or dirt collected behind brake pads
*Loose parts

quently and replace any excessively worn or damaged parts immediately. When replacing or refilling the brake fluid, use only DOT 3 or DOT 4 brake fluid, as specified in Chapter Three, from a closed and sealed container. See Chapter Fourteen for additional information on brake fluid and disc brake service. The troubleshooting procedures in **Figure** 36 will help you isolate the majority of disc brake troubles.

When checking brake pad wear, check that the brake pads in each caliper contact the disc squarely. If one of the brake pads is wearing unevenly, suspect a warped or bent brake disc, a damaged caliper or damaged caliper bracket pins.

2

CHAPTER THREE

LUBRICATION, MAINTENANCE, AND TUNE-UP

This chapter covers all of the required periodic service procedures that do not require major disassembly. Regular, careful maintenance is the best guarantee for a trouble-free, long lasting motorcycle. All motorcycles designed for off-road use require proper lubrication, maintenance and tune-up to maintain a high level of performance and extend engine, suspension and chassis life. Procedures at the end of this chapter also describe steps on how to store your Kawasaki for long periods of nonuse.

You can do your own lubrication, maintenance and tune-ups if you follow the correct procedures and use common sense. Always remember that damage can result from improper tuning and adjustment. In addition, where special tools or testers are specified during a particular maintenance or adjustment procedure, use the correct tool or refer service to a qualified Kawasaki dealership or repair shop.

Tables 1-13 are at the end of this chapter.

SERVICE INTERVALS

The factory specified intervals shown in **Table 1** and **Table 2** are based on a number of races completed. Strict adherence to these recommendations will help ensure long service from your motorcycle.

TUNE-UP

The number of definitions of the term "tune-up" is probably equal to the number of people defining it. For the purpose of this book, a tune-up is a general adjustment and maintenance to insure peak engine and suspension performance.

Kawasaki does not list a specific tune-up procedure to be followed in any set order. However, if you follow the service intervals listed in **Table 1** and **Table 2**, you will effectively keep the engine, steering, suspension and brakes in tune.

Tune-up procedures are usually listed in some logical order. For example, some procedures should be done with the engine cold and others with the engine hot. For example, check the cylinder head nuts when the engine is cold and adjust the carburetor and drain the transmission oil when the engine is hot. Also, because the engine needs to run as well as possible when adjusting the carburetor, service the air filter and spark plug first. If you adjust the carburetor and then find that the air filter needs service, you may have to readjust the carburetor.

After completing a tune-up, record the date, the motorcycle operating time or number of races completed, and the type of service performed. This information will provide an accurate record on the type of service performed. This record can also be used to schedule future service procedures at the correct time.

To perform a tune-up on your Kawasaki, service the following engine and chassis items as described in this chapter:

Engine Tune-Up Procedure

1. Tighten cylinder head nuts (Chapter Four).
2. Repack silencer (Chapter Four).
3. Check exhaust pipe fasteners for tightness (Chapter Four).
4. Clean and re-oil air filter.
5. Check and service spark plug.
6. Check compression.
7. Adjust carburetor.
8. Check throttle operation and cable.
9. Check clutch operation and cable.
10. Start engine and allow to warm to normal operating temperature.
11. Adjust carburetor.
12. Change transmission oil.
13. Check all exposed engine nuts and bolts for tightness.

Chassis Tune-Up Procedure

1. Clean and lubricate drive chain.
2. Check drive chain tension and alignment.
3. Check brake operation and cable adjustment.
4. Check rims, hubs and tires.
5. Check operation of front and rear suspension.
6. Check steering play.
7. Check all exposed steering and suspension nuts and bolts for tightness.

Test Ride

The test ride is an important part of the tune-up or service procedure because it is where you will find out whether the motorcycle is ready to ride or if it needs more work. When test riding a motorcycle, always start slowly and ride in a safe place away from all other vehicles and people. Concentrate on the areas that were worked on and how they can affect other systems. If the brakes were worked on, never apply full brake pressure at high speeds (emergencies excepted). It is safer to check the brakes at slower speeds and with moderate pressure. Do not continue to ride the motorcycle if the engine, brakes or any suspension or steering component is not working correctly.

PRE-RIDE INSPECTION

Perform the following checks before each race or before the first ride of the day. All of these checks, unless noted otherwise, are described in this chapter. If a component requires service, refer to the appropriate section.

1. Inspect the fuel hose and fittings for leakage. Check that each hose end is secured with a hose clamp.

> *WARNING*
> *When performing any service work to the engine or cooling system, never remove the radiator cap, coolant drain bolt or disconnect any hose while the engine and radiator are hot. Scalding fluid and steam may escape under pressure and cause serious injury.*

2. Check the coolant level with the engine cold. Check the cooling system for leaks.

3. Make sure the radiator cap is installed and tightened correctly.

4. Remove the spark plug and check its firing tip. Regap the plug, if necessary. Install the spark plug and tighten securely.

5. Check the spark plug cap and high tension lead for tightness.

6. Make sure the cylinder head and cylinder flange nuts are tightened correctly.

7. Make sure the air filter is clean and that the air box and carburetor boots are secured tightly. Check also that the subframe mounting bolts are tight.

8. Check the transmission oil level.

9. Check the front and rear sprockets for excessive wear.

10. Check the clutch and brake levers and replace damaged levers.

> *WARNING*
> *If the ball is broken off the end of the brake or clutch lever, replace the damaged lever immediately. The lever ball (Figure 1) is designed to prevent the lever from puncturing your hand or arm during a crash.*

11. Check the throttle for proper operation. Open the throttle all the way and release it. The throttle must close quickly with no binding or roughness. Repeat this step with the handlebar facing straight ahead and at both full lock positions. Start the engine and open and release the throttle. It must open and close smoothly.

12. Check the clutch free play adjustment. Start the engine and check the clutch operation by pulling the clutch lever in and shifting the transmission into gear. If the engine stalls or if the bike creeps forward, adjust the clutch as described in this chapter.

13. Check the front and rear brake fluid levels. Add the correct type of brake fluid, as specified in this chapter, to bring the levels to their FULL mark.

14. Check that the front and rear brakes work properly.

15. Check the front forks and rear shock absorber for oil leaks.

16. Check the front and rear suspension adjustments; adjust if necessary as described in Chapter Twelve or Chapter Thirteen.

17. Place the bike on a stand so the front wheel clears the ground and check steering play.

18. With the front wheel off the ground, turn the handlebar from side to side. Check that the control cables are routed properly and do not interfere with the handlebar or the handlebar controls.

19. Check the tires for damage.

20. Check each wheel for loose or damaged spokes. Check that the rim locks are tight.

21. Check the tire pressure.

22. Check for excessively worn, damaged or missing drive chain sliders and rollers.

23. Lubricate the drive chain.

24. Check the drive chain alignment and adjustment.

25. Check the tightness of all exposed fasteners.

26. Make sure the fuel tank is mounted securely. Check the fuel tank and fuel hose for leaks.

27. Make sure the fuel tank is full and has the correct fuel/oil mixture. Refer to *Engine Lubrication* in this chapter.

28. Start the engine, then operate the engine stop switch. The engine should turn off.

29. Before trail riding, check your tool belt to make sure that all of your tools and spare parts are in place.

ENGINE LUBRICATION

WARNING
A serious fire hazard always exists around gasoline and other petroleum products. Do not allow any smoking in areas where fuel is being mixed or while refueling your machine. Always have a fire extinguisher, rated for gasoline and electrical fires, within reach.

Your Kawasaki's engine is lubricated by oil mixed with gasoline. Refer to **Table 3** for recommended oil and fuel types. Mix the oil and gasoline thoroughly in a separate clean, sealable container larger than the quantity being mixed to allow room for agitation. Always measure the quantities exactly. **Table 4** lists the factory recommended fuel/oil mixture ratio for all models. **Table 5** lists the amount of oil to add to different amounts of fuel to obtain the correct fuel/oil mixture ratio. **Table 6** lists the fuel tank capacity for all models. Use a good grade of premium fuel as specified in **Table 3**.

Use a bottle with graduations in both milliliters (ml) or fluid ounces (oz.) on the side. Pour the

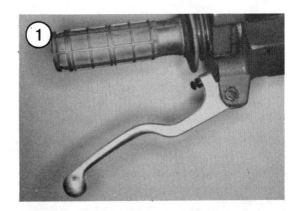

required amount of oil into the mixing container and add approximately 1/2 the required amount of gasoline. Agitate the mixture thoroughly, then add the remaining fuel and agitate again until well mixed..

NOTE

Always mix a fresh amount of fuel the morning of the race or ride; do not mix more than you will use that day. To avoid fuel system contamination, use a funnel with a filter when pouring the fuel into the fuel tank.

CAUTION

Do not mix castor bean oils with petroleum lubricants. A gum will form and may cause serious engine damage.

TRANSMISSION OIL

The transmission oil lubricates all of the components that operate behind the clutch cover and within the transmission portion of the crankcase. The transmission oil does not lubricate the two-stroke engine

components (piston, rings, cylinder, connecting rod, crankshaft and main bearings).

Kawasaki suggests the use of a high-quality engine oil (**Table 3**). The quality rating is stamped or printed on top of the can or label on plastic bottles (**Figure 2**).

Another type of oil to consider is a gear oil designed exclusively for use in two-stroke transmissions. These oils have the same lubricating qualities as API motor oils but are formulated with different load carrying agents and extreme pressure additives that prevent oil break down and foaming caused by clutch and transmission operation. For example, the Bel-Ray Gear Saver SAE 80W transmission oil shown in **Figure 3** is a light bodied oil that corresponds to motor oil grades SAE 30, SAE 10W-30 and SAE 10W-40. There are a number of two-stroke gear oils available for use in your motorcycle's transmission. However, do not confuse this type of gear oil with a Hypoid gear oil used in motorcycle and ATV shaft drive units. Before using a specific gear oil, pay attention to its service designation, making sure it is designed for use in two-stroke transmissions.

Try to use the same brand of oil at each oil change. Do not use an oil additive as it may cause clutch slippage.

Oil Level Check

1. If the engine has just been run, turn it off and wait three minutes to allow the oil to drain down into the crankcase.

2. Place the bike in an upright position on level ground.

3. Check the oil level through the oil level gauge (**Figure 4**) mounted on the right crankcase cover. The oil level must be between the upper and lower levels. If the oil level is too high or low, perform Step 4.

4. Adjust the oil level as follows:

  a. Remove the oil fill cap (**Figure 5**).

  b. If the oil level is too high, remove excess oil with a syringe.

  c. If the oil level is low, add oil through the oil fill hole to bring the level to the upper level mark. Top off the oil with the correct type of transmission oil listed in **Table 3**. Do not overfill.

  d. Install and tighten the oil fill cap (**Figure 5**).

Oil Change

To drain the oil you need the following:
  a. Drain pan.
  b. Funnel.
  c. Correct quantity of transmission oil (**Table 7**).

There are a number of ways to discard the old oil safely. The easiest way is to pour it from the drain pan into a half-gallon plastic bleach or milk bottle. Tighten the cap and take the oil to a service station or oil retailer for recycling. *Do not* discard the oil in your household trash or pour it onto the ground.

1. Start and run the engine for three minutes, then shut it off.

2. Park the bike on a level surface and place a drain pan underneath the engine.

3. Wipe all dirt and debris from around the drain plug. Then remove the drain plug (**Figure 6**) and washer and allow the oil to drain.

4. Replace the sealing washer if leaking or damaged.

5. Replace the drain plug if the if the hex portion on the plug is starting to round off.

6. After all of the oil has drained, install the transmission drain plug and washer and tighten as specified in **Table 8**.

7. Add the recommended weight (**Table 3**) and quantity transmission oil (**Table 7**).

8. Install the oil filler cap. Start the engine and run it for three minutes.

9. Shut the engine off and check the drain plug for leaks. Check the oil level as described in this chapter. Adjust the level if necessary.

> *WARNING*
> *Prolonged contact with used oil may cause skin cancer. Wash your hands and arms with soap and water as soon as possible after handling or coming in contact with any type of engine or transmission oil.*

AIR FILTER

The job of an air filter is to trap dirt and other abrasive particles before they enter the engine. Even though the air filter is one of the cheapest parts on your Kawasaki, it is often neglected at the expense of engine performance and wear. Never run the engine without a properly oiled and installed air

filter element. Likewise running the engine with a dry or damaged air filter element will allow unfiltered air to enter the engine. A well-oiled but dirty or clogged air filter will reduce the amount of air that enters the engine and cause a rich air/fuel mixture, resulting in poor engine starting, spark plug fouling and reduced engine performance. Frequent air filter inspection and cleaning service is critical part of minimizing engine wear and maintaining engine performance. **Figure 7** shows how dirt can pass through an improperly installed or damaged air filter.

Table 1 lists intervals for cleaning the air filter. Clean the air filter more often when riding in sand or in wet and muddy conditions.

1. Remove the seat (Chapter Fifteen).

2. Remove the wingbolt and washer (**Figure 8**) securing the air filter to the housing and remove the air filter.

3. Use a flashlight and check inside the air box and carburetor boot for dirt and other debris that may have passed through the air filter.

4. Wipe the inside of the air box with a clean rag. If you cannot clean the air box with it mounted on the

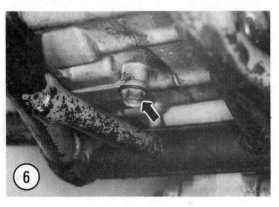

bike, remove and clean the air box thoroughly with solvent. Clean the air box with hot soapy water and rinse with water from a garden hose.

5. Cover the air box opening with a clean shop rag.

6. Inspect all air box fittings for damage.

7. Pull the foam element off its frame (**Figure 9**).

8. Before cleaning the air filter element, check it for brittleness, separation or other damage. Replace the filter if excessively worn or damaged. If there is no visible damage, clean the air filter element as follows.

> *WARNING*
> *Do not clean the air filter element with gasoline or any type of low flash point solvent..*

9. Soak the air filter in a container filled with kerosene or an air filter cleaner. Gently squeeze the filter to dislodge and remove the oil and dirt from the filter pores. Swish the filter around in the cleaner while repeating this step a few times, then remove the air filter and set aside to air-dry.

10. Fill a clean pan with warm soapy water.

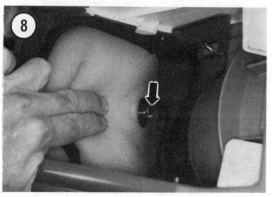

11. Submerge the filter into the cleaning solution and gently work the cleaner into the filter pores. Soak and gently squeeze the filter to clean it.

> *CAUTION*
> *Do not wring or twist the filter when cleaning it. This could damage a filter pore or tear the filter loose at a seam and allow unfiltered air to enter the engine.*

12. Rinse the filter under warm water while gently squeezing it.

13. Repeat these steps until there are no signs of dirt being rinsed from the filter.

14. After cleaning the filter, inspect it carefully and replace if torn or damaged.

> *CAUTION*
> *Do not run the engine with a damaged air filter as it will allow dirt to enter and damage the engine.*

15. Set the air filter aside and allow it to dry thoroughly.

> *CAUTION*
> *A damp filter will not trap fine dust. Make sure the filter is dry before oiling it.*

16. Properly oiling an air filter is a messy job. You may want to wear a pair of disposable rubber gloves when performing this procedure. Oil the filter as follows:

    a. Purchase a box of gallon size storage bags. The bags can be used when cleaning the filter as well as for storing engine and carburetor parts during disassembly.

b. Place the air filter into a storage bag (**Figure 10**).

NOTE
Motor oils are too thin to be used on air filters. If a motor oil is applied to an air filter, some of the oil drains from the filter and collects in the bottom of the air box and carburetor boot. When the engine is running, this oil and some of the other oil in the filter pores is drawn into the engine, thus richening the air/fuel mixture and causing the engine to sputter and run rough. The engine will eventually smooth out after this excess oil is consumed, but because there is less oil on the filter, dirt is more likely to pass through the air filter and into the engine. Foam air filter oils are specially formulated for use in polyurethane foam air filters. A low viscosity solvent in the filter oil helps the oil to be applied easily and thoroughly into the filter pores. This solvent evaporates after application and leaves behind a tacky, viscous fluid that stays in the filter pores while allowing maximum air flow through the filter.

c. Pour foam air filter oil onto the filter until the filter is soaked with oil.

d. Gently squeeze and release the filter to disperse the filter oil into the filter's pores. Repeat until all of the filter's pores are saturated.

e. Remove the filter from the bag and check the pores for uneven oiling. This is indicated by light or dark areas on the filter. If necessary, soak the filter and squeeze it again.

f. When the filter oiling is even, squeeze the filter a final time.

g. Remove the air filter from the bag.

17. Install the air filter onto its frame. Align the two holes in the filter with the two pins on the frame (**Figure 9**).

18. Apply a coat of grease onto the filter's sealing surface (**Figure 11**).

19. Make sure the lockwasher and flat washer are installed on the air filter wingbolt.

20. Install the air filter into the air box—align the tab on the air filter with the index mark inside the air box (**Figure 12**).

CAUTION
If the air filter is not aligned correctly with the air box, dirt may enter the engine and damage it.

21. Install the air filter wingbolt (Figure 8) and tighten securely. Check that the air filter element seats evenly against the air box.

22. Pour the leftover filter oil from the bag back into the bottle for reuse.

23. Dispose of the plastic bag.

24. Install the seat (Chapter Fifteen).

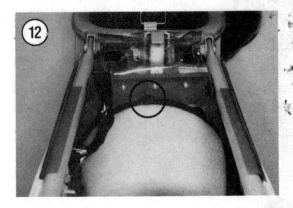

SPARK PLUG

Table 9 lists the standard heat range spark plug for the models covered in this manual.

Correct Spark Plug Heat Range

Spark plugs are available in various heat ranges, hotter or colder (**Figure 13**) than the plug originally installed at the factory.

Select a spark plug of the heat range designed for the loads and conditions in which your Kawasaki will be operating. Use of incorrect heat ranges can cause plug fouling, engine overheating and piston damage.

In general, use a hot plug for low speeds and low temperatures. Use a cold plug for high speeds, high engine loads and high temperatures. The plug must operate hot enough to burn off unwanted deposits, but not so hot that it causes engine overheating and preignition. A spark plug of the correct heat range will show a light tan color on the portion of the insulator within the cylinder after the plug has been in service. See *Reading Spark Plugs* in this section.

The reach (length) of a plug is also important. A too short plug will cause excessive carbon buildup, hard starting and plug fouling (**Figure 14**).

Spark Plug Removal

1. Grasp the spark plug lead (**Figure 15**) as near the plug as possible and pull it off the plug . If it is stuck to the plug, twist it slightly to break it loose.

2. Blow any dirt and other debris away from the spark plug and spark plug hole in the cylinder head.

CAUTION
Dirt that falls through the spark plug hole will cause engine wear and damage.

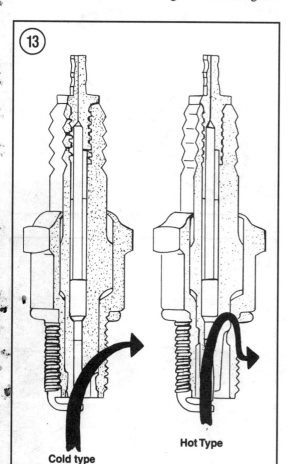

Cold type   Hot Type

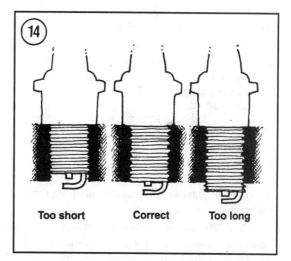

Too short   Correct   Too long

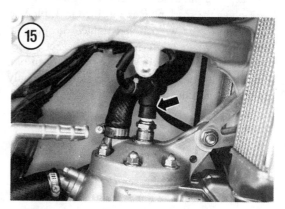

3. Remove the spark plug with a 14 mm spark plug wrench.

NOTE
If the plug is difficult to remove, apply penetrating oil, like WD-40 or Liquid Wrench, around the base of the plug and let it soak in about 10-20 minutes.

4. Inspect the plug carefully. Look for a broken center porcelain insulator, excessively eroded electrode, and excessive carbon or oil fouling. See *Reading Spark Plugs* in this section.

Gapping and Installing the Plug

Gap used and new spark plugs to ensure a reliable, consistent spark. Use a spark plug gapping tool and a wire feeler gauge as described in this procedure.

1. Install the small cap adapter onto the spark plug (**Figure 16**) if required.

2. Refer to the spark plug gap listed in **Table 9**. Insert a round feeler gauge between the center and side electrode (**Figure 17**). If the gap is correct, you will feel a slight drag as you pull the wire through. If there is no drag, or the gauge will not pass through, bend the side electrode with a gapping tool (**Figure 18**) to set the proper gap.

NOTE
Do not use a flat feeler gauge to check the spark plug gap on a used spark plug or too wide of a gap will result.

3. Apply an antiseize lubricant to the plug threads before installing the spark plug.

4. Screw the spark plug in by hand until it seats. Very little effort is required. If force is necessary, the plug may be cross-threaded. Unscrew it and try again.

5. Tighten the spark plug as specified in **Table 8** or use a spark plug wrench and tighten the plug an additional 1/4 to 1/2 turn after the gasket makes contact with the head. If you are installing an old, the original plug and reusing the old gasket, only tighten an additional 1/4 turn.

NOTE
Do not overtighten. This may crush the gasket and cause a compression leak.

6. Install the spark plug cap (**Figure 15**) onto the spark plug. Make sure it is on tight.

CAUTION
Make sure the spark plug wire is pulled away from the exhaust pipe.

Reading Spark Plugs

Careful examination of the spark plug can determine valuable engine and spark plug information. This information is only valid after performing the following steps.

1. Ride the motorcycle at full throttle in a suitable area.

NOTE
You must ride the motorcycle long enough to obtain an accurate reading or color on the spark plug. If the original plug was fouled, use a new plug.

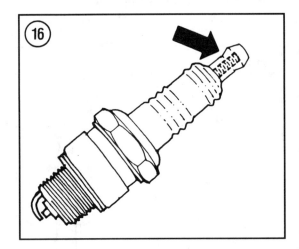

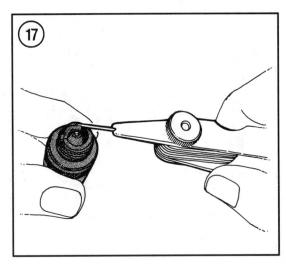

2. Push the engine stop switch, close the throttle and coast to a stop.

3. Remove the spark plug and examine it. Compare it to **Figure 19** and note the following:

Normal condition

If the plug has a light tan- or gray-colored deposit and no abnormal gap wear or erosion, good engine, carburetion and ignition condition are indicated. The plug in use is the proper heat range and may be serviced and returned to use.

Carbon fouled

Soft, dry, sooty deposits covering the entire firing end of the plug are evidence of incomplete combustion. Even though the firing end of the plug is dry, the plug's insulation decreases. An electrical path is formed that lowers the voltage from the ignition system. Engine misfiring is a sign of carbon fouling. Carbon fouling can be caused by one or more of the following:

a. Too rich fuel mixture.

b. Spark plug heat range too cold.

c. Clogged air filter.

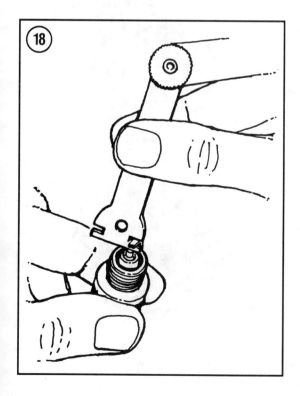

d. Over-retarded ignition timing.

e. Ignition component failure.

f. Low engine compression.

g. Prolonged idling.

Oil fouled

The tip of an oil fouled plug has a black insulator tip, a damp oily film over the firing end and a carbon layer over the entire nose. The electrodes will not be worn. Common causes for this condition are:

a. Incorrect carburetor jetting.

b. Low idle speed or prolonged idling.

c. Ignition component failure.

d. Spark plug heat range too cold.

e. Engine still being broken in.

Oil fouled spark plugs may be cleaned in an emergency, but is better to replace them. It is important to correct the cause of fouling before you return the engine to service.

Gap bridging

Plugs with this condition exhibit gaps shorted out by combustion deposits between the electrodes. The engine can still run with a bridged spark plug, but it will miss badly. If you encounter this condition, check for an improper oil type or excessive carbon in the combustion chamber or exhaust valve. Be sure to find and correct the cause of this condition.

Overheating

Badly worn electrodes and premature gap wear are signs of overheating, along with a gray or white "blistered" porcelain insulator surface. The most common cause for this condition is using a spark plug of the wrong heat range (too hot). If you have not changed to a hotter spark plug and the plug is overheated, consider the following causes:

a. Lean fuel mixture.

b. Ignition timing too advanced.

c. Engine air leak.

d. Improper spark plug installation (overtightening).

e. No spark plug gasket.

⑲

SPARK PLUG CONDITIONS

NORMAL USE

OIL FOULED

CARBON FOULED

GAP BRIDGED

SUSTAINED PREIGNITION

WORN OUT

OVERHEATED

Photos courtesy of Champion Spark Plug Company.

Worn out

Corrosive gases formed by combustion and high voltage sparks have eroded the electrodes. Spark plugs in this condition require more voltage to fire under hard acceleration. Replace with a new spark plug.

Preignition

If the electrodes are melted, preignition is almost certainly the cause. Check for carburetor mounting or intake manifold leaks and advanced ignition timing. It is also possible a plug of the wrong heat range (too hot) is being used. Find the cause of the preignition before returning the engine into service.

CARBURETOR

This section describes service to the fuel hose, shutoff valve, intake manifold, choke and carburetor.

Fuel Hose and Shutoff Valve Inspection

Inspect the fuel hose (A, **Figure 20**) for any leaks or damage. Make sure each end of the hose is secured with a hose clamp. Replace the fuel hose and hose clamps if damaged.

Inspect the fuel shutoff valve for any leaks or damage. O-rings installed in the valve can go bad and cause the valve to leak fuel. If there is insufficient fuel flow, the screen mounted at the top of the pickup tube may be partially clogged. To service the fuel valve, refer to Chapter Eight.

> *WARNING*
> *A leaking fuel hose may cause the engine to catch on fire. Do not start the*

engine with a leaking or damaged fuel hose or fuel shutoff valve.

Fuel Hose Replacement

Replace the fuel hose (A, **Figure 20**) at the intervals specified in **Table 1**.

Carburetor Cleaning

Disassemble, clean and reassemble the carburetor at the intervals specified in **Table 1**.

Carburetor Choke

Check the choke by lifting up and then pushing down the choke lever (B, **Figure 20**). The choke valve inside the carburetor should move smoothly in both directions. To check the choke, perform the following:

1. Start the engine and allow to warm to its normal operating temperature.

2. When the engine can run cleanly without the choke, lift the choke lever to open the choke circuit inside the carburetor. When doing so the engine should stall. If the engine does not stall, the choke may not be working correctly.

> *NOTE*
> *Lifting the choke lever opens the choke circuit. Pushing the choke lever down closes the choke circuit.*

3. If necessary, service the choke as described in Chapter Eight.

Intake Manifold Inspection

The intake manifold mounts against the cylinder and connects the reed valve and carburetor to the engine. Loose intake manifold mounting bolts or a damaged intake manifold will allow air to leak into the engine and cause a lean air/fuel mixture. To accurately check for a loose or damaged intake manifold, perform the *Leak Down Test* in Chapter Two.

Carburetor Idle Speed and Mixture Adjustment

Proper idle speed is a balance between a low enough idle to give adequate compression braking and a high enough idle to prevent engine stalling (if desired). The idle air/fuel mixture affects transition from idle to 1/8 throttle openings.

Turning the pilot air screw in enriches the fuel mixture and turning it out leans the mixture.

1. Make sure the throttle cable free play is correct. Check and adjust as described in this chapter.
2. Turn the pilot air screw (A, **Figure 21**) in until it seats lightly, then back it out the number of turns indicated in **Table 10**.

> *CAUTION*
> *Never turn the pilot air screw in tight; otherwise, you will damage the screw or the soft aluminum seat in the carburetor.*

3. Start the engine and allow to warm thoroughly.

> *NOTE*
> *The idle speed screw on some models is secured in place with a locknut. When a locknut is used, loosen it before adjusting the idle speed screw, then tighten it after making the adjustment.*

4. Turn the idle speed screw (B, **Figure 21**) in or out to obtain the desired idle speed. If you do not want the engine to idle, turn the idle speed screw out until the engine stops.
5. Adjust the pilot air screw (A, **Figure 21**) as follows:

   a. Turn the pilot air screw in one direction until the engine speed begins to drop quickly. Note the position of the screw.

   b. Next, turn the screw in the opposite direction until the engine speed increases and begins to drop again. Note the position of the screw.

   c. Last, turn the screw to a mid-point between the earlier settings.

> *NOTE*
> *Do not open the pilot air screw more than three turns or it may vibrate out. If you cannot get the bike to idle properly, check that the air filter is clean. If the air filter is good and other engine systems are operating correctly, the pilot jet size may be incorrect (Chapter Eight).*

> *NOTE*
> *After this adjustment is complete, test ride the bike. Throttle response from idle must be rapid without any hesitation. If there is hesitation, turn the pilot air screw in or out in 1/8 turn increments until the engine accelerates cleanly.*

> *WARNING*
> *With the engine idling, move the handlebar from side to side. If the idle speed increases during this movement, the throttle cable needs adjusting or it may be incorrectly routed through the frame. Correct this problem immediately. Do not ride the bike in this unsafe condition.*

EXHAUST SYSTEM

Inspect and service the exhaust system at the intervals specified in **Table 1**.

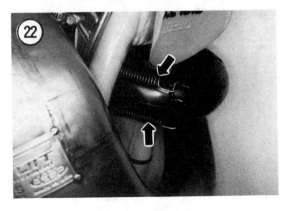

Inspection

Refer to Chapter Four for the service and repair procedures called out in this section.

1. Inspect the exhaust pipe for cracks or dents which could alter performance. Refer all repair to a qualified dealership or welding shop.

2. Check all of the exhaust pipe fasteners and mounting points for loose or damaged parts.

3. Check the exhaust pipe where it is bolted against the exhaust port on the front of the cylinder. Make sure the two springs (**Figure 22**) are in place and that there are no exhaust leaks. If the exhaust pipe is leaking at this point, remove the exhaust pipe and replace the gasket (A, **Figure 23**).

Exhaust System
O-ring Replacement

Remove the exhaust pipe (Chapter Four) and replace the O-rings (B, **Figure 23**) at the intervals specified in **Table 1**.

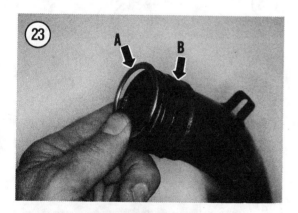

Silencer Repacking

Repack the silencer at the intervals specified in **Table 1**. Refer to Chapter Four for instructions.

COOLING SYSTEM

Cooling System Inspection

Once a year, or whenever troubleshooting the cooling system, check the following items. If you do not have the test equipment, refer testing to a Kawasaki dealership.

> *WARNING*
> *Never remove the radiator cap, coolant drain screw or disconnect any hose while the engine and radiators are hot. Scalding fluid and steam may be blown out under pressure and cause serious injury.*

1. With the engine cold, remove the radiator cap (**Figure 24**).

2. Check the rubber washers on the radiator cap (**Figure 25**). Replace the cap if the washers show signs of deterioration, cracking or other damage. If the radiator cap in good condition, perform Step 3.

> *CAUTION*
> *Do not exceed the cooling system pressure specified in Step 3 or Step 4 or you can damage the cooling system components.*

3. Pressure test the radiator cap (**Figure 26**) with a cooling system tester. The specified radiator cap relief pressure is 95-125 kPa (14-18 psi). The cap

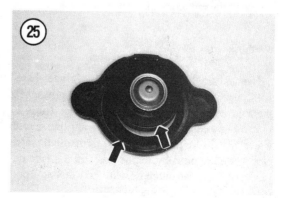

must be able to sustain this pressure for at least six seconds. Replace the radiator cap if it does not hold pressure.

4. Leave the radiator cap off and pressure test the cooling system to 125 kPa (18 psi). The system must be able to hold this pressure for at least six seconds. If the system fails to hold the specified pressure, check for the following conditions:

    a. Leaking or damaged hoses.

    b. Leaking water pump seal.

    c. Loose water pump mounting bolts.

    d. Warped water pump sealing surface.

    e. Warped cylinder head or cylinder mating surfaces.

5. Check all cooling system hoses for damage or deterioration. Replace any questionable hose. Make sure all hose clamps are tight.

6. Carefully clean the radiator core. Use a whisk broom, compressed air or low-pressure water. Straighten bent radiator fins with a screwdriver.

Coolant Check

WARNING
Never remove the radiator cap, coolant drain screw or disconnect any hose while the engine and radiators are hot. Scalding fluid and steam may be blown out under pressure and cause serious injury.

Before starting the bike, check the coolant level in the radiator. Remove the radiator cap (**Figure 24**). The coolant level must be at the bottom of the radiator filler neck as shown in **Figure 27**. If the level is low, add a sufficient amount of antifreeze and water (in a 50:50 ratio) as described under *Coolant*. Reinstall the radiator cap.

Coolant

Use only a high quality ethylene glycol-based antifreeze compounded for aluminum engines. Mix the antifreeze with water in a 50:50 ratio. **Table 11** lists coolant capacity. When mixing antifreeze with water, make sure to use only soft or distilled water. Never use tap or saltwater, as this will damage engine parts. You can purchase distilled water at supermarkets in gallon containers.

Coolant Change

Change the engine coolant at the intervals specified in **Table 1**.

CAUTION
Use only a high quality ethylene glycol antifreeze specifically labeled for use with aluminum engines. Do not use an alcohol-based antifreeze.

WARNING
Antifreeze is classified as an environmental toxic waste by the EPA and cannot be legally disposed of by flushing down a drain or pouring it onto the ground. Place antifreeze in a suitable container and dispose of it according to local EPA regulations. Do not store coolant where it is accessible to children or animals.

Perform the following procedure when the engine is *cold*.

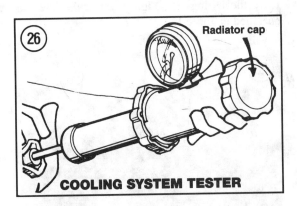

COOLING SYSTEM TESTER

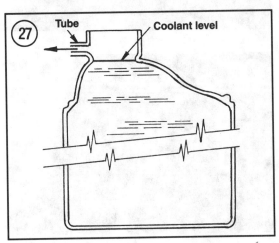

CAUTION
Be careful not to spill antifreeze on painted surfaces, as it will destroy the surface. Wash immediately with soapy water and rinse thoroughly with clean water.

1. Place a clean container under the water pump.

WARNING
When draining the coolant in this section, never remove the radiator cap, coolant drain screw or disconnect any hose while the engine and radiators are hot. Scalding fluid and steam may be blown out under pressure and cause serious injury.

2. Remove the radiator cap (**Figure 24**). This will speed up the draining process.
3. Remove the coolant drain plugs and washers. See **Figure 28** (water pump) and **Figure 29** (cylinder). Allow all coolant to drain.
4. Flush the cooling system with clean tap water directed through the radiator filler neck. Allow this water to drain completely.

NOTE
If any type of colored residue drains out with the coolant, flush the cooling system for at least 10 minutes (Step 4).

5. Install the coolant drain plugs and washers (**Figure 28** and **Figure 29**) and tighten as specified in **Table 8**.
6. Refill the radiator by adding a 50:50 mixture of antifreeze and distilled water through the radiator filler neck. See **Table 11** for coolant capacity for your model. Do not install the radiator cap at this time.
7. Lean the bike from side to side to bleed air trapped in the cooling system. When the bike is level, observe the coolant level in the radiator. Repeat this step until the coolant level stops dropping in the radiator.
8. Install and tighten the radiator cap (**Figure 24**).

WARNING
Never remove the radiator cap while the engine and radiators are hot. Scalding fluid and steam may be blown out under pressure and cause serious injury.

NOTE
Step 9 helps to bleed trapped air out of the cooling system.

9. Start the engine and allow to idle for a few minutes, then shut it off. After the engine cools down, remove the radiator cap and check the coolant level. Add coolant up to the filler neck (**Figure 27**), if necessary. Reinstall the radiator cap. Check the coolant drain plugs for leakage.

ENGINE COMPRESSION CHECK

A cylinder cranking compression check is the quickest way to check the internal condition of the engine (piston rings, piston and cylinder bore). It is a good idea to record the compression at each tune-up, and compare it with the reading you get at the next tune-up. This will help you spot any developing problems.

1. Clean the area around the spark plug, then remove it from the cylinder head.
2. Thread the tip of a compression gauge into the cylinder head spark plug hole (**Figure 30**). Make sure the gauge is seated properly.

3. Push the engine stop switch when kicking the engine over in Step 4.

4. Hold the throttle wide open and kick the engine over until the gauge needle gives its highest reading. The compression reading must be between 780-1220 kPa (114-176 psi).

   a. If the compression reading is low, disassemble the engine top end and measure the parts (Chapter Four).

   b. If the reading is excessively high, there may be excerssive of carbon deposits in the combustion chamber or on the piston crown. Disassemble the top end and clean the parts of all carbon as described in Chapter Four.

NOTE
If the compression is low, the engine cannot be tuned to provide maximum performance. The worn parts must be replaced and the engine rebuilt.

5. Push the release button on the compression gauge, then remove it from the cylinder. Reinstall the spark plug and connect its spark plug cap.

IGNITION TIMING

Refer to Chapter Nine.

CONTROL CABLE LUBRICATION

This section describes complete lubrication procedures for the control cables and clutch cable lever assembly.

Control Cable Lubrication

Clean and lubricate the clutch and throttle cables at the intervals indicated in **Table 1**. At the same time, check the cables for signs of wear and damage or fraying that could cause the cables to bind or break. The most positive method of control cable lubrication involves the use of a cable lubricator, like the one shown in **Figure 31**, and a can of cable lube.

CAUTION
Do not use chain lube to flush and lubricate the control cables.

1. Disconnect the clutch cable (**Figure 32**) at the handlebar and at the engine.

2. Disconnect the throttle cable at the handlebar and at the carburetor (**Figure 33**). Refer to Chapter Eight for instructions.

WARNING
Do not lubricate the throttle cable with its lower cable end mounted in the carburetor. The lubricant, dirt and other residues that flush out of the end of the cable will enter the carburetor and can

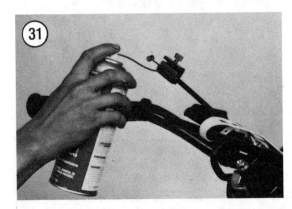

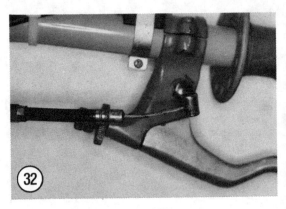

cause the throttle valve to stick open or cause rapid throttle valve and carburetor bore wear.

3. Attach a cable lubricator to the upper end of the cable following the manufacturer's instructions (**Figure 31**).

4. Insert the lubricant can nozzle into the hole in the lube tool, then press the button on the can and hold down until the lubricant begins to flow out the other end of the cable.

NOTE
Place a shop cloth at the end of the cable to catch the lubricant as it runs out.

5. Disconnect the lubricator from the end of the cable.

6. Apply a light coat of grease to the upper cable ball before reconnecting it.

7. Reconnect the clutch cable at the engine and handlebar. Adjust the clutch cable as described in this chapter.

8. Reconnect the throttle cable at the carburetor and handlebar as described in Chapter Eight. Adjust the

throttle cable as described in this chapter. Operate the throttle, checking that it opens and closes smoothly.

Clutch Lever
Pivot Bolt Lubrication

Periodically, remove the clutch lever pivot bolt at the handlebar and lubricate the bolt with 10W-30 motor oil. Replace the pivot bolt, if damaged.

THROTTLE CABLE ADJUSTMENT

Cable wear and stretch will affect the operation of the throttle cable and carburetor. Normal amounts of cable wear and stretch can be controlled by the free play adjustments described in this section. When you cannot adjust a cable within its adjustment limits, the cable is excessively worn or damaged and requires replacement.

Free play is the distance the throttle grip moves before the throttle valve moves.

Throttle Cable Adjustment
and Operation

Some throttle cable play is necessary to prevent changes in the idle speed when you turn the handlebars. Kawasaki specifies a throttle cable free play of 2-3 mm (1/8 in.).

In time, the throttle cable free play will increase due to cable stretch. This will delay throttle response and affect low speed operation. Conversely, if there is no throttle cable free play, an excessively high idle can result.

Minor adjustments can be made at the throttle grip adjuster. Major adjustments can be made at the throttle cable adjuster attached to the carburetor cap.

1. Open and release the throttle grip (**Figure 34**) with the handlebar pointed in different steering positions. In each position, the throttle must open and close smoothly. If the throttle cable binds or moves roughly, inspect the cable for kinks, bends or other damage. Replace a damaged cable. If the cable moves smoothly and is not damaged, continue with Step 2.

2. Slowly open the throttle and measure the free play at the throttle grip flange until resistance is felt.

If resistance is felt as soon as you turn the throttle grip, there is no cable free play.

3. If adjustment is necessary, slide the upper rubber cover away from the cable adjuster. Loosen the locknut and turn the cable adjuster (**Figure 35**) in or out to achieve the correct free play measurement. Tighten the locknut.

4. If the correct amount of free play cannot be achieved at the throttle grip flange, perform the following:

    a. Loosen the locknut and turn the throttle cable adjuster (**Figure 35**) in all the way. Tighten the locknut.

    b. At the carburetor cap, slide the lower rubber cover up the throttle cable and away from the cable adjuster. Loosen the cable adjuster locknut and turn the adjuster (**Figure 36**) as required. Tighten the locknut. If necessary, fine-tune the adjustment at the upper throttle cable adjuster (**Figure 35**).

    c. Make sure both adjuster locknuts are securely tightened.

    d. Slide the lower rubber cover (**Figure 36**) down the throttle cable and seat it onto the carburetor cap shoulder.

NOTE

The lower rubber cover must be installed correctly as it prevents dirt from entering the carburetor from around the cable.

    e. Slide the upper rubber cover over throttle housing at the handlebar.

5. If the correct amount of free play cannot be achieved after performing this adjustment procedure, the throttle cable has stretched to the point where it needs to be replaced. Replace the throttle cable as described in Chapter Eight.

6. Make sure the throttle grip rotates freely from a fully closed to fully open position.

7. Start the engine and allow it to idle in NEUTRAL. Turn the handlebar from side to side. If the idle increases, the throttle cable is routed incorrectly or there is not enough throttle cable free play.

CLUTCH

Clutch Cable Adjustment

The clutch adjustment takes up slack caused by cable stretch and clutch plate wear. Maintain the clutch cable free play within the specification listed in this procedure. Insufficient free play will cause clutch slippage and rapid clutch disc wear.

1. Pull the clutch lever toward the handlebar until resistance is felt and measure the free play between the clutch lever and its perch (A, **Figure 37**). The

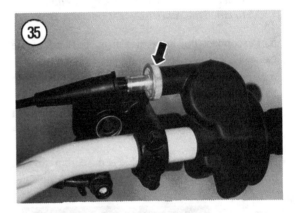

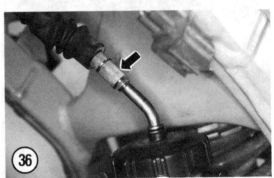

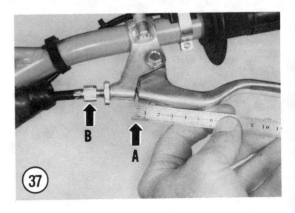

correct free play measurement is 2-3 mm (1/8 in.). If resistance was felt as soon as you pulled the clutch lever, there is no cable free play.

2. At the hand lever, loosen the locknut and turn the clutch cable adjuster (B, **Figure 37**) in or out to obtain the correct of free play. Tighten the locknut.

3. If the proper of free play cannot be achieved at the clutch lever adjuster, perform the following:

   a. At the clutch lever, loosen the locknut and turn the adjuster (B, **Figure 37**) in all the way. Tighten the locknut.

   b. Loosen the midcable adjuster locknut and turn the adjuster (**Figure 38**) as required to obtain the correct amount of cable free play. Tighten the locknut. If necessary, fine-tune the adjustment at the clutch lever adjuster (B, **Figure 37**).

4. If the proper amount of free play cannot be achieved by using this adjustment procedure, either the cable has stretched to the point that it needs to be replaced or the friction discs inside the clutch are worn and need replacing. Refer to Chapter Six for clutch cable and clutch plate service.

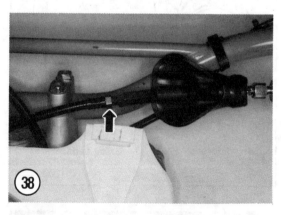

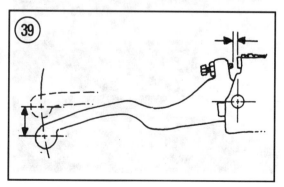

Clutch Plate Replacement

Refer to **Table 1** for clutch plate inspection and replacement intervals. Refer to Chapter Six for clutch service.

ENGINE TOP END INSPECTION

To maintain engine performance and reliability, perform the following engine top end inspection and service procedures at the intervals specified in **Table 1**. Refer to Chapter Four for service procedures.

1. Clean the exhaust valve assembly.
2. Clean and inspect the cylinder head.
3. Clean and inspect the piston, rings and cylinder bore.
4. Inspect the small end bearing for damage.

Piston and Ring Replacement

Replace the piston and rings at the intervals listed in **Table 1**.

KICK PEDAL AND SHIFT PEDAL

Inspect the kick pedal and shift pedal for looseness or damage. Tighten the kick pedal mounting bolt as specified in **Table 8**.

BRAKES

This section describes routine service procedures for the front and rear disc brakes. Refer to **Table 2** for service intervals.

Front Brake Lever Adjustment

Brake pad wear in the front brake caliper is automatically compensated for as the pistons move outward in the caliper. However, you can adjust the brake lever's position to move it closer to or farther away from the throttle grip. Adjust the lever to best suit your own personal preference.

> *CAUTION*
> *Be sure to maintain some front brake lever free play (**Figure 39**) when adjusting the brake lever. If there is no brake lever free play, the front brakes*

will drag on the brake disc. This will cause rapid brake pad wear and overheating of the front brake disc.

1A. On 1992-1996 models, adjust the front brake lever as follows:

  a. Loosen the locknut and turn the adjuster (**Figure 39**) in or out to position the brake lever closer to or farther away from the grip.

  b. Tighten the locknut and check the free play.

1B. On 1997 and later models, adjust the front brake lever as follows:

  a. Remove the cotter pin from the adjuster (**Figure 40**).

  b. Loosen the locknut and turn the adjuster in or out to position the brake lever closer to or farther away from the grip.

  c. Tighten the locknut and check the free play.

  d. Install a new cotter pin. Bend its arms over to lock it in place.

2. Support the bike with the front wheel off the ground. Then rotate the front wheel and check for brake drag. Operate the front brake lever several times to make sure it returns to the at-rest position after releasing it.

Rear Brake Pedal Adjustment (1992-1993)

The rear brake pedal can be adjusted two ways: rear brake pedal height and rear brake pedal play.

1. To check and adjust the rear brake pedal height position, perform the following:

  a. The rear brake pedal must be adjusted so it is within a range of 10 mm (0.39 in.) above or 10 mm (0.39 in.) below the top of the footpeg (**Figure 41**).

NOTE
A bent rear brake pedal will affect this adjustment and measurement.

  b. To adjust the rear brake pedal height position, loosen the locknut (A, **Figure 42**) and turn the adjuster (B, **Figure 42**) as necessary.

  c. Tighten the locknut and recheck the measurement.

2. To check and adjust the rear brake pedal free play, perform the following:

  a. The rear brake pedal must have 10-20 mm (0.39-0.78 in.) of free play when pushed down lightly by hand.

  b. To adjust the rear brake pedal play, loosen the locknut (A, **Figure 43**) and turn the pushrod adjuster (B, **Figure 43**) as necessary.

  c. Tighten the locknut and recheck the measurement.

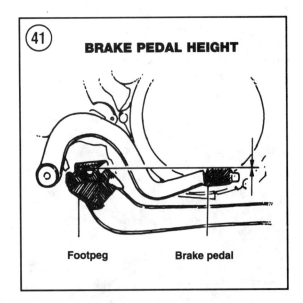

(41) **BRAKE PEDAL HEIGHT**

Footpeg   Brake pedal

(40)

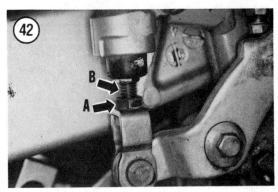

(42)

3. Support the bike with the rear wheel off the ground. Rotate the rear wheel and check for brake drag. Operate the rear brake pedal several times to make sure it returns to the at-rest position after releasing it.

Rear Brake Pedal Adjustment (1994-on)

On these models, there is no routine adjustment or specification provided for brake pedal position and

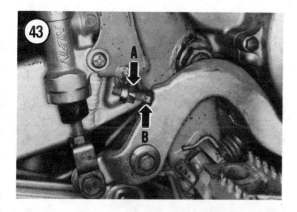

play. The only adjustment provided is for the length of the rear master cylinder pushrod. Because the pushrod length is adjusted when the master cylinder is rebuilt, periodic adjustment is not usually required. However, you can measure the pushrod length and adjust it with the master cylinder assembled and installed on the bike. To do so, perform the following:

1. Check that the rear brake pedal is in its at-rest position.

2. Measure the pushrod length, from the bottom master cylinder surface to the center of the clevis pin, as shown in **Figure 44**. The correct pushrod length is 52 mm (2.05 in.). If out of specification, adjust as follows:

3. To adjust the pushrod length, perform the following:

    a. Remove the cotter pin, washer and clevis pin (A, **Figure 45**).

    b. Loosen the pushrod locknut (B, **Figure 45**).

    c. Turn the clevis (C, **Figure 45**) as required to obtain the correct pushrod length measurement.

    d. Tighten the pushrod locknut. Install the clevis pin (A, **Figure 45**) and washer. Secure with a new cotter pin. Bend the cotter pin arms over to lock it.

4. Support the bike with the rear wheel off the ground. Rotate the rear wheel and check for brake drag. Operate the rear brake pedal several times to make sure it returns to the at-rest position after releasing it.

Brake Fluid Level Check

The brake fluid level in the front and rear master cylinder reservoirs must be kept above their minimum level line. If the fluid level is low in any reservoir, check for loose or damaged hoses or loose banjo bolts. If there are no visible fluid leaks, check the brake pads for excessive wear. As the brake pads wear, the caliper piston(s) moves farther out of its bore, causing the brake fluid level to drop in the reservoir. Also, check the master cylinder bore and the brake caliper piston areas for leaking brake fluid. If there is a noticeable fluid leak, that component requires overhaul to replace the damaged part. Check the brake pads for wear as described in this chapter. Refer to Chapter Fourteen for brake service.

WARNING
*If any reservoir is empty, or if the brake
fluid level is so low that air is entering
the brake system, you must bleed the
brake system as described in Chapter
Fourteen. Simply adding brake fluid to
the reservoir will not restore the brake
system to full effectiveness.*

1. Park the bike on level ground.
2. Clean any dirt from the master cylinder cover
prior to removing it.

WARNING
*Use brake fluid clearly marked DOT 3
or DOT 4 and specified for disc brakes.
Other types of brake fluid may cause
brake failure. Do not intermix different
brands or types of brake fluid as they
may not be compatible. Do not intermix
a silicone based (DOT 5) brake fluid
with DOT 3 or DOT 4 brake fluids. They
are incompatible and it can cause brake
system failure.*

CAUTION
*Be careful when handling brake fluid.
Do not spill it on painted or plastic
surfaces as it will destroy the surface.
Wash the area immediately with soap
and water and thoroughly rinse it off.*

3A. *Front*—Perform the following:
  a. Turn the handlebar so the master cylinder reservoir is level.
  b. On 1992-1996 models, remove the two top cover screws and remove the cover to check the brake fluid level . On 1997 and later models, observe the brake fluid level through the inspection window (**Figure 46**) on the master cylinder reservoir.
  c. The brake fluid level must be above the lower level line. If the brake fluid level is low, add brake fluid as described in the following steps.
  d. Remove the two top cover screws and remove the cover and diaphragm.
  e. Add DOT 3 or DOT 4 brake fluid to bring the level to the upper level mark (**Figure 47**) inside the reservoir.
  f. Inspect the cover and diaphragm and replace if damaged.
  g. Install the diaphragm and cover and tighten the screws securely.

3B. *Rear*—Perform the following:
  a. Unbolt and remove the rear master cylinder cover.
  b. Check that the brake fluid is above the lower level mark on the reservoir (**Figure 48**). To add brake fluid, continue with the following steps.
  c. Remove the master cylinder cap and diaphragm (**Figure 48**).
  d. Add DOT 3 or DOT 4 brake fluid to bring the level to the upper level mark on the reservoir.

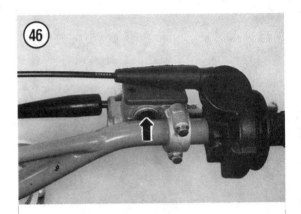

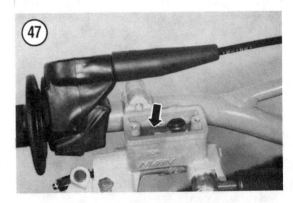

e. Inspect the cap and diaphragm and replace if damaged.

f. Install the diaphragm and cap. Tighten the cap securely.

g. Install and tighten the rear master cylinder cover.

Disc Brake Pad Wear

Inspect the brake pads for uneven wear, scoring, grease or oil contamination or other damage. See **Figure 49** (front) and **Figure 50** (rear). Measure the thickness of the friction material on each pad. Replace both brake pads as a set if the thickness of any pad is approximately 1 mm (0.04 in.), or if any pad is worn to its wear limit groove. Refer to Chapter Fourteen for brake pad service.

> *NOTE*
> *When you measure the brake pads, measure the thickness of the friction material only. Do not include the thickness of the pad's backing plate.*

Disc Brake Hose Replacement

Replace the brake hoses at the intervals specified in **Table 2**. Refer to Chapter Fourteen for service procedures.

Brake Fluid Change

Every time a master cylinder reservoir cover or cap is removed, a small amount of dirt and moisture enters the brake fluid. The same thing happens if a leak occurs or any part of the hydraulic system is loosened or disconnected. Dirt can clog the system and cause unnecessary wear. Water in the brake fluid can vaporize at high temperature, impairing the hydraulic action and reducing the brake's stopping ability.

To maintain peak performance, change the brake fluid every year and when rebuilding a caliper or master cylinder. To change brake fluid, follow the brake bleeding procedure in Chapter Fourteen.

> *WARNING*
> *Use brake fluid clearly marked DOT 3 or DOT 4 only. Others may cause brake failure. Dispose of any unused fluid according to local EPA regulations—never reuse brake fluid. Contaminated brake fluid can cause brake failure.*

Master Cylinder Cup and Dust Seal Replacement (Front and Rear)

Replace the master cylinder piston assembly if the master cylinder is leaking or at the intervals specified in **Table 2**. Refer to Chapter Fourteen for instructions.

Brake Caliper Seal Replacement (Front and Rear)

Replace the brake caliper piston seals if the caliper is leaking or at the intervals specified in **Table 2**. Refer to Chapter Fourteen.

DRIVE CHAIN AND SPROCKETS

Table 2 lists service intervals for the drive chain and sprockets.

Drive Chain
Cleaning

There is no maintenance interval for cleaning the drive chain. However, clean the chain before each race or if it is caked with mud and other debris.

1. Support the bike with the rear wheel off the ground.
2. Shift the transmission into NEUTRAL.

NOTE
*If the drive chain is equipped with a press fit master link, remove and install it as described under **Drive Chain** in Chapter Eleven.*

3. Remove the spring clip (**Figure 51**). Disconnect the master link (**Figure 52**). Remove the chain from the motorcycle. If your bike is equipped with an O-ring drive chain, remove the four O-rings installed on the master link.

4A. O-ring chain—Clean the drive chain in a plastic pan partially filled with kerosene. If necessary, remove dirt from the outside of the chain with a soft nylon brush. Do not use a steel or similar hard brush as its bristles will damage the O-rings.

CAUTION
*Do not clean an O-ring drive chain with anything but kerosene. Most solvents and gasoline will cause the O-rings (**Figure 53**) to swell and deteriorate, permanently damaging the chain.*

4B. Except-O-ring chain—Immerse the chain in a plastic pan containing a non-flammable or high flash point solvent. Allow the chain to soak for about a half hour. If necessary, remove dirt from the outside of the chain with a brush.

5. After the chain is clean, hang it up to allow the cleaning solution to drip off. Lubricate the chain as described in this chapter.

6. Reinstall the chain on the motorcycle. Use a new master link spring clip (**Figure 52**) and install it with the closed end of the clip facing the direction of chain travel (**Figure 54**). On O-ring drive chains, assemble

the master link following the manufacturer's instructions.

WARNING
Always check the master link spring clip after rolling the bike backwards, such as when unloading from a truck or trailer. The master link clip may snag on the chain guide, pulling it away from the chain. Losing a chain while riding can cause a serious spill not to mention the chain damage which may occur.

Drive Chain Lubrication
(Except O-ring Chain)

Lubricate the drive chain before each ride and then throughout the day as required. A properly maintained chain will provide maximum service life and reliability.

1. Support the bike on a workstand with the rear wheel off the ground.
2. Shift the transmission into NEUTRAL.
3. Turn the rear wheel and lubricate the chain with a commercial type chain spray. Do not overlubricate as this will cause dirt to collect on the chain and sprockets.
4. Wipe off all excess oil from the rear hub, wheel and tire.
5. Check that the master link is properly installed and secured.

Drive Chain Lubrication
(O-Ring Chain)

NOTE
If you previously lubricated the O-ring chain with a tacky chain lubricant,

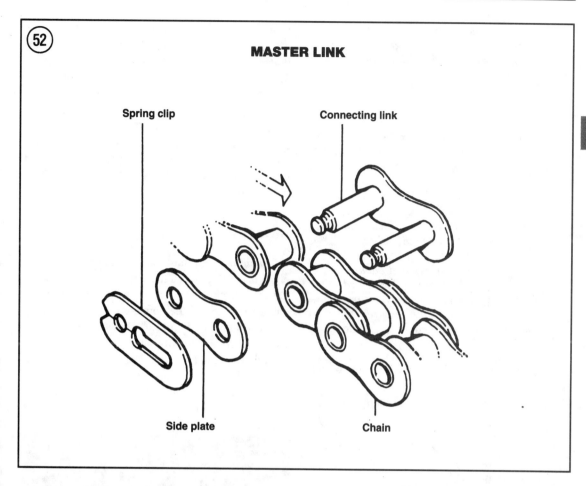

MASTER LINK

Spring clip

Connecting link

Side plate

Chain

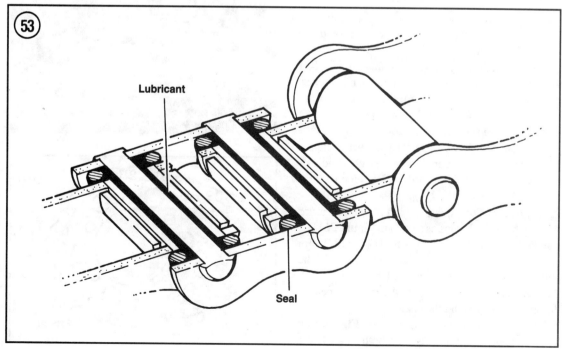

Lubricant

Seal

clean the chain (and sprockets) to remove all residue, dirt and grit. Clean the chain as described in this chapter.

1. Support the bike with the rear wheel off the ground.
2. Shift the transmission into NEUTRAL.
3. Externally lubricate the chain with a SAE 30-50 weight motor oil, WD-40, or a good grade of chain lubricant (non-tacky) specifically formulated for O-ring chains.

> *CAUTION*
> *Do not use a tacky chain lubricant on O-ring chains. Dirt and other abrasive materials that stick to the lubricant will stick against the O-rings and damage them. An O-ring chain is lubricated during its assembly at the factory. External oiling is only required to prevent chain rust and to keep the O-rings pliable.*

4. Wipe off all excess oil from the rear hub, wheel and tire.
5. Check that the master link is properly installed and secured.

Drive Chain/Sprocket Wear Inspection

Check chain and sprocket wear frequently and replace the parts when excessively worn or damaged.

A quick check will give you an indication of when to actually measure chain wear. At the rear sprocket, pull one of the links away from the sprocket. If the link pulls away more than 1/2 the height of a sprocket tooth, the chain is excessively worn (**Figure 55**).

To measure chain wear, perform the following:
1. Loosen the axle nut and tighten the chain adjusters to move the wheel rearward until the chain is tight (no slack).
2. Lay a scale along the top chain run and measure the length of any 21 pins as shown in **Figure 56**. The standard length measurement is 317.5-318.2 mm (12.50-12.53 in.). Replace the drive chain if the length measurement exceeds 323 mm (12.72 in.). Turn the rear wheel and repeat the measurement at different points around the chain.
3. Check the inner plate chain faces (**Figure 57**). They must be lightly polished on both sides. If the

chain shows considerable uneven wear on one side, the sprockets are not aligned. Excessive wear requires chain and sprocket replacement.
4. If the drive chain is worn, inspect the drive and driven sprockets for the following defects:
    a. Undercutting or sharp teeth (**Figure 58**).
    b. Broken teeth (**Figure 59**).
5. If excessive wear or damage is evident, replace the chain and sprockets as a set (**Figure 60**). Rapid chain wear will occur if a new chain is installed on worn sprockets.

Drive Chain Adjustment

The drive chain must have adequate slack so the chain is not tight when the swing arm is horizontal. On the other hand, too much slack may cause the chain to jump off the sprockets, with potentially disastrous results. **Figure 61** shows an engine case damaged from a thrown chain.

Riding in mud and sand will make the chain tighter. Under these conditions, stop and recheck chain slack. If necessary, loosen the chain adjustment so that it is not too tight.

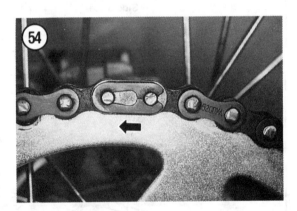

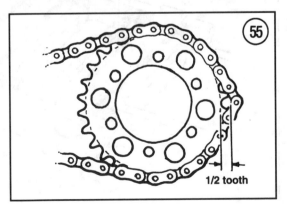

1/2 tooth

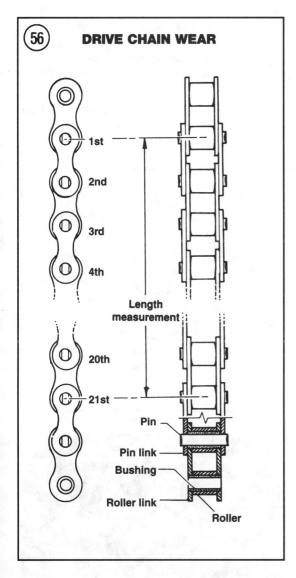

56 **DRIVE CHAIN WEAR**

1st

2nd

3rd

4th

Length
measurement

20th

21st

Pin

Pin link

Bushing

Roller link

Roller

Check the drive chain slack before riding the bike.
Table 12 lists drive chain slack specifications.

1. Place the bike on a workstand with the rear wheel
off the ground.

2. Spin the wheel and check the chain for tightness
at several spots. Check and adjust the chain at its
tightest point (the chain wears unevenly).

3. Measure the drive chain slack between the chain
and swing arm at the rear of the chain slider as shown
in **Figure 62**.

4. Compare the drive chain slack with the specifications listed in **Table 12**. If necessary, adjust the drive
chain as follows.

NOTE
*When adjusting the drive chain, you
must also maintain rear wheel
alignment. A misaligned rear wheel can
cause poor handling and pulling to one
side or the other, as well as increased
chain and sprocket wear. All models
have wheel alignment marks on the
swing arm and chain adjusters.*

5. Remove the cotter pin and loosen the axle nut
(**Figure 63**).

6. Loosen both chain adjuster locknuts (A, **Figure
64**).

7. Turn the adjuster bolts (B, **Figure 64**) to tighten
or loosen the drive chain. Turn both adjuster bolts so
the chain adjuster plate index marks (C, **Figure 64**)
align with the same marks on each side of the swing
arm (D, **Figure 64**). Recheck chain slack.

8. When the chain slack is correct, check wheel
alignment by sighting along the chain from the rear

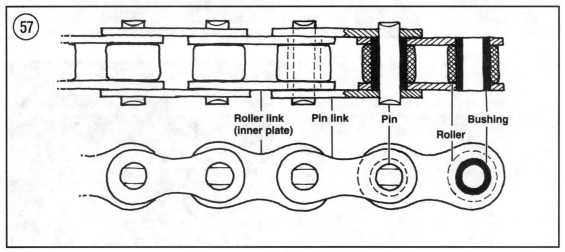

57

Roller link
(inner plate)

Pin link

Pin

Bushing

Roller

sprocket. The chain must leave the sprocket in a straight line (A, **Figure 65**). If it is turned to one side or the other (B and C, **Figure 65**), perform the following:

a. Adjust wheel alignment by turning one adjuster or the other. Recheck chain play.

b. Confirm swing arm accuracy by measuring from the center of the swing arm pivot shaft to the center of the rear axle. If necessary, make a tool, like the one shown in **Figure 66**, to accurately check chain alignment.

9. Tighten the rear axle nut (**Figure 63**) as specified in **Table 8**. Secure the axle nut with a new cotter pin.

10. Tighten the adjuster (B, **Figure 64**) against the chain adjuster plates, then tighten their locknuts (A, **Figure 63**) securely.

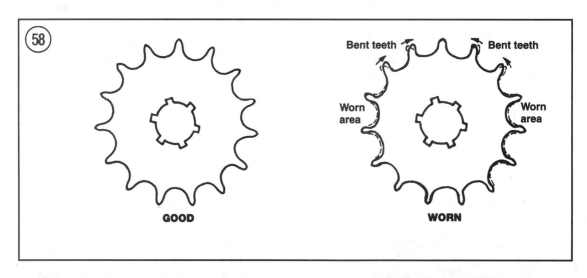

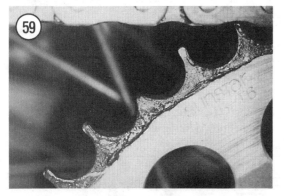

11. Spin the wheel several times and recheck the free play at its tightest point once again. Make sure the free play is within specification.

Drive Chain Sliders
Inspection

Inspect the drive chain slider (A, **Figure 67**) and replace when excessively worn or damaged.

Drive Chain Rollers
Inspection

Inspect the upper and lower drive chain rollers (B, **Figure 67**) for excessive wear, loose mounting bolts or excessively worn or damaged bushings. Replace if necessary.

Chain Guide and Slider
Inspection

1. Inspect the chain guide for loose mounting bolts or damage.
2. Check the chain guide slider, mounted inside the chain guide, for excessive wear or damage. Replace the slider if excessively worn.

TIRES AND WHEELS

Tire Pressure

Check and set the tire pressure to maintain good traction and handling and to prevent rim damage.

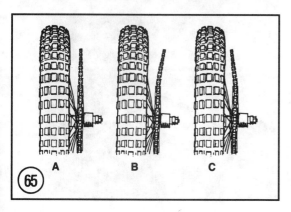
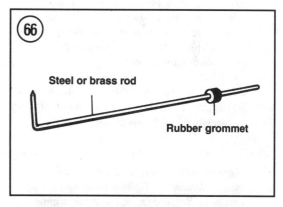

Store an accurate tire gauge (**Figure 68**) in your tool box. **Table 13** lists the standard tire pressure for the front and rear wheels.

Tire Inspection

The tires take a lot of punishment due to the variety of terrain they encounter. Inspect them weekly for excessive wear, cuts and abrasions. To check for internal sidewall damage, remove the tire from the rim as described in Chapter Eleven. Run your hand around the inside tire casing, checking for tears or sharp objects imbedded in the casing.

While checking the tires, also check the position of the valve stem. If a valve stem is turned sideways (**Figure 69**), the tire and tube have slipped on the rim. The valve will eventually pull out of the tube, causing a flat. Straighten the tube as described under *Tube Alignment* in this chapter.

Wheel Spoke Tension

> *NOTE*
> *During break-in for a new or a respoked wheel, check the spoke tension at the end of each 15 minute interval for the first hour of riding. Most spoke seating takes place during initial use.*

Check each spoke for tightness with a spoke wrench (**Figure 70**). If the spokes are loose, tighten them as described in Chapter Eleven.

> *NOTE*
> *Most spokes loosen as a group rather than individually. Tighten loose spokes carefully. Burying just a few spokes tight into the rim will put improper pressure across the wheel.*

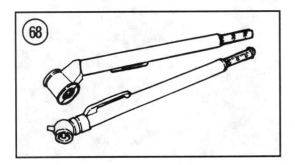

> *NOTE*
> *Excessive pressure when tightening spokes can round off spoke nipple flats.*

Rim Inspection and Runout

Inspect the rims for cracks, warpage or dents (**Figure 71**). Replace damaged rims.

Wheel rim runout is the amount of wobble a wheel shows as it rotates. You can check runout with the wheels on the bike by simply supporting the wheel off the ground and turning the wheel slowly while you hold a pointer solidly against a fork leg or the swing arm. If there is any runout, true the wheel as described in Chapter Eleven.

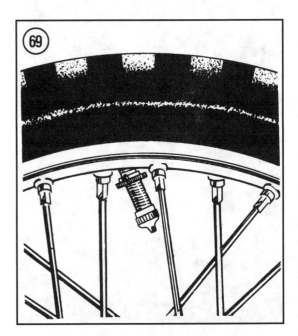

Tube Alignment

Check the tube's valve stem alignment. **Figure 69** shows a valve stem that has slipped with the tire. If the tube is not repositioned, the valve stem will eventually pull away from the tube, causing a flat. To realign the tube and tire:

1. Wash the tire and rim.

2. Remove the valve stem core and release all air pressure from the tube.

3. Loosen the rim lock nut(s) (**Figure 72**).

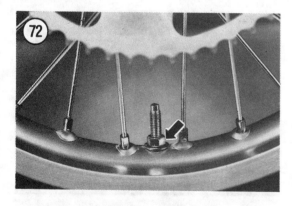

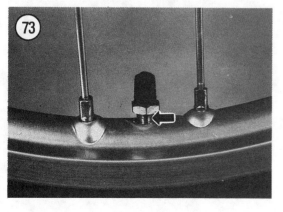

4. With an assistant steadying the bike, break the tire-to-rim seal all the way around the wheel on both sides.

5. After the tire seal is broken, put the bike on a stand with the wheel off the ground.

6. Spray some soapy water along the tire bead on both sides of the tire.

7. Have an assistant apply the brake.

8. Using your hands, grab the tire and turn it and the tube until the valve stem is straight up (90°). See **Figure 73**.

9. When the valve stem is straight up, install the valve stem core and inflate the tire. If the soap and water solution dries, reapply it to help the tire seat on the rim. Check the tire to make sure it seats evenly all the way around the rim.

> *WARNING*
> *Do not overinflate the tire and tube. If the tire will not seat properly remove the valve stem core and lubricate the tire again.*

10. Tighten the rim lock(s) securely.

11. Adjust the tire pressure (**Table 13**). Install the valve stem nut and cap (**Figure 73**).

WHEEL BEARINGS

Inspection

The stock wheel bearings are sealed on their outer side (**Figure 74**) and do not require periodic lubrication. At the intervals listed in **Table 2**, check the condition of the seals and bearings. If the seals are reusable, wipe off their outer surface. Pack the lip of each seal with grease. To replace the seals and wheel bearings, refer to Chapter Eleven.

STEERING

Steering Bearings

Clean and lubricate the steering bearings (**Figure 75**) and races at the intervals specified in **Table 2**. You must remove the steering stem to clean and lubricate the bearings. Refer to Chapter Twelve for complete service procedures.

Steering Head Adjustment Check

The steering head on all models includes upper and lower tapered roller bearings. Because the bike is subjected to rough terrain and conditions, check the bearing play at the specified maintenance intervals (**Table 2**) or whenever it feels loose. A loose bearing adjustment will hamper steering and cause premature bearing and race wear. In excessive conditions, a loose bearing adjustment can cause loss of control. Refer to *Steering Play Check and Adjustment* in Chapter Twelve.

Front Suspension Check

1. Apply the front brake and pump the suspension up and down as vigorously as possible. Check fork movement, paying attention for any abnormal noise or resulting oil leakage.
2. Check that the upper and lower fork tube pinch bolts are tight.
3. Check that the handlebar holder bolts are tight.
4. Check that the front axle and the axle holder fasteners are tight.

> *NOTE*
> *If any of the previously mentioned fasteners are loose, refer to Chapter Twelve for correct procedures and torque specifications.*

FRONT FORK

Oil Change

Change the oil in the front fork tubes at the intervals specified in **Table 2**. The design of the cartridge fork used on these models does not allow draining or replacement of the fork oil while the fork is assembled or installed on the bike. You must remove and partially disassemble the fork tubes to drain and change the oil. Refer to Chapter Twelve.

REAR SHOCK ABSORBER

Oil Change

Change the oil in the rear shock absorber at the intervals specified in **Table 2**. Refer this service to a Kawasaki dealership.

REAR SWING ARM AND LINKAGE

Rear Suspension Check

1. Support the bike on a stand with the rear wheel off the ground.
2. Check swing arm bearing play as described in Chapter Thirteen.
3. Check the tightness of all rear suspension mounting bolts.
4. Check that the rear axle nut is tight.

> *NOTE*
> *If any of the previously mentioned fasteners are loose, refer to Chapter Thirteen for correct tightening procedures and torque specifications.*

Swing Arm Bearing Assembly Lubrication

Service and lubricate the swing arm bearings, pivot collars and pivot bolts (**Figure 76**, typical) at the intervals specified in **Table 2**. You must remove the swing arm and partially disassemble it to lubri-

3

cate the bushings and bearings. Do not remove the needle bearing cages (**Figure 77**) to lubricate them. Refer to Chapter Thirteen for complete service procedures.

Shock Linkage Lubrication

Service and lubricate the rocker arm (**Figure 78**) and tierod (**Figure 79**) bearings, pivot collars and pivot bolts at the intervals specified in **Table 2**. Do not remove the needle bearing cages to lubricate them. Refer to Chapter Thirteen for complete service procedures.

Rear Shock Absorber
Bearing and Pivot Bolt Lubrication

At the same time you lubricate the shock linkage, lubricate the shock absorber pivot bolts, collar (**Figure 80**) and needle bearing (**Figure 81**). Do not remove the bearing for lubrication. Refer to Chapter Thirteen for service procedures.

GENERAL LUBRICATION

At the intervals specified in Table 2, lubricate the following components with 10W-30 motor oil:
1. Clutch lever pivot bolt.
2. Front brake lever pivot bolt.
3. Rear brake pedal pivot bolt or frame shoulder.
4. Kick pedal splines.

NUTS, BOLTS AND OTHER FASTENERS

Constant vibration can loosen many of the fasteners on the motorcycle. Check the tightness of all fasteners, especially those on:
1. Engine mounting hardware.
2. Cylinder head hanger bolts.
3. Engine crankcase covers.
4. Handlebar and front forks.
5. Shift pedal.
6. Kickstarter pedal.
7. Brake pedal and lever.
8. Exhaust system.

STORAGE

Several months of inactivity can cause serious problems and a general deterioration of the motorcycle's condition. This is especially true in areas of weather extremes. During long periods of nonuse, it is advisable to prepare your motorcycle for storage.

Selecting a Storage Area

Most riders store their motorcycles in home garages. If you do not have a home garage, facilities

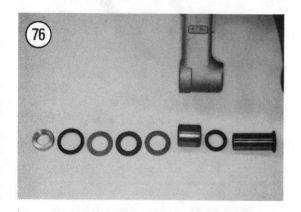

suitable for long-term storage are readily available for rent or lease in most areas. In selecting a building, consider the following points.

1. The storage area must be dry.

2. Avoid buildings with large window areas. Mask the windows if necessary.

Preparing Motorcycle for Storage

Careful preparation will minimize deterioration and make it easier to restore the motorcycle to service later. Use the following procedure.

1. Wash the motorcycle completely. Make certain to remove dirt in all the hard to reach parts. Completely dry the bike to remove all moisture.

2. Run the engine for about five minutes to warm the transmission oil. Drain the oil, regardless of the time since the last oil change. Refill with the normal quantity and type of oil.

3. Drain all gasoline from the fuel tank, interconnecting hose, and the carburetor.

4. Clean and lubricate the drive chain and control cables; refer to specific procedures in this chapter.

5. Remove the spark plug and add about one teaspoon of engine oil into the cylinder. Reinstall the spark plug and turn the engine over to distribute the oil to the cylinder wall and piston.

6. Tape or tie a plastic bag over the end of the silencer to prevent the entry of moisture.

7. Check the tire pressure, inflate to the correct pressure and move the motorcycle to the storage area. Place it securely on a stand with both wheels off the ground.

8. Cover the motorcycle with a tarp, blanket or heavy plastic drop cloth. Place this cover over the bike mainly as a dust cover—do not wrap it tightly, especially any plastic material, as it may trap condensation. Leave room for air to circulate around the motorcycle.

Inspection During Storage

Try to inspect the motorcycle weekly while in storage. Correct any deterioration as soon as possible. For example, if you find any corrosion, cover the area with a light coat of grease or silicone spray.

Turn the engine over a couple of times, but do not start it.

Restoring Motorcycle to Service

A motorcycle that has been properly prepared and stored in a suitable area requires only light maintenance to restore to service.

1. Before removing the motorcycle from the storage area, reinflate the tires to the correct pressures. Air loss during storage may have caused flattened tires.

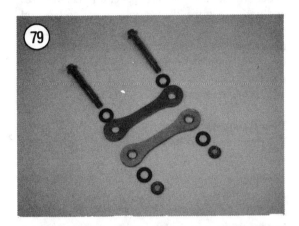

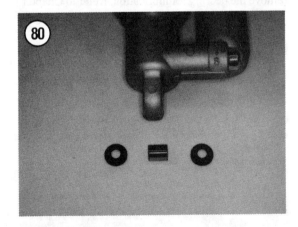

2. Clean and reoil the air filter.

3. When the motorcycle is brought to the work area, refill the tank with freshly mixed gasoline.

4. Install a fresh spark plug and start the engine.

5. Check the operation of the engine stop switch. Oxidation of the switch contacts during storage may make it inoperative.

6. Test ride the motorcycle.

Table 1 ENGINE MAINTENANCE SCHEDULE

After each race
Clean air filter element, replace if damaged
Clean and inspect spark plug
Clean and inspect the carburetor, then adjust
Check the exhaust system
Check the cooling system
Check the coolant level in the radiator
Check the throttle adjustment and operation
Check the clutch adjustment and operation
Check the kick pedal and shift pedal
After every 3 races
Change the transmission oil
Replace the spark plug
Replace the exhaust pipe O-rings
Repack the silencer
Check the clutch plates
Clean and inspect the engine top end
After every 5 races
Replace the clutch plates
Replace the piston and ring
Once a year
Change the engine coolant
Every 4 years
Replace the fuel hose

Table 2 CHASSIS MAINTENANCE SCHEDULE

After each race
Check the brake adjustment
Lubricate the drive chain
Adjust the drive chain
Check the front and rear sprockets
Check the spokes and wheel runout
Check the steering play
Check the front fork
Perform the general lubrication
Check all exposed nuts, bolts and fasteners
Initial 2 races, then every 5 races
Change fork oil
Change shock oil
Every 3 races
Check the brake fluid level
Every 5 races
Check brake pad wear
Check drive chain wear
Check wheel bearings
Lubricate steering stem
Check and lubricate rear swing arm and linkage
Every 2 years
Replace brake fluid
Replace front and rear master cylinder cups and seals
Replace front and rear brake caliper seals
Every 4 years
Replace brake hoses
When required
Replace chain rollers and guide

Table 3 RECOMMENDED LUBRICANTS AND FUEL

Engine oil	Kawasaki 2-stroke racing oil or equivalent
Transmission oil	SE, SF or SG SAE 10W-30 or 10W-40 motor oil
Air filter	Foam air filter oil
Drive chain	Non-tacky O-ring chain lubricant or SAE 30-50 engine motor oil
Brake fluid	DOT 3 or DOT 4
Steering and suspension lubricant	Multipurpose grease
Fuel	Pump gasoline with Octane rating of 90 or higher
Control cables	Cable lube

Table 4 FUEL/OIL PREMIX RATIO

Model	Premix ratio
All models	32:1

Table 5 FUEL/OIL PREMIX QUANTITIES (32:1)

Gasoline U.S. gal.	Oil mL	Oil U.S. oz.
1	118	4
2	237	8
3	355	12
4	473	16
5	591	20

Table 6 FUEL TANK CAPACITY

	Liters	U.S. gal.	Imp. gal.
All models	8.5	2.2	1.9

Table 7 TRANSMISSION OIL CAPACITY

	mL	U.S. oz.	Imp. oz.
All models	850	28.7	23.9

Table 8 MAINTENANCE TORQUE SPECIFICATIONS

	N•m	in.-.lb.	ft.-lb.
Coolant drain screws			
Cylinder block drain plug			
1992	22	–	16
1993	21	–	15
1994-1995	22	–	16
1996-on	8.8	78	–
Water pump drain plug	8.8	78	–
Cylinder base nuts	34	–	25
Cylinder head nuts	25	–	18
Front axle nut			
1992-1993	54	–	40
1994-on	78	–	58
Front axle clamp nuts	9.3	82	–
Kick pedal			
Mounting nut			
1992-1993	49	–	36
Allen bolt			
1994-on	8.8	78	–
Rear axle nut			
1992-1994	98	–	72
1995-on	115	–	87
Spark plug	27	–	20
Transmission oil drain plug	20	–	14.5

3

Table 9 SPARK PLUG TYPE AND GAP

Spark plug gap	
1992-1993	0.5-0.6 mm (0.019-0.024 in.)
1994-on	0.6-0.7 mm (0.024-0.028 in.)
Spark plug type	
1992-1993	
U.S. models	NGK R6254E-9
All other models	NGK R6252E-9
1994-1996	
U.S. models	NGK B8EVX
All other models	NGK BR8EVX
1995-on	NGK BR8EVX

Table 10 CARBURETOR PILOT AIR SCREW ADJUSTMENT

Model	Initial adjustment* Turns out
1992-1993	1 1/2
1994-1997	2.0
1998	1 1/2
*See text for adjustment procedure.	

Table 11 COOLANT CAPACITY

Model	mL	U.S. qt.	Imp. qt.
All	1.18	1.25	1.04

Table 12 DRIVE CHAIN SLACK

	mm	in.
1992-1993	50-60	2-2 3/8
1994-on	60-70	2 3/8-2 3/4

Table 13 TIRE INFLATION PRESSURE

	psi (kPa)
Front and rear tire	11-14 (80-100)

CHAPTER FOUR

ENGINE TOP END

This chapter covers information on servicing the KX250 engine top end and exhaust system. Service to the engine lower end is covered in Chapter Five.

Before working on the engine, read the information listed under *Service Hints* in Chapter One.

The text often refers to the left and right sides of the engine as it sits in the motorcycle's frame, not as it happens to be sitting on your workbench. Left and right sides refer to the rider sitting on the seat and facing in the normal operating direction (forward).

Engine specifications are listed in **Tables 1-3** at the end of this chapter.

ENGINE OPERATING PRINCIPALS

Figure 1 explains how a typical two-stroke engine works. This information will be helpful when troubleshooting or repairing the engine.

CLEANLINESS

Repairs go much faster and easier if the engine is clean before you begin work. When servicing the engine top end with the engine installed in the frame, dirt trapped underneath the fuel tank and upper frame tubes can fall into the cylinder or crankcase opening. To prevent this, remove the fuel tank and wrap the frame tube with a large, clean cloth.

EXHAUST SYSTEM

The exhaust system is a critical part to the overall performance and operation of your 2-stroke engine. Check the exhaust system for deep dents and fractures and repair them or replace damaged parts immediately. Check the exhaust pipe and silencer for loose or missing fasteners. Running the engine with a loose exhaust system will increase the likelihood of damage to the exhaust pipe and frame mounting brackets. In addition, a loosely mounted exhaust pipe will increase the motorcycle's noise level. A loose exhaust pipe-to-cylinder head connection will reduce engine performance, cause excessive noise and possible piston seizure.

Refer to **Figure 2** when servicing the stock exhaust system.

Removal/Installation

1. Support the bike on a workstand.

2. Remove the seat and the right side cover (Chapter Fifteen).

3. Unbolt and remove the silencer (**Figure 3**).

4. Disconnect and remove the expansion chamber springs (**Figure 4**).

5. Remove the upper and lower expansion chamber mounting bolts, then remove the expansion chamber (**Figure 5**).

6. Remove the front gasket (A, **Figure 6**)

①

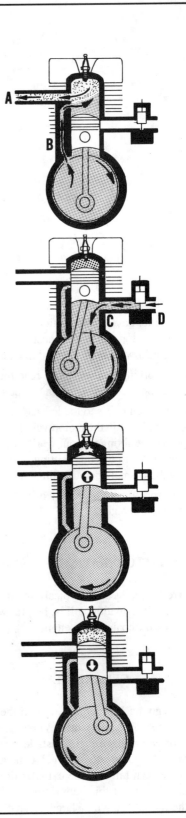

2-STROKE
OPERATING PRINCIPLES

The crankshaft in this discussion is rotating in a clockwise direction.

As the piston travels downward, it uncovers the exhaust port (A) allowing the exhaust gases, which are under pressure, to leave the cylinder. A fresh fuel/air charge, which has been compressed slightly, travels from the crankcase into the cylinder through the transfer port (B). Since this charge enters under pressure, it also helps to push out the exhaust gases.

While the crankshaft continues to rotate, the piston moves upward, covering the transfer port (B) and exhaust port (A). The piston is now compressing the new fuel/air mixture and creating a low pressure are in the crankcase at the same time. As the piston continues to travel, it uncovers the intake port (C). A fresh fuel/air charge, from the carburetor (D), is drawn into the crankcase through the intake port, because of the low pressure within it.

Now, as the piston almost reaches the top of it's travel, the spark plug fires, thus igniting the compressed fuel/air mixture. The piston continues top dead center (TDC) and is pushed downward by the expanding gases.

As the piston travels down, the exhaust gases leave the cylinder and the complete cycle starts all over again.

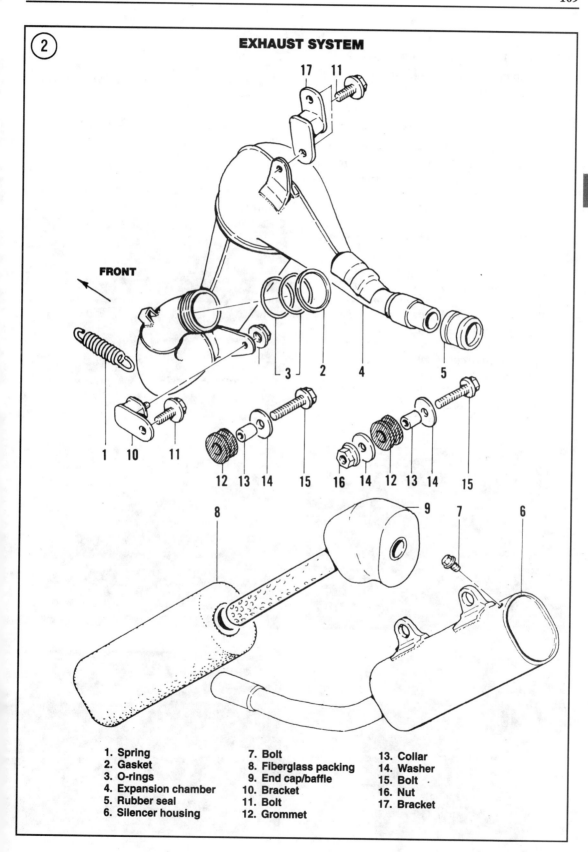

② **EXHAUST SYSTEM**

FRONT

1. Spring
2. Gasket
3. O-rings
4. Expansion chamber
5. Rubber seal
6. Silencer housing
7. Bolt
8. Fiberglass packing
9. End cap/baffle
10. Bracket
11. Bolt
12. Grommet
13. Collar
14. Washer
15. Bolt
16. Nut
17. Bracket

7. Install the expansion chamber and silencer by reversing the preceding steps, plus the following:

   a. Install the rubber seal where the silencer joins the expansion chamber.

   b. Replace any missing or damaged mounting bracket dampers and washers (**Figure 2**).

   c. Make sure the spark plug wire, fuel line, control cables and all water hoses are properly positioned to prevent damage from the hot expansion chamber.

   d. Install a new front gasket (A, **Figure 6**).

   e. Start the engine and check for exhaust leaks.

NOTE
Check the expansion chamber and silencer mounting bolts and brackets before each ride. **Figure 7** *shows the type of expensive damage that can occur from a hot exhaust system that is not installed or secured correctly. A loose silencer pipe fell on top of the rear master cylinder and melted the cap, diaphragm and reservoir housing, requiring replacement of the parts.*

Inspection

Replace parts that show excessive wear or damage as described in this section.

1. Inspect the O-rings (B, **Figure 6**) for leaks or damage.

2. Replace weak or damaged springs.

3. Inspect the mounting brackets for missing parts (**Figure 2**) or damage.

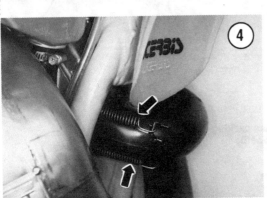

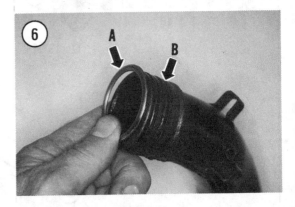

4. Inspect the expansion chamber for cracks, dents or other damage. Refer repair to a competent welding repair shop.

5. Inspect the silencer for damage. When necessary, repack the silencer as described in this chapter.

Repacking the Silencer

All models are equipped with a rebuildable silencer that uses replaceable fiberglass packing material (**Figure 8**). Repack the silencer after every

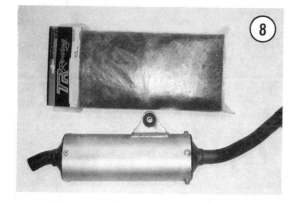

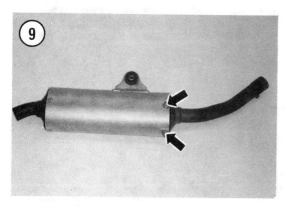

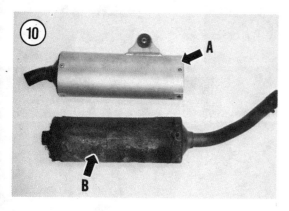

three races. If you are racing regularly, you should follow this recommendation. If you do not race, repack the silencer every six to eight hours of engine operation or when you notice the exhaust becoming increasingly louder. Because your engine is designed to be used with a silencer, do not remove it and expect an increase in power. Removing the silencer or operating with a blown out silencer will reduce engine performance and make the bike very loud.

NOTE
Because there are many stock and aftermarket silencers that can be used on the KX250, the following section describes repacking a typical silencer. Where screws are used to secure the silencer housing shown in this procedure, others may use circlips or rivets. To help with reassembly, make notes or drawings as required.

CAUTION
When removing rivets, make sure you drill through the rivet head and not into the silencer housing. Remove the loose rivet ends when cleaning out the silencer.

1. Remove the silencer as described in this chapter

2. Remove the screws (**Figure 9**) securing the silencer housing to the core (inner pipe).

3. Pull the silencer housing (A, **Figure 10**) off the core .

4. Pull the fiberglass packing (B, **Figure 10**) off the core pipe and discard it. Remove any fiberglass residue from inside the silencer housing.

5. Clean the core (**Figure 11**) with a wire brush to remove all rust and exhaust residue.

6. Take the new fiberglass packing out of its container and compare its width with the core and housing diameters. If necessary, cut the fiberglass to fit the housing.

7. Wrap the new fiberglass packing around the core (**Figure 12**), then slide the housing over the inner pipe and secure it with the mounting screws (**Figure 9**). Pack as much fiberglass around the core as possible.

8. Install the silencer as described in this chapter.

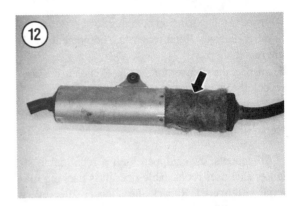

CYLINDER HEAD

The cylinder head can be serviced with the engine mounted in the frame.

Service Notes

Before servicing the top end, perform a leak down test as described in Chapter Two. This test will help you to spot air leaks that can cause problems later on.

Removal

> *CAUTION*
> *To prevent warpage and damage to any component, remove the cylinder head when the engine is cold.*

1. Remove the seat and fuel tank.

2. Clean the upper frame rails of all dirt and debris that could fall into the cylinder.

3. Remove the expansion chamber as described in this chapter.

4. Drain the cooling system (Chapter Three).

5. Disconnect the water hose (A, **Figure 13**) from the cylinder head.

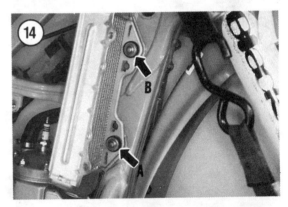

6. On 1994-on models, reposition both radiators as follows:

   a. Disconnect one side of the radiator hose (B, **Figure 13**).

   b. Remove the radiator lower mounting bolts (A, **Figure 14**) from each radiator.

   c. Loosen the radiator upper mounting bolts (B, **Figure 14**) from each radiator. Swing both radiators forward. See A, **Figure 15**.

7. Remove the cylinder head hanger bracket nuts and bolts and remove the hanger bracket (B, **Figure 15**).

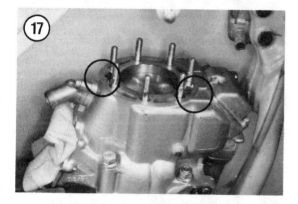

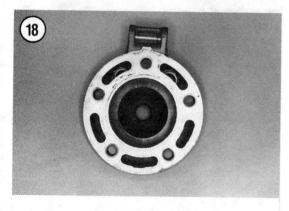

8. Disconnect the spark plug wire from the plug, then loosen the spark plug.

9. Loosen the cylinder head flange nuts (**Figure 16**) 1/4 turn at a time following a crisscross pattern.

10. Remove the cylinder head (**Figure 16**).

11. Check the cylinder head and its gasket for coolant leakage or other damage.

12. Remove and discard the cylinder head gasket.

13. Remove the two dowel pins (**Figure 17**), if necessary.

14. Turn the crankshaft and bring the piston to top dead center (TDC). Lay a clean rag over the cylinder to prevent dirt from falling into the cylinder.

15. Inspect the cylinder head as described in this chapter.

Inspection

1. Wipe away any soft deposits from the combustion chamber (**Figure 18**). Remove hard deposits with a wire brush mounted in a drill or drill press, or with a soft metal scraper.

> *CAUTION*
> *Do not gouge the gasket or combustion chamber surfaces when cleaning the cylinder head. Burrs created from improper cleaning may cause preignition and heat erosion.*

2. Measure the cylinder head flatness with a straightedge and feeler gauge (**Figure 19**). If the cylinder head warpage exceeds the service limit in **Table 2**, resurface the head as follows:

   a. Tape a piece of 400-600 grit wet emery sandpaper onto a piece of thick plate glass or a surface plate.

   b. Slowly resurface the head by moving it in figure-eight patterns on the sandpaper.

   c. Rotate the head several times to avoid removing too much material from one side. Check the progress often with the straightedge and feeler gauge.

   d. If the cylinder head warpage still exceeds the service limit, take the cylinder head to a Kawasaki dealership for further inspection.

3. Remove the spark plug and check the cylinder head threads (**Figure 18**) for carbon buildup or thread damage. Repair the threads with a spark plug tap.

4

NOTE
Repair damaged threads with a spark plug tap or install a thread insert.

4. Replace damaged cylinder head flange nuts.
5. Replace damaged cylinder head studs (Chapter One).
6. Wash the cylinder head in hot soapy water and rinse with clean, cold water.

Cylinder Head Hanger Bracket Inspection

1. Inspect the cylinder head hanger brackets for cracks, warpage or other defects and replace if damaged.
2. Clean the bolts, washers and nuts in solvent and dry thoroughly.
3. Replace damaged fasteners as required.

Installation

1. Clean the cylinder head as described under *Inspection* in this chapter.
2. Remove all gasket residue from the cylinder gasket surface.

NOTE
Before installing the dowel pins in Step 3, position the piston at TDC. Then block off the cylinder water jackets holes so you do not accidentally drop a dowel pin into the engine.

3. Install the two dowel pins (**Figure 17**), if removed.
4. Install a new cylinder head gasket. If the stock head gasket has an EX mark like the one shown in **Figure 20**, install it with the mark at the front of the cylinder. See **Figure 21**. Make sure both dowel pins align with the mating holes in the gasket.

CAUTION
Cylinder head gaskets are directional and must be installed correctly because the cooling passage openings are larger on the exhaust side of the gasket. Installing the head gasket incorrectly will cause the engine to overheat.

NOTE
Kawasaki sells two different thickness head gaskets for most KX250 models. A

Kawasaki dealership can tell you what the stock thickness gasket is for your model.

5. Install the cylinder head onto the cylinder with its bracket boss facing forward (**Figure 16**).
6. Install the cylinder head flange nuts (**Figure 16**) and tighten finger-tight. Tighten the nuts in 2-3 steps following in a crisscross pattern as specified in **Table 3**.
7. Install the spark plug and connect the spark plug lead.

NOTE
Spray the cylinder head hanger bracket bolts with a rust inhibitor before installing them in Step 8.

8. Install the cylinder head hanger brackets, bolts and nuts (B, **Figure 15**). Tighten the nuts as specified in **Table 3**.
9. Reconnect the coolant hose (A, **Figure 13**) at the cylinder head .
10. Reposition the radiators as follows:

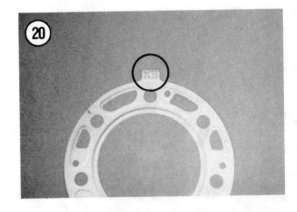

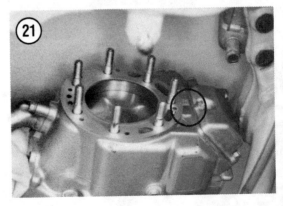

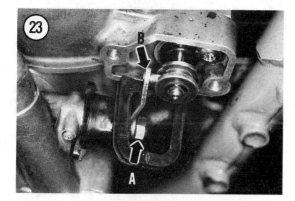

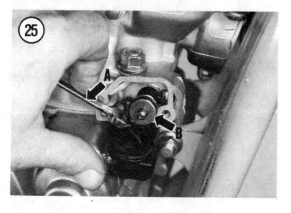

a. Push both radiators back into place along the frame, then reconnect the lower radiator hose (B, **Figure 13**) to the radiator.

b. Install the bottom radiator mounting bolt (A, **Figure 14**) at each radiator.

c. Tighten the upper and lower radiator mounting bolts (**Figure 14**) securely.

11. Refill the cooling system (Chapter Three).

12. Install the radiator covers and tighten their mounting bolts securely.

13. Install the expansion chamber as described in this chapter.

14. Install the fuel tank and seat.

15. Start the engine and check for coolant leaks.

CYLINDER

The cylinder can be removed with the engine mounted in the frame. The cylinder must be removed to service the exhaust valve assembly.

Removal

1. Remove the expansion chamber as described in this chapter.

2. Disconnect the coolant hose (C, **Figure 13**) from the cylinder block.

3. Unbolt and remove the exhaust valve cover (**Figure 22**).

4A. On 1992 models, remove the shaft lever nut (A, **Figure 23**) and shaft lever (B).

4B. On 1993 and later models, disconnect the shaft lever as follows:

a. Remove the E-clip, washer and wave washer (**Figure 24**) from the operating rod.

b. Put a 9 mm open end wrench on the shaft lever as shown in A, **Figure 25** and turn the shaft lever counterclockwise. Push the operating rod into the cylinder and remove the operating rod collar (B, **Figure 25**).

c. Before releasing the shaft lever, turn the operating rod so that its remaining E-clip will be out of the way of the shaft lever when it returns to its at-rest position. See **Figure 26**.

5. Remove the cylinder head as described in this chapter.

6. Loosen the cylinder base nuts in a crisscross pattern, then remove them.

7. Loosen the cylinder (**Figure 27**) by tapping it with a rubber or plastic mallet.

> *CAUTION*
> *When removing the cylinder in Step 8, do not twist the cylinder so far that the piston rings could snap into the intake port. This would cause the cylinder to bind and damage the piston and rings.*

> *NOTE*
> *Two dowel pins are lightly pressed into the bottom right side of the cylinder block (**Figure 28**). If the cylinder block is difficult to remove, the dowel pins are probably corroded, locking the cylinder in place. When removing a stubborn cylinder block, do not pry it away from the crankcase as this will damage both mating surfaces. Instead, spray a penetrating liquid down the cylinder studs at each dowel pin position. After allowing the liquid to soak in, rap the cylinder with a plastic mallet and try to work the cylinder off the crankcase.*

> *NOTE*
> *Stuff a shop towel around the connecting rod and under the cylinder before the cylinder is completely removed from the piston. The towel will prevent dirt or any loose parts from falling into the crankcase. The towel will also prevent the connecting rod from falling when the cylinder is removed.*

8. Rotate the engine so the piston is at BDC and pull the cylinder straight up and off the crankcase studs and piston.
9. Remove and discard the cylinder base gasket.
10. Remove any remaining gasket material on the crankcase by scraping it off with a gasket removal tool. Be careful not to gouge the gasket surfaces.
11. Place a clean shop cloth into the crankcase opening to prevent the entry of foreign material.
12. If necessary, service the exhaust valve as described in this chapter.

> *NOTE*
> *If you do not plan on servicing the exhaust valve assembly, but some of the components fell out the bottom of the cylinder as it was removed from the*

engine, install them as described under **Exhaust Valve Service** *in this chapter.*

Inspection

To accurately measure the cylinder bore in this procedure, use a bore gauge and a 50-75 mm (2-3 in.) micrometer, an inside micrometer or a telescoping gauge and micrometer. If you do not have these tools, have the measurements performed at a Kawasaki dealership or motorcycle service shop.

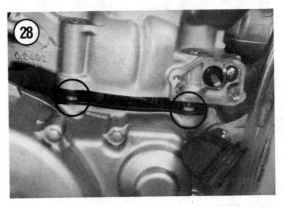

1. Remove all carbon residue from the exhaust port and exhaust valve operating areas.

2. Remove all gasket residue from the upper and lower cylinder block gasket surfaces.

3. Measure the cylinder bore with a bore gauge (**Figure 29**) or an inside micrometer at a depth of 30 mm (1 3/16 in.) from the top of the cylinder as shown in **Figure 30**. Measure inline with the piston pin and at 90° to the pin. Note the following:

   a. Measure the cylinder bore when the cylinder is cold (room temperature).

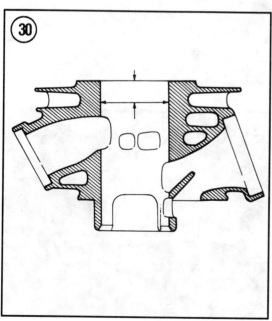

   b. If the cylinder bore measurement exceeds the service limit in **Table 2**, you must replace the cylinder or have it resleeved. The stock plated cylinder liner cannot be bored to accept a new piston. It can only be bored to install a new sleeve. Replacement cylinder sleeves, however, can be bored to fit a new piston. Refer to *Cylinder Bore Service* in this chapter.

NOTE
When repairing or replacing the cylinder head studs in Step 4, install the old head gasket over the cylinder to protect the upper mating surface from damage.

4. Check each cylinder stud for thread damage or looseness. Repair minor thread damage with the correct size metric die. If the studs are loose or damaged, remove or replace them as described in Chapter One.

5. Inspect the cylinder dowel pins (**Figure 31**) for rust and corrosion. Clean the dowel pins by removing rust with a small fine-cut file. If a dowel pin is damaged, replace it as described in Step 6.

NOTE
The cylinder dowel pins are a light press fit in the cylinder. Do not remove them unless necessary.

6. Replace damaged cylinder dowel pins (**Figure 31**) as follows:

   a. Remove the old dowel pin with a pair of locking pliers or a dowel pin removal tool.

NOTE
If you cannot remove a dowel pin, do not cause further damage by crushing it with locking pliers or other tools. Take

the cylinder to a dealership and have it removed.

b. Install the new dowel pin and center it in the cylinder. Then install a bolt, nut and two washers over the stud as shown in **Figure 32**. Hold the bolt and tighten the nut to install the dowel pin into the cylinder until it bottoms.

7. When installing new piston rings, hone the cylinder to deglaze the bore surface and to help the new rings to seat. If necessary, refer this service to a dealership or motorcycle repair shop.

> *CAUTION*
> *Clean the cylinder bore thoroughly before installing the exhaust valve (if removed) and cylinder. This step is important whenever the cylinder has been removed from the engine, and especially when the bore was honed. Failure to clean the cylinder bore correctly can leave abrasive material in the cylinder, which will cause rapid wear to the piston, rings and cylinder bore.*

8. Clean the cylinder bore as follows:
   a. You will do a more thorough job of cleaning the cylinder if the exhaust valve assembly is first removed from the cylinder.
   b. Flush the cylinder coolant passages to remove sludge and other residue.
   c. Clean the exhaust valve area thoroughly. If the exhaust valve is installed in the cylinder, flush the area with water and then with compressed air. Repeat until you are sure there are no more carbon particles being released from the exhaust valve or its operating surfaces.
   d. Wash the bore in a bucket of hot soapy water (**Figure 33**). Take a soft rag and wipe the bore surface repeatedly. Rinse with clear water.
   e. Rub a clean white cloth against the cylinder bore and then check it (**Figure 34**). If the cloth does not come out clean, the cylinder bore is still dirty. Rewash the bore until the cloth comes out clean—no smudge or dark marks.
   f. Dry the cylinder with compressed air. Lubricate the bore with two-stroke oil.

9. When installing a new cylinder or an old cylinder with a new liner, follow the same break-in procedure you would use on a new machine. See *Break-in* in this chapter.

Cylinder Bore Service

If the cylinder bore is going to be honed or bored out to accept a replacement sleeve, first remove the exhaust valve assembly as described in this chapter. Clean the exhaust valve area thoroughly. Do not leave the exhaust valve assembly in the cylinder

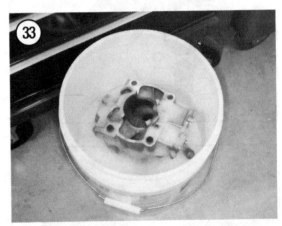

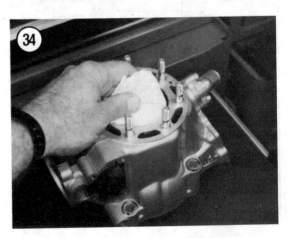

when honing the cylinder, as it will be difficult to remove all of the fine abrasive grit material left over from the honing job.

Installation

Make sure all engine parts are clean before starting assembly.

1. If removed, install the piston as described in this chapter.

2. Clean the cylinder bore as described under *Cylinder Inspection* in this chapter.

3. If removed, install the exhaust valve assembly, as described in this chapter.

4. Check that the crankcase and both cylinder surfaces are clean.

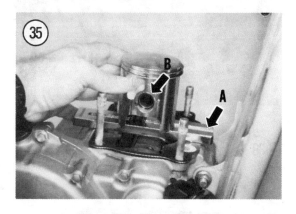

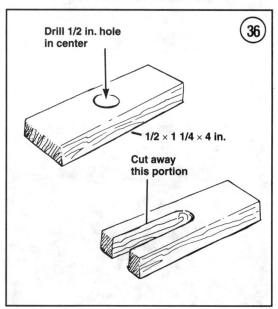

Drill 1/2 in. hole
in center

1/2 × 1 1/4 × 4 in.

Cut away
this portion

5. Make sure the two dowel pins (**Figure 31**) are installed into the bottom of the cylinder. Lubricate them with grease to help with cylinder removal the next time.

NOTE
*If removed, install the dowel pins as described under **Inspection** in this section.*

6. Install a new base gasket.

7. Lubricate the piston skirt, piston rings and cylinder bore with 2-stroke engine oil.

8. Install a piston holding fixture (A, **Figure 35**) under the piston. Rotate the crankshaft until the piston skirt seats against the fixture.

NOTE
*While a piston holding fixture is not necessary to install the cylinder, its use makes it easier to install the cylinder without damaging the piston rings, especially if your are doing the work by yourself. A piston holding fixture can be made of wood as shown in **Figure 36**.*

9. Check that the piston pin clips (B, **Figure 35**) are seated in the piston grooves completely.

10. Check that the piston ring end gaps align with the piston ring locating pins (**Figure 37**).

CAUTION
Do not rotate the cylinder while installing it over the piston. The piston rings could snag in the intake port and break.

11. Install the cylinder as follows:

a. Compress the rings with your fingers. Start the bottom edge of the cylinder over the top ring, then the bottom ring. Hold the piston and slide the cylinder down over the crankcase mounting studs and seat it against the piston holding fixture (**Figure 38**).

b. Remove the piston holding fixture and slide the cylinder down so the two dowel pins (**Figure 28**) pass through the base gasket without tearing it. Seat the cylinder against the base gasket. Make sure both dowel pins seat into the crankcase and do not pinch or cut the base gasket.

c. Hold the cylinder in place with one hand and operate the kick pedal with your other hand. The piston should move up and down the cylinder bore smoothly.

NOTE
If the piston catches or stops in the cylinder, one or both piston ring end gaps were not properly aligned with their locating pin. Remove the cylinder and check for damage.

NOTE
*Because of the cylinder's design, all of the cylinder base nuts cannot be tightened with a torque wrench and socket. To accurately tighten the cylinder base nuts, a torque adapter (Figure 39) must be used with a torque wrench. However, because the torque adapter can increase the length of the torque wrench, the torque applied may be greater than the torque or dial reading on the torque wrench. When using a torque adapter and it increases the length of the torque wrench, the torque specification **must be** recalucated. To do this, follow the tool manufacturer's instructions or use the information listed under **Torque Wrench Adapters** in Chapter One. If the torque adapter is placed at a 90° angle (Figure 40) on the torque wrench, the length of the torque wrench is not increased and the torque specification does not have to be recalculated.*

12. Install the cylinder base nuts and tighten them (**Figure 40**) in two or three steps and in a crisscross pattern as specified in **Table 3**.

13A. On 1992 models, install the shaft lever as follows:

a. Install the gasket onto the operating rod.

b. Set the governor lever (A, **Figure 41**) onto the governor shaft with the end of the lever centered in the operating rod collar groove.

c. Install the shaft lever nut (B, **Figure 41**) and tighten securely.

13B. On 1993 and later models, install the shaft lever as follows:

a. Install the gasket onto the operating rod.

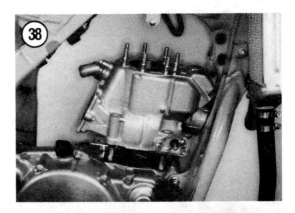

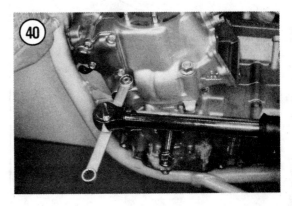

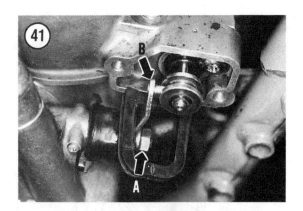

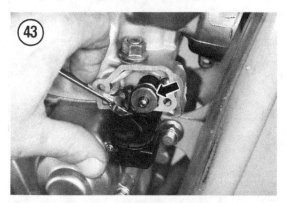

b. The operating rod is equipped with two E-clip grooves. Make sure an E-clip is installed in the inner groove (A, **Figure 42**) before installing the shaft lever.

c. Turn the shaft lever counterclockwise with a 9 mm wrench (B, **Figure 42**) and install the operating rod collar (**Figure 43**) over the operating rod. At the same time, use the wrench to guide the end of the shaft lever into the groove in the operating rod.

d. Install the wave washer and flat washer onto the operating rod and install the E-clip into the operating rod groove (**Figure 44**).

NOTE
Make sure the E-clips seat in their grooves completely.

14. Install the exhaust valve cover (**Figure 45**) and tighten its mounting bolts securely.

15. Install the cylinder head as described in this chapter.

16. Perform the *Leak Down Test* in Chapter Two to ensure that the engine is air tight.

17. Install the exhaust system as described in this chapter.

18. Follow the *Break-in Procedure* in this chapter if new parts were installed (piston, rings, cylinder, etc.).

EXHAUST VALVE

The Kawasaki exhaust valve system broadens the engine's power band throughout the speed range without sacrificing peak engine power. Main parts of the exhaust valve system are the exhaust valves

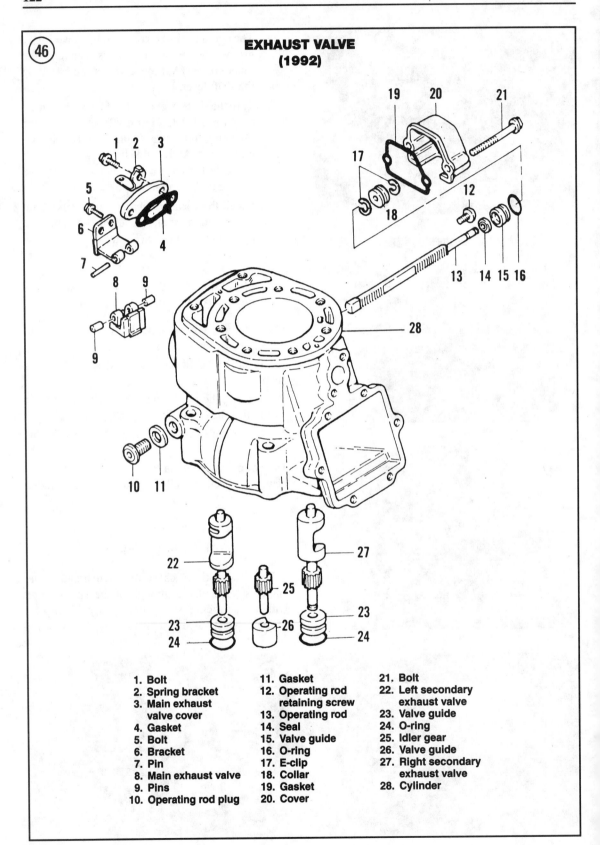

EXHAUST VALVE (1992)

1. Bolt
2. Spring bracket
3. Main exhaust valve cover
4. Gasket
5. Bolt
6. Bracket
7. Pin
8. Main exhaust valve
9. Pins
10. Operating rod plug
11. Gasket
12. Operating rod retaining screw
13. Operating rod
14. Seal
15. Valve guide
16. O-ring
17. E-clip
18. Collar
19. Gasket
20. Cover
21. Bolt
22. Left secondary exhaust valve
23. Valve guide
24. O-ring
25. Idler gear
26. Valve guide
27. Right secondary exhaust valve
28. Cylinder

(installed in the cylinder block) and the governor (installed behind the right crankcase cover).

This system varies the height of the exhaust port with sliding exhaust valves at the top of the exhaust port. The exhaust port timing is changed relative to engine speed. At low engine speed, the exhaust valves are closed, and as the engine speed increases the exhaust valves begin to open until they are completely open at high engine speed.

As the engine speed increases, steel balls within the governor move out due to centrifugal force. As the balls move out, so does the face of the governor, which is connected to the exhaust valves by a simple linkage system. When the governor face opens, it also opens the exhaust valves installed in the exhaust port. When engine speed decreases, the exhaust valves begins to close. The overall effect provides the best exhaust valve timing for power and torque throughout the engine's speed range.

The exhaust valve system consists of a number of parts. Before beginning the following procedures, study the exploded view drawings for your model.

EXHAUST VALVE SERVICE (1992)

This section describes service for the exhaust valve installed on 1992 models.

Refer to **Figure 46** when servicing the exhaust valve in the following section.

Exhaust Valve Disassembly

1. Remove the cylinder as described in this chapter.
2. Remove the operating rod plug and gasket (**Figure 47**).
4. Pull the operating rod (**Figure 48**) out until its stops
5. Remove the operating rod retaining screw (**Figure 49**).
6. Remove the secondary exhaust valves, idler gear and their guides as follows:

> *NOTE*
> *The secondary exhaust valves and idler gear can be very difficult to remove if they are heavily coated with carbon and oil residue. If you must use force on the exhaust valve and idle gear shafts to remove them, first wrap the shafts with a piece of shim stock or similar material. Doing so may help to prevent damage to the shaft surfaces.*

   a. Pull up the exhaust valves and idler gear and remove the valve guides (**Figure 50**).
   b. Remove the idler gear (A, **Figure 51**).
   c. Lift the two exhaust valves (B, **Figure 51**) slightly and remove the operating rod (**Figure 52**) past the exhaust valves and out of the cylinder.
   d. Remove the two exhaust valves (**Figure 53**).

7. Unbolt and remove the main exhaust valve cover (**Figure 54**) and its gasket.

8. Remove the main exhaust valve mounting bolts (**Figure 55**) and remove the main exhaust valve assembly (**Figure 56**).

Inspection

Replace parts that are excessively worn or damaged as described in this procedure.

1. Clean the exhaust valve assembly as described under *Exhaust Valve Cleaning and Decarbonizing* in this chapter.

2. Inspect the operating rod (A, **Figure 57**) for nicks, burrs or damage. Check the rack teeth for damage.

3. To disassemble and inspect the operating rod assembly (**Figure 58**), perform the following:

    a. Remove the outer E-clip, collar, inner E-clip and valve guide.

    b. Inspect the collar and valve guide for nicks, burrs or damage.

    c. Inspect the valve guide O-ring (**Figure 59**) for cracks, flat spots or other damage.

4. To assemble the operating rod assembly, perform the following:

    a. Apply a high temperature grease to the oil seal lip on the valve guide.

    b. Lubricate the O-ring with two-stroke oil and install it into the valve guide groove (**Figure 58**).

    c. Install the valve guide onto the rod with its O-ring side next to the rod's rack teeth (**Figure 59**).

    d. Install the inner E-clip.

    e. Slide on the collar.

    f. Install the outer E-clip.

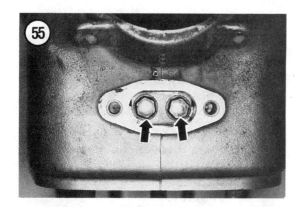

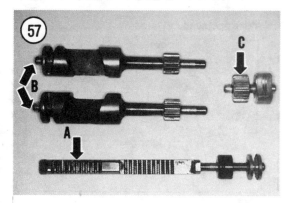

g. Make sure both E-clips seat in their grooves completely.

5. Inspect the exhaust valves (B, **Figure 57**) and idler gear (C) for scoring, nicks, burrs or gear damage. Install each valve guide onto its respective shaft to make sure the valve pivots smoothly. Remove any burrs with a fine-cut file.

6. To service the main exhaust valve, perform the following:

    a. Remove the pin (7, **Figure 46**) and separate the exhaust valve assembly.

    b. Inspect the valve for cracks or damage.

    c. Inspect the pins for wear or damage.

    d. Align the exhaust valve with the bracket and install the pin.

7. Inspect the exhaust valve operating areas in the cylinder block for excessive wear or damage.

Exhaust Valve Assembly

Refer to **Figure 46** when assembling the exhaust valve assembly.

> *NOTE*
> *Before installing the exhaust valve assembly, clean the cylinder bore as described under **Cylinder Inspection** in this chapter.*

> *NOTE*
> *When oil is specified to lubricate the exhaust valve components in the following steps, use a two-stroke engine oil.*

1. Lubricate the following parts with a two-stroke engine oil:

    a. Inside the valve guides (A, **Figure 60**).

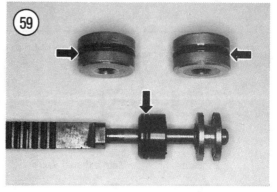

b. Exhaust valve and idler gear pinions (B, **Figure 60**).

c. Operating rod rack and journals (C, **Figure 60**).

d. Idler gear and exhaust valve upper and lower journals (D, **Figure 60**).

2. Install the main exhaust valve (**Figure 56**) into the cylinder. Install the mounting bolts (**Figure 55**) and tighten securely. Check that there is no clearance between the main exhaust valve bracket and the cylinder as shown in **Figure 61**.

NOTE
If there is clearance between the bracket and cylinder, remove the main exhaust valve and check the bracket for bending or other damage. If the bracket is not bent, check the area inside the cylinder for carbon buildup that is causing the clearance between the parts.

NOTE
If a cast iron liner was just installed, check the main exhaust valve's open and closed positions. Operate the main exhaust valve by hand. If the valve sticks, locate the problem area, then repair it with a file or grinder. Remove

only a small amount of material at a time, then recheck valve operation.

3. When installing and timing the secondary exhaust valve assembly in the following steps, first note the following:

a. **Figure 62** shows the exhaust valve timing marks.

b. The left and right side exhaust valves are different. The right exhaust valve (B, **Figure 63**) has a groove machined at the top of its shaft; see C, **Figure 63**.

c. The short gear tooth (**Figure 64**) on each secondary exhaust valve is its timing mark. Mark each timing mark with white paint.

d. The operating rod is marked with two grooves that represent its timing marks. Mark each groove with white paint.

4. Install the left exhaust valve (A, **Figure 63**) into the cylinder (A, **Figure 65**).

5. Install the right exhaust valve (B, **Figure 63**) into the cylinder (B, **Figure 65**).

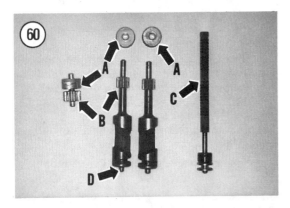

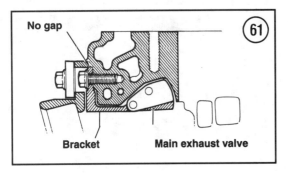

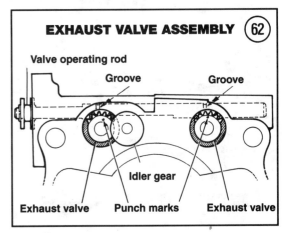

EXHAUST VALVE ASSEMBLY 62

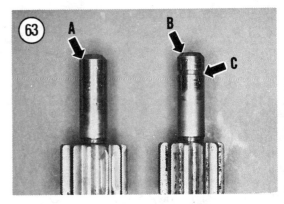

6. Turn each exhaust valve so its index mark faces forward. See **Figure 66**, typical.

7. Install the operating rod as follows:

    a. Lift both exhaust valves slightly (**Figure 65**) and install the operating rod (**Figure 67**) into the cylinder. The rack portion of the rod should face toward the back of the cylinder.

    b. When the operating rod is pushed in all the way, seat the valve guide into the cylinder (**Figure 68**) and secure it with its mounting screw (**Figure 49**).

8. Align the left exhaust valve index mark with the groove in the operating rod. See **Figure 62** and **Figure 69**.

9. Align the right exhaust valve index mark with the groove in the operating rod. See **Figure 62** and **Figure 70**.

10. Install the idler gear, meshing it with the right exhaust valve pinion and the operating rod (**Figure 71**).

NOTE
Because you have not yet installed the valve guides the operating rod may bind when you move it in Step 11. If this happens, install the two valve guides (with their O-rings) halfway into their bores, then try moving the operating rod. Partially installing the valve guides helps to center the exhaust valves and idler gear in their bores. However, do not install the valve guides all the way at this time as you will disturb the valve timing when trying to remove them.

11. Slide the operating rod back and forth and check the index marks when the rod is pushed all the way in. The index marks should align as described in Steps 8 and 9 and as shown in **Figure 62**. Note the following:

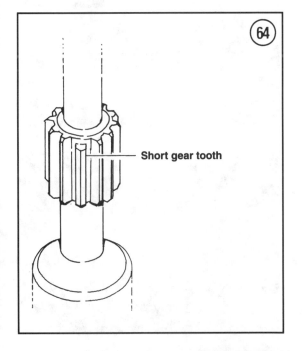

64

Short gear tooth

66

65

67

a. If the index marks align properly, continue with Step 12.

b. If the index marks do not align properly, retime the secondary exhaust valves.

12. Install an O-ring into each outer valve guide groove (**Figure 59**). Lubricate the O-rings with oil.

NOTE
The idler gear valve guide does not use an O-ring.

13. Install the three valve guides as shown in **Figure 72**.

14. Install the operating rod plug and gasket (**Figure 73**) and tighten as specified in **Table 3**.

15. Install the main exhaust valve cover, gasket and mounting bolts (**Figure 54**). Tighten the bolts securely.

16. Install the cylinder as described in this chapter.

EXHAUST VALVE SERVICE (1993-ON)

This section describes service for the exhaust valve assembly installed on 1993 and later models.

Refer to **Figure 74** when servicing the exhaust valve in the following section.

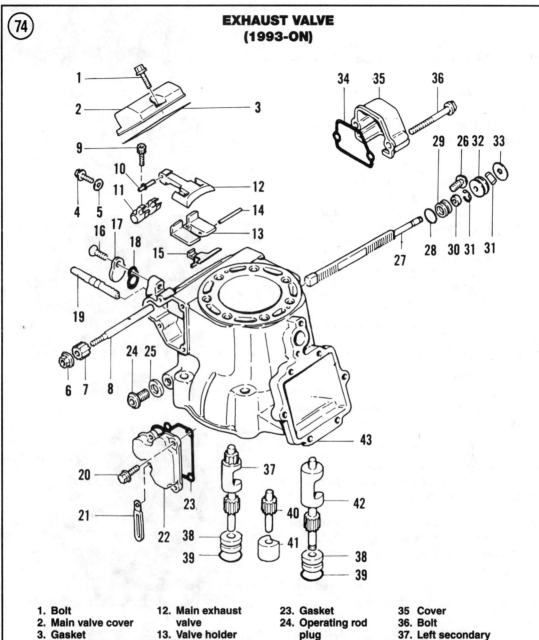

**EXHAUST VALVE
(1993-ON)**

4

1. Bolt
2. Main valve cover
3. Gasket
4. Main exhaust valve mounting bolt
5. Washer
6. Mainshaft nut
7. Main valve gear
8. Mainshaft
9. Main lever Allen bolt
10. Pin
11. Main lever
12. Main exhaust valve
13. Valve holder
14. Pin
15. Small main exhaust valve
16. Screw
17. Main valve rod cover
18. Gasket
19. Main valve rod
20. Bolt
21. Clamp
22. Resonator cover
23. Gasket
24. Operating rod plug
25. Gasket
26. Operating rod retaining screw
27. Operating rod
28. O-ring
29. Valve guide
30. Seal
31. E-clip
32. Collar
33. Washer
34. Gasket
35 Cover
36. Bolt
37. Left secondary exhaust valve
38. Valve guide
39. O-ring
40. Idler gear
41. Valve guide
42. Right secondary exhaust valve
43. Cylinder

Exhaust Valve Disassembly

1. Remove the cylinder as described in this chapter.
2. Remove the operating rod plug and gasket (**Figure 75**).
3. Pull the operating rod (A, **Figure 76**) out until it stops
4. Remove the operating rod retaining screw (B, **Figure 76**).

> *NOTE*
> *The secondary exhaust valves and idler gear can be very difficult to remove if they are heavily coated with carbon and oil residue. If you must use force on the exhaust valve and idle gear shafts to remove them, first wrap the shafts with a piece of shim stock or similar material. Doing so may help to prevent damage to the shaft surfaces.*

5. Remove the idler gear, secondary exhaust valves and their valve guides as follows:
   a. Lift and remove the idler gear and its valve guide (**Figure 77**).
   b. Lift the two secondary exhaust valves and remove their valve guides and O-rings (**Figure 78**).

> *NOTE*
> *You will not be able to remove the secondary exhaust valves until after removing the operating rod.*

   c. Lift the two secondary exhaust valves and remove the operating rod (**Figure 79**).
   d. Remove the two secondary exhaust valves (**Figure 80**).
6. Remove the following covers and their gaskets:
   a. Main valve cover (A, **Figure 81**).

b. Resonator cover (B, **Figure 81**).

c. Main valve rod cover (C, **Figure 81**).

NOTE

The mainshaft nut removed in Step 7 has left-hand threads.

7. Turn the mainshaft nut (**Figure 82**) *clockwise* and remove it and the main valve gear. See **Figure 83**.

8. Remove the main valve rod (**Figure 84**).

NOTE

Before removing the main lever Allen bolt in Step 9, remove all carbon residue from inside the bolt head.

9. Loosen and remove the main lever Allen bolt (**Figure 85**), then remove the main shaft (**Figure 86**).

10. Remove the main lever (A, **Figure 87**) and pin (B).

11. Remove the two main exhaust valve mounting bolts (C, **Figure 87**).

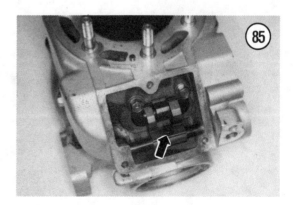

NOTE
The main exhaust valve can be very difficult to remove if it is heavily coated with carbon and oil residue.

12. Remove the main exhaust valve assembly (**Figure 88**).

CAUTION
If you cannot remove the main exhaust valve from the cylinder block, do not force it as it may damage the cylinder. Push the exhaust valve in (toward the cylinder) and check its outer edges for carbon buildup. Remove any carbon buildup from these areas with a file.

Inspection

Replace parts that are excessively worn or damaged as described in this procedure.

1. Clean the exhaust valve assembly as described under *Exhaust Valve Cleaning and Decarbonizing* in this chapter.

2. Inspect the operating rod (A, **Figure 89**) and the main valve rod (B) for nicks, burrs or damage. Check the rack teeth for damaged teeth.

3. Inspect the operating rod seal (**Figure 90**) for excessive wear or damage. Replace the seal as follows:

   a. Pry the seal out with a small screwdriver.

   b. Clean the mounting bore.

   c. Pack the lips of the new seal with a high temperature grease.

   d. Press the new seal into the cylinder with its closed side facing out (**Figure 90**).

4. Inspect the exhaust valves and idler gear (**Figure 91**) for scoring, nicks, burrs or gear damage. Install

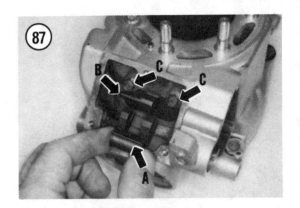

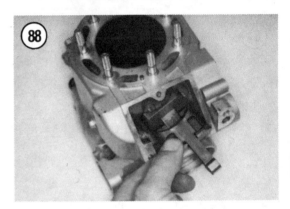

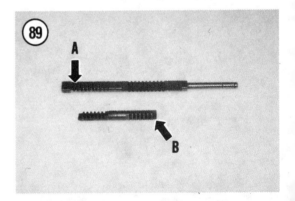

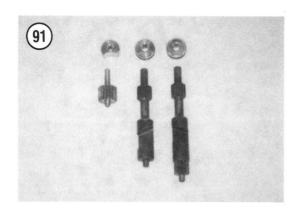

each valve guide (**Figure 92**) onto its respective shaft to make sure the valve pivots smoothly. Remove any burrs with a fine-cut file.

5. Inspect the mainshaft, main valve gear, main lever and pin (**Figure 93**) for excessive wear or damage.

6. To service the main exhaust valve (**Figure 94**), perform the following:

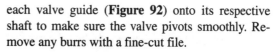

a. Lift the main exhaust valve (A, **Figure 95**) off of the valve holder.

b. Remove the pin (B, **Figure 95**) and the small main exhaust valve (C) from the valve holder (D).

c. Remove all carbon residue from the valve components.

d. Inspect the parts for cracks or damage.

e. Secure the small main exhaust valve (A, **Figure 96**) onto the holder (B) with the pin.

f. Place the main exhaust valve (C, **Figure 96**) onto the valve holder. See **Figure 94**.

7. Inspect the exhaust valve operating areas in the cylinder block for excessive wear or damage.

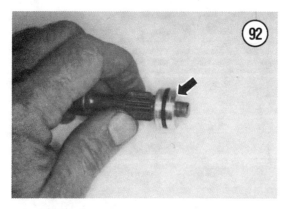

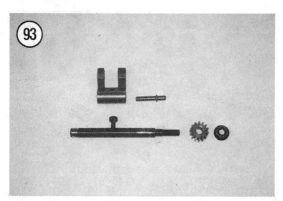

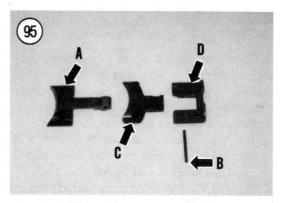

Exhaust Valve Assembly

Refer to **Figure 74** when assembling the exhaust valve assembly.

> *NOTE*
> *Before installing the exhaust valve assembly, clean the cylinder bore as described under Cylinder Inspection in this chapter.*

> *NOTE*
> *When oil is specified to lubricate the exhaust valve components in the following steps, use a 2-stroke engine oil.*

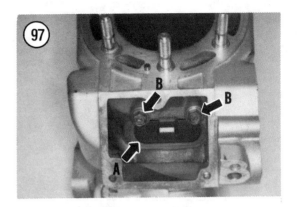

1. Install the main exhaust valve assembly as follows:

    a. Assemble the main exhaust valve assembly (**Figure 94**) as described under *Inspection* in this section.

    b. Lubricate the main exhaust valve and its cylinder operating chamber with oil.

    c. Install the main exhaust valve (**Figure 88**) into the cylinder. See A, **Figure 97**.

    d. Install and tighten the main exhaust valve mounting bolts (B, **Figure 97**).

    e. Operate the main exhaust valve to make sure it slides smoothly.

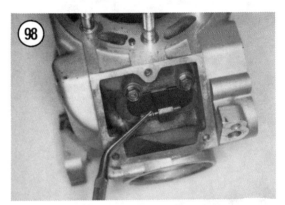

2. Install the pin—shoulder side facing right—through the main exhaust valve hole (**Figure 98**).

3. Install the main lever over the pin as shown in **Figure 99**.

4. Lubricate the main valve rod with oil.

5. Install the mainshaft (**Figure 100**) through the cylinder block and into the main lever with its threaded end facing toward the left side.

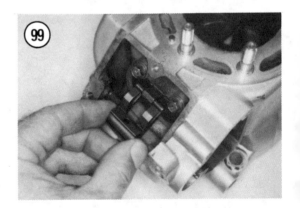

6. Align the main lever and mainshaft rod holes and install the Allen bolt (**Figure 101**). Tighten the main lever Allen bolt as specified in **Table 3**. Operate the main lever to make sure the exhaust valve slides smoothly.

7. Insert the main valve rod into the cylinder with its groove end (A, **Figure 102**) facing out and its end rack (B) facing down. Push the main valve rod all the way into its cylinder bore until it stops.

8. Turn the cylinder over so its base surface faces up.

9. Install a new O-ring into each secondary exhaust valve guide groove (**Figure 91**). Lubricate the O-rings with oil.

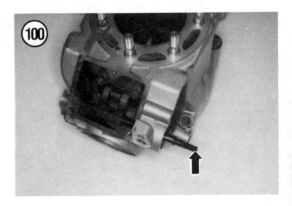

10. Lubricate and identify the secondary exhaust valves and idler gear as follows:

NOTE
If you had to remove the idler gear and both secondary exhaust valves with pliers, install a guide onto each shaft to make the shafts pivot smoothly. Remove any burrs with a fine-cut file.

a. Lubricate the secondary exhaust valve and idler gear pivot shoulders and gear teeth with oil.

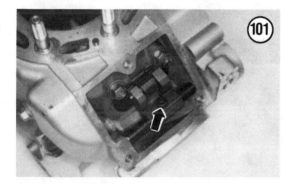

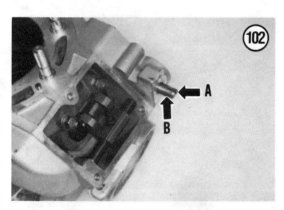

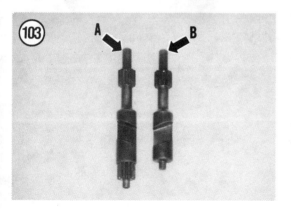

b. The left side secondary exhaust valve (A, **Figure 103**) is longer than the right side valve (B).

c. The short gear tooth (**Figure 104**) on each secondary exhaust valve is its timing mark. Mark each timing mark with white paint. See **Figure 105**.

d. The operating rod is marked with 2 grooves that represent its timing marks. Mark each groove with white paint on the side of the rod shown in **Figure 105**.

11. Install the secondary exhaust valves as follows:

a. Install the left exhaust valve (**Figure 106**).

b. Install the right exhaust valve (**Figure 107**).

c. Turn each valve so its timing mark faces forward (**Figure 108**).

4

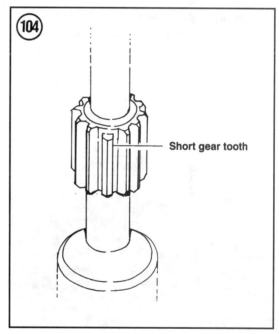

Short gear tooth

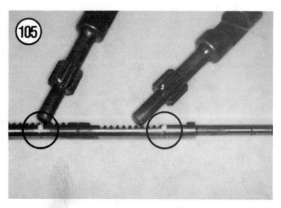

12. Install the operating rod and time the secondary exhaust valves as follows:

   a. When installing the operating rod, align it so its timing marks face up with its rod teeth facing toward the secondary exhaust valve gears as shown in **Figure 109**.

   b. Lift up the left and right secondary exhaust valves so the operating rod can pass under their pinion gears, then install the operating rod into the cylinder (**Figure 110**).

   c. Lower the left secondary exhaust valve and align its timing mark with the operating rod timing mark (**Figure 111**). When doing so, you will also be meshing the exhaust valve with the main valve rod.

   d. Lower the right secondary exhaust valve and align its timing mark with the operating rod timing mark (**Figure 112**). Install the idler gear (**Figure 113**), making sure it did not change the secondary exhaust valve timing marks.

   e. Install the guides over the secondary exhaust valve and idle gear shafts. Install the guide with the cutout over the idle gear shaft. Install

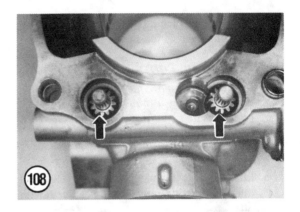

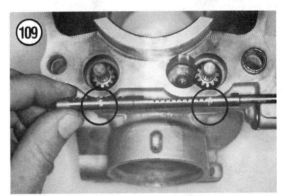

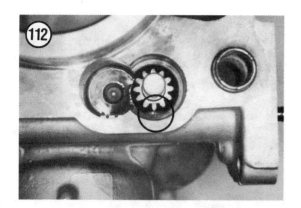

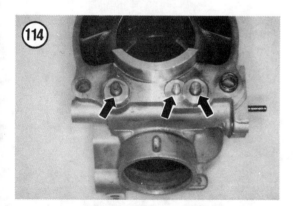

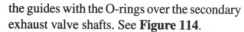

the guides with the O-rings over the secondary exhaust valve shafts. See **Figure 114**.

13. Install the main valve rod cover (without gasket) and its mounting screw (**Figure 115**).

NOTE
Installing the cover in Step 13 prevents the main valve rod from moving out of the cylinder when tightening the mainshaft nut later in this procedure.

14. Pull the operating rod (A, **Figure 116**) all the way out to open the secondary exhaust valves.

NOTE
The mainshaft nut installed in Step 15 has left-hand threads.

15. Pull the main lever (B, **Figure 116**) to open the main exhaust valve all the way. Install the main valve gear (**Figure 117**) and the mainshaft nut (**Figure 118**). Turn the mainshaft nut *counterclockwise* to install it, then tighten as specified in **Table 3**.

16. Remove the screw and the main valve rod cover (**Figure 115**).

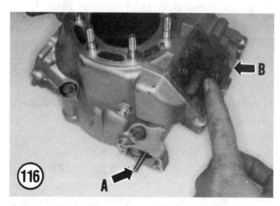

17. Pull the operating rod (A, **Figure 116**) all the way out to open the main and secondary exhaust valves. Check that the end of the main valve rod end is flush with the cylinder block surface (**Figure 119**). Note the following:

   a. If the main valve rod end is flush with the cylinder as described, the exhaust valve timing is correct. Confirm this by visually inspecting the main and secondary exhaust valves. When the main exhaust valve is all the way open, it will be aligned with the top of the exhaust port (**Figure 120**). When the secondary exhaust valves are open all the way, you will be able to see past the valves when looking through the exhaust port from the front of the cylinder and both edges of the secondary valves will be flush with the port openings (**Figure 121**).

   b. If the main valve rod is not flush with the cylinder block as described, the exhaust valve timing is incorrect. Disassemble the exhaust valve assembly, then reinstall it as described in this section.

18. Install the operating rod retaining screw (**Figure 122**). Tighten securely.

19. Install the operating rod plug (A, **Figure 123**) and gasket, then tighten as specified in **Table 3**.

20. Install the following covers and new gaskets. Tighten the fasteners securely:

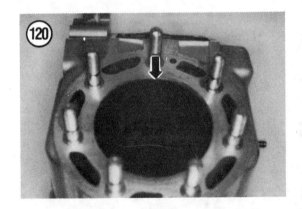

   a. Main valve cover (B, **Figure 123**).
   b. Main valve rod cover (C, **Figure 123**).
   c. Resonator cover (D, **Figure 123**).

21. Install the cylinder as described in this chapter.

EXHAUST VALVE CLEANING AND DECARBONIZING

The exhaust valve components are subjected to a lot of carbon and oil residue. This condition is made worse when the residue is allowed to accumulate over a period of time. If this residue is not removed periodically, the accumulation will cause the exhaust valve components to bind or seize. To prevent this type of damage, the exhaust valve system must be removed and cleaned regularly. For a recommended time interval, refer to the maintenance table at the end of Chapter Three.

One way you can tell when the exhaust valve system needs cleaning is if the engine becomes hard to start (exhaust valve stuck open) or if the engine operates with less power (exhaust valve stuck closed). Because of the close operating clearance between the main exhaust valves and cylinder operating surfaces and between the secondary exhaust valve gears, any carbon buildup can cause the parts to seize. Another problem that occurs from a seized exhaust valve assembly is trying to remove the components from the cylinder. If the components are seized, they are often damaged during removal.

To thoroughly clean the exhaust valve, the complete assembly must be removed from the cylinder.

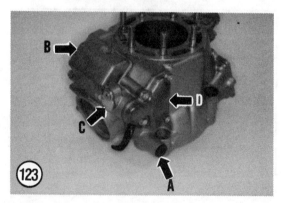

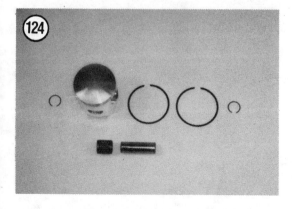

The exhaust valve operating chambers within the cylinder block must also be cleaned. At the same time, remove, clean and inspect the piston, ring and cylinder bore.

1. Remove all gasket residue from the cylinder block and cover gasket surfaces.

2. Clean the exhaust valve assembly as follows:

   a. Disassemble the main exhaust valve as described under the appropriate procedure for your model.

   b. Soak all of the exhaust valve components in solvent to loosen the oil and carbon residue. Use a parts cleaning brush to clean the oil from the parts.

   c. Parts covered with a heavy carbon buildup will require longer soaking times.

   d. Remove the parts from the solvent and inspect them. Remove carbon with a wire brush, making sure you work carefully to avoid damaging the part.

3. Clean the exhaust valve chambers in the cylinder block. When cleaning around the cylinder ports, work carefully to avoid damaging the cylinder bore surface.

PISTON, PISTON PIN, AND PISTON RINGS

Figure 124 shows the piston components.

Piston and Piston Ring Removal

1. Remove the cylinder as described in this chapter.

2. Before removing the piston, hold the rod tightly and rock the piston to detect excessive clearance between the piston, piston pin and connecting rod (**Figure 125**). Any rocking motion (do not confuse with the normal sliding motion) indicates wear on the piston pin, needle bearing, piston pin bore, or more likely, a combination of all three.

3. Wrap a clean shop cloth under the piston so the clips cannot fall into the crankcase.

> *WARNING*
> *Wear safety glasses when performing Step 4.*

4. Remove the clip from each side of the piston pin bore (**Figure 126**). Hold your thumb over one edge

of the clip when removing it to prevent it from springing out.

5. Use a proper size wooden dowel or socket extension and push the piston pin (**Figure 127**) out of the piston.

CAUTION
If the engine ran hot or seized, piston warpage may lock the piston pin in place, making it difficult to remove. However, do not drive the piston pin out of the piston as this will damage the piston, needle bearing and connecting rod. If you cannot remove the piston pin by hand, remove it as described in Step 6.

6. If the piston pin is tight, fabricate the tool shown in **Figure 128**. Assemble the tool onto the piston and pull the piston pin out of the piston. Install a pad between the piston and piece of pipe to prevent the tool from damaging the piston.

7. Lift the piston (**Figure 127**) off the connecting rod.

8. Remove the needle bearing (**Figure 129**).

9. Place a piece of foam insulation tube or shop cloth over the end of the connecting rod to protect it.

NOTE
If you are going to reuse the piston rings, mark their top side after removing them.

10. Spread the upper piston ring ends with your fingers and slide the ring out of the ring land and up

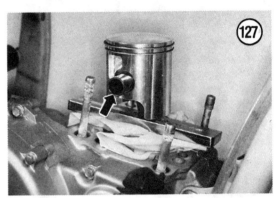

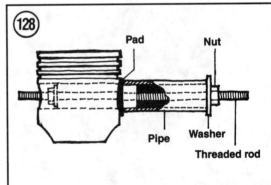

Pad   Nut

Pipe   Washer

Threaded rod

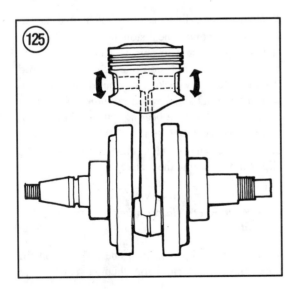

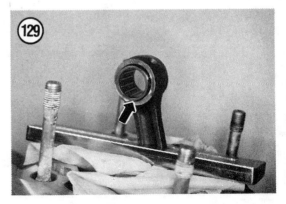

and off the piston (**Figure 130**). Repeat for the lower ring.

Piston Pin and Needle Bearing Inspection

When measuring the parts in this section, compare the actual measurements to the specifications in **Table 2**. Replace parts that are out of specification or show damage as described in this section.

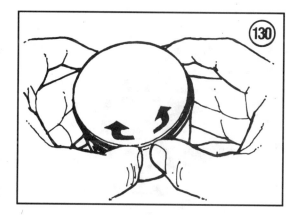

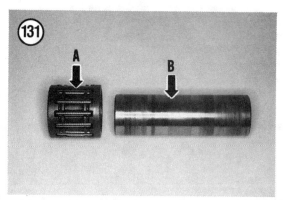

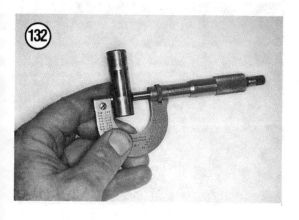

1. Clean the piston pin and needle bearing in solvent and dry thoroughly.

2. Inspect the needle bearing (A, **Figure 131**) and replace if worn or damaged.

3. Check the piston pin (B, **Figure 131**) for wear, scoring and cracks along its outer diameter. Replace the piston pin if necessary.

4. Measure the piston pin outside diameter at its piston contact areas (**Figure 132**).

5. Measure the piston pin hole inside diameter with a small hole gauge (**Figure 133**). and micrometer.

Connecting Rod Inspection

When measuring the connecting rod in this section, compare the actual measurements to the specifications in **Table 2**. Replace the connecting rod if it is out of specification or shows damage as described in this section.

1. Check the connecting rod small end for galling, cracks or other damage.

2. Measure the connecting rod small end inside diameter with a telescoping gauge (**Figure 134**). Measure the telescoping gauge with a micrometer.

3. Measure the connecting rod big end side clearance with a feeler gauge. **Figure 135** shows the clearance being measured with the crankshaft removed from the engine.

NOTE
*To replace the connecting rod, the crankshaft must be removed from the engine and then disassembled. Refer to **Crankcase and Crankshaft** in Chapter Five.*

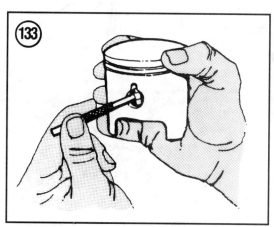

Piston and Ring Inspection

When measuring the piston and rings in this section, compare the actual measurements to the specifications in **Table 2**. Replace parts that are out of specification or show damage as described in this section.

1. Check the piston for cracks at the transfer cutaways and along the piston skirt (**Figure 136**).

2. Check the piston skirt (**Figure 136**) for galling and abrasion. Replace the piston if there is any damage.

NOTE

Figure 137 shows a piston with seizure marks on the intake skirt.

3. Check for a loose or damaged ring locating pin. Each pin must be tight and the piston must show no signs of cracking around the pins. Replace the piston if a pin is loose or damaged.

CAUTION

A loose or damaged piston locating pin can fall out and cause engine damage.

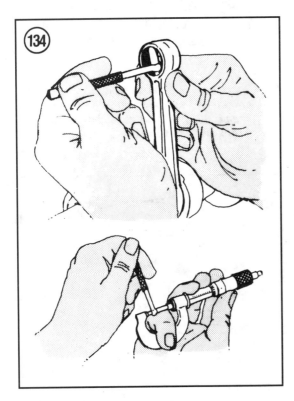

4. Check the piston pin clip grooves for excessive wear or damage. Replace the piston, if necessary.

5. Check the condition and color of the piston crown (**Figure 138**). Remove normal carbon buildup with a wire wheel mounted in a drill.

CAUTION

Do not use a wire brush to clean the piston skirt or gouge the piston when cleaning it.

NOTE

If the piston shows signs of overheating, pitting or other abnormal conditions, the engine may be experiencing preignition or detonation. Refer to Chapter Two for information on both conditions.

6. Remove carbon buildup from the ring groove with a broken ring (**Figure 139**). Work carefully so

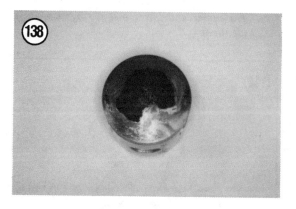

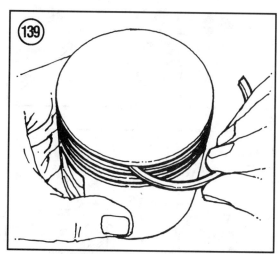

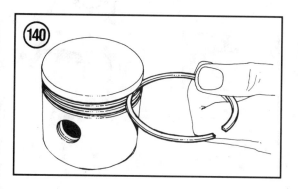

you do not remove any aluminum material from the groove.

7. Inspect the ring grooves for burrs, nicks or broken and cracked lands. Replace the piston if the ring groove is excessively worn or damaged.

8. Measure the piston ring thickness with a micrometer.

9. Roll the ring around its groove (**Figure 140**) and check for binding. Repair minor binding with a fine-cut file.

10. Measure the piston ring-to-groove side clearance (**Figure 141**).

11. Measure the piston ring end gap as follows. Place the ring into the bottom of the cylinder and push it in to a point where cylinder wear is minimal. Measure the ring gap with a flat feeler gauge (**Figure 142**).

12. Measure the piston outside diameter as described under *Piston/Cylinder Clearance* in this chapter.

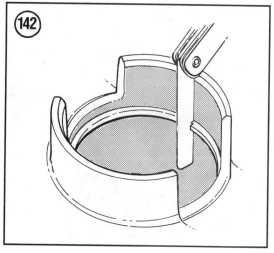

Piston/Cylinder Clearance

1. Measure the piston diameter at a point 20.5 mm (0.81 in.) from the bottom of the piston skirt. Measure at a 90° angle to the piston pin as shown in **Figure 143** and compare to the dimension in **Table 2**. Note the following:
   a. Install a new piston if the diameter is less than the service limit in **Table 2**.
   b. If the piston diameter is within service specifications, continue with Step 2.
2. Measure the cylinder bore with a bore gauge (**Figure 144**) or an inside micrometer at a depth of 30 mm (1.18 in.) from the top of the cylinder as shown in **Figure 145**. Measure in line with the piston pin and at 90° to the pin. Note the following:
   a. Measure the cylinder bore when the cylinder is cold (room temperature).
   b. If the cylinder bore measurement exceeds the service limit in **Table 2**, you must replace the cylinder block or have it resleeved. The stock plated cylinder liner cannot be bored to accept a new piston. It can only be bored to install a new sleeve.
3. Subtract the piston skirt diameter from the maximum cylinder bore diameter to determine the piston-to-cylinder clearance. Compare this measurement with the dimension listed in **Table 2**. Resleeve or replace the cylinder if the clearance exceeds the service limit in **Table 2** and the piston diameter is within specification.

NOTE
*Excessive piston clearance can cause piston slap and engine damage when the piston skirt breaks. **Figure 146** shows a piston damaged from excessive piston skirt clearance.*

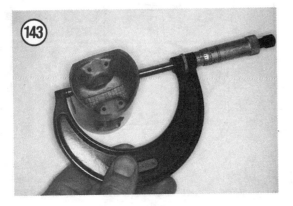

Piston Ring Installation

1. Check the piston ring end gap before assembling the piston and ring; refer to *Piston and Ring Inspection* in this chapter. The end gap measurement must not exceed the service limit in **Table 2**.
2. Wash the piston and rings in solvent, then in soapy water to remove any oil and carbon particles. Dry with compressed air.

NOTE
The upper and lower piston rings are identical.

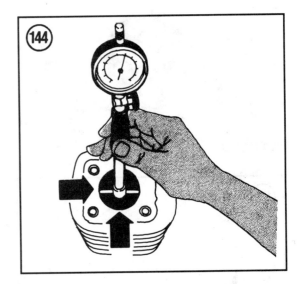

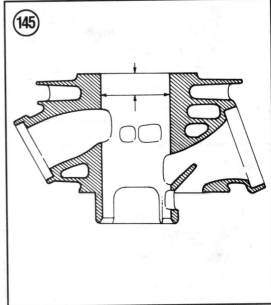

3. Install the lower piston ring with its stamped mark (**Figure 147**) facing up.

4. Install the piston ring by carefully spreading its ends your thumbs and slipping it over the top of the piston (**Figure 148**). Position the ring gap around the pin in the ring groove (**Figure 149**).

5. Check that the ring floats smoothly in its ring groove.

6. Repeat the preceding steps to install the upper piston ring.

Piston Installation

Use a two-stroke engine oil when oil is specified in the following steps.

1. Lubricate the needle bearing with oil and install it in the connecting rod (**Figure 150**).

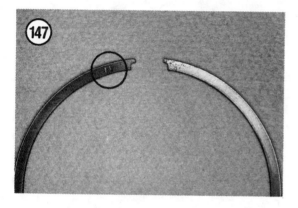

> *WARNING*
> *Wear safety glasses when performing Step 2.*

2. Install one piston pin clip into the piston. Make sure the clip seats in the groove completely. Turn the clip so its open end does not align with the piston slot.

3. Oil the piston pin and install it partway into the piston (**Figure 151**).

4A. On 1992-1993 models, install the piston onto the connecting rod with the arrow mark on the piston crown facing forward. Align the piston pin with the bearing and push the pin (**Figure 152**) into the piston.

4B. On 1994 and later models, install the piston so the IN mark (A, **Figure 153**) on the side of the piston faces toward the right side of the engine. Align the

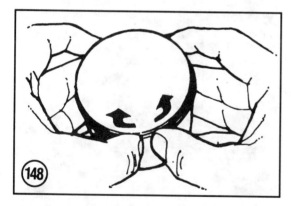

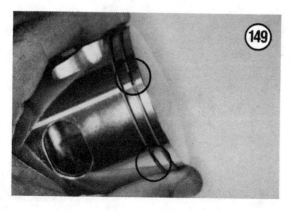

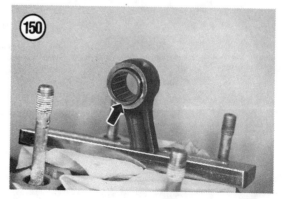

piston pin with the bearing and push the pin (**Figure 152**) into the piston.

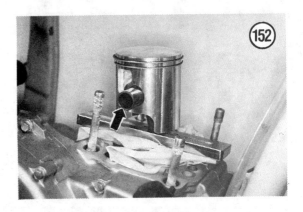

> *NOTE*
> *If the piston mark is not visible, install the piston with its piston ring locating pins facing toward the intake side of the engine.*

> *CAUTION*
> *If the piston pin will not slide in the piston smoothly, use the home-made tool described during **Piston Removal** to install the piston pin.*

5. Wrap a clean shop cloth under the piston so the clip cannot fall into the crankcase.

> *WARNING*
> *Safety glasses must be worn when performing Step 6.*

6. Install the second *new* piston pin clip (**Figure 154**) into the clip groove in the piston. Make sure the clip is seated in the groove completely. Turn the clip so its open end does not align with the piston slot.

7. Make sure the rings are seated completely in their grooves with their end gap (B, **Figure 153**) positioned around the ring locating pins.

REED VALVE ASSEMBLY

Figure 155 shows the reed valve components.

> *NOTE*
> *If your model is equipped with an aftermarket reed valve, refer to the manufacturer's instructions for removal, installation and inspection procedures.*

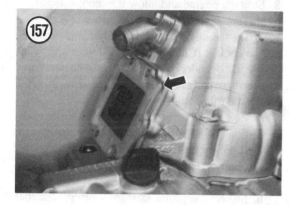

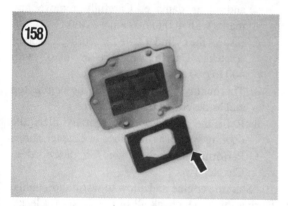

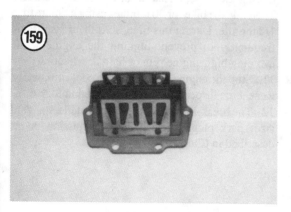

Removal/Installation

1. Remove the carburetor (Chapter Eight).

2. Remove the intake manifold mounting bolts and remove the manifold (**Figure 156**).

3. Remove the reed block and gasket (**Figure 157**).

4. Remove the spacer (**Figure 158**) from the reed block.

5. Inspect the reed valve assembly as described in this chapter.

6. Remove all gasket residue from the crankcase mating surface.

7. Install the spacer (**Figure 158**) into the reed block.

8. Install a new gasket onto the reed block, then install the reed block into the cylinder (**Figure 157**).

9. Install the intake manifold (**Figure 156**) and its mounting bolts. Tighten the intake manifold mounting bolts in 2-3 steps and in a crisscross pattern as specified in **Table 3**.

10. Install the carburetor (Chapter Eight).

Inspection/Reed Valve Replacement

1. Carefully examine the reed valve assembly (**Figure 159**) for wear, distortion or damage.

2. Use a flat feeler gauge and measure the clearance between the reed valve and the reed block sealing surface (**Figure 160**). Compare to the service limit in **Table 2**. Replace the reed valve if the clearance exceeds the service limit.

3. Remove the screws securing the reed stop to the reed block and disassemble the reed assembly.

4. Clean all parts in solvent and dry thoroughly. Remove all thread sealer residue from the mounting screws and the threaded holes in the reed block.

5. Check the reed valves and replace them if cracked or excessively worn.

6. Check the intake manifold and replace it if damaged.

7. Replace damaged screws and lockwashers.

8. Reassemble the reed cage as follows:
   a. The reeds are not perfectly flat, but instead, one side will bow out slightly. Install the reed so the bowed section faces out.
   b. Apply ThreeBond threadlock TB1342 or equivalent to the mounting screws prior to installation. Assemble the reed valves, reed stops and secure with the mounting screws. Tighten the screws securely.

ENGINE BREAK-IN

If the rings were replaced, a new piston installed, the cylinder replaced, the crankshaft rebuilt or replaced or new engine bearings installed, perform the following engine break-in procedure.

Before breaking-in the engine, note the following:
   a. Perform the break-in procedure on flat ground. To prevent engine overheating, avoid riding in sand, mud or up hills.
   b. Do not run the engine with the throttle in the same position for more than a few seconds.
   c. Check the spark plug frequently during the break-in procedure. The electrode should be dry and clean and the color of the insulation should be light to medium tan. Because slow riding may cause the spark plug to foul, install a hotter spark plug during the break-in period if necessary. Refer to Chapter Three for further information on spark plug reading.

1. Remove and clean the air filter and air box assembly (Chapter Three).

2. Check the engine coolant level and top off as required.

3. Check the transmission oil level and top off as required.

4. Start the engine and allow to run at idle speed until it is thoroughly warmed. Stop the engine and allow it to cool completely.

5. Start the engine and allow to warm thoroughly. Ride the bike for 10 minutes using no more than 1/2 throttle. During this time, shift the transmission fre-

quently to prevent lugging the engine while avoiding high engine rpm or hard acceleration.

6. Stop the engine and allow it to cool completely. During this time, check the chain tension and alignment and spoke tightness. Check all of the other exposed engine fasteners, especially engine and sprocket mounting bolts, for looseness.

7. Start the engine and allow it to warm thoroughly. Ride the bike for 20 minutes using no more than 1/2 throttle. During this time, shift the transmission frequently to prevent lugging the engine while avoiding high engine rpm or hard acceleration.

8. Stop the engine and allow it to cool completely. Repeat the inspection check described in Step 6.

9. When the engine is completely cool, drain the engine coolant (Chapter Three). Remove the cylinder head, cylinder and piston (this chapter) and inspect these parts for scoring or other damage while noting the following:
   a. Remove all carbon build-up from the combustion chamber, piston crown and exhaust port. If the exhaust valve seems heavily carboned, remove and clean it as described in this chapter.
   b. Inspect the piston skirt for scoring, scratches and other damage. Carefully remove any marks with 400 to 600 emery cloth.
   c. Inspect the cylinder bore for scoring and other scratches. Carefully remove any marks with 400 to 600 emery cloth.
   d. Thoroughly clean and install the engine top end as described in this chapter.
   e. Refill the engine with coolant and bleed the cooling system as described in Chapter Three.
   f. Perform the *Leak Down Test* described in Chapter Two.

10. Start the engine and allow to warm thoroughly. During this time, check all of the gasket for leaks. Then ride the bike for 30 minutes using no more than 1/2 throttle. During this time, shift the transmission frequently to prevent lugging the engine while avoiding high engine rpm or hard acceleration.

11. Stop the engine and allow it to cool completely. Repeat the inspection check described in Step 6.

12. The break-in is now complete. Install a standard size spark plug. Replace the transmission oil as described in Chapter Three.

Table 1 GENERAL ENGINE SPECIFICATIONS

Displacement	249 ml (15.2 cu. in.)
Bore × stroke	66.4 × 72.0 mm (2.61 × 2.83 in.)
Compression ratio	
1992	
Low speed	10.9:1
High speed	9.3:1
1993	
Low speed	10.2:1
High speed	8.7:1
1994	
Low speed	10.3:1
High speed	8.8:1
1995-on	
Low speed	
U.S models	10.4:1
All other models	10.8:1
High speed	
U.S. models	8.7:1
All other models	9.0:1
Port timing	
1992	
Intake	
Open	Full open
Close	–
Transfer	
Open	61.0° BBDC
Close	61.0° ABDC
Exhaust	
Open	
Low speed	80.5° BBDC
High speed	92.5° BBDC
Close	
Low speed	80.5° ABDC
High speed	92.5° ABDC
1993	
Intake	
Open	Full open
Close	–
Transfer	
Open	60.0° BBDC
Close	60.0° ABDC
Exhaust	
Open	
Low speed	80.5° BBDC
High speed	92.5° BBDC
Close	
Low speed	80.5° ABDC
High speed	92.5° ABDC
1994	
Intake	
Open	Full open
Close	–
Transfer	
Open	60.0° BBDC
Close	60.0° ABDC
Exhaust	
Open	
Low speed	79.5° BBDC
High speed	91.5° BBDC
	(continued)

Table 1 GENERAL ENGINE SPECIFICATIONS (continued)

Port timing	
1994	
Exhaust (continued)	
Close	
Low speed	79.5° ABDC
High speed	91.5° ABDC
1995	
Intake	
Open	Full open
Close	–
Transfer	
Open	58.4° BBDC
Close	58.4° ABDC
Exhaust	
Open	
Low speed	76.9° BBDC
High speed	91.4° BBDC
Close	
Low speed	76.9° ABDC
High speed	91.4° ABDC
1996-on	
Intake	
Open	Full open
Close	–
Transfer	
Open	59.1° BBDC
Close	59.1° ABDC
Exhaust	
Open	
Low speed	76.9° BBDC
High speed	91.4° BBDC
Close	
Low speed	76.9° ABDC
High speed	91.4° ABDC
Lubrication system	
System type	Fuel/oil
Premix ratio	32:1

Table 2 ENGINE SERVICE SPECIFICATIONS

	New mm (in.)	Service limit mm (in.)
Cylinder head warpage limit	–	0.03 (0.0012)
Cylinder bore diameter	66.400-66.415 (2.6141-2.6147)	66.48 (2.617)
Piston diameter		
1992	66.323-66.338 (2.6111-2.6117)	66.17 (2.605)
1993-on	66.336-66.351 (2.6116-2.6122)	66.19 (2.606)
Piston-to-cylinder clearance		
1992	0.072-0.082 (0.0028-0.0032)	–
1993-on	0.059-0.069 (0.0023-0.0027)	–
	(continued)	

Table 2 ENGINE SERVICE SPECIFICATIONS (continued)

	New mm (in.)	Service limit mm (in.)
Piston ring-to-groove clearance		
1992-1997	0.04-0.08 (0.0016-0.0031)	0.18 (0.007)
1998	0.025-0.06 (0.0009-0.0024)	0.18 (0.007)
Piston ring groove width		
1992-1996	1.23-1.25 (0.048-0.049)	1.30 (0.051)
1997	1.03-1.05 (0.040-0.041)	1.13 (0.044)
1998	1.01-1.03 (0.039-0.040)	1.13 (0.044)
Piston ring thickness		
1992-1996	1.17-1.19 (0.046-0.047)	1.10 (0.043)
1997-on	0.970-0.985 (0.038-0.039)	0.90 (0.035)
Piston ring end gap		
1992-1993	0.25-0.45 (0.0098-0.018)	0.75 (0.029)
1994-on	0.25-0.45 (0.0098-0.018)	0.80 (0.030)
Piston pin outside diameter	17.995-18.000 (0.7084-0.7087)	17.96 (0.707)
Piston pin bore diameter		
1992-1997	18.000-18.020 (0.7087-0.7094)	18.07 (0.711)
1998	18.005-18.015 (0.7089-0.7092)	18.07 (0.711)
Connecting rod big end side clearance	0.45-0.55 (0.018-0.022)	0.70 (0.028)
Conecting rod small end inside diameter	22.003-22.012 (0.8663-0.8666)	22.05 (0.868)
Reed valve clearance	– –	0.2 (0.008)

Table 3 ENGINE TOP END TORQUE SPECIFICATIONS

	N•m	in.-lb.	ft.-lb.
Coolant drain plugs			
Cylinder block drain plug			
1992	22	–	16
1993	21	–	15
1994-1995	22	–	16
1996-on	8.8	78	–
Water pump drain plug	8.8	78	–
Cylinder base nuts	34	–	25
Cylinder head flange nuts	25	–	18
Cylinder head hanger nuts			
1992-1993			
At engine	34	–	25
At frame	26	–	19.5
(continued)			

Table 3 ENGINE TOP END TORQUE SPECIFICATIONS (continued)

	N•m	in.-lb.	ft.-lb.
1994-on			
8 mm	26	–	19
10 mm	39	–	29
Exhaust valve			
1992			
Operating rod plug	15	–	11
Shaft lever nut	7.8	69	–
1993			
Main lever Allen bolt	3.9	35	–
Mainshaft nut	8.8	78	–
Operating rod left side plug	15	–	11
Shaft lever nut	8.8	78	–
1994-on			
Main lever Allen bolt	3.9	35	–
Mainshaft nut	8.8	78	–
Operating rod plug	22	–	16
Intake manifold mounting bolts	8.8	78	–
Spark plug	27	–	20

5

ENGINE BOTTOM END

This chapter covers information on servicing the KX250 engine bottom end. Clutch, kickstarter, primary drive and external shift mechanism service is covered in Chapter Six. Transmission service (other than removal and installation) is covered in Chapter Seven.

Before working on the engine, read the information listed under *Service Hints* in Chapter One.

Table 1 lists crankshaft specifications. **Table 2** lists engine tightening torques. **Tables 1** and **2** are at the end of the chapter.

SERVICING ENGINE IN FRAME

Some of the components can be serviced while the engine is mounted in the frame (the bike's frame is a great holding fixture—especially for breaking loose stubborn bolts and nuts):

1. Cylinder head.
2. Cylinder.
3. Piston.
4. Carburetor.
5. Reed valve.
6. Flywheel and stator plate.
7. Water pump.
8. Clutch.
9. External shift mechanism.
10. Primary drive gear.
11. Kickstarter.

ENGINE

Removal/Installation

1. Remove the radiator side covers and seat (Chapter Fifteen).
2. Remove the fuel tank (Chapter Eight).
3. Drain the transmission oil (Chapter Three)
4. Drain the coolant (Chapter Three).
5. Support the bike on a workstand.
6. Remove the carburetor (Chapter Eight)
7. Remove the exhaust pipe (Chapter Four).
8. Disconnect the drive chain and remove the drive sprocket, if necessary (Chapter Eleven).
9. Disconnect the clutch cable as follows:
   a. Loosen the clutch cable adjuster at the handlebar.
   b. Disconnect the clutch cable from the left side of the engine (**Figure 1**).
10. Remove the shift pedal pinch bolt and the shift pedal.
11. Disconnect the water hose (A, **Figure 2**) from the cylinder head.
12. Disconnect the water hose (**Figure 3**) from the water pump.
13. On 1994-on models, reposition both radiators as follows:
   a. Disconnect the radiator lower connecting hose (B, **Figure 2**) from one of the radiators.
   b. Remove the radiator lower mounting bolts (A, **Figure 4**) from each radiator.

c. Loosen the radiator upper mounting bolts (B, **Figure 4**) from each radiator. Pivot both radiators forward. See A, **Figure 5**.

14. Remove the cylinder head hanger bracket bolts and the hanger bracket (B, **Figure 5**).

15. If you are going to disassemble the crankcases, remove the following engine sub-assemblies before removing the engine from the frame:

a. Cylinder head (Chapter Four).
b. Cylinder (Chapter Four).
c. Piston (Chapter Four).
d. Flywheel and stator plate (Chapter Nine).
e. Clutch (Chapter Six).
f. Kickstarter and idler gear (Chapter Six).
g. External shift mechanism (Chapter Six).
h. Primary drive gear (Chapter Six).

16. If you are going to remove the stator plate, disconnect the stator plate electrical connectors. Remove its wiring harness from around the frame so it can be removed with the engine.

17. Remove the rear brake pedal pivot bolt (**Figure 6**), spring and allow the brake pedal to hang down.

18. Remove the swing arm pivot shaft nut. Do not remove the pivot shaft (A, **Figure 7**) at this time.

NOTE
Before removing the front and lower engine mounting bolts in step 19, check for any washers placed between the engine and frame. These washers are used to shim gaps between the engine and frame to help prevent vibration and frame mount damage. If any are found, they should be installed in their original mounting positions.

19. Remove the front (B, **Figure 7**) and lower (C) engine mount nuts and bolts.

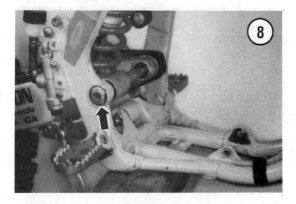

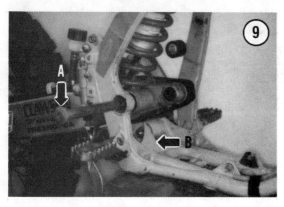

20. Slide the pivot shaft (A, **Figure 7**) out until it is free of the engine. Do not pull it all the way out of the swing arm.

21. Lift the engine (**Figure 7**) out of the frame and remove it.

NOTE
*After removing the engine, reinstall the swing arm pivot shaft through the frame and swing arm (**Figure 8**). The pivot shaft will keep the swing arm in position while steadying the bike.*

22. Clean all corrosion and rust from the engine mount bolts and hanger bracket. Inspect these parts for cracks or other damage and replace if necessary.

23. Check the frame and engine brackets (**Figure 8**) for cracks or other damage.

NOTE
While the engine is removed from the frame, check the swing arm pivot bosses for cracks or other damage.

24. Install the engine by reversing the preceding removal steps. Note the following.

25. Lubricate the pivot shaft with grease and insert it partway through one side of the swing arm (A, **Figure 9**).

26. Push the left and right side pivot collars (B, **Figure 9**) all the way into the swing arm pivot bosses.

27. Lubricate the engine mount bolts with grease or with a spray-type lubricant.

28. Install the engine into the frame. Secure it with the pivot shaft (A, **Figure 7**). Make sure the flat on the pivot shaft seats against the tab welded to the frame.

29. Install the engine mount bolts and nuts (B and C, **Figure 7**). Install the washers between the engine and frame, if used.

NOTE
If you are installing a new set of crankcases or a different engine, shims used between the engine and frame may or may not be required. Check carefully before installing the engine mounting fasteners.

30. Tighten the swing arm pivot shaft nut as specified in **Table 2**.

31. Hold the engine mounting bolts and tighten the nuts (B and C, **Figure 7**) as specified in **Table 2**.

32. Hold the engine hanger (B, **Figure 5**) bracket bolts and tighten the nuts as specified in **Table 2**.

33. Before starting the engine, refill or adjust the following items as described in Chapter Three:

   a. Transmission oil level.

   b. Coolant level.

   c. Clutch adjustment.

   d. Throttle adjustment.

   e. Drive chain adjustment.

34. Start the engine and check for leaks.

COUNTERSHAFT SEAL REPLACEMENT

Because of the countershaft seal's (**Figure 10**) location behind the engine sprocket, it is susceptible to damage from rocks, dirt and other debris thrown off from the chain and sprocket. An oil leak from this area is a certain indication that the seal is damaged. With care, you can replace this seal without having to split the crankcase.

1. Remove the drive sprocket, spacer and O-ring as described in Chapter Eleven.

2. Clean the engine case around the countershaft seal thoroughly. Do not force any water past the seal.

3. Remove the seal with a hooked tool or a seal removal tool. Do not pry between crankcase and seal, but instead, apply pressure to the inside of the seal between the seal and countershaft. If the seal is tight, thread one or two small sheet metal screws into the seal and pull the seal out with a pair of pliers. Do not install the screws too deeply or you may score the countershaft bearing.

4. Wipe the seal sealing area in the crankcase with a clean rag. Check the crankcase for cracks or other damage. If the case half is damaged, you will have to disassemble the engine and repair the crankcase.

5. Pack the inner seal lip with grease.

6. Slide the seal over the countershaft with its manufacturer's marks facing out, and tap it squarely into the crankcase bore with a long, hollow driver. Seat the seal so it is flush with the crankcase.

7. Install the O-ring, spacer and drive sprocket as described in Chapter Eleven.

8. Recheck the clutch/transmission oil level as described in Chapter Three.

LEFT SIDE MAIN BEARING SEAL REPLACEMENT

A leaking left side main bearing seal (A, **Figure 11**) will allow some of the fuel mixture to escape during crankcase compression while drawing in air with crankcase vacuum. This condition results in a lean air/fuel mixture, reduced power and erratic idling. If this seal is damaged, it is usually discovered during a two-stroke leakdown test or through visual inspection. The main cause of this seal failure is usually related to age deterioration or dirt entering past the flywheel cover.

On the KX250 engine, the left side main bearing seal is installed from inside the crankcase and cannot be replaced with the engine assembled. To replace this seal, it is necessary to split the crankcase halves and remove the crankshaft and bearing as described in this chapter.

CRANKCASE AND CRANKSHAFT

The crankcase is made in two halves of a precision diecast aluminum alloy. The crankcase halves are

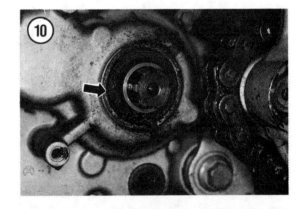

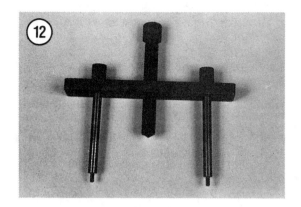

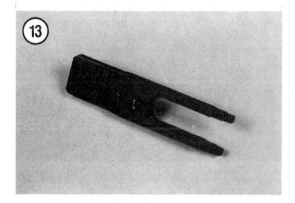

sold as a matched set only. If one crankcase half is damaged and cannot be repaired, you must replace both as an assembly.

The crankshaft assembly is made up of two full-circle flywheels pressed together on a hollow crankpin. The connecting rod big end bearing on the crankpin is a needle bearing assembly. The crankshaft assembly is supported by two ball bearings in the crankcase.

Special Tools

To disassemble and reassemble the crankcase assembly you will need the following special tools or their equivalents. These tools allow easy disassembly and reassembly of the engine.

    a. Kawasaki crankcase separating tool part No. 57001-1098 (**Figure 12**). This tool is used to separate the crankcase halves.

    b. A hydraulic press with suitable adapters are required to assemble the crankcase assembly.

    c. Kawasaki crankshaft jig part No. 57001-1174 (**Figure 13**). This tool is used to prevent the crankshaft halves from pressing inward when removing and installing the crankshaft and assembling the crankcase halves.

    d. When handling the engine cases, a wooden fixture (**Figure 14**) will assist in engine disassembly and reassembly and will help to prevent damage to the crankshaft and transmission shafts.

Crankcase Disassembly

This procedure describes disassembly of the crankcase halves and removal of the crankshaft, transmission and internal shift mechanism.

1. Remove all exterior engine assemblies as follows:

    a. Cylinder top end (Chapter Four).

    b. Clutch, kickstarter, external shift mechanism and primary drive gear (Chapter Six).

    c. Drive sprocket (Chapter Eleven).

    d. Flywheel and stator plate (Chapter Nine).

2. Place the engine assembly on a couple of wooden blocks with the left side facing up (**Figure 15**). Remove the crankcase breather hose.

3. Remove the Woodruff key (B, **Figure 11**) from the crankshaft keyway.

4. Loosen the crankcase bolts one-quarter turn at a time in a crisscross pattern.

NOTE
Before removing the crankcase bolts in Step 5, draw an outline of the left side crankcase on cardboard, and then punch a hole along the outline to represent the position of each crankcase bolt. Install each bolt in its correct position after removing it (Figure 16).

5. Remove the crankcase bolts loosened in Step 4. Install them into the cardboard holder (**Figure 16**).

6. Mount the crankcase separating tool onto the crankcase and over the crankshaft as shown in **Figure 15**. Apply some grease onto the end of the crankshaft before tightening the tool's pressure bolt against it.

7. Run the tool's pressure bolt against the end of the crankshaft. Check to make sure the tool's body is parallel with the crankcase. If not, readjust the tool's mounting bolts.

CAUTION
If the separating tool is not parallel with the crankcase surface, it will put an uneven stress on the case halves and may damage them.

8. Turn the tool's pressure bolt *clockwise* until the left case half begins to separate. You may hear a small pop when the case halves separate. This is normal, but stop and investigate all the way around the case halve mating surfaces. If everything is normal, continue with Step 9. If there is a problem, release tension from the pressure bolt and make sure all of the screws are removed.

NOTE
As the left case half is pulled up, the countershaft may ride up with its left case bearing, causing the case halves to bind. After every turn of the tool's pressure bolt, tap the countershaft with a plastic or rubber mallet to release any binding. This will help the case halves to separate more easily.

CAUTION
*Crankcase separation requires only hand pressure on the pressure bolt. If extreme pressure is needed, **stop immediately**. Check for crankcase bolts*

not removed, an external part that is still attached or a binding transmission shaft.

9. Continue to operate the pressure bolt, making sure the crankcase halves separate evenly (**Figure 17**) until the left case is free. Then remove the left crankcase half and the special tool. See **Figure 18**.

10. Remove the two dowel pins (A, **Figure 19**).

11. Remove the transmission assembly as follows:

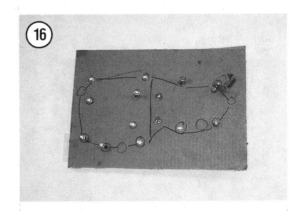

a. Remove the two shift fork shafts (B, **Figure 19**).

b. Pivot the shift forks away from the shift drum, then remove the shift drum (C, **Figure 19**).

c. Remove the three shift forks.

d. Reposition the right crankcase so both transmission shafts are parallel with the workbench. Tap against the mainshaft and remove the mainshaft and countershaft assemblies together from the crankcase half (**Figure 20**).

NOTE
*Step 12 describes crankshaft removal. As explained under **Special Tools** in this chapter, special tools will be required to remove and install the crankshaft. If you do not have these tools, take the case half and crankshaft to a dealership and have them remove the crankshaft.*

12. Remove the crankshaft as follows:

a. Place the connecting rod at bottom dead center (BDC) and install the crankshaft jig between the crankshaft wheels as shown in **Figure 21**. Position the tool with its arms contacting the inside of the crank wheels evenly (in four places), then tighten the wingnut securely.

b. Support the right side crankcase half in a press on two wooden blocks (**Figure 22**).

CAUTION
Make sure the wooden blocks are tall enough so that the crankshaft or the connecting rod will not contact the press bed during removal.

b. Center the crankshaft under the press ram and press it out of the crankcase (**Figure 23**).

c. Remove the right side crankcase half from the press.

13. Clean and inspect the crankcase halves, bearings and crankshaft as described in this chapter.

14. Service the transmission and internal shift mechanism as described in Chapter Seven.

Crankcase
Cleaning and Inspection

1. Remove the crankcase seals as described in this chapter.

2. Remove all gasket and sealer residue from all mating surfaces.

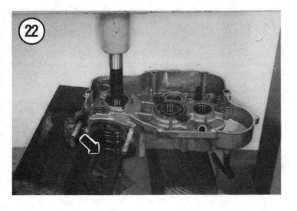

3. Clean both crankcase halves and bearings with solvent. Reclean in hot, soapy water and rinse in clear, cold water.

4. Dry the case halves and bearings with compressed air, if available. When drying the bearings with compressed air, do not allow the air jet to spin the bearings, but instead, hold the inner bearing races to prevent them from turning. When the bearings are dry, lubricate them with oil.

5. Turn each bearing by hand (**Figure 24**). The bearings must turn smoothly with no roughness, catching, binding or excessive play. Replace damaged bearings as described in this chapter.

6. Carefully inspect the case halves for cracks and fractures, especially in the lower areas where they are vulnerable to rock damage.

7. Inspect machined surfaces for burrs, cracks or other damage. You may be able to repair minor damage with a fine-cut file or oilstone. Major damage may require welding and machining work or replacement of the crankcase halves.

8. Check the cylinder studs and threaded holes for stripping, cross-threading or deposit buildup. Clean threaded holes with compressed air. If necessary, repair threads with the correct size tap or die.

9. Check all bearing holder bolts, the shift shaft pin bolt and kickstarter ratchet guide for damage or looseness.

Seal Replacement

Install new crankcase seals (**Figure 24**) before reassembling the engine.

Seals are mounted in the following areas:
a. Left main bearing seal (A, **Figure 25**).
b. Left countershaft bearing seal (B, **Figure 25**).
c. Shift shaft seal (C, **Figure 25**).
d. Clutch release lever seal (**Figure 26**).
e. Right main bearing seal (A, **Figure 27**).

Before removing the seals, note and record the direction in which the closed side of each seal faces for proper assembly.

1. To remove the left (A, **Figure 25**) and right (A, **Figure 27**) main bearing seals, perform the following:
a. These seals are installed behind and from the same direction as the main bearings. If the main bearings came off with the crankshaft, remove the seals as described in this step. If the main bearing bearing(s) did not come off

with the crankshaft but stayed in the crankcase, remove the seal and main bearing at the same time; refer to *Crankcase Bearing Replacement* in this chapter.
b. Position the crankcase with the seal's closed side facing up, then drive the seal out with a socket or bearing driver (**Figure 28**).

NOTE
Step 2 describes how to remove the remaining crankcase seals.

NOTE
Except for the clutch release lever seal, the countershaft bearing and shift shaft seals use a metal ring shoulder which makes it difficult to remove the seal. To prevent damaging the crankcase, remove these seals with a seal removal tool as shown in Step 2.

2. To remove the countershaft bearing (B, **Figure 25**) and shift shaft (C) seals, perform the following:
a. Pry out the seal with a seal removal tool (**Figure 29**), taking care not to damage the case bore. Pad the pry area under the tool with a shop cloth to avoid damaging the seal mounting bore.
b. Repeat for the other seal.

3. Remove the clutch release lever seal (**Figure 26**).

4. Inspect the engine case bearings and replace damaged bearings before installing the new seals. Refer to *Crankcase Bearing Replacement* in this section.

NOTE
*The new main bearing seals (A, **Figure 25**) and (A, **Figure 27**) must be installed before the main bearings.*

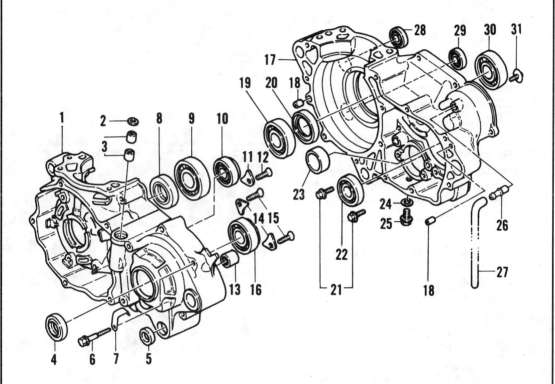

CRANKCASE

1. Left crankcase half
2. Oil seal
3. Bearings
4. Seal
5. Seal
6. Bolt
7. Hose guide
8. Seal
9. Bearing
10. Bearing
11. Holder
12. Screw
13. Bearing
14. Holders
15. Screws
16. Bearing
17. Right crankcase half
18. Dowel pin
19. Bearing
20. Seal
21. Bolts
22. Bearing
23. Bushing
24. Gasket
25. Plug
26. Hose fitting
27. Hose
28. Bearing
29. Bearing
30. Bearing
31. Screw

5

5. Pack a high-temperature grease between the lips of each seal.

6. Install the new main bearing seals (A, **Figure 25**) and (A, **Figure 27**) as follows:

   a. The left and right side main bearing seals are different. Make sure you install each seal in its correct position.

   b. Place the seal into its mounting bore with its open side facing in (toward crankshaft).

   c. Place a washer (**Figure 30**) or bearing driver across the seal.

   d. Drive the oil seal into its mounting bore (**Figure 31**) until it bottoms against the crankcase. See **Figure 27**.

7. Install the new countershaft bearing, shift shaft and clutch release shaft seals as follows:

   a. Some seals can be installed by hand and others will require force from a hammer and a bearing driver or socket. When using a driver, place it against the seals outer surface. See **Figure 32**, typical.

   b. Press in the seal until its outer surface is flush with its mounting bore surface.

   c. Repeat for the remaining seals.

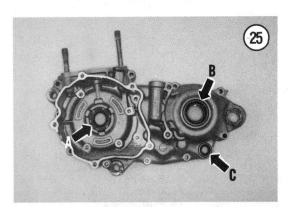

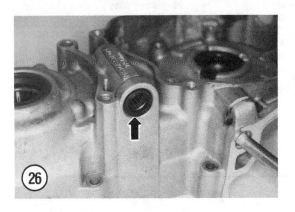

Crankcase Bearing Replacement

The left side crankcase bearings are identified as follows:

   a. Left main bearing (A, **Figure 33**).
   b. Left mainshaft bearing (B, **Figure 33**).
   c. Left countershaft bearing (C, **Figure 33**).
   d. Left shift drum bearing (D, **Figure 33**).
   e. Clutch release bearing (**Figure 34**).

The right side crankcase bearings are identified as follows:

   a. Right main bearing (A, **Figure 35**).
   b. Right mainshaft bearing (B, **Figure 35**).
   c. Right countershaft bushing (C, **Figure 35**).
   d. Right shift drum bearing (D, **Figure 35**).
   e. Exhaust advancer bearing (B, **Figure 27**).
   f. Water pump bearing (C, **Figure 27**).

1. If a bearing came off with the crankshaft (**Figure 36**), remove it with a bearing splitter and press as follows:

   a. Mount a bearing splitter against the main bearing as shown in A, **Figure 37**.
   b. Place the connecting rod at bottom dead center (BDC) and install the crankshaft jig between the crankshaft wheels as shown in B, **Figure 37**. Position the tool with its arms contacting the inside of the crank wheels evenly (in four places), then tighten the wingnut securely.
   c. Mount the sides of the bearing splitter on two wooden block in the press (**Figure 38**). Center the crankshaft under the press ram.

CAUTION
Make sure the wooden blocks are tall enough so that the crankshaft or the connecting rod will not contact the press bed during removal.

CAUTION
The crankshaft will fall once it is free of the bearing. Catch the crankshaft before it falls to the floor.

d. Press the crankshaft off its bearing.

e. Repeat for the other bearing, if necessary.

NOTE
Use an impact driver with a Phillips bit (described in Chapter One) to loosen the Phillips screws described in Step 2. These screws are normally secured with a threadlocking compound and can be difficult to remove. Trying to loosen these screws with a screwdriver may damage the screw heads.

2. Some transmission bearings are held in position by retainer plates, bolts and screws; see **Figure 39**, typical. Remove these before removing the bearing(s).

NOTE
*Two methods of replacing the crankcase bearings are described below. Before you begin, read the **Ball Bearing Replacement** section in Chapter One for additional information on bearing removal.*

3A. To replace the bearings using heat, perform the following steps:

a. Read this step through completely, then collect all of the correct size bearing drivers or sockets you will need before starting. Have all of your tools and other supplies on hand so you can quickly replace the bearings while the crankcase is hot.

b. Before heating the crankcase to replace the bearings, place the new bearings in a freezer if possible. Chilling them will slightly reduce their overall diameter, while the hot crankcase is slightly larger due to heat expansion. This will make installation much easier.

c. Wash the cases thoroughly to remove all traces of oil and other chemical deposits.

d. The bearings are installed with a slight interference fit. Heat the crankcase to a temperature of about 212° F (100° C) in a shop oven or on a hot plate. Heat only one case at a time.

CAUTION
Do not heat the cases with a torch (propane or acetylene)—never bring a flame into contact with the bearing or case. The direct heat will destroy the case hardening of the bearing and will likely warp the case half.

e. Remove the case from the shop oven or hot plate and hold onto the two crankcase studs with welding gloves—*it is hot.*

NOTE

Suitable size sockets and extensions work well for removing and installing bearings.

f. Support the crankcase on wooden blocks, then drive the bearing out from its opposite side. Use a bearing driver or socket to remove the

bearing. Use a blind bearing removal tool to remove bearings installed in blind holes.

NOTE
*When you remove the crankcase main bearings, you will also remove the seals (**Figure 40**) at the same time.*

NOTE
Install new bearings so their manufacturer's name and size code faces in the same direction recorded during disassembly. If you did not note this information prior to removing the bearings, install the new bearings so their marks will be visible after the bearing has been installed.

g. Install the two main bearing seals (**Figure 31**) before installing the main bearings. See *Seal Replacement* in this section.

h. While the crankcase is still hot, install the new bearing(s) into the crankcase. Install the bearings by hand, if possible. If necessary, lightly tap the bearing(s) into the case with a bearing driver or socket placed on the outer bearing race. *Do not* install the bearings by driving on their inner race. Install the bearing(s) until it seats completely in its mounting bore.

3B. To replace bearings with a press:

a. Support the crankcase on two wooden blocks and center the bearing under the press ram.

b. Press the bearing out of the crankcase; see **Figure 41**, typical.

NOTE
*When you remove the crankcase main bearings, you will also remove the seals (**Figure 40**) at the same time.*

c. Support the crankcase on two wooden blocks and center the bearing and bearing bore under the press ram.

d. Install the two main bearing seals (**Figure 31**) before installing the main bearings. See *Seal Replacement* in this section.

e. Place a bearing driver on the outer bearing race (**Figure 42**, typical). Press the bearing into the crankcase until it bottoms.

4. If you removed the bearing retainers, install them as follows:

a. Remove all threadlock residue from the retainer screws and screw hole threads.

b. Apply ThreeBond threadlock TB1360 (or equivalent) onto the retainer screw threads, then install and tighten the bearing retaining screws as specified in **Table 2**.

5. Install the remaining crankcase seals as described under *Seal Replacement* in this chapter.

Crankshaft Inspection

When measuring the crankshaft in this section, compare the actual measurements to the new and service limit specifications in **Table 1**. Replace the connecting rod assembly if it is out of specification or damaged as described in this section. To replace the connecting rod assembly, a 20-30 ton press and adapters, V-blocks or crankshaft truing stand, and dial indicator are required. If necessary, refer crankshaft overhaul to a dealership. You can save considerable expense by disassembling the engine and just taking the crankshaft in for repair.

Figure 43 shows an exploded view of the crankshaft and the individual parts that can be replaced. When rebuilding the crankshaft, always install a new connecting rod, pin, bearing and both washers as a set.

1. Clean the crankshaft in solvent and dry thoroughly. Lubricate the bottom end bearing and crankshaft journals with two-cycle engine oil.

2. Check the crankshaft journals (**Figure 44**) for scratches, heat discoloration or other defects.

3. Check the flywheel taper, threads and keyway (**Figure 44**) for damage. If one crankshaft half is damaged, the crankshaft can be disassembled and the damaged part replaced by a dealership.

4. Check the crankshaft seal surfaces (**Figure 44**) for grooving, pitting or scratches.

5. Check the crankshaft bearing surfaces for chatter marks and excessive or uneven wear. Clean minor damage with 320 grit carborundum cloth.

6. Check the lower end bearing and connecting rod (A, **Figure 45**) for signs of heat damage. Check the needles and cage for visible damage.

7. Check the crankshaft weights (B, **Figure 45**) for loose rivets or other damage.

8. Measure the connecting rod big end side clearance between the connecting rod and washer with a flat feeler gauge (**Figure 46**). Compare to the service limit in **Table 1**. If the clearance is greater than

specified, have the crankshaft rebuilt and the connecting rod replaced at a dealership.

9. Place the crankshaft in V-blocks and position it with the connecting rod at TDC. Attach a dial indicator to the bottom of the connecting rod big end as shown in **Figure 47**. While holding the crankshaft in position, push the connecting rod forward and then backward. The difference between the two readings is the connecting rod radial clearance. If the radial clearance exceeds the service limit in **Table 1**, replace the connecting rod assembly.

10. Check crankshaft runout with a dial indicator and a truing stand or V-blocks (**Figure 48**). Have a dealership retrue the crankshaft if the runout exceeds the service limit in **Table 1**.

11. Measure the crank wheel width every 90° at its machined edge with a micrometer or vernier caliper (**Figure 49**). If the measurement is not the same at all four positions, have the crankshaft retrued by a dealership.

Crankcase Assembly

This procedure describes installation of the crankshaft and transmission assembly and assembly of the crankcase halves. Special tools are required to install the crankshaft and the left crankcase half. If necessary, have the crankshaft installed and the engine assembled by a dealership.

1. Clean all parts before assembly.

2. Pack all of the crankcase seals with a high-temperature grease.

3. Lubricate both crankshaft main bearings with two-stroke engine oil.

NOTE
Install the crankshaft before installing the transmission assembly.

4. Install the crankshaft with a press as follows:

CAUTION
Do not install the crankshaft without a press. Do not drive the crankshaft into

the right main bearing with a hammer as this will damage the crankshaft and crankcase, causing expensive and permanent damage.

a. Install the crankshaft into the right side crankcase half until it stops (**Figure 50**). The tapered crankshaft end (A, **Figure 50**) should be

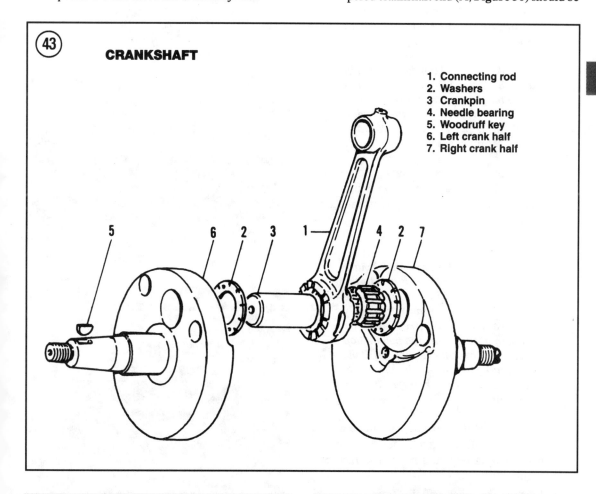

CRANKSHAFT

1. Connecting rod
2. Washers
3 Crankpin
4. Needle bearing
5. Woodruff key
6. Left crank half
7. Right crank half

facing up (away from crankcase.) Screw the flywheel nut onto the end of the crankshaft threads to protect the threads during the following steps.

b. Position the connecting rod at BDC and install the Kawasaki crankshaft jig between the crank wheels as shown in B, **Figure 50**.

CAUTION
The crankshaft can be forced out of alignment if the crankshaft jig is not used. Also, if the crankshaft jig is not used, make sure you keep the connecting rod at BDC or TDC so it does not contact the side of the crankcase when the crankshaft is being installed. Doing so will bend the connecting rod and damage the crankcase.

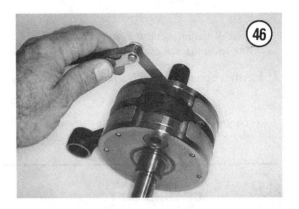

c. Install the crankcase assembly onto two wooden blocks placed in the press bed, then center the crankshaft under the press ram (**Figure 51**).

NOTE
When installing the crankshaft, make sure the crankshaft is pressed into the bearing evenly. After aligning the crankshaft with the crankcase, apply pressure from the press so the crankshaft moves a small amount. Stop and recheck crankshaft alignment. If the crankshaft is pinched to one side, realign the crankshaft before continuing.

d. Check the alignment once again, then press the crankshaft into the right crankcase until it bottoms against the bearing's inner race. See **Figure 52**.

e. Remove the crankshaft jig from the crankshaft.

5. Remove the right crankcase from the press and place it onto two wooden blocks (**Figure 53**). Make sure the blocks are deep enough to allow the transmission to be installed without the mainshaft contacting the workbench.

6. Lubricate all of the transmission bearings with transmission oil.

7. Check the transmission shafts to make sure the gears, washers and circlips are properly installed (**Figure 54**). See Chapter Seven.

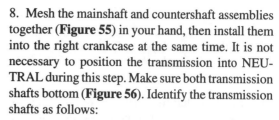

8. Mesh the mainshaft and countershaft assemblies together (**Figure 55**) in your hand, then install them into the right crankcase at the same time. It is not necessary to position the transmission into NEUTRAL during this step. Make sure both transmission shafts bottom (**Figure 56**). Identify the transmission shafts as follows:

   a. Mainshaft (A, **Figure 56**).

   b. Countershaft (B, **Figure 56**).

9. Identify the shift forks as follows:

   a. Mainshaft third gear shift fork: The fork fingers are shorter than the fingers on the other two shift forks (A, **Figure 57**). A, **Figure 58** shows another view of the shift fork.

   b. Countershaft fourth gear shift fork: The fork fingers are longer than the fingers on the other two shift forks (B, **Figure 57**). The guide pin is also positioned to the left side of the fork fingers (B, **Figure 58**).

   c. Countershaft fifth gear shift fork: One fork finger is longer than the other finger (C, **Figure 57**). The guide pin is also positioned in the center of the shift fork (C, **Figure 58**).

NOTE
*In Step 10, install all of the shift forks
with their guide pins facing toward the
inside (toward the shift drum) of the
engine.*

10. Install the shift forks and shift drum as follows:
   a. Install the mainshaft third gear shift fork (A,
      Figure 57) into the third gear groove. See A,
      Figure 59.
   b. Install the countershaft fifth gear shift fork (C,
      Figure 57) into the fifth gear groove. See B,
      Figure 59.
   c. Install the shift drum (A, **Figure 60**) into its
      right crankcase bearing.
   d. Engage each shift fork pin with its respective
      shift drum groove.
   e. Install the countershaft fourth gear shift fork
      (B, **Figure 57**) into the fourth gear groove. See
      B, **Figure 60**. Engage the fourth gear shift fork
      with its shift drum groove.

11. Lubricate the shift fork shafts with oil.

12. Install the short shift fork shaft (A, **Figure 61**)
through the mainshaft shift fork.

13. Install the long shift fork shaft (B, **Figure 61**)
through the two countershaft shift forks.

NOTE
*Make sure both shift fork shafts bottom
solidly after installing them.*

14. Lubricate the transmission gears and shift forks
with transmission oil.

15. Thoroughly clean both crankcase mating surfaces of all oil residue with an electrical contact
cleaner.

16. Install the two dowel pins (**Figure 62**) into the
right crankcase. Both dowel pins are the same size.

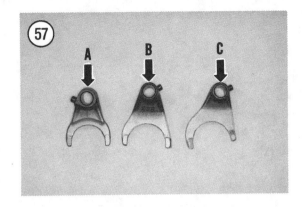

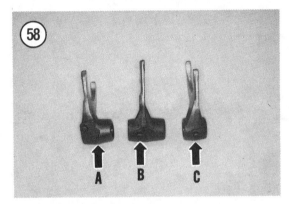

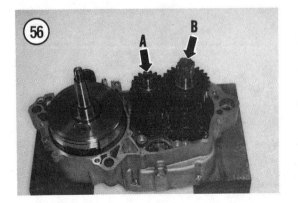

5

17. Install the right crankcase half assembly onto two wooden blocks placed in the press bed, then center the crankshaft under the press ram (A, **Figure 63**).

18. Position the connecting rod at BDC and install the Kawasaki crankshaft jig between the crank wheels as shown in B, **Figure 63**.

CAUTION
The crankshaft can be forced out of alignment if the crankshaft jig is not used. Also, if the crankshaft jig is not used, make sure you keep the connecting rod at BDC or TDC so it does not contact the side of the crankcase when the left crankcase is being installed. Doing so will bend the connecting rod and damage the crankcase.

NOTE
Before applying gasket sealer and assembling the engine cases in the following steps, check the working clearance between the press ram and engine to make sure you have enough room to install the left crankcase with the bearing driver you will be using.

NOTE
Suitable gasket sealers to use in Step 19 are ThreeBond Liquid Gasket 1104 and Yamabond No. 4. Both gasket sealers are available through motorcycle dealerships.

19. Apply a light coat of a nonhardening liquid gasket sealer to the left crankcase mating surface (**Figure 64**). This type of gasket sealer is thin and runs easily. Make sure it does not contact any of the crankcase bearings.

20. Without touching the gasket sealer installed in Step 19, install the left crankcase half over the countershaft and crankshaft as shown in C, **Figure 63**. These two shafts will align the crankcase with the remaining transmission assembly shafts.

21. Place a bearing driver between the press ram and left crankcase as shown in **Figure 65**. Make sure the bearing driver seats squarely against the left crankcase.

22. Press the left side crankcase against the opposite case half. When doing so, stop often and check that both case surfaces remain parallel (**Figure 66**). You may have to tap the left side case near the counter-

shaft to maintain this alignment. Check that both dowel pins engage the left side crankcase when the cases come together. When the case halves bottom, release the pressure against the engine. Check that the gasket surfaces are flush (**Figure 67**) all the way around the engine. Check also that the mainshaft, countershaft, shift drum and crankshaft rotate freely. There must be no binding with any shaft.

CAUTION
The crankcase halves must fit together completely. If not, do not try to pull them together with the crankcase screws. Separate the crankcase halves and investigate the cause of the interference. If the transmission shafts were disassembled, check to make sure that a gear was not installed backward. Do not risk damage by trying to force the cases together.

23. Remove the crankcase jig and then place the engine on two wooden blocks on your workbench with the left case half facing up (**Figure 68**).

24. Install all of the crankcase bolts (**Figure 69**) and tighten finger-tight. Place any clips under the bolts in the locations recorded during disassembly.

25. Tighten the crankcase mounting bolts in two stages and in a crisscross pattern to the final torque specification listed in **Table 2**.

NOTE
Do not worry if the crankshaft becomes tight when tightening the crankcase bolts in Step 26. The crankshaft can be recentered as described in Step 26.

26. Rotate the crankshaft and check for binding. The crankshaft should rotate freely. If the crankshaft is tight, it is probably not centered correctly (**Figure 70**) between the two crankcase halves. Center the crankshaft as follows:

a. Install the flywheel nut onto the crankshaft threads (A, **Figure 70**). Install the water pump drive gear on the right crankshaft end (B, **Figure 70**).

NOTE
Because you must tap against the crankshaft shaft ends to center the crankshaft, the parts installed in **substep a** *help to protect the crankshaft*

ends and to remove any burrs that may be produced during contact.

b. Visually inspect the gap between the crankshaft flywheels and both case halves to see which gap is larger.

CAUTION
Tap the crankshaft ends squarely in the next step. Hitting either crankshaft end at an angle can damage the shaft.

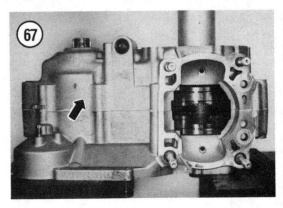

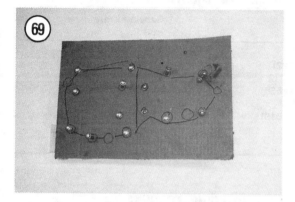

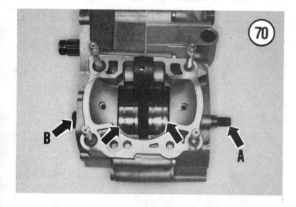

c. Carefully tap the appropriate end of the crankshaft squarely with a brass mallet to center it.

d. Repeat until the crankshaft is centered correctly and rotates freely.

NOTE
If the crankshaft is centered but it still turns roughly, there are three possible causes to consider: either one or both main bearings are not centered correctly; the crankshaft was assembled with too much side clearance; and one or both main bearings are damaged.

27. Rotate the crankshaft and each transmission shaft and check for binding. Each shaft must turn freely.

28. Check the shifting as described under *Transmission Shifting Check* in this chapter.

29. Install the crankcase breather hose.

30. Install the engine in the frame as described in this chapter.

31. Install all exterior engine assemblies as follows:
    a. Flywheel and stator plate (Chapter Nine).
    b. Drive sprocket (Chapter Eleven).
    c. Primary drive gear, external shift mechanism, kickstarter and clutch (Chapter Six).
    d. Cylinder top end (Chapter Four).

32. After filling the engine with oil and the cooling system with coolant, start the engine and check for leaks. Check the throttle and clutch operation and adjust if necessary as described in Chapter Three.

TRANSMISSION SHIFTING CHECK

You can check the transmission shifting with the engine mounted in the frame or with it sitting on the workbench. Always check the shifting after reassembling the crankcase.

1. Install the shift drum cam (A, **Figure 71**) as described in Chapter Six.

2. Install the stopper lever (B, **Figure 71**) over its mounting stud (without the spring, washer or nut).

3. Turn the mainshaft while moving the shift drum by hand to align the raised shift drum detent with the stopper lever roller as shown in C, **Figure 71**. The raised shift drum detent position is its NEUTRAL position. Lower detent ramp positions on the shift drum cam represent different gear positions (1 through 5). When the shift drum and stopper lever are aligned as shown in C, **Figure 71**, the transmission is in NEUTRAL. In this position, the mainshaft

and countershaft assemblies can be turned separately, indicating that they are not engaged or meshed together.

4. Check each gear position by turning the mainshaft and shift drum by hand. Each time the stopper lever roller seats into a shift drum detent ramp, the transmission is in gear. When the transmission is in gear, the countershaft and mainshaft are engaged and will turn together.

5. If the transmission does not shift properly into each gear, disassemble the engine and check the transmission and the internal shift mechanism.

Table 1 CRANKSHAFT SERVICE SPECIFICATIONS

	New mm (in.)	Service limit mm (in.)
Connecting rod big end side clearance	0.45-0.55 (0.018-0.022)	0.70 (0.028)
Conecting rod small end inside diameter	22.003-22.012 (0.8663-0.8666)	22.05 (0.868)
Connecting rod radial clearance	0.037-0.049 (0.0015-0.0019)	0.10 (0.004)
Crankshaft runout limit	0-0.03 (0-0.001)	0.05 (0.0020)

Table 2 ENGINE BOTTOM END TIGHTENING TORQUES

	N•m.	in.-lb	ft.-lb
Crankcase bearing retaining screws			
1992-1993			
Countershaft bearing	5.4	48	–
Mainshaft bearing	8.8	78	
Shift drum bearing	8.8	78	–
1994-on	8.8	78	
Crankcase mounting bolts	8.8	78	–
Engine hanger nuts			
1992-1993			
At engine	34	–	25
At frame	26	–	19
1994-on			
8 mm	26	–	19
10 mm	39	–	29
Engine mounting nuts			
1992-1993	34	–	25
1994	39	–	29
1995-on	44	–	33
Flywheel nut	78	–	58
Shift drum cam mounting bolt	22	–	16
Swing arm pivot shaft nut	98	–	72
Transmission oil drain bolt	20	–	15

CHAPTER SIX

CLUTCH

This chapter contains service procedures for the following components:

1. Clutch cover.

2. Clutch release lever.

3. Right crankcase cover.

4. Exhaust valve governor.

5. Clutch.

6. Primary drive gear.

7. Kickstarter.

8. External shift mechanism.

Clutch specifications are listed in **Table 1**. Tightening torques are listed in **Table 2**. Both tables are at the end of the chapter.

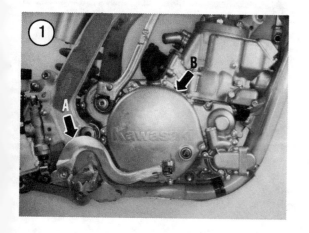

CLUTCH COVER

The clutch cover is mounted on the right crankcase cover assembly and can be removed to service the clutch plates. To service the clutch housing or any of the other parts installed on the right side of the engine, remove the right crankcase cover instead of the clutch cover.

Removal/Installation

1. Drain the transmission oil (Chapter Three).

2. Remove the rear brake pedal (A, **Figure 1**) as described in Chapter Fourteen.

3. Unbolt and remove the clutch cover (B, **Figure 1**). Remove the dowel pins and gasket.

4. Install the clutch cover by reversing the preceding removal steps, plus the following:

    a. Remove all gasket residue from the clutch cover and crankcase cover mating surfaces.

    b. Replace the clutch cover gasket if leaking or damaged.

    c. Tighten the clutch cover (B, **Figure 1**) mounting bolts securely.

    d. Fill the transmission with the recommended type and quantity of oil (Chapter Three).

    e. Install the rear brake pedal (Chapter Fourteen).

CLUTCH RELEASE ARM

The clutch release arm is mounted in the left crankcase and can be removed with the engine mounted in the frame.

Removal/Installation

1. Remove the carburetor (Chapter Eight).
2. Disconnect the clutch cable as follows:
   a. Loosen the clutch cable locknut (A, **Figure 2**) at the handlebar and loosen the adjuster (B), then disconnect the clutch cable at the handlebar.
   b. Disconnect the clutch cable from the engine, then from the clutch release arm (**Figure 3**).
3. Remove the clutch release arm (**Figure 3**) from the engine.
4. Install the clutch release arm by reversing the preceding removal steps, plus the following:
   a. Lightly grease the top of the clutch release arm where it contacts the seal.
   b. Install the clutch release arm (**Figure 3**) into the engine. Turn it so the notch on the bottom of the arm engages the clutch pushrod. When the engagement is correct, the clutch release arm will drop down, then becomes hard to turn counterclockwise (away from engine).
   c. Adjust the clutch (Chapter Three).

Inspection

1. Inspect the release arm for cracks, deep scoring or excessive wear.
2. Inspect the seal (**Figure 4**) for damage. If the seal is torn or leaking, replace it as described in the following procedure.

Seal and Needle Bearing Replacement

1. Replace the seal (**Figure 4**) as follows:
   a. Carefully pry the seal (**Figure 4**) out of the crankcase.
   b. If necessary, replace the needle bearings before installing the new seal. Replace the bearings as described in Step 2.
   c. Pack the seal lips with a waterproof grease, then press the seal into the crankcase until it

bottoms. Install the seal with its closed side facing out.

2. Replace the needle bearings as follows:

NOTE

The two needle bearings are identical (same part number).

   a. Remove the engine from the frame.
   b. Remove the seal (**Figure 4**).

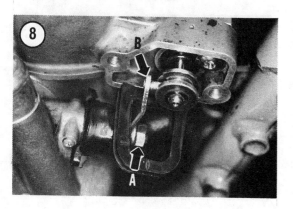

c. Measure the depth of the upper bearing (**Figure 5**) and record the measurement for reassembly.

d. Remove the upper bearing with a pilot bearing remover.

e. Measure the depth of the lower bearing and record the measurement for reassembly.

f. Remove the lower bearing with a pilot bearing remover.

g. Press in the lower bearing to the depth recorded during removal.

h. Press in the upper bearing to the depth recorded during removal.

RIGHT CRANKCASE COVER

The right crankcase cover houses the water pump, exhaust valve governor and the exhaust valve lever assembly.

Right Crankcase Cover
Removal

1. Drain the transmission oil (Chapter Three).
2. Remove the exhaust system (Chapter Four).
3. Drain the cooling system (Chapter Three).
4. Disconnect the two coolant hoses from the water pump (**Figure 6**).
5. Remove the rear brake pedal (A, **Figure 1**) as described in Chapter Fourteen.
6. Unbolt and remove the linkage cover (**Figure 7**).
7A. On 1992 models, remove the shaft lever nut (A, **Figure 8**) and shaft lever (B).
7B. On 1993 and later models, disconnect the shaft lever as follows:

a. Remove the E-clip, washer and wave washer (**Figure 9**) from the operating rod.

b. Put a 9 mm open end wrench on the shaft lever as shown in A, **Figure 10** and turn the shaft lever counterclockwise. Push the operating rod into the cylinder and remove the operating rod collar (B, **Figure 10**).

c. Before releasing the shaft lever, turn the operating rod so that its remaining E-clip will be out of the way of the shaft lever when it returns to its at-rest position. See **Figure 11**.

8. Remove the nut or the bolt and washer and remove the kickstarter pedal.

> *NOTE*
>
> *You can remove the right crankcase cover without removing the water pump cover (A, **Figure 12**) or its three flange bolts.*

> *NOTE*
>
> *If you are going to service the water pump, remove the water pump cover (A, **Figure 12**) and loosen the impeller bolt as described in Chapter Ten.*

9. Remove the right crankcase cover mounting bolts and the cover (B, **Figure 12**).

10. A washer is installed on the kickstarter shaft (A, **Figure 13**). Check the crankcase cover to see if the washer came off with the cover. If so, reinstall it onto the kickstarter shaft.

11. Remove the crankcase cover gasket and both dowel pins (B, **Figure 13**).

12. Lift the governor lever and remove the exhaust valve governor (A, **Figure 14**).

Inspection

1. Remove all gasket residue from the cover and crankcase gasket surfaces (B, **Figure 14**).

2. Inspect the kickstarter shaft seal (**Figure 15**) for damage. If necessary, replace the seal as described in this section.

3. If necessary, service the exhaust valve governor (A, **Figure 14**) as described in this chapter.

4. If necessary, service the water pump (C, **Figure 14**) as described in Chapter Ten.

Kickstarter Shaft Seal Replacement

If the kickstarter shaft seal (**Figure 15**) is leaking, replace it as follows:

1. Pry the seal out of the cover with a wide-blade screwdriver (**Figure 16**). Pad the screwdriver to prevent damage to the cover.
2. Clean the seal bore.
3. Pack the lips of the new seal with grease.
4. Press the new seal into the cover with its closed side facing out. Drive the seal into its mounting bore with a hammer and socket or bearing driver. Install the seal until it bottoms.

Right Crankcase Cover Installation

1. If removed, install the water pump assembly as described in Chapter Ten. Do not install the water pump cover at this time.
2. Install the exhaust valve governor as follows:
   a. Lubricate the bearing (installed in cover) with transmission oil.
   b. Raise the governor lever (A, **Figure 17**) and install the exhaust valve governor groove (B, **Figure 17**) onto the lever.
   c. Hold the exhaust valve governor in place. Turn the governor shaft to lower the exhaust valve governor shaft into the bearing.
   d. Make sure the exhaust valve governor is still engaged with the governor lever.
3. Turn the exhaust valve governor to level its drive pin (**Figure 18**) with the right crankcase cover.

> *CAUTION*
> *If the pin is not level when the right crankcase cover is installed, it may fall*

6

*out. The pin could then catch between
two gears, causing engine damage.*

4. Install the governor boot (**Figure 19**), if removed.

5. Install the two dowel pins (B, **Figure 13**).

6. If removed, install the washer onto the kickstarter shaft (A, **Figure 13**).

7. Install the right crankcase cover gasket.

8. Install the right crankcase cover (B, **Figure 12**) and its mounting bolts. Tighten the bolts as specified in **Table 2**.

NOTE
*If the crankcase cover will not fit flush
against the crankcase in Step 8, the
water pump drive gear or exhaust valve
governor gear is not meshing properly
with the primary drive gear. If this
happens, remove the cover and turn the
gears to align them.*

9. Install the kickstarter pedal onto the kickstarter shaft. Install the nut or mounting bolt and washer and tighten as specified in **Table 2**.

10. Tighten the impeller mounting bolt and install the water pump cover, if removed, as described in Chapter Ten.

11. Reconnect the two coolant hoses (**Figure 6**) to the water pump.

12A. On 1992 models, install the shaft lever as follows:

   a. Install the gasket over the operating rod.

   b. Set the governor lever (B, **Figure 8**) onto the governor shaft with the end if the lever centered in the operating rod collar groove.

   c. Install the shaft lever nut (A, **Figure 8**) and tighten securely.

12B. On 1993 and later models, install the shaft lever as follows:

   a. Install the gasket over the operating rod.

   b. The operating rod is equipped with two E-clip grooves. Make sure an E-clip is installed in the inner groove (A, **Figure 20**).

   c. Turn the shaft lever counterclockwise with a 9 mm wrench (B, **Figure 20**) and install the operating rod collar (B, **Figure 10**) into the operating rod. At the same time, use the wrench to guide the end of the shaft lever into the groove in the operating rod collar.

   d. Install the wave washer and flat washer over the operating rod and install the E-clip into the operating rod groove (**Figure 9**).

13. Install the linkage cover (**Figure 7**) and tighten its mounting bolts securely.

14. Install the rear brake pedal (Chapter Fourteen).

15. Install the exhaust system (Chapter Four).

16. Refill the cooling system (Chapter Three).

17. Fill the transmission with the recommended type and quantity of oil (Chapter Three).

18. Start the engine and check for coolant and oil leaks.

EXHAUST VALVE GOVERNOR

The exhaust valve governor is controlled by engine speed to open and close the exhaust valves in the cylinder. A linkage system connects the exhaust valves to the exhaust valve governor.

Removal/Installation

1. Remove the right crankcase cover as described in this chapter.

2. Lift the governor shaft (A, **Figure 17**) and remove the exhaust valve governor (B).

3. Inspect the exhaust valve governor as described in this chapter.

4. Lubricate the bearing (installed in cover) with transmission oil.

5. Raise the governor lever (A, **Figure 17**) and install the exhaust valve governor groove (B, **Figure 17**) onto the lever.

6. Hold the exhaust valve governor in place and turn the governor shaft to lower the exhaust valve governor shaft into the bearing.

7. Make sure the exhaust valve governor is still engaged with the governor lever.

8. Install the right crankcase cover as described in this chapter.

Governor Shaft
Removal/Inspection/Installation

Refer to **Figure 21** for this procedure.

1. Remove the two Allen bolts and remove the governor lever (**Figure 22**).

2. Remove the Phillips screw (A, **Figure 23**), then turn the cover over to drop the small pin (**Figure 24**) out of the governor shaft.

3. Remove the governor shaft (B, **Figure 23**).

4. Replace the seal (**Figure 21**) if leaking or damaged. Note the following:

    a. Pack the lips of the new seal with grease.

    b. Install the seal with its closed side facing out.

5. Inspect the governor shaft and governor lever for excessive wear or damage.

6. Reverse the preceding steps to install the governor shaft assembly, plus the following:

    a. Make sure the pin (**Figure 24**) seats into the hole in the governor shaft.

    b. Tighten the governor lever Allen bolts as specified in **Table 2**.

    c. Pivot the governor shaft back and forth by hand to make sure it moves smoothly.

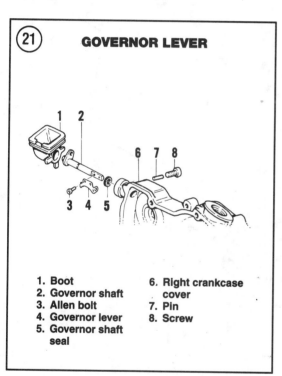

(21) GOVERNOR LEVER

1. Boot
2. Governor shaft
3. Allen bolt
4. Governor lever
5. Governor shaft seal
6. Right crankcase cover
7. Pin
8. Screw

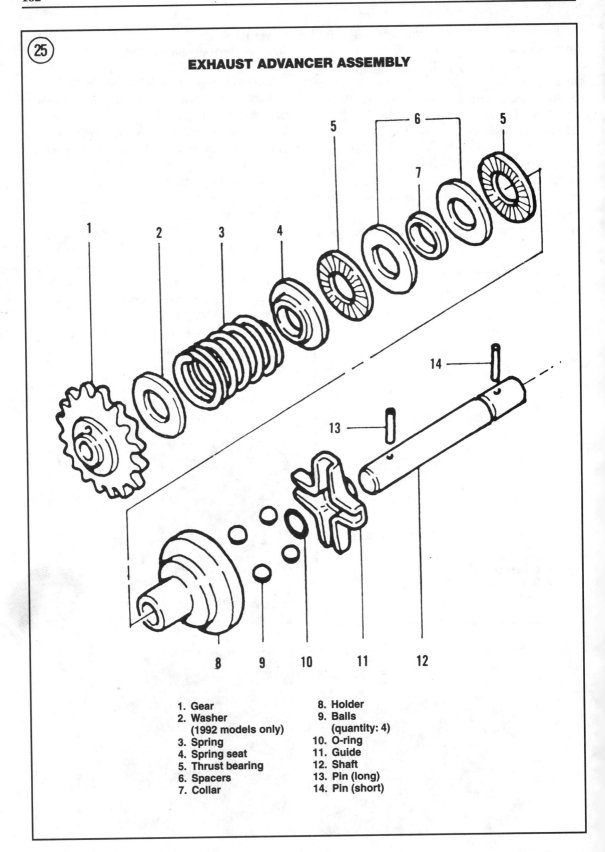

EXHAUST ADVANCER ASSEMBLY

1. Gear
2. Washer
   (1992 models only)
3. Spring
4. Spring seat
5. Thrust bearing
6. Spacers
7. Collar
8. Holder
9. Balls
   (quantity: 4)
10. O-ring
11. Guide
12. Shaft
13. Pin (long)
14. Pin (short)

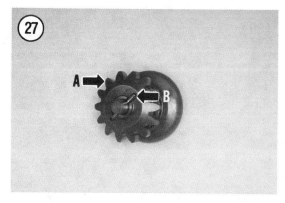

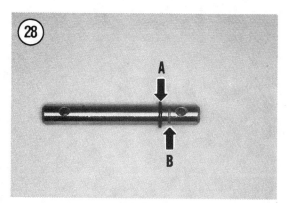

Exhaust Valve Governor
Disassembly and Inspection

Refer to **Figure 25** for this procedure.

NOTE
The exhaust valve governor (Figure 26)
is comprised of a number of parts. Make
sure you store the parts in their order of
removal to ease assembly.

1. Compress the gear (A, **Figure 27**) and remove the pin (B). Disassemble the exhaust valve governor assembly in the order shown in **Figure 25**.
2. Clean and dry all parts.

NOTE
Replace parts that show excessive wear
or damage.

3. Inspect the thrust bearings for cracks, heat damage (blue color) or excessive wear.
4. Inspect the balls, holder and guide for flat spots, cracks or excessive wear.
5. Inspect the spring for cracks or excessive wear.
6. Check all machined surfaces for cracks, excessive wear or heat damage (blue color).
7. Check the O-ring for cracks or excessive wear.

Exhaust Valve Governor
Assembly

Refer to **Figure 25** for this procedure.
1. Lubricate all of the governor parts with transmission oil.
2. Install the O-ring (A, **Figure 28**) onto the shaft and position it next to the shaft groove (B).

NOTE
When installing the pins in the following
steps, note that two different length pins
are used. See 13 and 14, Figure 25 to
identify each pin.

3. Install the guide (A, **Figure 29**) onto the shaft and secure it with its pin (B). Seat the O-ring (C, **Figure 29**) into the shaft groove (B, **Figure 28**).
4. Install a ball into each of the four guide slots (**Figure 30**).
5. Install the holder and seat it over the balls and guide as shown in **Figure 31**.

6

NOTE
*When installing the thrust bearing assembly in the following steps, note that the two thrust bearings (5, **Figure 25**) are identical as are the two spacers (6, **Figure 25**).*

6. Install the following parts in order:
   a. Thrust bearing (A, **Figure 32**).
   b. Spacer (B, **Figure 32**).
   c. Collar (C, **Figure 32**).
7. Install the following parts in order:
   a. Spacer (A, **Figure 33**).
   b. Thrust bearing (B, **Figure 33**).
   c. Spring seat (C, **Figure 33**). Install the spring seat with its shoulder (**Figure 34**) facing away from the thrust bearing.
8. Install the following parts in order:
   a. On 1992 models, install the washer (2, **Figure 25**) and seat it against the spring seat shoulder.
   b. Spring (A, **Figure 35**).
   c. Install the gear (B, **Figure 35**) with its pin holder groove facing out.

WARNING
Parts installed under spring tension can fly apart. Wear safety glasses when compressing the spring and installing the pin in Step 9.

9. Set the governor assembly with its gear side facing up. Compress the gear and spring. Install the pin (C, **Figure 35**) through the gear and shaft. Release the gear, making sure the pin is secured in the gear and shaft (B, **Figure 27**).
10. Check the governor assembly to make sure all of the parts are installed correctly (**Figure 26**).

CLUTCH

The clutch is a multiplate type which operates immersed in the oil supply it shares with the transmission. The clutch hub is splined to the transmission mainshaft and the clutch housing can rotate freely on the mainshaft. The clutch housing is geared to the primary drive gear attached to the crankshaft.

CLUTCH SERVICE

Refer to **Figure 36** when servicing the clutch in this section.

NOTE
You can service the clutch through the clutch cover opening in the right crankcase cover. This section shows clutch service with the right crankcase cover removed for clarity.

Removal

1. Drain the transmission oil (Chapter Three).
2. Remove the clutch cover or right crankcase cover as described in this chapter.

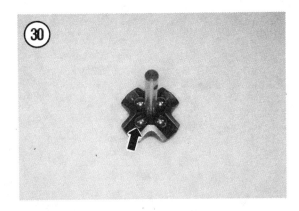

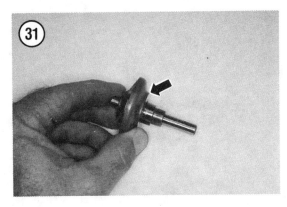

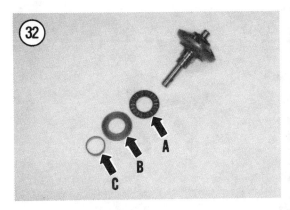

3. Loosen the clutch spring bolts (A, **Figure 37**) in a crisscross pattern. Remove the bolts and springs.

4. Remove the pressure plate (B, **Figure 37**).

NOTE
*A bearing (**Figure 38**) is installed in the pressure plate and can easily fall out.*

5. Remove the pushrod holder (A, **Figure 39**) and washer (B) from the pushrod.

6. Remove the pushrod (A, **Figure 40**) from inside the mainshaft.

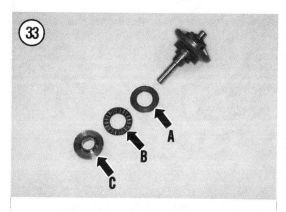

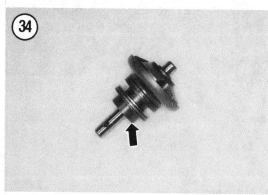

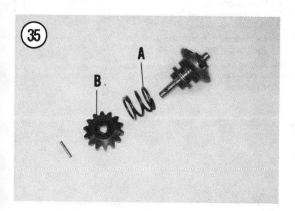

7. Remove the clutch plates and friction discs (B, **Figure 40**) from the clutch housing. See **Figure 41**.

CAUTION
When using the clutch holder in Step 8, make sure you secure it squarely onto the clutch hub. If the clutch holder starts to slip, stop loosening the clutch nut and reposition the clutch holder. If the clutch holder slips when you loosen the clutch, it may damage the clutch hub splines. If you have access to compressed air, it will be easier to loosen the clutch nut with an impact driver and impact socket.

8. Hold the clutch hub with a clutch holder (A, **Figure 42**). Loosen and remove the clutch nut (B).

9. Remove the spline washer (**Figure 43**).

10. Remove the clutch hub (**Figure 44**).

11. Remove the thrust washer (A, **Figure 45**).

12. Remove the clutch housing (B, **Figure 45**).

13A. On 1992-1993 models, remove the needle bearing and sleeve (**Figure 46**).

13B. On 1994 and later models, remove the two needle bearings and sleeve (**Figure 47**).

14. Remove the flat washer (**Figure 48**).

15. Inspect the clutch assembly as described under *Clutch Inspection* in this chapter.

Installation

1. Coat all clutch parts with transmission oil before reassembly.

NOTE
Make sure you thoroughly lubricate the friction discs and clutch plates with oil before installing them.

2. Install the flat washer (**Figure 48**) onto the mainshaft and seat it against the bearing.

3. Lubricate the outside of the sleeve (15, **Figure 36**) with molybdenum disulfide grease and slide it onto the mainshaft. Seat it against the washer.

4A. On 1992-1993 models, install the needle bearing (**Figure 46**) over the sleeve.

4B. On 1994 and later models, install the two needle bearings (**Figure 47**) over the sleeve.

5. Install the clutch housing (B, **Figure 45**) over the mainshaft and mesh it with the kickstarter idler gear and primary drive gear.

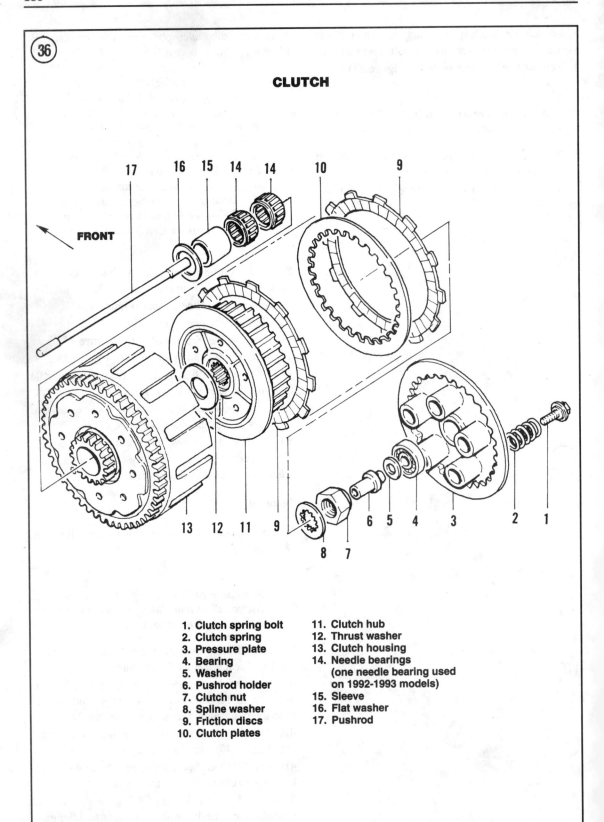

CLUTCH

17 16 15 14 14 10 9

FRONT

13 12 11 9

8 7

6 5 4 3 2 1

1. Clutch spring bolt
2. Clutch spring
3. Pressure plate
4. Bearing
5. Washer
6. Pushrod holder
7. Clutch nut
8. Spline washer
9. Friction discs
10. Clutch plates
11. Clutch hub
12. Thrust washer
13. Clutch housing
14. Needle bearings
    (one needle bearing used
    on 1992-1993 models)
15. Sleeve
16. Flat washer
17. Pushrod

6

NOTE
If you are having trouble meshing the clutch housing with the two gears described in Step 5, turn the clutch housing with one hand to mesh it with the primary drive gear while at the same time slowly operating the kickstarter to turn the kickstarter idler gear.

6. Install the thrust washer (A, **Figure 45**) and seat it against the clutch housing.

7. Install the clutch hub (**Figure 44**) over the main-shaft splines and seat it against the thrust washer.

8. Install the spline washer (**Figure 43**) and seat it against the clutch hub.

9. Install a new clutch nut with its shoulder side facing out (**Figure 49**). Tighten finger-tight.

10. Hold the clutch hub with a clutch holder tool (A, **Figure 42**), then tighten the clutch nut (B, **Figure 42**) as specified in **Table 2**. Remove the clutch holder tool.

CAUTION
The clutch nut must be staked to alternate splines on the mainshaft. When doing so, do not hit the mainshaft

or the impact may damage the mainshaft and/or bearings.

11. Hold a punch against the clutch nut (**Figure 50**) at a point where it aligns with one of the mainshaft splines. Hit the punch with a hammer to stake the nut

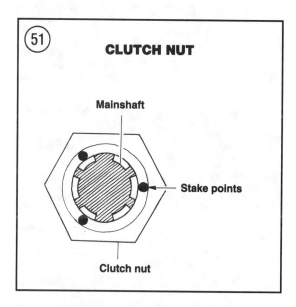

(51) **CLUTCH NUT**

Mainshaft

Stake points

Clutch nut

to the mainshaft splines. Repeat at two alternate points around the clutch nut as shown in **Figure 51**.

NOTE
If the mainshaft splines are not visible past the clutch nut, stake the nut at three places (every 120°) as shown in **Figure 51**.

12. Install the clutch plates as follows:
   a. Lubricate the clutch plates with transmission oil.
   b. Install a friction disc (**Figure 52**), then a clutch plate (**Figure 53**). Continue to alternately install the friction discs and clutch plates. The last plate installed must be a friction disc. **Table 1** lists the correct number of clutch plates used in the stock clutch assembly.

13. Lubricate the pushrod shoulders and ends with transmission oil. Install the pushrod into the mainshaft (A, **Figure 40**) until it seats against the clutch release lever. Operate the clutch release lever (**Figure 54**) back and forth by hand to make sure the pushrod moves in and out.

NOTE
The pushrod can be installed either end first. Both ends are symmetrical.

14. Install the pushrod holder assembly as follows:
   a. Install the bearing (**Figure 38**) into the pressure plate mounting bore.
   b. Lubricate the washer and pushrod holder operating surfaces with molybdenum disulfide grease.
   c. Install the washer (B, **Figure 39**) onto the pushrod holder and install the pushrod holder (A, **Figure 39**) onto the end of the pushrod. See **Figure 55**.

6

52

53

54

15. Align the pressure plate and clutch hub splines, then install the pressure plate (B, **Figure 37**) onto the clutch hub.

> *NOTE*
>
> *Make sure the pressure plate seats flush against the outer friction disc as shown in **Figure 56**. If not, the pressure plate is not installed correctly.*

16. Install the clutch springs and clutch spring bolts (A, **Figure 37**). Tighten the clutch spring bolts in a crisscross pattern in 2 or 3 steps as specified in **Table 2**.

17. Install the clutch cover or right crankcase cover as described in this chapter.

18. Refill the transmission with the correct type and quantity of oil (Chapter Three).

19. Check and adjust the clutch (Chapter Three).

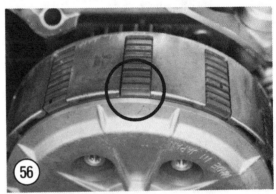

20. Shift the transmission into NEUTRAL and start the engine. After the engine warms, pull the clutch in and shift the transmission into first gear. Note the following:

    a. If you hear a loud grinding and spinning noise coming from the clutch immediately after starting the engine, you either forgot to fill the crankcase with transmission oil or you installed new clutch plates and did not lubricate them with oil.

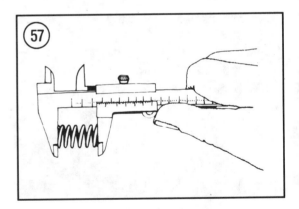

    b. If the bike jumps forwards and stalls or creeps with the transmission in gear and the clutch lever pulled in, recheck the clutch adjustment. If the clutch will not adjust properly, either the clutch cable or friction plates are excessively worn and require replacement.

    c. If the clutch adjustment is correct, operate the clutch lever while watching the clutch release lever (**Figure 54**) at the engine. The lever should move in and out as the clutch lever is operated by hand.

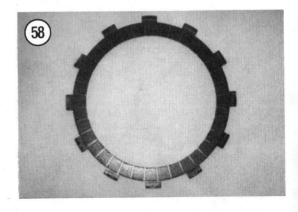

    d. If the clutch adjustment, clutch cable and clutch release lever seem to be working correctly, but a problem is evident you may have assembled the clutch incorrectly or there is a broken part in the clutch. Disassemble the clutch as described in this chapter and inspect the parts.

Clutch Inspection

When measuring the clutch components, compare the measurements to the specifications in **Table 1**. Replace worn or damaged parts as described in this section.

1. Clean and dry all parts.

2. Measure the free length of each clutch spring (**Figure 57**) with a vernier caliper. Replace the springs as a set if any one spring is too short.

3. Inspect the friction discs (**Figure 58**) as follows:

NOTE
If any friction disc is damaged or out of specification as described in the following steps, replace all of the

*friction discs as a set. Never replace only one or two discs. See **Table 1** for the number of friction discs used in the stock clutch assembly.*

a. The friction material used on the friction discs (**Figure 58**) is bonded onto an aluminum plate for warp resistance and durability. Inspect the friction material for excessive or uneven wear, cracks and other damage. Check the disc tangs for surface damage. The sides of the disc tangs where they contact the clutch housing fingers (**Figure 59**) must be smooth; otherwise, the discs cannot engage and disengage correctly.

NOTE
If the disc tangs are damaged, inspect the clutch housing fingers carefully as described later in this section.

b. Measure the thickness of each friction disc with a vernier caliper (**Figure 60**). Measure at several places around the disc.

c. Place a friction disc into the clutch housing and measure the friction disc-to-clutch housing clearance between the friction disc tang and the clutch housing finger with a feeler gauge (**Figure 61**). Repeat for all friction discs.

d. Place each friction disc on a flat surface and measure warpage with a feeler gauge (**Figure 62**).

4. Inspect the steel and aluminum clutch plates (**Figure 63**) as follows:

a. Inspect the clutch plates for cracks, damage or color change. Overheated clutch plates will have a blue discoloration.

b. Check the clutch plates for an oil glaze buildup. Remove by lightly sanding both sides of each plate with 400 grit sandpaper placed on a surface plate or piece of glass.

c. Place each clutch plate on a flat surface and check warpage with a feeler gauge (**Figure 64**).

d. The clutch plate inner teeth mesh with the clutch hub splines (**Figure 65**). Check the clutch plate teeth for any roughness or damage. The teeth contact surfaces must be smooth; otherwise, the plates cannot engage and disengage correctly.

6

NOTE
If the clutch plate teeth are damaged, inspect the clutch hub splines carefully as described later in this section.

5. Inspect the clutch hub (A, **Figure 66**) for the following conditions:

    a. The clutch plate teeth slide in the clutch hub splines (**Figure 65**). Inspect the splines for rough spots, grooves or other damage. Repair minor damage with a file or oil stone. If the damage is excessive, replace the clutch hub.

    b. Damaged spring towers and threads.

6. Check the clutch housing (B, **Figure 66**) for the following conditions:

    a. The friction disc tangs slide in the clutch housing grooves (**Figure 59**). Inspect the grooves for cracks or galling. Repair minor damage with a file. If the damage is excessive, replace the clutch housing.

    b. Check the two clutch housing gears (A, **Figure 67**) for excessive wear, pitting, chipped gear teeth or other damage.

    c. Check the clutch housing bore (B, **Figure 67**) for cracks, pitting or other damage.

7. Check the sleeve and needle bearing(s) for excessive wear and damage.

8. Check the pushrod holder assembly (**Figure 68**) for excessive wear or damage. Replace the bearing if it does not spin smoothly.

9. Check the pressure plate for cracks or other damage. Check the bearing bore for excessive wear or damage.

NOTE
*The bearing (**Figure 38**) is a light press fit and can be removed and installed by hand.*

10. Check the pushrod as follows:

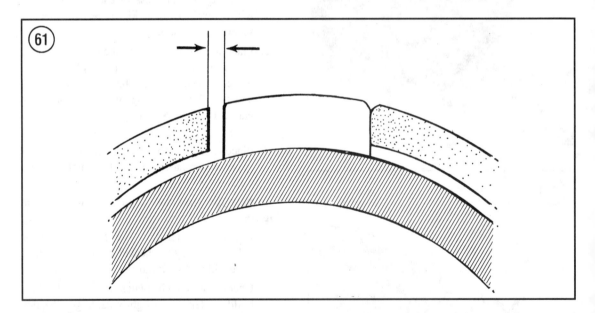

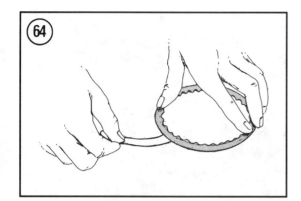

a. Inspect the pushrod ends for cracks or severe wear.

b. Roll the pushrod on a flat surface and check it for bending or other damage. Replace the pushrod if bent. Do not try to straighten it.

11. Check each washer for nicks, burrs or damage.

WATER PUMP AND PRIMARY DRIVE GEARS

Refer to **Figure 69** when servicing the water pump drive gear and primary drive gear.

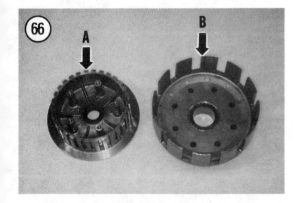

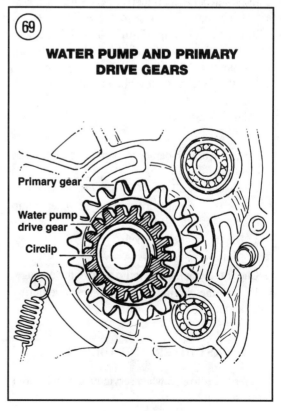

WATER PUMP AND PRIMARY DRIVE GEARS

Primary gear

Water pump drive gear

Circlip

Removal/Installation

1. Remove the clutch as described in this chapter.
2. Remove the circlip (**Figure 70**) from the crank-shaft groove.
3. Remove the water pump drive gear (A, **Figure 71**).
4. Remove the primary drive gear (B, **Figure 71**).

NOTE
If the gears are hard to slide off the crankshaft, first check the circlip groove for any burrs and repair with a file. If this area is in good condition, check the crankshaft end for spreading or other damage. Crankshaft end spreading can occur after reassembling the engine and centering the crankshaft in the crankcase. If there is some crankshaft end spreading, remove the two gears with a puller.

5. Inspect the gears as described under *Inspection* in this section.
6. Install the primary drive gear with its chamfered side (**Figure 72**) facing out. See B, **Figure 71**.
7. Install the water pump drive gear with its chamfered side (**Figure 73**) facing out. See A, **Figure 71**.
8. Install a *new* circlip (**Figure 70**) and seat it into the crankshaft groove. Install the circlip with its flat side facing out.
9. Install the clutch as described in this chapter.

Inspection

Replace worn or damaged parts as described in this section.
1. Clean and dry all parts (**Figure 74**).
2. Check the primary drive gear and water pump drive gear (**Figure 74**) for:
    a. Broken or chipped teeth.
    b. Damaged splines.
3. Check the crankshaft circlip groove for damage.
4. Discard the circlip and install a new one during installation.

KICKSTARTER AND IDLE GEAR

Refer to **Figure 75** when servicing the kickstarter in this section.

Kickstarter
Removal/Installation

> *NOTE*
> *If you are servicing the kickstarter because it is not working correctly, examine its mounting position before removing it in the following steps. Make sure the return spring is mounted in the crankcase hole.*

1. Remove the clutch as described in this chapter.
2. Remove the washer (A, **Figure 76**) from the kick shaft.

> *WARNING*
> *Wear safety glasses when disconnecting the return spring and removing the kickstarter in Step 3.*

3. Unhook the return spring (**Figure 77**) and remove the kickstarter assembly.
4. If necessary, unbolt and remove the ratchet guide (**Figure 78**).
5. If necessary, service the kickstarter as described later in this section.

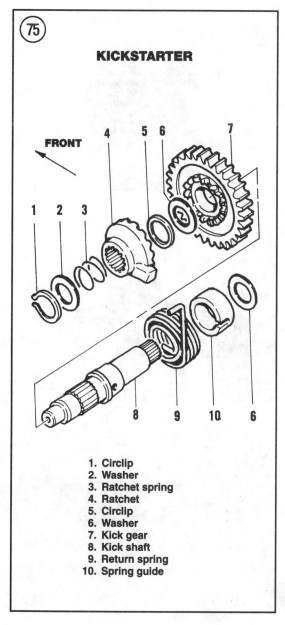

KICKSTARTER

FRONT

1. Circlip
2. Washer
3. Ratchet spring
4. Ratchet
5. Circlip
6. Washer
7. Kick gear
8. Kick shaft
9. Return spring
10. Spring guide

6. If the ratchet guide (**Figure 78**) was removed, install it as follows:

    a. Install the ratchet guide hole over the pin in the crankcase.

    b. Apply a medium strength threadlock onto the ratchet guide mounting bolt, then install the mounting bolt and tighten securely.

NOTE
Steps 7-12 describe kickstater installation.

7. Check the kickstarter to make sure the return spring end is installed in the hole in the kick shaft (**Figure 79**). Check that the spring guide is pushed forward (**Figure 80**) and that its slot is installed around the return spring end.

8. Lubricate both kick shaft ends with transmission oil.

9. Install the kickstarter assembly as follows:

WARNING
Wear safety glasses when installing the kickstarter and connecting the return spring.

    a. Install the kick pedal onto the kickstarter as shown in **Figure 81**.

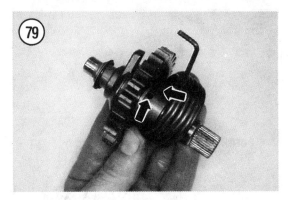

NOTE
Figure 82 identifies the ratchet arm (A) and ratchet guide (B).

    b. Install the return spring (A, **Figure 83**) into the hole in the crankcase and hold it in place with your hand. Do not install the ratchet arm (A, **Figure 82**) behind the ratchet guide (B, **Figure 82**) at this time.

    c. Turn the kick pedal (B, **Figure 83**) counterclockwise and push the kickstarter into the crankcase so that the ratchet arm fits behind the ratchet guide.

    d. Release the kick pedal and allow the kick shaft to return.

10. After installing the kickstarter, check the kickstarter and idle gear operation as follows:

    a. Turn the idle gear (B, **Figure 76**) by hand. The idle gear and kick gear should turn freely.

    b. Operate the kickstarter (B, **Figure 83**) by hand. Make sure the ratchet operates correctly and engages the kick gear with the idle gear. Also make sure the return spring returns the

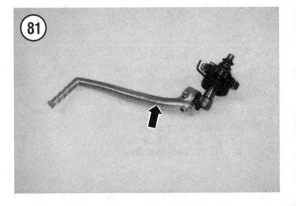

kick shaft under sufficient spring tension and that the ratchet disengages from the kick gear.

c. If the gears do not engage or disengage properly, remove the kickstarter and inspect the parts for correct assembly. If the kickstarter was disassembled, make sure the ratchet gear was properly indexed with the kick shaft. See the *Assembly* procedure in this section.

11. Install the washer (A, **Figure 76**) onto the kick shaft.

12. Install the clutch as described in this chapter.

Kickstarter
Disassembly

1. Wash the kickstarter assembly in solvent and dry thoroughly.

2. Disassemble the kickstarter assembly in the order shown in **Figure 75**. See **Figure 84**.

3. Discard both circlips.

Kickstater
Inspection

Replace worn or damaged parts as described in this section.

1. Check the kick shaft (A, **Figure 85**) for:
   a. Worn or damaged splines. Install the ratchet onto the kick shaft splines and slide it back and forth. The ratchet must slide freely.
   b. Elongation of the circlip grooves.
   c. Elongation of the return spring hole.
   d. Scored or cracked operating surfaces. Install the kick gear onto the kick shaft and spin it by hand. The gear must turn freely.

2. Check the ratchet (B, **Figure 85**) for:
   a. Cracks or other damage.
   b. Worn, damaged or rounded-off ratchet teeth.
   c. Worn or damaged splines.

3. Check the kick gear (C, **Figure 85**) for:
   a. Chipped or missing gear teeth.
   b. Worn, damaged or rounded-off ratchet teeth.
   c. Worn or damaged gear bore.

4. Inspect the ratchet spring (3, **Figure 75**) and return spring (9) for cracks or other visible damage. Check both return spring ends for damage.

5. Check the spring guide (10, **Figure 75**) for excessive wear or damage.

6. Inspect the washers for burrs, excessive thrust wear and other damage.

7. Inspect the ratchet guide (**Figure 78**) for damage or a loose mounting bolt.

Kickstarter
Assembly

1. Lubricate all of the sliding surfaces with transmission oil.
2. Identify the circlips and washers as follows:
   a. The outer circlip (1, **Figure 75**) is smaller than the circlip used between the ratchet and kick gear (5, **Figure 75**).

> *NOTE*
> *Install new circlips when assembling the kickstarter.*

   b. The washer (2, **Figure 75**) installed between the outer circlip and ratchet spring is smaller than the other two washers (6, **Figure 75**).

3. Install the kick gear (A, **Figure 86**) with its ratchet teeth facing toward the inside of the shaft. Seat the kick gear against the kick shaft shoulder.

4. Install the washer (B, **Figure 86**) and circlip (C, **Figure 86**). Seat the circlip in the groove shown in **Figure 87**. Spin the kick gear to make sure it turns smoothly. Make sure the circlip seats in the groove completely.

5. Align the index mark on the ratchet with the index mark on the kick gear and install the ratchet (**Figure 88**).

> *NOTE*
> *The kickstarter will not work if the two index marks (Step 5) are not properly aligned.*

6. Install the ratchet spring (A, **Figure 89**) and seat it against the ratchet.

7. Install the washer (B, **Figure 89**) and seat it against the ratchet spring.

8. Install the circlip (C, **Figure 89**) into the groove in the end of the kick shaft so its flat side faces toward the ratchet spring. See **Figure 90**. Make sure the circlip seats in the groove completely.

9. Install the return spring end into the hole in the kick shaft as shown in **Figure 91**.

10. Install the spring guide over the kick shaft and push it forward so its slot (**Figure 92**) seats around the return spring end (A, **Figure 93**).

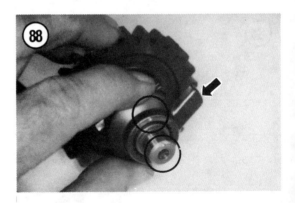

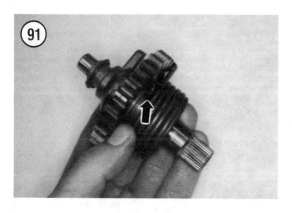

11. Install the washer (B, **Figure 93**) and seat it against the spring guide.

Kick Pedal
Disassembly/Reassembly

If the kick pedal fails to lock in place after returning it to its locked position, refer to **Figure 94** to service the detent ball and spring assembly. Note the following when servicing the kick pedal assembly:

    a. Replace the seal (2, **Figure 94**) if damaged.

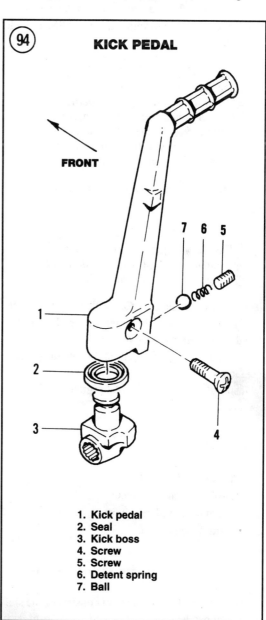

KICK PEDAL

FRONT

1. Kick pedal
2. Seal
3. Kick boss
4. Screw
5. Screw
6. Detent spring
7. Ball

b. Lubricate the kick boss shoulder (3, **Figure 94**) with grease.

c. Lubricate the detent spring (6, **Figure 94**) with grease.

Idle Gear
Removal/Installation

The idle gear engages the kick gear with the clutch. The idle gear can be serviced with the kickstarter installed in the engine.

1. Remove the clutch as described in this chapter.

2. Remove the outer circlip (A, **Figure 95**) and idle gear (B).

> *NOTE*
> *The inner circlip (**Figure 96**) secures the countershaft needle bearing in place. Do not remove the inner circlip (**Figure 96**) unless you are going to replace it. Leave this circlip in place when splitting the engine cases.*

3. Inspect the idle gear as described under *Inspection*.

> *NOTE*
> *The two idle gear circlips are identical. Install new circlip(s) when installing the idle gear in the following steps.*

4. Lubricate the idle gear bore with transmission oil.

5. If removed, install the inner circlip (**Figure 96**) into the countershaft groove.

6. Install the idle gear with its shoulder side (**Figure 97**) facing in.

7. Install the outer circlip (A, **Figure 95**) into the countershaft groove.

Inspection

1. Inspect the idle gear for:
   a. Broken or chipped teeth.
   b. Worn or scored gear bore.

2. Discard the circlip(s).

EXTERNAL SHIFT MECHANISM

The external shift mechanism consists of the shift shaft, stopper lever assembly and shift drum cam.

These parts can be removed with the engine mounted in the frame.

Refer to **Figure 98** (1992-1996) or **Figure 99** (1997-on) when servicing the external shift mechanism in this section.

Removal

1. Remove the clutch as described in this chapter.

2. Remove the shift pedal (**Figure 100**).

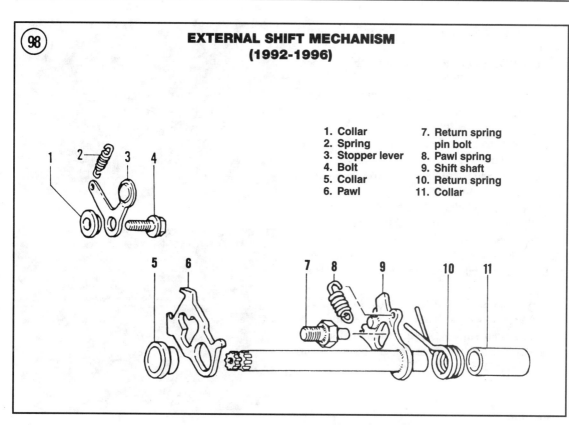

**EXTERNAL SHIFT MECHANISM
(1992-1996)**

1. Collar
2. Spring
3. Stopper lever
4. Bolt
5. Collar
6. Pawl
7. Return spring
   pin bolt
8. Pawl spring
9. Shift shaft
10. Return spring
11. Collar

6

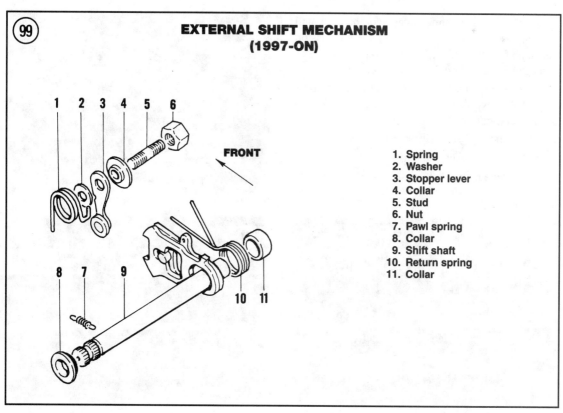

**EXTERNAL SHIFT MECHANISM
(1997-ON)**

FRONT

1. Spring
2. Washer
3. Stopper lever
4. Collar
5. Stud
6. Nut
7. Pawl spring
8. Collar
9. Shift shaft
10. Return spring
11. Collar

3. Pull the shift shaft assembly (**Figure 101**) out of the crankcase.

4A. On 1992-1996 models, remove the stopper lever assembly as follows:

    a. Disconnect the spring (A, **Figure 102**) and remove the bolt and stopper lever (B) assembly. See **Figure 98**.

    b. If necessary, remove the return spring pin bolt (C, **Figure 102**).

4B. On 1997 and later models, remove the stopper lever assembly as follows:

    a. Remove the bolt (A, **Figure 103**) and remove the stopper lever (B) assembly. See **Figure 99**.

    b. If necessary, remove the return spring pin bolt (C, **Figurc 103**).

5. Remove the shift drum cam (A, **Figure 104**) as follows:

    a. Turn the shift drum cam bolt (B, **Figure 104**) counterclockwise until the shift drum cam locks in position. Loosen and remove the bolt.

    b. Remove the shift drum cam and its dowel pin (**Figure 105**).

Inspection

Worn or damaged shift linkage components will cause missed shifts and wear to the transmission gears, shift forks and shift drum. Replace worn or damaged parts as described in this section.

1. Clean the components in solvent and dry thoroughly. Remove all threadlock residue from the shift drum cam mounting bolt threads.

2. Check the shift shaft (**Figure 106**) for:

    a. Loose or broken shaft arm.

    b. Corroded, twisted or otherwise damaged shaft.

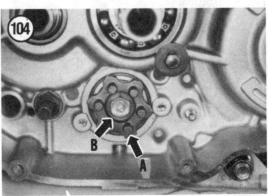

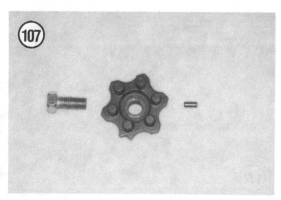

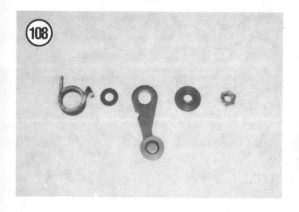

c. Weak or damaged spring.
3. Check the stopper lever assembly for:
  a. Weak or damaged spring.
  b. Bent, cracked or damaged stopper lever.
  c. Bent or damaged washer.
4. Check the shift drum cam (**Figure 107**) assembly for:
  a. Excessively worn or damaged mounting bolt.
  b. Excessively worn or damaged shift drum center ramps.
  c. Damaged dowel pin.
5. Check the shift shaft seal in the left crankcase half for excessive wear or damage. Replace the seal if leaking. Note the following:
  a. Pry the seal out of the crankcase with a screwdriver. Make sure you do not damage the crankcase.
  b. Pack the seal lips with grease, then press the seal into the case with its closed side facing out. Install the seal so it seats squarely in the case bore.

6

Installation

NOTE
On 1992-1996 models, it is easier to install the shift drum cam first, then the stopper lever assembly. On 1997 and later models, it is easier to install the stopper lever assembly first, then the shift drum cam.

1. On 1997 and later models, install the stopper lever assembly (**Figure 108**) as follows:
  a. Install the washer (**Figure 109**) over the stopper lever stud.
  b. Hook the return spring onto the stopper lever as shown in **Figure 110**. Note how the stopper

lever roller faces toward the crankcase (**Figure 110**).

c. Install the stopper lever and spring onto the stopper lever stud (A, **Figure 111**), then position the spring end against the crankcase boss (B).

d. Install the collar—shoulder side facing in (**Figure 112**)—onto the stud and center it into the stopper lever. Install the stopper lever nut and tighten as specified in **Table 2**.

e. Push the stopper lever down and release it. It should move and return under spring tension. If the stopper lever is stuck, remove the nut and reinstall the stopper lever assembly.

2. Install the shift drum cam as follows:

a. On 1997 and later models, pry the stopper lever assembly away from the shift drum cam with a screwdriver (A, **Figure 113**).

NOTE
While there are two holes in the end of the shift drum cam, the pin will only fit into one of the holes.

b. Install the pin into the hole in the shift drum cam. Install the shift drum cam, aligning its hole with the pin (B, **Figure 113**).

c. Apply a medium strength threadlock onto the shift drum cam mounting bolt. Install the bolt (B, **Figure 104**) and tighten finger-tight.

d. On 1997 and later models, remove the screwdriver and allow the stopper lever to return and sit against the shift drum cam.

e. Turn the shift drum cam mounting bolt clockwise until the shift drum cam locks in place. Tighten the bolt as specified in **Table 2**.

3. On 1992-1996 models, install the stopper lever assembly as follows:

a. Install the collar onto the back of the stopper lever as shown in 1, **Figure 98**.

b. Install the collar and stopper lever onto the crankcase and secure the lever with its mounting bolt (B, **Figure 102**). Tighten the mounting bolt finger-tight, then move the stopper lever back and forth. If there is any binding, the collar is not centered correctly against the stopper lever. If the stopper lever moves freely, tighten the stopper lever mounting bolt as specified in **Table 2**.

c. Connect the spring between the stopper lever arm and the crankcase pin (A, **Figure 102**).

4. Install the shift shaft assembly as follows:

    a. Make sure the return spring is centered on the plastic collar and against the shift shaft arm as shown in A, **Figure 114**.

    b. Make sure the pawl spring is connected between the two pawl arms as shown in B, **Figure 114**.

    c. Make sure the metal collar is centered on the inner pawl (**Figure 115**).

    d. Lubricate the shift shaft with transmission oil.

    e. Install the shift shaft through the crankcase and center its return spring on the return spring pin bolt. See **Figure 101**.

5. Install the shift pedal (**Figure 100**) and its pinch bolt. Tighten the bolt securely.

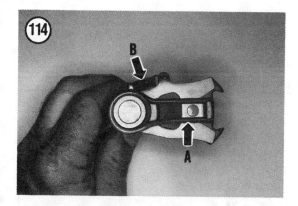

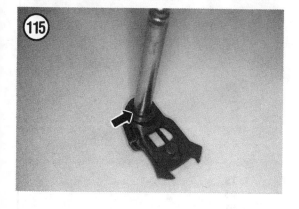

6. Install the clutch as described in this chapter.

7. Raise the rear wheel off the ground. Check the shifting as follows:

    a. Slowly turn the rear wheel and shift the transmission into first gear. Shift into NEUTRAL and the remaining forward gears.

    b. If the shift shaft locks in place, the return spring may not be centered on the return spring pin bolt (**Figure 101**).

    c. If the transmission overshifts, the stopper lever assembly may not have been installed correctly.

    d. If the transmission does not shift correctly, remove the clutch and recheck the external shift mechanism.

CLUTCH CABLE REPLACEMENT

1. Remove the fuel tank (Chapter Eight).

2. Loosen the clutch cable adjuster locknut and adjuster at the handlebar, then disconnect the clutch cable.

3. Disconnect the clutch cable from the clutch release lever.

NOTE
Prior to removing the cable make a drawing of the cable routing through the frame. It is easy to forget the cable's routing path after removing it. Replace the cable exactly as it was, avoiding any sharp turns.

4. Pull the cable out of any retaining clips on the frame.

5. Remove the cable and replace it with a new one.

6. Lubricate the clutch cable before reconnecting it in the following steps. Refer to Chapter Three.

7. Install by reversing the preceding removal steps. Make sure the clutch cable is correctly routed with no sharp turns. Adjust the clutch cable as described in Chapter Three.

6

Table 1 CLUTCH SERVICE SPECIFICATIONS

	New mm (in.)	Service limit mm (in.)
Clutch spring free length	35.0 (1.378)	33.6 (1.323)
Friction disc thickness	2.92-3.08 (0.114-0.121)	2.8 (0.110)
Friction disc warpage	0-0.15 (0-0.005)	0.3 (0.011)
Friction disc-to-clutch housing clearance	0.15-0.45 (0.006-0.018)	0.8 (0.031)
Steel plate thickness	1.46-1.74 (0.057-0.068)	1.36 (0.053)
Steel plate warpage	0-.2 (0-0.007)	0.3 (0.011)
Number of clutch plates		
Clutch plates (steel or aluminum)	7	
Friction discs (fiber)	8	

Table 2 TIGHTENING TORQUES

	N•m	in.-lb.	ft.-lb.
Clutch nut	98	–	72
Clutch spring bolts	8.8	78	–
Governor lever Allen bolts	3.9	35	–
Kickstarter pedal			
1992-1993	49	–	36
1994-on	8.8	78	–
Kickstarter ratchet guide bolt	8.8	78	–
Rear brake pedal			
1992-1997	8.8	78	–
1998	25	–	19
Right crankcase cover mounting bolts	8.8	78	–
Shaft lever nut			
1992-1993	7.8	69	–
1994-on	8.3	85	–
Shift drum cam mounting bolt	22	–	16
Shift shaft return spring pin			
1992-1993	22	–	16
1994	37	–	27
1995-on	42	–	31
Stopper lever			
Bolt (1992-1996)	8.8	78	–
Nut (1997-on)	8.8	78	–
Water pump impeller mounting bolt	69	61	–

CHAPTER SEVEN

TRANSMISSION AND
INTERNAL SHIFT MECHANISM

This chapter describes disassembly and reassembly of the transmission shafts and internal shift mechanism. Before you can remove these parts, you must remove the engine and separate the crankcase halves (Chapter Five).

Table 1 lists transmission gear ratios. Service specifications are listed in **Table 2**. **Tables 1** and **2** are at the end of the chapter.

TRANSMISSION OPERATION

The basic transmission has five pairs of constantly meshed gears (**Figure 1**) on the mainshaft (A) and countershaft (B). Each pair of meshed gears provides one gear ratio. In each pair, one of the gears is locked to its shaft and always turns with it. The other

gear is not locked to its shaft and can spin freely on it. Next to each free spinning gear is a another gear, which is splined to the same shaft, always turning with it. This gear can slide from side to side along the shaft splines. The side of the sliding gear and the free spinning gear have mating dogs and slots. When the sliding gear moves up against the free spinning gear, the two gears lock together, fixing the free spinning gear to its shaft. Since both meshed mainshaft and countershaft gears are now locked to their shafts, power is transmitted at that gear ratio.

Shift Drum and Forks

Each sliding gear has a deep groove machined around its outside (**Figure 2**). The curved shift fork arm rides in this groove, controlling the side-to-side sliding of the gear; therefore, the selection of different gear ratios. Each shift fork (A, **Figure 3**) slides back and forth on a shaft, and has a pin (B, **Figure 3**) that rides in a groove machined in the shift drum (**Figure 4**). When the shift linkage rotates the shift drum, the zigzag grooves move the shift forks and sliding gears back and forth.

TRANSMISSION TROUBLESHOOTING

Refer to *Transmission* in Chapter Two.

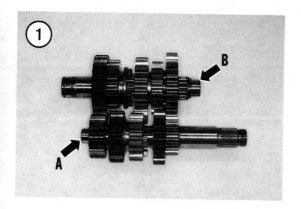

TRANSMISSION

Removal/Installation

Remove and install the transmission and internal shift mechanism as described under *Crankcase Disassembly/Reassembly* in Chapter Five.

TRANSMISSION OVERHAUL

Transmission Service Notes

1. After removing the transmission shafts, place one of the shafts into a large can or plastic bucket and clean with solvent. Dry with compressed air or let sit on rags to drip dry. Repeat for the opposite shaft.

2. If you have intermixed gears from both shafts (mainshaft and countershaft), use the gear ratio information in **Table 1** and the transmission illustration (in this chapter) to identify the gears.

3. Store the transmission gears, washers and circlips in a divided container, such as an egg carton (**Figure 5**), to help maintain their correct alignment and position as you remove them from the transmission shafts.

4. Replace all of the transmission circlips during reassembly. Do not reuse circlips, as removal may distort them and cause them to fail.

5. To avoid bending and twisting the new circlips when installing them, open the new circlip with a pair of circlip pliers while holding the back of the circlip with a pair of pliers (**Figure 6**). Slide the circlip down the shaft and seat it into its correct transmission groove. This technique can also be used to remove the circlips from a shaft once they are free from their grooves.

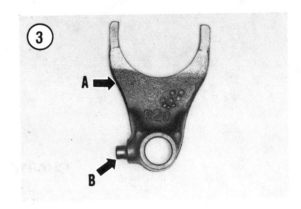

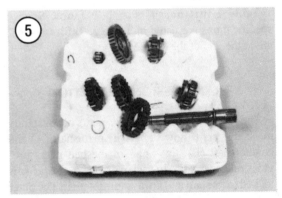

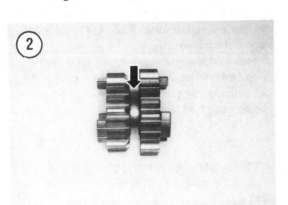

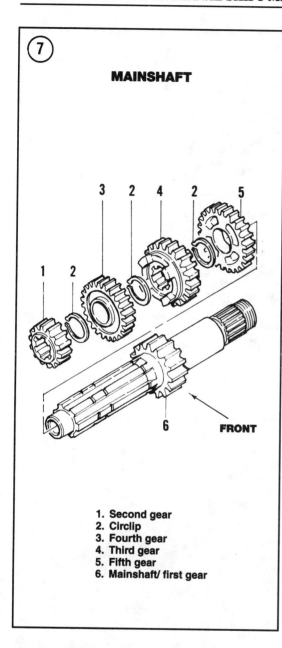

⑦

MAINSHAFT

3 2 4 2 5

1 2

6 **FRONT**

1. Second gear
2. Circlip
3. Fourth gear
4. Third gear
5. Fifth gear
6. Mainshaft/ first gear

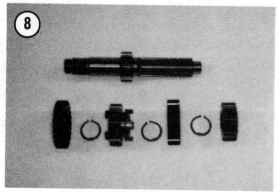

⑧

Mainshaft Disassembly

Refer to **Figure 7**.

1. Disassemble the mainshaft (**Figure 8**) in the following order:
   a. Second gear.
   b. Circlip.
   c. Fourth gear.
   d. Circlip.
   e. Third gear.
   f. Circlip.
   g. Fifth gear.

NOTE
First gear is an integral part of the mainshaft.

2. Inspect the mainshaft assembly as described under *Transmission Inspection* in this chapter.

7

Mainshaft Assembly

Before assembling the mainshaft assembly, note the following:

   a. The mainshaft uses three circlips (2, **Figure 7**). Each circlip is identical (same part number).
   b. Always install new circlips.
   c. Install the circlips with their chamfered edge facing *away* from the thrust load.
   d. Install the circlips with the gap aligned with a groove in the shaft (**Figure 9**)

1. Lubricate all sliding surfaces with transmission oil to ensure initial lubrication.

2. Install fifth gear (**Figure 10**) with its gear dogs facing away from first gear.

3. Install the circlip (**Figure 11**) into the groove next to fifth gear.

4. Install third gear (**Figure 12**) with its shift fork groove facing away from fifth gear.

5. Install the circlip (A, **Figure 13**) into the groove next to third gear. See **Figure 14**.

6. Install fourth gear with its gear dogs (**Figure 15**) facing toward third gear.

7. Install the circlip (**Figure 16**) into the groove next to fourth gear.

8. Install second gear (**Figure 17**) and seat it next to the circlip.

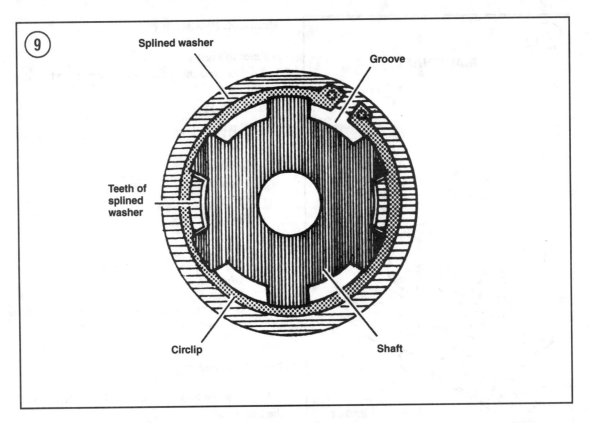

(9)

Splined washer

Groove

Teeth of
splined
washer

Circlip

Shaft

(10)

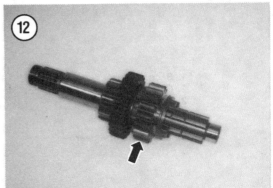

(12)

(11)

(13)

A

B

C

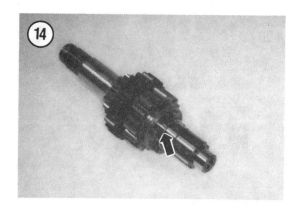

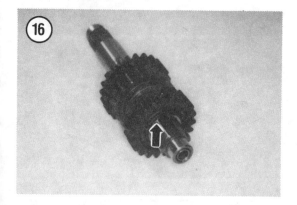

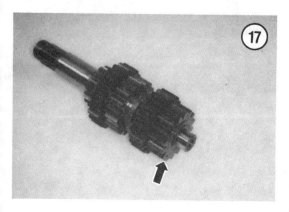

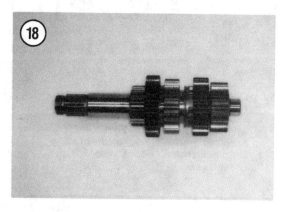

NOTE
On the transmission shown in this procedure, the gear teeth on both sides of second gear are symmetrical (same shape). If second gear on the model you are working with has chamfered gear teeth on one side, install the gear so the chamfered side faces toward fourth gear.

9. Refer to **Figure 7** and **Figure 18** for the correct placement of the mainshaft gears.

Countershaft Disassembly

Refer to **Figure 19**.

1. Disassemble the countershaft (**Figure 20**) in the following order:
   a. Second gear.
   b. Fourth gear.
   c. Circlip.
   d. Needle bearing
   e. First gear.
   f. Fifth gear.
   g. Circlip.
   h. Third gear.

2. Inspect the countershaft assembly as described under *Transmission Inspection* in this chapter.

Countershaft Assembly

Refer to **Figure 19** for this procedure.

Before assembling the countershaft assembly, note the following:
   a. The countershaft uses two different circlips.
   b. Always install new circlips.
   c. Install the circlips with their chamfered edge facing *away* from the thrust load.

7

d. Install the circlips with the gap aligned with a shaft groove as shown in **Figure 9**.

1. Lubricate all sliding surfaces with transmission oil.

2. Install third gear with its dog recess (**Figure 21**) facing toward the left side of the shaft.

3. Install the circlip (**Figure 22**) into the groove next to third gear.

4. Install fifth gear with its shift fork groove (**Figure 23**) facing toward third gear.

5. Install first gear (**Figure 24**) with its longer shoulder facing away from fifth gear.

6. Install the needle bearing and circlip (**Figure 25**).

7. Install fourth gear (**Figure 26**) with its shift fork groove facing toward third gear.

8. Install second gear (2, **Figure 19**) and its bushing (1) as follows:

    a. Install the bushing into second gear as shown in **Figure 27**.

    b. Install second gear (**Figure 28**) with its dog recess facing toward fourth gear.

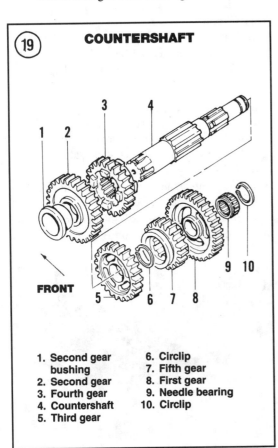

COUNTERSHAFT

FRONT

1. Second gear bushing
2. Second gear
3. Fourth gear
4. Countershaft
5. Third gear
6. Circlip
7. Fifth gear
8. First gear
9. Needle bearing
10. Circlip

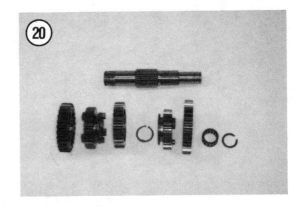

9. Refer to **Figure 19** and **Figure 29** for the correct placement of the countershaft gears.

TRANSMISSION INSPECTION

Maintain the alignment of the transmission components when cleaning and inspecting the individual parts in the following section. To prevent intermixing the parts, work on only one shaft at a time.

Replace parts that show excessive wear or damage as described in this section.

1. Clean and dry the shaft assembly.

2. Inspect the mainshaft (**Figure 30**) and countershaft (**Figure 31**) for:

    a. Worn or damages splines.

    b. On the mainshaft, missing, broken or chipped first gear teeth.

    c. Excessively worn or damaged bearing surfaces.

    d. Cracked or rounded-off circlip grooves.

3. Check each gear for excessive wear, burrs, pitting, or chipped or missing teeth. Check the splines on sliding gears and the bore on stationary gears for excessive wear or damage.

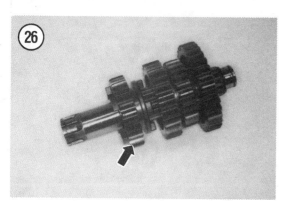

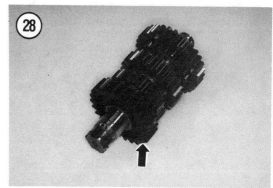

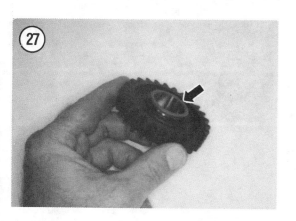

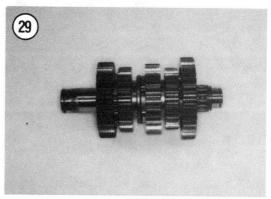

4. Check second gear and its bushing (**Figure 32**) for excessive wear, cracks or other damage.

5. To check stationary gears for wear, install them on their correct shaft and in their original operating position. If necessary, use the old circlips to secure them in place. Spin the gear by hand. The gear should turn smoothly. A rough turning gear indicates heat damage—check for a dark blue color or galling on the operating surfaces. Rocking indicates excessive wear, either to the gear or shaft or both.

6. To check the sliding gears, install them on their correct shaft and in their original operating position. The gear should slide back and forth without any binding or excessive play.

7. Check the dogs (**Figure 33**) on the gears for excessive wear, rounding, cracks or other damage. When wear is noticeable, make sure it is consistent on each gear dog. If one dog is worn more than the others, the others will be overstressed during operation and will eventually crack and fail. Check engaging gears as described in Step 9.

8. Check each gear dog recess (**Figure 34**) for cracks, rounding and other damage. Check engaging gears as described in Step 9.

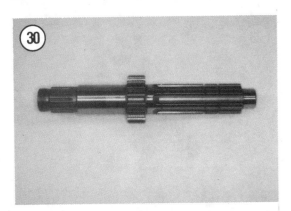

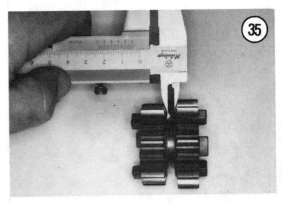

9. Check engaging gears by installing the two gears on their respective shaft and in their original operating position. Mesh the gears together. Twist one gear against the other and then check the dog engagement. Reverse the thrust load to check in the other operating position. Make sure the engagement in both directions is positive and without any slippage. Check that there is equal engagement across all of the engagement dogs.

NOTE
If there is excessive or uneven wear to the gear engagement dogs, check the shift forks carefully for bending and other damage. Refer to **Internal Shift Mechanism** *in this chapter.*

10. Measure each sliding gear shift fork groove width (**Figure 35**) and compare to the service limit in **Table 2**. If a groove width is excessive, replace the gear and check the shift fork finger thickness as described under *Internal Shift Mechanism* in this chapter.

NOTE
Replace defective gears along with their mating gears, though they may not show as much wear or damage.

11. Check the countershaft needle bearing (**Figure 25**) for needle or cage damage and wear. Check the mating bushing (**Figure 36**) in the right crankcase-half for cracks and severe wear.
12. Replace all of the circlips during reassembly.

INTERNAL SHIFT MECHANISM

Refer to **Figure 37** when servicing the internal shift mechanism.

Removal/Installation

Remove and install the transmission and internal shift mechanism as described in Chapter Five.

Shift Drum
Inspection

1. Clean and dry the shift drum assembly.
2. Check the shift drum for:

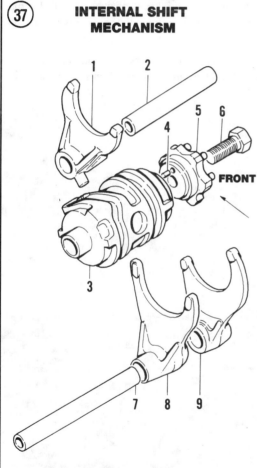

INTERNAL SHIFT MECHANISM

FRONT

1. Mainshaft third gear shift fork
2. Shift fork shaft (short)
3. Shift drum
4. Pin
5. Shift drum segment
6. Bolt
7. Shift fork shaft (long)
8. Countershaft fourth gear shift fork
9. Countershaft fifth gear shift fork

a. Scored or damaged bearing surfaces (A, **Figure 38**).

b. Excessively worn or damaged grooves (B, **Figure 38**).

3. Measure the width of each shift drum groove (B, **Figure 38**) and compare to the service limit in **Table 2**. Replace the shift drum if any groove is out of specification.

Shift Fork
Inspection

Table 2 lists new and service limit specifications for the shift forks. Replace the shift forks if out of specification or if they show damage as described in this section.

1. Inspect each shift fork (C, **Figure 38**) for wear or damage. Examine the shift forks at the points where they contact the slider gear (C, **Figure 38**). These surfaces must be smooth with no signs of excessive wear, bending, cracks, heat discoloration or other damage.

2. Check each shift fork for arc-shaped wear or burn marks. These marks indicate a bent shift fork.

3. Check the shift fork shafts for bending or other damage. Install each shift fork on its shaft (**Figure 39**) and slide it back and forth. Each shift fork must slide smoothly with no binding or tight spots. If you notice any binding, check the shaft closely for bending.

4. Measure the thickness of each shift fork finger (**Figure 40**) and compare to the dimension in **Table 2**.

5. Measure each shift fork guide pin diameter (**Figure 41**) and compare to the dimension in **Table 2**.

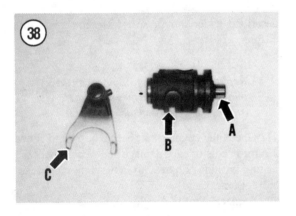

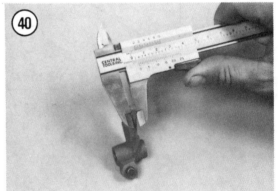

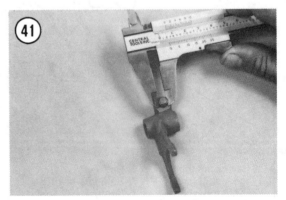

Table 1 TRANSMISSION GEAR RATIOS

Primary reduction system	
Type	Gear
Reduction ratio	2.750 (55/20)
Transmission	
Type	5-speed constant mesh
Gear ratios	
First	2.133 (32/15)
Second	
1992-1996	1.687 (27/16)
1997-on	1.625 (26/16)
Third	
1992-1996	1.388 (25/18)
1997-on	1.333 (24.18)
Fourth	1.136 (25/22)
Fifth	1.000 (24/24)
Final reduction ratio	
1992-1996	3.500 (49/14)
1997	
U.S. models	3.500 (49/14)
All other models	3.769 (49/13)
1998	
U.S. models	3.500 (49/14)
All other models	3.692 (48/13)
Overall drive ratio @ top gear	
1992-1996	9.625
1997	
U.S. models	9.625
All other models	10.365
1998	
U.S. models	9.625
All other models	10.153

7

Table 2 TRANSMISSION SERVICE SPECIFICATIONS

	Standard mm (in.)	Service limit mm (in.)
Shift drum groove width	6.05-6.20 (0.2381-0.2441)	6.25 (0.246)
Shift fork finger thickness	4.40-4.50 (0.173-0.177)	4.30 (0.169)
Shift fork guide pin diameter	5.90-6.00 (0.2323-0.0.2362)	5.80 (0.228)
Sliding gear shift fork groove width	4.55-4.65 (0.179-0.183)	4.75 (0.187)

CHAPTER EIGHT

FUEL SYSTEM

The fuel system consists of the fuel tank, fuel shutoff valve, carburetor and air filter.

This chapter includes service procedures for all parts of the fuel system. Air filter service is covered in Chapter Three.

Table 1 lists stock carburetor specifications. **Tables 1** and **Table 2** are at the end of the chapter.

CARBURETOR

Removal

1. Support the bike on a workstand.
2. On 1998 models, disconnect the powerjet valve electrical connector (**Figure 1**).
3. Loosen, but do not remove, the carburetor cap (A, **Figure 2**).
4. Disconnect the fuel hose (B, **Figure 2**) from the fuel tank. Plug the end of the hose to prevent dirt from entering the hose.
5. Loosen the front and rear carburetor hose clamps (C, **Figure 2**).
6. Pull the carburetor to the left and remove it.
7. If there is fuel in the carburetor, drain it into a suitable container. Dispose of it properly.
8. Remove the carburetor cap, then the throttle valve assembly (A, **Figure 3**).
9. To service the throttle valve assembly, refer to *Throttle Valve and Jet Needle Removal/Inspection/Installation* in this chapter.

NOTE

*If you are not going to remove the jet needle (B, **Figure 3**), slide a piece of hose over it to protect it from damage.*

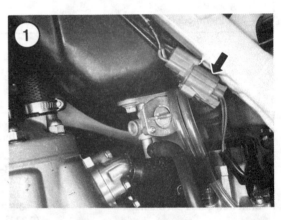

10. Plug the intake manifold and air box openings to prevent dirt and dust from entering the carburetor or air box.

Installation

1. Assemble the jet needle and throttle valve assembly as described in this chapter.

2. Remove all dirt and other residue from the throttle valve and jet needle.

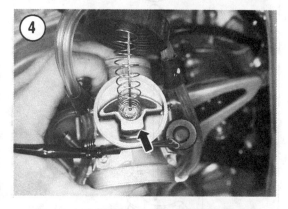

3. Install the throttle valve into the carburetor body as shown in **Figure 4**. Install and tighten the carburetor cap.

4. If necessary, slide the rubber boot (**Figure 5**) down the throttle cable and over the cable adjuster. Make sure the throttle cable is seated correctly in the cable adjuster.

NOTE
After you tighten the carburetor cap, turn and release the throttle grip a few times. The throttle valve must open and close smoothly. If the throttle grip operates roughly, or if the throttle valve does not return smoothly, check the throttle cable, throttle valve and throttle grip for damage or incorrectly installed parts.

5. Remove the covers from the intake manifold and air box. Install the carburetor into the intake manifold, and then into the air box hose boot (**Figure 2**). Align the lug on the carburetor body with the groove in the intake manifold. Tighten both hose clamps securely.

CAUTION
Make sure the air box hose boot did not fold over when you installed the carburetor. If so, dirt will enter the carburetor at this point and cause rapid carburetor bore, throttle valve and engine wear.

6. Tighten the carburetor cap (A, **Figure 2**) securely.

7. Route all of the carburetor vent hoses through the bracket on the rear of the engine, then down and away from the drive chain and shock absorber.

8. On 1998 models, reconnect the powerjet valve electrical connector (**Figure 1**).

9. Reconnect the fuel hose at the carburetor. Secure the hose with its spring clamp.

10. Check the throttle valve operation once again.

11. Turn the fuel valve on, then check the hose and carburetor for leaks.

Throttle Valve and Jet Needle
Removal/Inspection/Installation

Figure 6 shows an exploded view of the throttle valve assembly.

1. Clean the carburetor cap of all dirt and other debris.

2. Loosen, but do not remove, the carburetor cap (A, **Figure 2**).

3. Loosen both carburetor hose clamp screws (C, **Figure 2**), then pivot the carburetor toward the left side.

4. Unscrew the carburetor cap and remove the throttle valve assembly (A, **Figure 3**).

5. Compress the spring, then push down and disconnect the throttle cable (**Figure 7**) from the slot in the cable holder. Remove the throttle valve assembly.

6. Remove the cable lock collar and spring (**Figure 8**) from the throttle cable.

7. Loosen and remove the cable holder (**Figure 9**).

8. Remove the jet needle (**Figure 10**).

9. To remove the E-clip:

    a. Record the jet needle's clip position.

    b. Install the E-clip into one of the jet needle clip grooves. **Table 1** lists the standard clip position.

    c. Drop the jet needle (**Figure 10**) into the throttle valve.

10. Replace the cable holder if damaged.

11. Replace the cable lock collar if damaged.

12. Replace the carburetor cap gasket if it is missing or damaged.

NOTE
*The cable lock collar has an inner tab that fits into a notch in the cable holder. This engagement locks the cable holder in place when installing the throttle cable. **Figure 11** shows these parts assembled with the cable holder removed for clarity. To ensure that this alignment is made during assembly, make a mark on the outside of the cable lock collar that aligns with its inner tab (**Figure 12**). When you install the cable lock collar in Step 13, align the mark with the notch in the cable holder.*

13. Install the cable lock collar into the end of the spring. Install the spring over the throttle cable and seat it into the cap's inner shoulder (**Figure 8**).

14. Compress the spring and then install the throttle cable and into the notch in the cable holder. Release the spring so the tab on the cable lock collar seats into the notch in the cable holder (**Figure 13**).

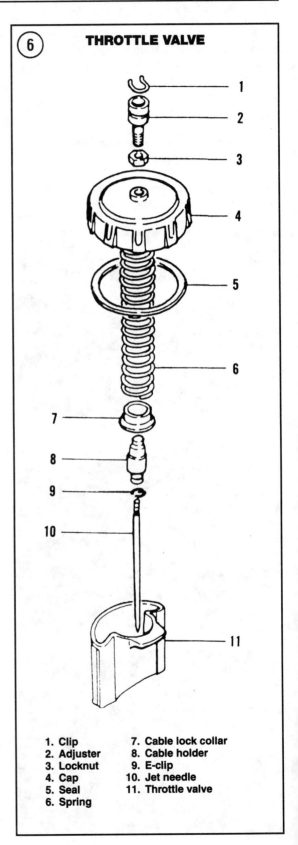

⑥ **THROTTLE VALVE**

1. Clip	7. Cable lock collar
2. Adjuster	8. Cable holder
3. Locknut	9. E-clip
4. Cap	10. Jet needle
5. Seal	11. Throttle valve
6. Spring	

15. Open and close the throttle grip a few times to make sure the cable does not pop out of the throttle valve.

16. Install the throttle valve into the carburetor body as shown in **Figure 4**. Install and tighten the carburetor cap.

17. If necessary, slide the rubber boot (**Figure 5**) down the throttle cable and over the cable adjuster. Make sure the throttle cable is seated correctly in the cable adjuster.

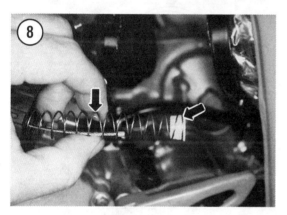

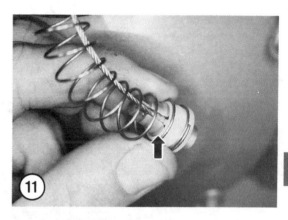

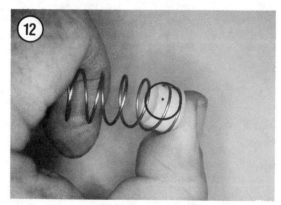

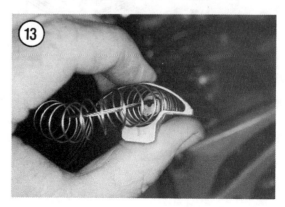

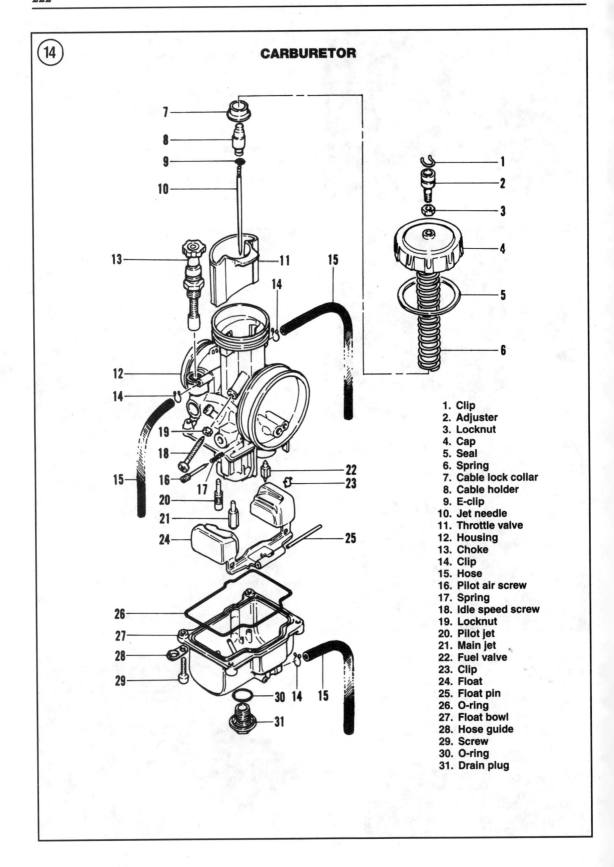

CARBURETOR

1. Clip
2. Adjuster
3. Locknut
4. Cap
5. Seal
6. Spring
7. Cable lock collar
8. Cable holder
9. E-clip
10. Jet needle
11. Throttle valve
12. Housing
13. Choke
14. Clip
15. Hose
16. Pilot air screw
17. Spring
18. Idle speed screw
19. Locknut
20. Pilot jet
21. Main jet
22. Fuel valve
23. Clip
24. Float
25. Float pin
26. O-ring
27. Float bowl
28. Hose guide
29. Screw
30. O-ring
31. Drain plug

NOTE

After you tighten the carburetor cap, turn and release the throttle grip a few times. The throttle valve must open and close smoothly. If the throttle grip operates roughly, or if the throttle valve does not return smoothly, check the throttle cable, throttle valve and throttle grip for damage or incorrectly installed parts.

18. Turn the carburetor and aligns its body lug with the groove in the intake manifold. Tighten both hose clamps securely.

19. Tighten the carburetor cap (A, **Figure 2**) securely.

Disassembly

Refer to **Figure 14**.

1. Remove the carburetor as described in this chapter.

2. Label and then disconnect the hoses from the nozzles on the carburetor body and float bowl.

3. On 1998 models, loosen and remove the powerjet assembly (**Figure 15**).

4. Remove the idle speed screw and spring (A, **Figure 16**).

5. Lightly seat the pilot air screw, counting the number of turns required for reassembly reference. Back the screw out and remove it from the carburetor (B, **Figure 16**).

6. Loosen and remove the choke valve assembly (C, **Figure 16**).

NOTE

Before removing the float bowl screws, record the position and direction of the vent hose brackets mounted on the bottom of the float bowl. See A, Figure 17.

7. Remove the float bowl screws and float bowl (B. **Figure 17**).

CAUTION

The float pin removed in Step 8 should be a slip fit. However, burrs on the pin or pedestal holes may make pin removal difficult. If the pin is tight, do not apply too much force when trying to remove it or you may damage one of the pedestals. Doing so would require replacement of the carburetor body.

8. Remove the float pin (**Figure 18**) and float assembly (**Figure 19**). Remove the fuel valve attached to the bottom of the float.

NOTE

Before removing the pilot jet in Step 9, make sure the screwdriver fits the groove in the top of the jet securely. If the screwdriver tip is too small, it can break the top of the brass jet, making removal very difficult. A good

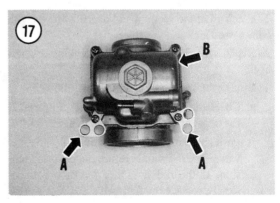

screwdriver to use when removing the pilot jets installed in Keihin PWK carburetors is the Craftsman 3/16 × 4 slotted screwdriver. You will have to grind the sides of the screwdriver to fit into the carburetor jet channel, but its tip is wide and thick enough to grip the jet securely without damaging it.

9. Remove the pilot jet (A, **Figure 20**).
10. Remove the main jet (B, **Figure 20**).

NOTE
*The needle jet (**Figure 21**) is pressed into the carburetor housing and cannot be removed.*

11. Clean and inspect all parts as described in this chapter.

Cleaning and Inspection

You can purchase a gasket kit to replace all of the carburetor's rubber parts. O-rings become hardened after prolonged use and heat, and lose their ability to seal properly.
1. Initially clean all parts in a petroleum-based solvent, then clean in hot soapy water. Rinse parts with cold water and blow dry with compressed air.

CAUTION
Do not clean the float or any of the O-rings in a carburetor cleaner or other solution that can damage them.

CAUTION
*Do **not** use wire or drill bits to clean the jets as minor gouges in a jet can alter flow rate and change the air/fuel mixture.*

2. Clean all of the vacuum and overflow tubes with compressed air.
3. Replace the float bowl O-ring if leaking or damaged.
4. Inspect the fuel valve assembly as follows:
   a. Check the end of the fuel valve (A, **Figure 22**) for steps, excessive wear or damage.
   b. Push and release the rod in the end of the fuel valve. The rod should return under spring tension. If the rod does not return or returns slowly, replace the fuel valve.

CAUTION
*The fuel valve seat (B, **Figure 22**) is an integral part of the carburetor body. Any attempt to remove or repair the seat will permanently damage the carburetor body.*

   c. Check the fuel valve seat (B, **Figure 22**) in the carburetor for steps, uneven wear or other damage. Because the fuel valve seat is an integral part of the carburetor body, the carburetor body must be replaced if the fuel valve seat is excessively worn or damaged.

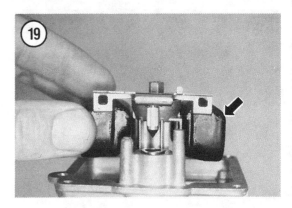

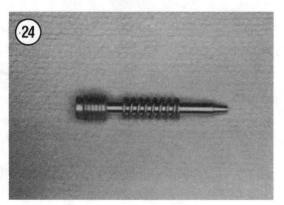

NOTE
A worn or damaged fuel valve and seat assembly will cause a rich fuel mixture and/or carburetor flooding.

5. Inspect the float (**Figure 23**) for deterioration or damage. Check the float by submersing it in a container of water. If the float absorbs water, replace it.

6. Inspect the pilot air screw tip (**Figure 24**) for damage. Check the spring for stretched coils or other damage.

7. Inspect the idle adjust screw and spring for damage.

8. Inspect thespeed knob assembly (**Figure 25**). Check the spring and choke knob for severe wear or damage. Hold the plastic body and operate the choke knob by hand. The choke is damaged if it does not move smoothly or if it fails to lock into position.

9. Make sure all openings in the carburetor body are clear. Clean with compressed air.

10. Check the float bowl for fuel sediment and other debris. Clean thoroughly.

8

11. If necessary, test the powerjet assembly (**Figure 26**) as described under *Powerjet Valve Testing* in Chapter Nine.

NOTE
A faulty powerjet valve can cause hard starting (valve does not open correctly) and poor low speed performance (valve does not open fully).

12. Replace the O-ring on the end of the powerjet valve if cracked or damaged.

13. On powerjet carburetors, make sure the joining carburetor and float bowl fuel passages (**Figure 27**) are clear.

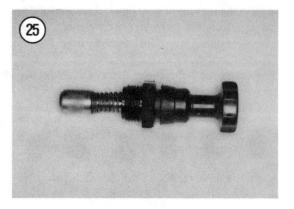

Assembly

Refer to **Figure 14** when assembling the carburetor body.

1. Install the main jet (B, **Figure 20**).
2. Install the pilot jet (A, **Figure 20**).
3. Hook the fuel valve onto the float (**Figure 19**), then install the fuel valve into the fuel valve seat (**Figure 19**).
4. Install the float pin through both carburetor pedestals and float (**Figure 18**).
5. Check the float level as described under *Float Level Adjustments* in this chapter.
6. Install the float bowl (B, **Figure 17**) and O-ring, then secure it with its mounting screws. Install the vent hose brackets (A, **Figure 17**) in their original mounting position.
7. Install and tighten the choke (C, **Figure 16**).
8. Install the pilot air screw (B, **Figure 17**) and lightly seat it. Back the screw out the number of turns recorded during removal or set it to the specification listed in **Table 1** for your model.
9. Install the idle speed screw and spring (A, **Figure 16**).
10. On 1998 models, install and tighten the powerjet valve. Route the valve's wiring harness through the bracket as shown in **Figure 15**.
11. Reconnect the vacuum and overflow hoses onto the carburetor body and float bowl nozzles. See **Figure 28**, typical.
12. Install the carburetor as described in this chapter.
13. Perform the *Carburetor Idle Speed and Mixture* in Chapter Three.

FLOAT HEIGHT ADJUSTMENT

The fuel valve and float maintain a constant fuel level in the carburetor float bowl. Because the float height affects the fuel mixture throughout the engine's operating range, maintain the height within factory specifications.

1. Remove the carburetor as described in this chapter.

> *NOTE*
> *Before removing the float bowl screws, record the position and direction of the vent hose brackets mounted on the bottom of the float bowl. See A, Figure 17.*

2. Remove the float bowl screws and float bowl (B, **Figure 17**).

3. Hold the carburetor so the fuel valve just touches the float arm. At the same time, fully seat the fuel valve into the fuel valve seat. Then measure the distance from the float bowl gasket surface to the float (**Figure 29**) using a float level gauge, ruler or vernier caliper. See **Table 1** for the correct float level. Note the following:

   a. If the float level is incorrect, perform Step 4.

   b. If the float level is correct, go to Step 5.

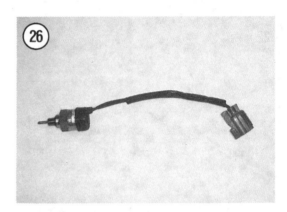

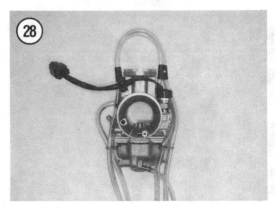

4. Adjust the float height as follows:

CAUTION

The float pin should be a slip fit. However, burrs on the pin or pedestal arm holes may make pin removal difficult. If the pin is tight, do not apply too much force when trying to remove it or you may crack or break one of the pedestal arms. Doing so would require replacement of the carburetor body.

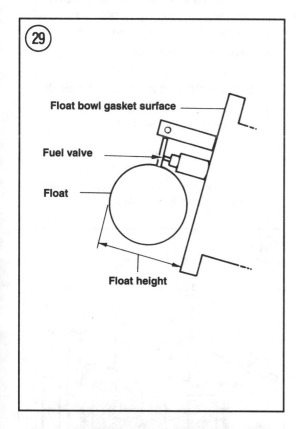

Float bowl gasket surface

Fuel valve

Float

Float height

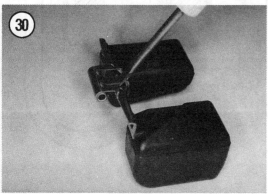

a. Remove the float pin (**Figure 18**) and float assembly (**Figure 19**).
b. Remove the fuel valve attached to the bottom of the float (**Figure 19**).
c. Bend the float arm with a screwdriver (**Figure 30**) to adjust the float height.
d. Hook the fuel valve onto the float (**Figure 19**), then install the fuel valve into the fuel valve seat (**Figure 19**).
e. Install the float pin through both carburetor pedestal arms and float (**Figure 18**).
f. Recheck the float height and readjust the float if necessary. Repeat until the float height is correct.

5. Install the float bowl (B, **Figure 17**) and O-ring. Secure the bowl with its mounting screws. Install the vent hose brackets (A, **Figure 17**) in their original mounting position.

6. Install the carburetor as described in this chapter.

CARBURETOR FUEL LEVEL ADJUSTMENT

The fuel level in the float bowl is critical to engine performance. The fuel flow rate from the float bowl up to the carburetor bore depends not only on the vacuum in the throttle bore and the size of the jets, but also upon the fuel level in the carburetor. Kawasaki gives a specification of the actual *fuel level*, measured from the top edge of the float bowl with the carburetor mounted on the bike (**Figure 31**).

The fuel level measurement is more useful than a simple float height measurement because the actual fuel level can vary from bike to bike, even when their floats are set at the same height. To check the fuel level, you will need the Kawasaki fuel level gauge (part No. 57001-122). This tool consists of a special fitting that screws into the bottom of the carburetor and a clear tube gauge. The fuel level is adjusted by bending the float arm tang.

WARNING
Some fuel will spill from the carburetor when performing this procedure. Because gasoline is an extremely flammable and explosive petroleum product, perform this procedure away from all open flames and sparks. Do not smoke or allow someone who is smoking in the work area. Always work

8

in a well-ventilated area. Wipe up fuel spills immediately.

1. Turn the fuel valve off and remove the carburetor from the bike, so it can be held level. Leave the fuel line connected to the fuel tank and carburetor.
2. Remove the drain plug (**Figure 32**) from the bottom of the float bowl and install the Kawasaki fuel level gauge onto the carburetor (**Figure 31**).
3. Hold the clear tube against the carburetor body so the 0 line on the tube is several millimeters higher than the bottom edge on the carburetor housing.
4. Turn the fuel valve on. Do not lower the tube until the fuel level in the tube settles.
5. When the fuel level in the tube settles, slowly lower the tube until the 0 line is even with the bottom edge of the carburetor housing (**Figure 31**). Read the level in the tube and compare it to the fuel level specification in **Table 1** for your model.

> *NOTE*
> *Do not lower the 0 line on the tube below the bottom edge on the carburetor housing and then raise it again, as this will cause the level to be higher than the actual fuel level in the carburetor. If the tube is lowered too far, turn the fuel valve off and pour the fuel from the tube into a suitable fuel container. Repeat this procedure.*

6. If the fuel level is incorrect, adjust the float/arm height setting as described under *Float Level Adjustment* in this chapter.

> *NOTE*
> *Increasing the float height lowers the fuel level. Decreasing the float height raises the fuel level.*

7. Repeat until the fuel level is correct.
8. Turn the fuel valve off. Lower the tube and drain the fuel into a suitable fuel container. Remove the fuel gauge and reinstall the drain plug and its O-ring into the carburetor. Tighten the drain plug securely.
9. Reinstall the carburetor as described in this chapter.

CARBURETOR REJETTING

Changes in altitude, temperature, humidity and track conditions can noticeably affect engine performance. This also includes changes that affect the engine's ability to breathe—jetting changes, different exhaust pipes or air filters. To obtain maximum performance from your Kawasaki, jetting changes may be necessary. However, before you change the jetting, make sure the engine is in good running condition. For example, if your bike is now running poorly under the same weather, altitude and track conditions where it once ran properly, it is unlikely the carburetor jetting is at fault. Attempting to tune the engine by rejetting the carburetor would only complicate matters.

If your bike shows evidence of one of the following conditions, rejetting may be necessary:

  a. Poor acceleration (too rich).
  b. Excessive exhaust smoke (too rich).
  c. Fouling spark plugs (too rich).
  d. Engine misfires at low speeds (too rich).
  e. Erratic acceleration (too lean).
  f. Ping or rattle (too lean).

> *NOTE*
> *Old gasoline or gasoline with a too low octane rating can also cause engine pinging. See Chapter Three.*

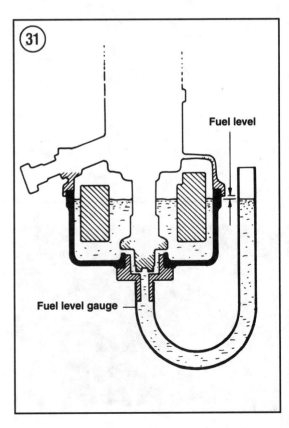

Fuel level

Fuel level gauge

g. Running hot (too lean).

h. The engine accelerates properly but misfires at high speed.

Before checking the carburetor for one of the previously listed operating conditions, consider the following tuning and adjustment variables:

a. Carburetor float level—an incorrect float level will cause the engine to run rich or lean.

b. Air filter element—a dirty air filter element will cause the engine to run rich. Attempting to jet the engine with a dirty air filter element will only complicate engine tuning.

c. Ignition timing—incorrect ignition will change the engine's performance.

d. Exhaust flow—a plugged exhaust pipe silencer, or a heavily carbonized engine top and exhaust valve system will reduce engine performance.

If the previously mentioned service items are okay, the carburetor may require rejetting if any of the following conditions hold true:

a. An aftermarket reed valve is being used.

b. An aftermarket exhaust system is being used.

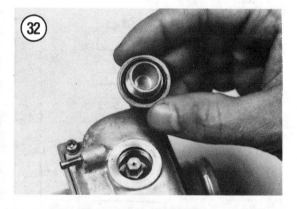

c. You have modified any of the top end parts (piston, porting, compression ratio, etc.).

d. You changed the fuel oil mixture from the standard 32:1 ratio to a different ratio.

e. The motorcycle is operating in a much higher or lower altitude, in hotter or colder temperature, or in a wetter or drier climate than in the past.

f. You are operating the motorcycle at considerably higher speeds than before (faster track conditions) and changing to a colder spark plug does not solve the problem.

g. A previous owner changed the jetting or the needle positions in your motorcycle. See **Table 1** for the original factory carburetor jetting and jet needle clip specifications.

Carburetor Variables

The following carburetor parts may be changed when rejetting the carburetor.

Pilot jet

The pilot jet (A, **Figure 20**) and pilot air screw (**Figure 33**) control the fuel mixture from closed throttle to about 1/8 throttle. Note the following:

a. As the pilot jet numbers increase, the fuel mixture gets richer.

b. Turning the pilot air screw clockwise richens the mixture.

c. Turning the pilot air screw counterclockwise leans the mixture.

Throttle valve

The throttle valve cutaway (A, **Figure 34**) affects airflow at small throttle openings. The smaller the cutaway, the richer the fuel mixture. The larger the cutaway, the leaner the fuel mixture. The Keihin PWK throttle valves are identified by their cutaway sizes. A larger size number results in a leaner mixture. For example 0 is rich and 9.0 is lean. The cutaway numbers are in millimeters and are listed as follows: 0 , 3.0, 4.0, 5.0, 6.0, 7.0, 8.0 and 9.0. See **Table 1** for stock throttle valve cutaway sizes.

Jet needle

The jet needle (B, **Figure 34**) controls the mixture at medium speeds from approximately 1/8 to 3/4 throttle. The Keihin jet needles used in the PWK carburetors have three different metering points. **Figure 35** shows the metering points. The top of the needle has five evenly spaced clip grooves (**Figure 35**). The bottom half of the needle is tapered; this portion extends into the needle jet. While the jet needle is fixed into position by the clip, fuel cannot flow through the space between the needle jet and jet needle until the throttle valve is raised approximately 1/8 open. As the throttle valve is raised, the jet needles tapered portion moves out of the needle jet. The grooves permit adjustment of the mixture ratio. If the clip is raised (thus dropping the needle deeper into the jet), the mixture will be leaner; lowering the clip (raising the needle) will result in a rich mixture.

Needle jet

On the Keihin carburetors described in this manual, the needle jet is an integral part of the carburetor housing and cannot be changed or adjusted.

Main jet

The main jet (B, **Figure 20**) controls the mixture from 3/4 to full throttle, and has some effect at lesser throttle openings. Each main jet is stamped with a number. Larger numbers provide a richer mixture, smaller numbers a leaner mixture. You can replace the main jet through the float bowl drain bolt hole.

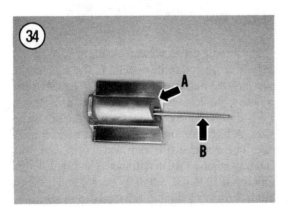

Rejetting

CAUTION
Serious engine damage can occur in a matter of seconds when running the engine with a main jet that is too small. When rejetting your Kawasaki, always start too rich and progress toward a leaner mixture, one jet size at a time. In addition, make sure the engine is at normal operating temperature when checking jetting. If you attempt to jet an engine that is not yet at operating temperature, the mixture will be incorrect once the engine does reach normal operating temperature.

When jetting the carburetor, perform the procedures in Steps 1-3 to ensure accurate results. Note the following before carburetor jetting:

    a. Referring to **Figure 36**, note the different jetting circuits and how they overlap with each

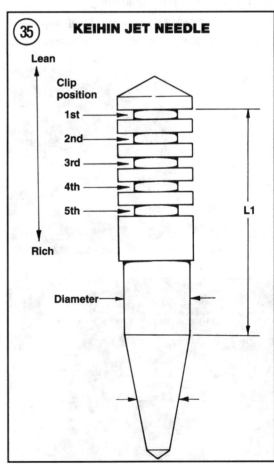

other in relation to the different throttle positions. Determine the throttle position at which the adjustment should be made.

b. An accurate way to determine throttle position is to mark the throttle housing and throttle grip with tape and a marking pen (**Figure 37**). Use the mark on the throttle grip as a pointer to align with the different throttle positions marked on the throttle housing when riding the bike. Make four marks on the throttle housing to represent closed, 1/4, 3/4 and full open throttle positions.

c. When checking the jetting, run the bike on a track or private road where you can safely run at top speed. Keep accurate records as to weather, altitude and track conditions.

d. Check the jetting in the following order: pilot air screw, main jet and jet needle.

1. Adjust the pilot air screw (if so equipped) and engine idle as described in Chapter Three.

2. Because the main jet controls the mixture from 3/4 to full throttle, run the bike at full throttle for a short distance. Stop the engine with the engine stop switch while the bike is running under full throttle. Pull the clutch lever in and coast to a stop. Remove and examine the spark plug after each test. The insulator must be a light tan color. If the insulator is soot black, the mixture is too rich; install a smaller main jet as described in this chapter. If the insulator is white, or blistered, the mixture is too lean; install a larger main jet. See **Figure 38**. Refer to *Main Jet Replacement* in this chapter.

3. Using the marked throttle housing, repeat the jetting check in Step 2 at different throttle positions. You may find that the full open throttle position is correct but that the 1/4 to 3/4 operating range is too rich or too lean. Refer to *Carburetor Variables*. If changing the jet needle clip position is necessary, refer to *Jet Needle Adjustment* in this chapter.

Main Jet Replacement

Refer to **Table 1** for standard main jet sizes.

> *WARNING*
> *If you are taking spark plug readings, the engine will be HOT! Use caution as the fuel in the float bowl will spill out when you remove the main jet cover from the bottom of the float bowl. Have a fire extinguisher and an assistant standing by when performing this procedure.*

> *WARNING*
> *Some fuel will spill from the carburetor when performing this procedure. Because gasoline is extremely flammable and explosive, perform this procedure away from all open flames and sparks. Do not smoke or allow someone who is smoking in the work*

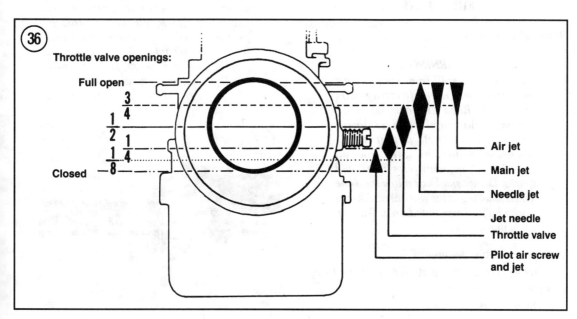

(36) Throttle valve openings:

Full open
3/4
1/2
1/4
1/8
Closed

Air jet
Main jet
Needle jet
Jet needle
Throttle valve
Pilot air screw and jet

area. Always work in a well-ventilated area. Wipe up any spills immediately.

1. If you have never removed the main jet with the carburetor mounted on the bike, practice removing the main jet while the engine is cold. When taking spark plug readings and making jetting changes, the engine will be hot.
2. Turn the fuel shutoff valve to the OFF position.
3. Loosen the drain plug from the bottom of the float bowl and drain out all fuel in the bowl.
4. The main jet is directly under the plug (**Figure 39**). Remove the main jet and replace it with a different one. Remember, change only one jet size at a time.
5. Install and tighten the drain plug securely.

Jet Needle Adjustment

See **Table 1** for the standard jet needle size for your model.
1. Remove the throttle valve and jet needle as described in this chapter.
2. Note the position of the clip. Raising the needle (lowering the clip) will enrich the mixture during mid-throttle opening, while lowering it (raising the clip) will lean the mixture. Refer to **Figure 35**.
3. Reverse the proceeding steps to install the jet needle.

FUEL TANK

Removal/Installation

WARNING

Some fuel may spill from the fuel tank and hose when performing this procedure. Because gasoline is an extremely flammable and explosive petroleum product, perform this procedure outside and away from all open flames (including pilot lights) and sparks. Do not smoke or allow someone who is smoking in the work area. Always work in a well-ventilated area. Wipe up spills immediately.

1. Support the bike securely.
2. Remove the following parts as described in Chapter Fifteen:
   a. Side covers.

b. Seat.
c. Radiator covers.
3. Turn the fuel valve off and disconnect the fuel line (**Figure 40**) from the fuel tank.
4. Pull the fuel tank vent tube (A, **Figure 41**) free from the steering head area.
5. Remove the fuel tank mounting bolt (B, **Figure 41**).
6. Disconnect the rubber strap (C, **Figure 41**) and remove the fuel tank (D).
7. Check for loose, missing or damaged fuel tank brackets and rubber dampers. Tighten or replace parts as required.
8. Reverse these steps to install the fuel tank while noting the following:
   a. When installing the fuel tank, check the throttle cable routing at the same time. If the throttle cable is pulled toward the center of the bike, it can become damaged when the fuel tank is installed over it.
   b. Check for fuel leaks.

FUEL VALVE

Removal/Installation

WARNING

Some fuel may spill from the fuel tank and hose when performing this procedure. Because gasoline is extremely flammable and explosive, perform this procedure outside and away from all open flames (including pilot lights) and sparks. Do not smoke or allow someone who is smoking in the work area. Always work in a

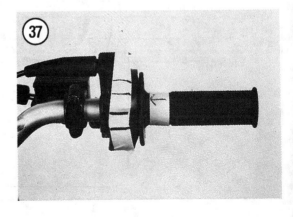

SPARK PLUG CONDITIONS

NORMAL USE

OIL FOULED

CARBON FOULED

OVERHEATED

GAP BRIDGED

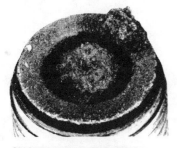

SUSTAINED PREIGNITION

WORN OUT

8

well-ventilated area. Wipe up spills immediately.

1. Remove the fuel tank as described in this chapter.
2. Drain the fuel into a fuel storage container.
3. Remove the bolts and washers and remove the fuel shutoff valve.
4. Remove the two handle screws and disassemble the valve (**Figure 42**). Clean all parts in solvent with a small soft brush, then dry. Check the small O-ring within the valve and the O-ring gasket; replace if they are deteriorated or hard. Inspect the wave spring and replace if weak or damaged.
5. Reassemble the valve and install it on the tank. Do not forget to install the O-ring between the valve and tank.
6. Install the fuel tank as described in this chapter.
7. Add a small amount of fuel to the tank and check for leaks.

THROTTLE CABLE REPLACEMENT

1. Support the bike on a workstand.
2. Remove the fuel tank as described in this chapter.

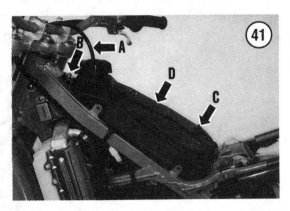

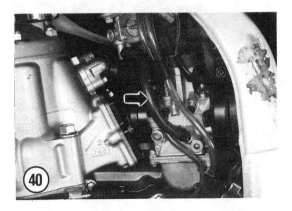

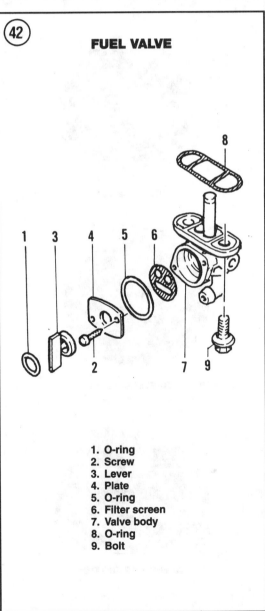

FUEL VALVE

1. O-ring
2. Screw
3. Lever
4. Plate
5. O-ring
6. Filter screen
7. Valve body
8. O-ring
9. Bolt

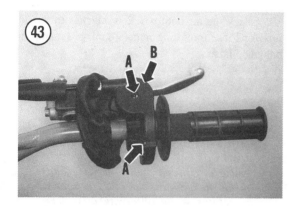

3. Disconnect the throttle cable from the throttle grip as follows:

    a. Pull the rubber cover away from the cable adjuster at the handlebar.

    b. Remove the two screws (A, **Figure 43**) and cable cover (B).

    c. Remove the wheel and collar (A, **Figure 44**).

    d. Loosen the cable adjuster locknut and unscrew the adjuster from the throttle housing.

    c. Remove the throttle housing cover screws and cover.

4. Remove the throttle valve as described under *Throttle Valve and Jet Needle Removal/Inspection/Installation* in this chapter.

5. Remove the U-clip (**Figure 45**) securing the throttle cable to the cap adjuster, then slide the cap off the throttle cable.

6. Disconnect the throttle cable from any clips holding the cable to the frame.

7. Remove the throttle cable.

8. Install the new throttle cable through the frame, routing it from the handlebar to carburetor. Secure the cable with its frame clips.

9. Lubricate the new cable as described in Chapter Three. Clean excessive cable lube from the bottom of the cable.

10. Slide the new cable through the cable adjuster on the carburetor cap (**Figure 45**). Secure the cable to the adjuster with the U-clip (**Figure 45**). Tug on the cable to make sure the cable is secured properly.

11. Install the throttle valve assembly (**Figure 46**) as described under *Throttle Valve and Jet Needle Removal/Inspection/Installation* in this chapter.

12. Reconnect the throttle cable to the throttle grip as follows:

    a. Screw the new cable adjuster (B, **Figure 44**) all the way into the throttle housing.

    b. Apply a small amount of grease onto the end of the throttle cable.

    c. Reconnect the cable end to the hole in the throttle grip. Install the wheel and collar, routing the cable around the roller as shown in **Figure 47**.

    d. Install the cover (B, **Figure 43**) and secure it with the two screws (A).

    e. Install the rubber cover (A, **Figure 48**) over the throttle housing.

    f. Slide back the cable adjuster cover (B, **Figure 48**) and adjust the throttle cable free play as

8

described in Chapter Three. Tighten the cable adjuster locknut securely.

g. Pull the cover (B, **Figure 48**) over the cable adjuster.

13. Install the fuel tank as described in this chapter.

14. Operate the throttle lever and make sure the carburetor cable, twist grip and throttle valve are operating correctly. If throttle operation is sluggish, check that you attached the cable correctly and that there are no tight bends in the cable.

AIR BOX

Removal/Installation

1. Support the bike on a stand.
2. Remove the silencer (A, **Figure 49**).
3. Remove the igniter (Chapter Nine).
4. Remove the seat and side covers (Chapter Fifteen).
5. Loosen the hose clamp securing the carburetor to the air box boot.
6. Remove the top subframe mounting bolts (B, **Figure 49**).
7. Loosen the lower subframe mounting bolts (C, **Figure 49**) and pivot the subframe assembly down.
8. Remove the bolts securing the air box to the sub-frame. Remove the air box (D, **Figure 49**).
9. Check the air boot to make sure that it is sealing properly and that no dirt is passing through the air filter. If there is dirt inside the air boot, check the boot and air filter for damage. If necessary, remove the air filter (Chapter Three) and clean the air box and boot thoroughly.

10. Check the air boot where it attaches to the air box for loose mounting nuts, a damaged clamp or damaged hose.

WARNING
Adequate ventilation must be provided when using a weatherstrip adhesive in Step 11. Do not use where there are sparks or any open flame. Vapor can cause flash fires as well as dizziness and headaches. Follow the manufacturer's directions while observing all safety precautions.

11. If you removed the air boot from the air box, apply a weatherstrip adhesive to the boot's sealing surface before installing the air boot.

12. Install the air box by reversing the preceding removal steps. Tighten the subframe mounting bolts as specified in **Table 2**.

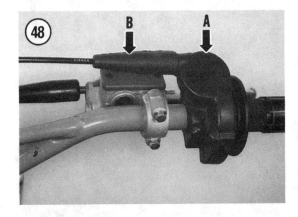

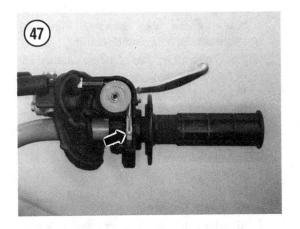

Table 1 CARBURETOR SPECIFICATIONS

Carburetor	Keihin
Carburetor type	PWK38
Jet needle	
1992	NOLB
1993	NOZF
1994	NIEE
1995	
U.S. models	NIEE
All other models	NOZE
1996	NIED
1997	N3WF
1998	NOZG
Jet needle clip position	
1992-1994	3rd
1995-1996	4th
1997-on	3rd
Main air jet	
1992-1993	200
1994-on	Not specified
Main jet	
1992-1993	162
1994	165
1995-1996	
U.S. models	162
All other models	160
1997	165
1998	158
Pilot air screw turns out	
1992-1993	1 1/2
1994-1997	2
1998	1 1/2
Pilot jet	
1992	58
1993	50
1994-on	45
Throttle valve cutaway	No. 7
Fuel level	
1992-1993	2 mm (0.078 in.) above mating surface 0 mm below mating surface
1994-on	0 - 1 mm (0 - 0.4 in.)
Float level	
1992-1993	14-18 mm (0.551-0.709 in.)
1994-on	14-18 mm (0.551-0.709 in.)

8

Table 2 TORQUE SPECIFICATIONS

	N•m	ft.-lb.
Sub-frame mounting bolts		
1992-1993	26	19
1994-on	29	21

IGNITION SYSTEM

This chapter describes service procedures for the ignition system.

Ignition system test specifications are in **Table 1** and **Table 2**. Both tables are located at the end of the chapter.

COMPONENT TESTING

Use an ohmmeter to test the ignition coil, stator plate coils, engine stop switch and wiring.

Resistance Testing

Kawasaki lists resistance specifications for the ignition coil and stator plate coils. See **Table 1**. By comparing your test readings with specifications in **Table 1**, you can determine the condition of the part.

Perform resistance tests after disconnecting the component from the main wiring harness. You do not have to remove the part to test it, but instead, locate its wiring connectors and disconnect them.

When using an ohmmeter, follow the manufacturer's instruction manual, while keeping the following guidelines in mind:

1. Make sure the test leads are connected properly. **Table 1** lists the test leads and wire connections for each test.
2. Make all ohmmeter readings when the engine is cold (ambient temperature of 68° F [20° C]). Read-

ings taken on a hot engine will show increased resistance and may lead you to replace parts that are not faulty without solving the basic problem.

> *NOTE*
> *With the exception of certain semiconductors, the resistance of a conductor increases as its temperature increases. In general, the resistance of a conductor increases 10 ohms per each degree of temperature increase. The opposite is true if the temperature drops. To ensure accurate testing, Kawasaki performs their tests at a controlled temperature of 68° F (20° C) and base their specifications on tests performed at this temperature.*

3. When switching to another ohmmeter scale on a analog ohmmeter, always cross the test leads and zero the needle to assure a correct reading.

CAPACITOR DISCHARGE IGNITION

All models are equipped with a capacitor discharge ignition (CDI) system. This solid state system, unlike conventional ignition system, uses no contact breaker points or other moving parts.

Alternating current from the magneto is rectified and used to charge the capacitor. As the piston approaches the firing position, a pulse from the pulse coil is rectified, shaped, and used to trigger the silicone controlled rectifier. This in turn allows the capacitor to discharge quickly into the primary side of the high-voltage ignition coil where it is increased, or stepped up, to a high enough voltage to jump the gap between the spark plug electrodes.

CDI Cautions

When servicing the CDI system, note the following:

1. Keep all connections between the various units clean and tight. Be sure that the wiring connectors are pushed together firmly (**Figure 1**).
2. Never disconnect any of the electrical connections while the engine is running. Otherwise, excessive voltage may damage the coils or igniter unit.
3. When kicking the engine over with the spark plug removed, make sure the spark plug is installed in the plug cap and grounded against the cylinder head (**Figure 2**). If not, excessive resistance may damage the igniter unit.
4. The igniter is mounted in a rubber vibration isolator or on rubber dampers. Make sure that the

igniter is mounted correctly. Handle the igniter unit carefully. The igniter unit is a sealed unit. Do not attempt to open it as this will cause permanent damage.

CDI Troubleshooting

Refer to *Ignition System* in Chapter Two for step-by-step troubleshooting procedures.

FLYWHEEL

Special Tools

You will two special tools to remove and install the flywheel:
1. Flywheel holder—This tool is used to hold the flywheel when removing and installing the flywheel nut. The Kawasaki flywheel holder part No. 57001-1313 is shown at A, **Figure 3**.

> *NOTE*
> *An impact wrench and socket can also be used to remove the flywheel nut. However, a flywheel holder is required to hold the flywheel when tightening the nut during reassembly.*

2. Flywheel puller—A flywheel puller is required to remove the flywheel from the crankshaft. Use the Kawasaki flywheel puller (part No. 57001-1313) or the Motion Pro flywheel puller (part No. 08-026). See B, **Figure 3**.

Removal

1. Place the bike on a workstand.
2. Remove the shift pedal and the flywheel cover (**Figure 4**).
3. Remove the two pickup coil screws and move the pickup coil (**Figure 5**) away from the flywheel. Do not disconnect the pickup coil wires.
4. Wipe the flywheel with a rag. Secure the flywheel with a flywheel holder as shown in A, **Figure 6**.
5. Hold the flywheel with the tool, then loosen and remove the flywheel nut (B, **Figure 6**). Remove the flywheel holder from the flywheel.

> *CAUTION*
> *If the flywheel nut is too tight, the flywheel holder may slip when pressure*

9

is applied to the nut, allowing the flywheel to turn. If the flywheel turns, you may have to remove the flywheel nut with an impact wrench and socket. Do not hold the flywheel with a chain wrench or similar tool as it may damage the flywheel.

CAUTION
Do not pry or hammer on the flywheel when trying to remove it. Do not remove the flywheel with a jaw-type puller. Using this type of tool can damage the flywheel and stator coils and may weaken the flywheel's magnetism. Use the proper type of puller described for your bike. If you do not have a puller, have a dealership remove the flywheel for you.

6. Place a dab of grease onto the end of the flywheel puller center bolt, then thread the puller into the flywheel until it bottoms (**Figure 7**). The flywheel puller has left-hand threads so turn it counterclockwise when installing it into the flywheel.

7. Hold the puller body with a wrench, then turn the center bolt until the flywheel pops free (A, **Figure 8**).

CAUTION
If normal flywheel removal attempts fail, do not exert excessive force against the puller. The threads may strip out of the flywheel causing expensive damage. Take the engine to a dealership and have the flywheel removed.

8. Remove the puller from the flywheel.

9. If necessary, remove the Woodruff key (**Figure 9**) installed in the crankshaft keyway.

NOTE
It will be necessary to remove the stator plate before removing the Woodruff key.

10. If necessary, remove the stator plate as described in this chapter.

Inspection

The flywheel is permanently magnetized and cannot be tested except by substituting a known good flywheel. A flywheel can lose magnetism due to old

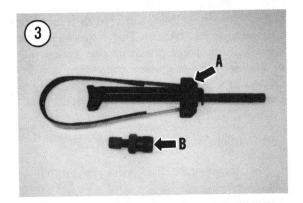

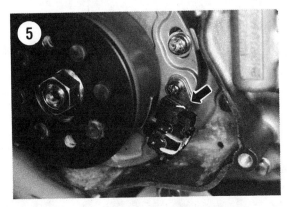

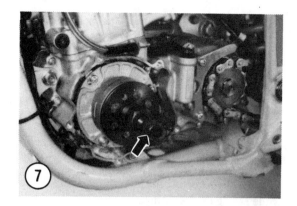

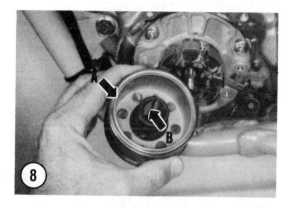

age or a sharp blow. A defective flywheel must be replaced; it cannot be remagnetized.

1. Check the flywheel (**Figure 10**) carefully for cracks or breaks and replace if damaged. Do not attempt to repair a cracked or otherwise damaged flywheel.

2. Check the flywheel weight for loose or missing rivets. Replace the flywheel if there are any loose or damaged rivets.

3. Check the flywheel for any rust or other contamination. Clean with sandpaper and solvent.

4. Inspect the flywheel nut and washer and replace if damaged.

5. Check the flywheel tapered bore and the crankshaft taper for cracks or other abnormal conditions.

6. Inspect the Woodruff key and replace if damaged.

Installation

1. Inspect the flywheel (**Figure 10**) for small bolts, washers or other metal debris that may have been picked up by the magnets.

> *CAUTION*
> *Installing a flywheel with a washer or other metal part inside it will damage the stator coils when the engine is started.*

2. Rotate the crankshaft so the keyway faces straight up (**Figure 9**).

3. If removed, install the Woodruff key (**Figure 9**) into the crankshaft keyway.

> *NOTE*
> *The Woodruff key must be a snug fit in the crankshaft keyway.*

> *CAUTION*
> *Do not lubricate the crankshaft or flywheel tapers with grease. Both surfaces must be dry.*

4. Align the keyway in the flywheel (B, **Figure 8**) with the Woodruff key (**Figure 9**), then install the flywheel onto the crankshaft. Check that the Woodruff key did not pop out when you installed the flywheel.

5. Install the flywheel nut (B, **Figure 6**).

6. Hold the flywheel with a flywheel holder (A, **Figure 6**) and tighten the flywheel nut (B) as specified in **Table 2**. Remove the flywheel holder.

9

7. Install and secure the pickup coil as follows:

  a. Turn the flywheel so its raised pickup surface (**Figure 11**) aligns with the pickup coil's mounting position.

  b. Install the pickup coil (**Figure 5**) and secure it with its mounting screws. Slowly turn the flywheel to make sure there is an air gap between the pickup coil and flywheel pickup surfaces.

NOTE
Kawasaki does not list an air gap measurement for the pickup coil.

8. Replace the flywheel cover gasket if damaged.

9. Install the flywheel cover and its gasket (**Figure 4**) and tighten its mounting bolts securely.

CAUTION
Do not overtighten the flywheel cover bolts in Step 9. The plastic cover will warp and allow dirt to pass through.

10. Install the shift pedal (**Figure 4**).

STATOR COILS

The stator coils are mounted on a plate installed on the left side of the engine. The individual stator coils cannot be replaced separately.

Stator Plate
Removal/Installation

1. Remove the fuel tank (Chapter Eight).

2. Remove the flywheel as described in this chapter.

3. Disconnect the stator plate electrical connectors from the main wiring harness. Pull the wiring harness out along with the rubber grommet from the crankcase and any clips on the frame.

4. Note the timing mark alignment on the stator plate and crankcase (**Figure 12**). You must realign these marks during installation.

NOTE
If you cannot loosen the stator plate mounting screws by hand in Step 5, loosen them with an impact driver and a No. 3 Phillips bit (described in Chapter One). Otherwise, you may

damage the screw heads and be forced to remove the screws with a chisel.

5. Loosen and then remove the stator plate mounting screws (A, **Figure 13**) and stator plate (B). See **Figure 14**.

6. Clean the electrical connectors with contact cleaner. Then check for corroded or damaged connectors. Make sure all of the connector pins are tight.

7. Install by reversing the preceding removal steps, while noting the following.

8. Route the electrical wires along their original path, keeping them away from the exhaust system.

9. Pack the electrical connectors with dielectric grease. Reconnect the connectors, making sure the wiring colors match. Retape the connectors with electrical tape.

10. Realign the stator plate and crankcase timing marks (**Figure 12**).

11. Check the ignition timing as described in this chapter.

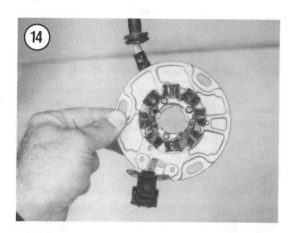

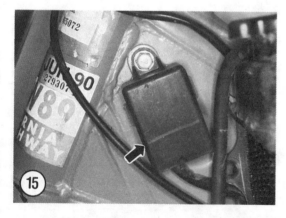

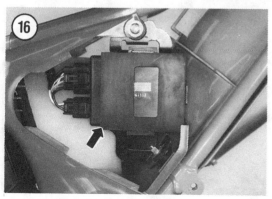

Stator Coil Testing

NOTE
Before testing the stator coils, refer to the information listed under Component Testing in this chapter.

You can test the stator coils without removing the stator plate from the bike.

1. Remove the fuel tank (Chapter Eight).

2. Disconnect the stator plate electrical connectors.

3. Using an ohmmeter, measure the resistance between the stator coil terminals listed in **Table 1**. If the resistance is zero (short circuit) or infinite (open circuit), check the wiring to the coils. Check for loose or damaged connector pins. If the wiring and connector pins are in good condition, replace the stator plate assembly.

NOTE
On all models, replace the stator plate assembly if one coil is bad. You cannot replace the coils separately.

4. Reverse Steps 1 and 2 to complete installation.

IGNITER

The igniter is mounted on the front frame tube on 1992-1997 models (**Figure 15**) or on the air box on 1998 models (**Figure 16**).

Removal/Installation

1. Support the bike on a workstand.

2A. On 1992-1997 models, remove the following components:

    a. Seat and side covers (Chapter Fifteen).

    b. Fuel tank (Chapter Eight).

    c. Radiator covers (Chapter Ten).

2B. On 1998 models, remove the left side cover (Chapter Fifteen).

3. Disconnect the igniter unit electrical connectors, then remove mounting bolts and igniter unit. See **Figure 15** (1992-1997) or **Figure 16** (1998).

4. Reverse the preceding steps to install the igniter unit, while noting the following.

5. Clean the igniter unit connectors with contact cleaner, then pack them with dielectric grease.

Testing

The igniter unit is the brain of your Kawasaki's ignition system. The semiconductors in the igniter that control the ignition spark advance and retard systems, as well as other ignition circuits. Because of the igniter unit's complex circuitry, it is difficult to accurately bench test it with an ohmmeter or other test instrument. Kawasaki specifies the Kawasaki tester (part No. 57001-983) to test the igniter unit. Using a different meter will result in incorrect readings. To isolate the igniter unit as a problem source, test all of the other ignition system components separately. If a problem or faulty part is not found during these tests, the igniter unit is probably faulty. Refer to *Ignition System* in Chapter Two.

IGNITION COIL

The ignition coil is mounted on the upper frame rail (**Figure 17** [1992-1993]) or between the front radiators (**Figure 18** [1994-on]).

Removal/Installation

1. Support the bike on a workstand.
2. Remove the fuel tank (Chapter Eight).
3. Disconnect the spark plug lead from the spark plug.
4. Disconnect the ignition coil electrical connectors.
5. Remove the screws securing the ignition coil to the frame and remove it. See **Figure 17** (1992-1993) or **Figure 18** (1994-on).
6. Install by reversing the preceding removal steps, plus the following.
7. Make sure all electrical connectors are tight and free of corrosion. Make sure the ground wire connection point on the frame is free of rust and corrosion.
8. Pack the electrical connectors with dielectric grease.

Testing

While the following steps measure the resistance of the ignition coil primary and secondary windings, the results are not a guarantee that the ignition coil is in top working order. Also, because the resistance value of the primary windings is very small, you can easily confuse your meter's reading with that taken from a shorted wire (zero resistance reading). If the ignition coil fails one or all of the following tests, take the coil to your local dealership and have them make an operational spark test using an ignition coil tester to see if the coil is producing an adequate spark and continues to do so after it heats up.

> *NOTE*
> *Before testing the ignition coil, refer to the information listed under **Component Testing** in this chapter.*

1. Remove the fuel tank (Chapter Eight).

2. Disconnect the ignition coil electrical connectors from the coil and the spark plug cap from the spark plug. See **Figure 17** (1992-1993) or **Figure 18** (1994-on).

3. Measure the coil primary resistance using an ohmmeter set at R × 1. Measure the resistance between the primary terminal and the coil's mounting flange as shown in **Figure 19**. See **Table 1** for test specifications.

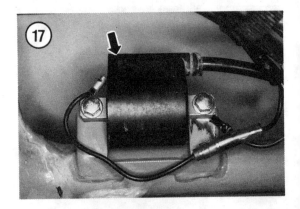

4. Measure the secondary resistance using an ohm-meter set at R × 1,000. Remove the spark plug cap from the coil wire before measuring resistance. Measure the resistance between the secondary lead (spark plug lead) and the coil's mounting flange (**Figure 19**). See **Table 1** for test specifications.

5. If either reading is out of specification, replace the ignition coil or take it to a dealership for further testing.

ENGINE STOP SWITCH

The engine stop switch (**Figure 20**) is mounted on the left side of the handlebar.

Testing

You can quickly isolate the engine stop switch when troubleshooting the ignition system by discon-necting the two engine stop switch leads from the main wiring harness. If there is no spark with the leads connected and a spark after disconnecting them, the engine stop switch is the problem. See *Spark Test* in Chapter Two.

1. Remove the fuel tank (Chapter Eight).

2. Disconnect the engine stop switch connector ter-minals.

3. Use an ohmmeter set at R × 1 and connect the two leads of the ohmmeter to the two electrical wires of the switch.

4. Push the stop switch button (**Figure 20**)—if the switch is good there will be continuity.

5. If there is no continuity the switch is faulty and must be replaced.

6. Remove the screw securing the switch (**Figure 20**) to the handlebar and remove the switch. Reverse to install a new switch, making sure to route the switch wiring harness along its original path.

IGNITION TIMING

The stator plate is scribed with three timing marks (**Figure 12**). The marks provide reference points if you advance or retard the ignition timing to better suit different riding conditions.

1. Support the bike on a workstand.

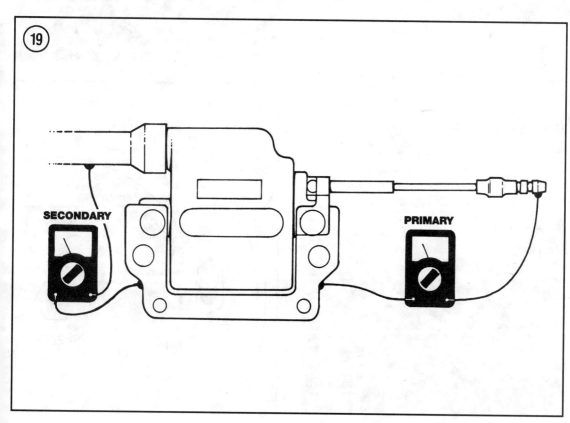
SECONDARY   PRIMARY

2. Remove the flywheel cover (**Figure 4**).

3. The stator plate has three timing marks (**Figure 12**). The center timing mark indicates the standard ignition timing. The two outer marks represent the adjustment limits for advancing or retarding the ignition timing.

> *NOTE*
> *If you cannot loosen the stator plate mounting screws by hand in Step 4, loosen them with an impact driver and a No. 3 Phillips bit (described in Chapter One). Otherwise you may damage the screw heads and be forced to remove the screws with a chisel.*

4. Adjust the timing by loosening the stator plate mounting screws (A, **Figure 21**) and moving the stator plate (B, **Figure 21**). The crankcase timing mark should remain within the area outlined by the two outer marks. Moving the stator plate clockwise advances the ignition timing. Moving the stator plate counterclockwise retards ignition timing. See **Figure 22**. Tighten the stator plate screws.

> *CAUTION*
> *Do not adjust the ignition timing outside of the marked range listed above or engine damage may occur.*

5. Replace the flywheel cover gasket if torn or damaged.

6. Install the flywheel cover and its gasket (Figure 4) and tighten its mounting bolts securely.

> *CAUTION*
> *Do not overtighten the flywheel cover bolts in Step 6. The plastic cover will warp and allow dirt to pass through.*

POWERJET ASSEMBLY (1998)

This section describes service to the powerjet assembly used on 1998 models. These components include the regulator/rectifier assembly and the powerjet valve.

Regulator/Rectifier Removal/Installation

1. Support the bike on a workstand.

2. Remove the seat and side covers (Chapter Fifteen).

3. Remove the fuel tank (Chapter Eight).

4. Remove the radiator covers (Chapter Ten).

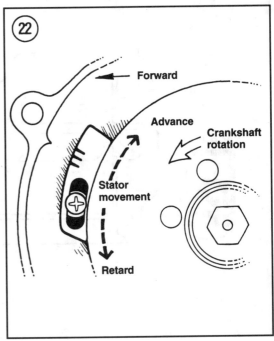

5. Disconnect the regulator/rectifier electrical connector.

6. Remove the mounting bolt and the regulator/rectifier (**Figure 23**).

7. Reverse these steps to install the regulator/rectifier unit, while noting the following.

8. Clean the regulator/rectifier unit electrical connector with contact cleaner, then pack it with dielectric grease.

Regulator/Rectifier Output Voltage Test

The regulator/rectifier (**Figure 23**) can be tested while mounted on the frame.

1. Start the engine and allow it to idle until it reaches normal operating temperature, then shut it off.

2. Remove the seat and side covers (Chapter Fifteen).

3. Remove the fuel tank (Chapter Eight).

4. Remove the radiator covers (Chapter Ten).

5. Disconnect the regulator/rectifier electrical connector.

6. Reconnect the regulator/rectifier electrical connector to its main wiring harness connector using four jumper wires as shown in **Figure 24**. Then connect a voltmeter to the two jumper wires identified as follows: Connect the positive voltmeter lead (+) to the red/white wire and the negative voltmeter lead (–) to the black/yellow wire. Make sure the meter leads do not touch or short across the other wires.

9

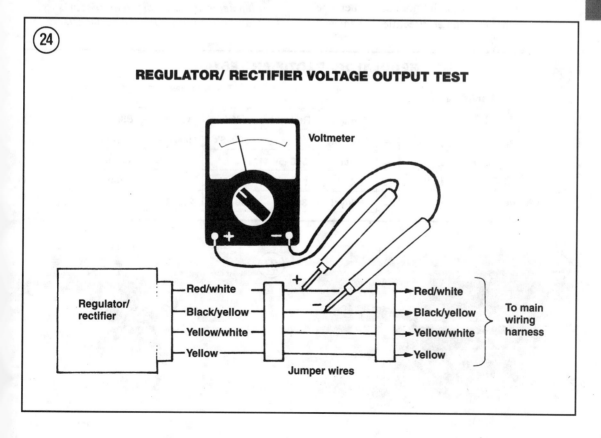

REGULATOR/ RECTIFIER VOLTAGE OUTPUT TEST

Voltmeter

Regulator/ rectifier

Red/white
Black/yellow
Yellow/white
Yellow

Red/white
Black/yellow
Yellow/white
Yellow

To main wiring harness

Jumper wires

NOTE
Make sure all of the jumper wires are connected correctly and securely attached to the mating connectors. A loose jumper wire connection at one of the electrical connectors can result in an incorrect meter reading. This may lead you to replace a good part.

7. Start the engine and allow to idle. Increase the engine speed while reading the voltmeter scale. The voltage reading should start at 14.2 volts and increase to a maximum of 15.2 volts as the engine speed is increased. Turn the engine off and note the following:

    a. If the output voltage reading stayed at 14.2 volts at low speed and then increased to a maximum reading of 15.2 volts as the engine speed was increased, the charging system is working correctly.

    b. If the output voltage reading exceeded the maximum reading, the regulator/rectifier is faulty or one of its wires are disconnected or open. Clean and repair the connectors or wiring harness, then repeat the test.

    c. If the output voltage did not rise with engine rpm, either the regulator/rectifier is damaged or the stator coil output is too low. Test the regulator/rectifier as described in this section. Test the stator coil as described under *Stator Coil* in this chapter.

8. Remove the voltmeter from the wiring harness.

9. Remove the jumper wires from the connectors, then reconnect the connectors.

10. Reverse Steps 1-4 to complete installation.

Regulator/Rectifier
Resistance Test

    Kawasaki specifies the use of their hand tester (part No. 57001-1394) for accurate testing of the regulator/rectifier unit. Because of the different resistance value characteristics of the semiconductors used in this meter, the use of a different meter may give you a false reading. You can purchase this meter through a Kawasaki dealership, or you can remove the regulator/rectifier unit and have them bench test it for you.

CAUTION
Kawasaki specifies the use of their hand tester for this test. If a different ohmmeter is used, different readings may be recorded. Using an ohmmeter

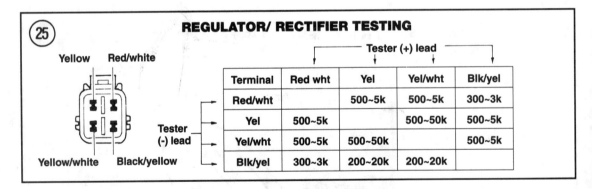

REGULATOR/ RECTIFIER TESTING

Terminal	Tester (+) lead			
	Red wht	Yel	Yel/wht	Blk/yel
Red/wht		500~5k	500~5k	300~3k
Yel	500~5k		500~50k	500~5k
Yel/wht	500~5k	500~50k		500~5k
Blk/yel	300~3k	200~20k	200~20k	

Yellow   Red/white

Tester (-) lead

Yellow/white   Black/yellow

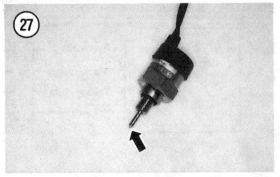

equipped with a large-capacity battery will damage the regulator/rectifier.

The regulator/rectifier (**Figure 23**) can be tested while mounted on the frame.

1. Warm up the engine until it reaches normal operating temperature, then shut it off.

2. Remove the seat and side covers (Chapter Fifteen).

3. Remove the fuel tank (Chapter Eight).

4. Remove the radiator covers (Chapter Ten).

5. Disconnect the regulator/rectifier electrical connector.

6. Set the Kawasaki tester to the R × 100 ohms scale.

7. Refer to **Figure 25** for test connections and values. If any of the meter readings differ from the stated values, first check the condition of the battery in the multimeter; an old battery can cause inaccurate readings. If the readings are still incorrect with a new battery, replace the regulator/rectifier unit as described in this chapter.

8. Reverse Steps 1-5 to complete assembly.

Powerjet Valve
Removal/Installation

The powerjet valve is mounted on the carburetor (**Figure 26**). Refer to *Carburetor* in Chapter Eight for removal and installation procedures.

Powerjet Valve
Testing

A fully charged 12-volt battery is required for this test.

1. Remove the powerjet valve (**Figure 26**) from the carburetor as described in Chapter Eight.

2. Measure the valve rod (**Figure 27**) length as follows:

   a. Connect a 12-volt battery to the powerjet electrical connector (**Figure 28**) and measure the valve rod length as shown in **Figure 28**. The correct length measurement with the battery connected is 21.3-21.7 mm (0.839-0.854 in.).

   b. Disconnect the battery leads and remeasure the valve rod length as shown in **Figure 28**. The correct length measurement with the battery disconnected is 19.4-19.6 mm (0.764-0.772 in.).

   c. If the valve rod measurement for either test is too long or too short, the powerjet valve is defective and must be replaced.

3. Reverse Step 1 to install the powerjet valve.

WIRING DIAGRAMS

Wiring diagrams for all models are located at the end of this book.

9

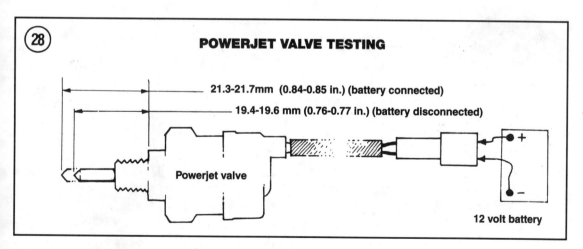

POWERJET VALVE TESTING

21.3-21.7mm (0.84-0.85 in.) (battery connected)
19.4-19.6 mm (0.76-0.77 in.) (battery disconnected)

Powerjet valve

12 volt battery

Table 1 ELECTRICAL SPECIFICATIONS*

Ignition timing	
1992-1994	14° BTDC @ 6000 rpm
1995-1996	13.4° BTDC @ 6000 rpm
1997	14° BTDC @ 6530 rpm
1998	11° BTDC @ 7000 rpm
Ignition coil	
Primary winding resistance	
1992-1993	0.25-0.37 ohm
1994	0.26-0.36 ohm
1995-on	0.45-0.61 ohm
Secondary winding resistance	
1992-1993	3300-4900 ohms
1994	3500-4700 ohms
1995-on	10,700-14,500 ohms
Stator coil resistance	
1992-1997	
White/red to white/green	396-594 ohms
Red to black/red	288-432 ohms
White to red	14-21 ohms
1998	
White/yellow to green/white	180-380 ohms
Red to white	7-15 ohms

* Resistance at of 68° F (20°C).

Table 2 FLYWHEEL TORQUE SPECIFICATIONS

	N•m	ft.-lb.
Flywheel nut	78	57

CHAPTER TEN

LIQUID COOLING SYSTEM

The liquid cooling system consists of two radiators, a radiator cap, water pump and hoses. During operation, the coolant heats up and expands, thus pressurizing the system. The radiator cap seals the system. Water cooled in the radiator is pumped down through the radiator and into the cylinder head where it passes through the cylinder water jackets and back into the radiator. The water drains down through the radiator where it is cooled once again.

The water pump requires no routine maintenance and can be serviced after first removing the right crankcase cover. There is no thermostat or cooling fan and you can service the cooling system with the engine mounted in the frame.

This chapter describes repair and replacement of cooling system components. Cooling system maintenance procedures are found in Chapter Three.

Cooling system specifications are listed in **Table 1** and **Table 2**.

SAFETY PRECAUTIONS

Certain safety precautions must be kept in mind to protect yourself from injury and the engine from damage. For your own personal safety, do not remove the radiator cap (**Figure 1**) when the engine is hot. Instead, wait until the system cools. When you remove the radiator cap, first place a rag over the cap, then stand off to one side of the radiator. Slowly turn the radiator cap to its safety stop to allow pressure in the system to escape, then push the cap down and turn it to release it from the groove in the top of the radiator. Always check the coolant level in the radiator *before* the first ride of the day.

> *WARNING*
> *Do not remove the radiator cap (**Figure 1**) when the engine is hot. The coolant is very hot and under pressure. If you remove the radiator cap from a hot engine, scalding steam and coolant will spray violently from the radiator, causing severe burns where it contacts your skin.*

To protect the engine and cooling system, drain and flush the cooling system at least once a year. Refer to Coolant Change in Chapter Three.

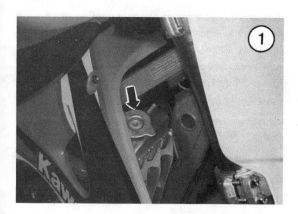

CAUTION
Never operate the cooling system with water only, even in climates where antifreeze protection is not required. While water is a better coolant than antifreeze, the antifreeze protects the engine and cooling system metal surfaces while acting as a lubricant.

WARNING
Antifreeze is classified as an environmental toxic waste by the EPA. Dispose of it according to local regulations. Antifreeze is poisonous and may attract animals. Do not store coolant where it is accessible to children or pets.

COOLING SYSTEM CHECK

1. Check the radiators for clogged or damaged fins.
2. To clean a clogged radiator, blow compressed air from the rear (engine side), keeping the air nozzle at least 51cm (20 in.) away from the radiator. Blow air directly through the radiator fins (perpendicular); never blow air at an angle against the fins.
3. Check the radiators for loose or missing mounting bolts.
4. Check all coolant hoses for cracks or damage. Replace any questionable part. Make sure the hose clamps are tight, but not so tight that they cut the hoses.
5. Make sure the overflow tube is connected to the radiator (next to the radiator cap) and is not clogged or damaged.
6. Pressure test the cooling system as described in Chapter Three.
7. If coolant loss is noted, there is a leak in the system. Check the cooling system hoses, water pump and water jackets (cylinder and cylinder head) carefully.

RADIATORS

Refer to **Figure 2** (1992-1993) or **Figure 3** (1994-on) when servicing the radiators and coolant hoses.

Removal/Installation

1. Place the bike on a workstand.
2. Remove the fuel tank (Chapter Eight).
3. Drain the cooling system (Chapter Three).

4. Remove the radiator covers.
5. Disconnect the radiator hoses at the radiators or cylinder head. Disconnect the hoses required to remove one or both radiators. See **Figure 4** and **Figure 5**, typical.
6. Remove the radiator mounting bolts and radiators (**Figure 6**, typical).
7. Perform the *Inspection* procedure in this section.
8. To install the radiators, reverse Steps 1-6 while noting the following.

NOTE
If you installed aftermarket radiator guards, you may need to install longer mounting bolts. Check the placement of each bolt, so you do not strip the bolt or frame threads.

9. Do not tighten the radiator mounting bolts until both radiators and all hoses are in place. Tighten the bolts securely.
10. Add engine coolant and bleed the cooling system as described in Chapter Three.

Inspection

1. Flush off the exterior of the radiator with a low-pressure stream of water from a garden hose. Spray the front and back of the radiator to remove all dirt and debris. Carefully use a whisk broom or stiff paint brush to remove any stubborn dirt.

CAUTION
Do not press too hard or you can damage the cooling fins and tubes.

2. Examine the radiator cooling surface for damage (**Figure 7**). Refer radiator service to a radiator repair shop.
3. Carefully straighten any bent cooling fins with a wide-blade screwdriver. Replace the radiator if it is damaged across 20% or more of its frontal area.
4. Check for cracks or leakage (usually a moss-green colored residue) at the filler neck, the inlet and outlet hose fittings and the upper and lower tank seams.
5. Check for missing or damaged radiator mounting bushings and collars (**Figure 8**). Replace if necessary.
6. Inspect the radiator cap (**Figure 9**) and seal for damage. Check for a bent or distorted cap. Raise the

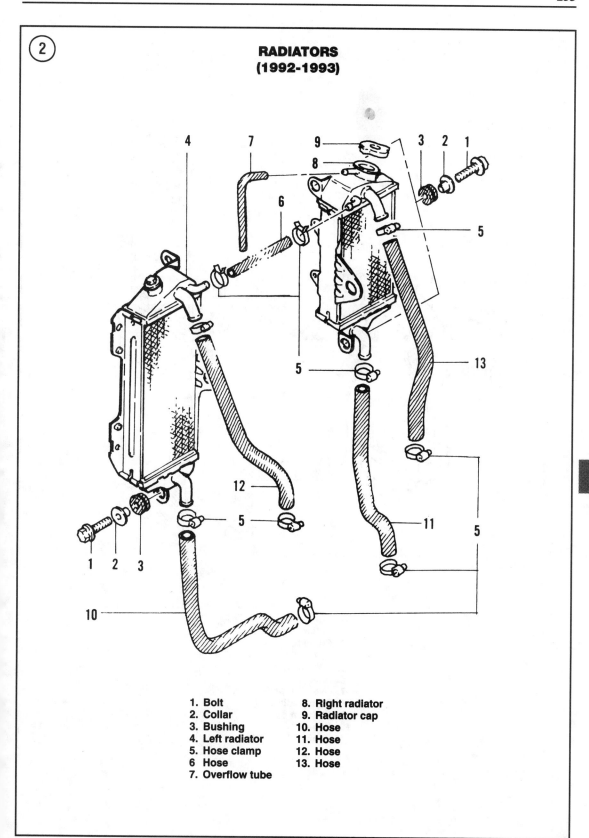

**RADIATORS
(1992-1993)**

1. Bolt
2. Collar
3. Bushing
4. Left radiator
5. Hose clamp
6. Hose
7. Overflow tube
8. Right radiator
9. Radiator cap
10. Hose
11. Hose
12. Hose
13. Hose

③

RADIATORS
(1994-ON)

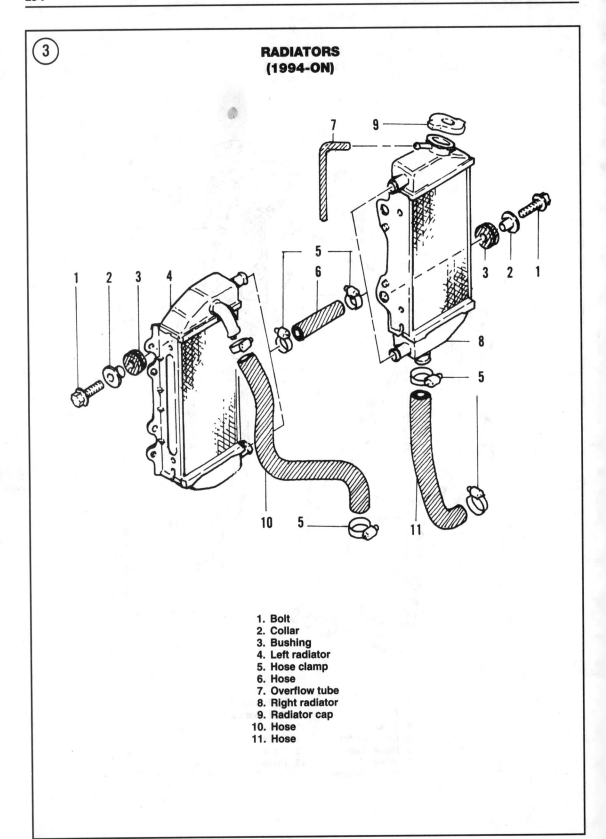

1. Bolt
2. Collar
3. Bushing
4. Left radiator
5. Hose clamp
6. Hose
7. Overflow tube
8. Right radiator
9. Radiator cap
10. Hose
11. Hose

vacuum valve and rubber seal and rinse the cap with water to flush away any loose rust or dirt particles.

7. Replace leaking or damaged coolant hoses.

8. Replace damaged or corroded hose clamps.

WATER PUMP

The water pump is mounted inside the right crankcase cover. **Figure 10** shows an exploded view of the water pump assembly.

Water Pump Cover and Impeller Removal/Installation

1. Drain the cooling system (Chapter Three).

2. Disconnect the coolant hoses from the water pump. See **Figure 11**, typical.

NOTE
*Do not remove the front hose elbow (A, **Figure 12**) unless necessary. The water pump cover can be removed with the*

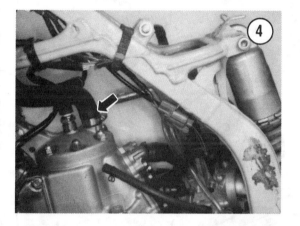

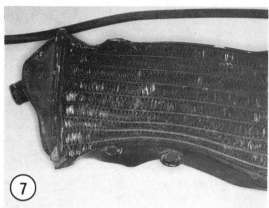

10

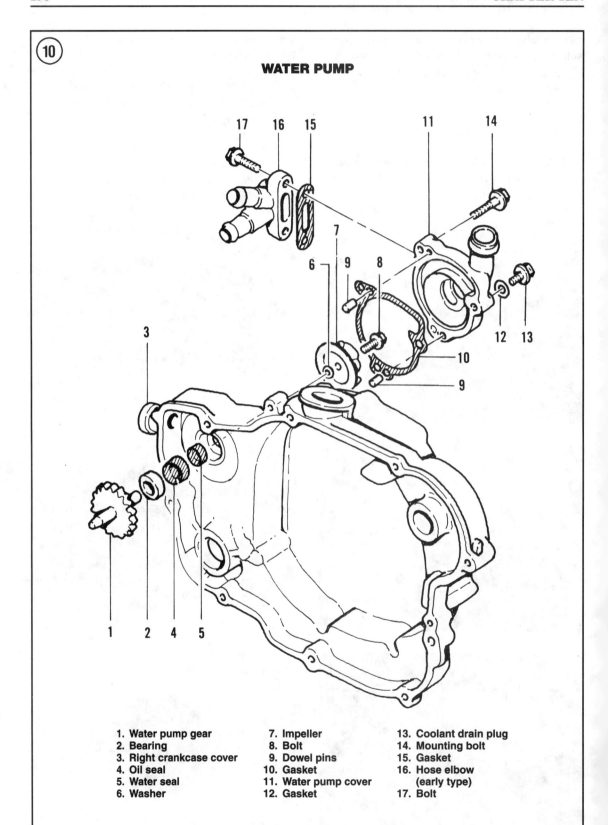

WATER PUMP

1. Water pump gear
2. Bearing
3. Right crankcase cover
4. Oil seal
5. Water seal
6. Washer
7. Impeller
8. Bolt
9. Dowel pins
10. Gasket
11. Water pump cover
12. Gasket
13. Coolant drain plug
14. Mounting bolt
15. Gasket
16. Hose elbow
    (early type)
17. Bolt

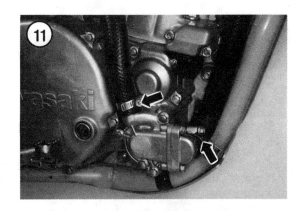

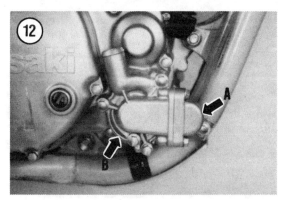

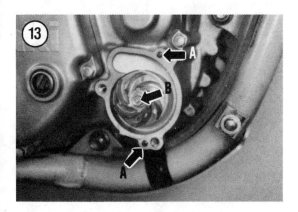

hose elbow in place. If you remove the front hose elbow, you must install a new gasket during installation.

3. Unbolt and remove the water pump cover (B, **Figure 12**). Remove and discard the water pump gasket.

4. If necessary, remove the two dowel pins (A, **Figure 13**).

5. Loosen and remove the impeller (B, **Figure 13**) and washer. See **Figure 14**.

6. Remove all gasket residue from the water pump cover and crankcase cover gasket surfaces.

7. Clean and dry all parts.

8. Inspect the impeller blades (**Figure 15**) for corrosion and damage.

9. Install the bolt through the front of the impeller, then install the washer behind the impeller (**Figure 14**).

10. Install the impeller (B, **Figure 13**) and tighten its mounting bolt as specified in **Table 2**.

11. If removed, install the two dowel pins (A, **Figure 13**).

12. Install a new gasket and the water pump cover (B, **Figure 12**). Install and tighten the water pump cover mounting bolts as specified in **Table 2**.

13. If the hose elbow (A, **Figure 12**) is removed, install it using a new gasket. Tighten both mounting bolts securely.

14. Install the hoses onto the water pump (**Figure 11**, typical). Tighten each hose clamp securely.

15. Fill and bleed the cooling system (Chapter Three). Check the water pump and hoses for leaks.

Disassembly

Refer to **Figure 10** for this procedure.

10

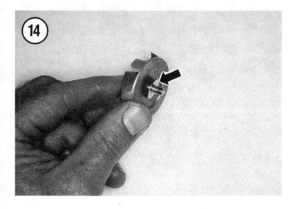

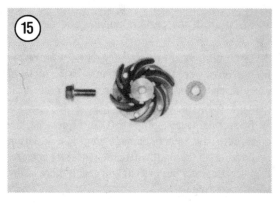

1. Remove the water pump cover as described in this section.

2. Loosen, but do not remove, the impeller mounting bolt (B, **Figure 13**).

3. Remove the right crankcase cover (Chapter Six).

4. Remove the mounting bolt, impeller (**Figure 16**) and washer (**Figure 14**).

5. Remove the water pump shaft and gear assembly (**Figure 17**).

> *CAUTION*
> *When removing the oil and water seals in the following steps, use care to avoid damage to the mounting bore. Such damage can cause the new seals to leak.*

> *NOTE*
> *Before removing the seals in Steps 6 and 7, record the direction in which its manufacturer's marks or numbers face for proper reinstallation.*

6. Pry the water seal (**Figure 18**) out of the mounting bore with a screwdriver.

7. Pry the oil seal out of the mounting bore as shown in **Figure 19**.

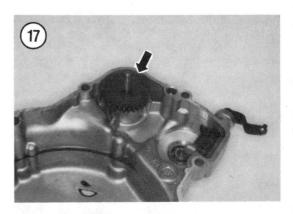

> *NOTE*
> *Because the oil seal is recessed into the mounting bore, use a seal removal tool like the one shown in **Figure 19** to avoid damaging the bore.*

8. Do not remove the bearing unless it requires replacement. Refer to *Inspection and Bearing Replacement* in this section.

Inspection and Bearing Replacement

1. Clean all of the parts in solvent and dry thoroughly.

2. Inspect the water pump shaft gear (A, **Figure 20**) for broken or worn teeth. If the transmission oil level ran low, check the gear for warpage or other heat damage.

3. Inspect the water pump shaft (B, **Figure 20**) for burrs, excessive wear or damage. Pay close attention to the point on the shaft where the two seals operate. Replace the water pump shaft and gear if there is any wear or scoring.

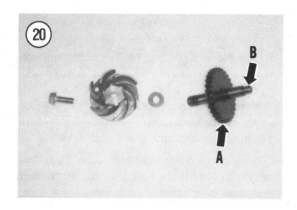

4. Turn the water pump bearing inner race (**Figure 21**) by hand. If the bearing turns roughly, replace it as follows:

a. Support the right crankcase cover on wooden blocks. Drive (**Figure 22**) the bearing out of its mounting bore (**Figure 23**).

b. Clean the mounting bore in solvent and dry thoroughly.

c. Inspect the bore for burrs or nicks that would make bearing installation difficult.

d. Support the crankcase cover on wooden blocks with the inside surface facing up.

e. Place the new bearing squarely against the bore opening. Place a bearing driver on the bearing's outer race and drive the bearing into the bore until it bottoms against the mounting bore shoulder (**Figure 24**).

> *CAUTION*
> *Applying pressure to the bearing's inner race will damage the bearing.*

Assembly

The water pump uses two different types of seals—an oil seal (A, **Figure 25**) and a water seal (B, **Figure 25**). Make sure you install each seal in its correct position and facing in its proper direction. This step is important because both seals are unique in their design and function. If a seal is installed incorrectly, it will leak.

1. If removed, install the bearing as described in this section.

> *NOTE*
> *Refer to **Figure 26** when installing the seals.*

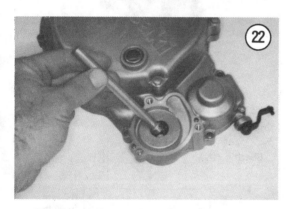

2. Install the oil seal (A, **Figure 25**) as follows:

    a. Pack the lip of the new oil seal with grease.

    b. Place the oil seal squarely against the bore opening with its marked side facing in (toward bearing). Select a driver with an outside diameter just slightly smaller than the seal's outside diameter. Drive the oil seal in the bore until it bottoms out against the bearing (**Figure 27**).

3. Install the water seal (B, **Figure 25**) as follows:

    a. Pack both lips of the new water seal with grease.

    b. Place the water seal squarely against the bore opening with its marked side facing in (toward bearing). Place a driver against the water seal's outer lip. Drive the water seal (**Figure 25**) in the bore until the edge of the seal is 0.5 mm (0.02 in.) below the surface of the mounting bore (**Figure 26**).

CAUTION

Before you install the water pump shaft in Step 4, check to see that the shaft is not nicked or burred. If nicks or burrs are found, remove them with a fine grade sandpaper or crocus cloth. Burrs or nicks on the shaft's shoulder may damage the seal lips.

4. Lubricate the water pump shaft with grease. Insert the shaft through the bearing, then turn it while it passes through both seals. Doing so will help to prevent the shaft from damaging the lips of the seals. Continue until the shaft bottoms against the bearing (**Figure 17**).

5. Install the bolt through the front of the impeller, then install the washer behind the impeller (**Figure 14**).

6. Install the impeller (**Figure 16**) and tighten its mounting bolt as specified in **Table 2**. Turn the impeller by hand, making sure the shaft turns smoothly. If the shaft turns roughly, make sure the washer (**Figure 14**) was installed between the impeller and water seal.

7. Install the right crankcase cover (Chapter Six).

8. Install the water pump cover as described in this chapter.

HOSES

Hoses deteriorate with age and should be replaced periodically or whenever they show signs of cracking or leakage. To be safe, replace the hoses every two years. The spray of hot coolant from a cracked hose can cause injury. Loss of coolant will also cause the engine to overheat and cause engine damage.

Whenever any component of the cooling system is removed, inspect the hoses(s) and determine if replacement is necessary.

Inspection

1. With the engine cool, check the cooling hoses for brittleness or hardness. A hose in this condition will usually show cracks and must be replaced.

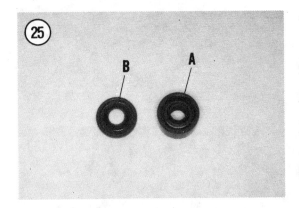

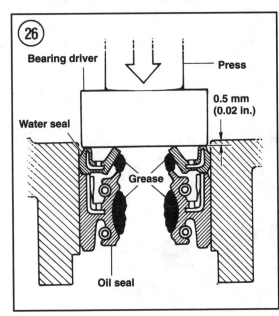

2. With the engine hot, examine the hoses for swelling along the entire hose length. Eventually a hose will rupture at this point.

3. Check the area around the hose clamps. Signs of rust around clamps indicate possible hose leakage.

Replacement

Replace the hoses when the engine is cold.

1. Drain the cooling system as described under *Coolant Change* in Chapter Three.

2. Loosen the hose clamps from the hose to be replaced. Slide the clamps along the hose and out of the way.

3. Twist the hose end to break the seal and remove from the connecting joint. If the hose has been on for some time, it may be fused to the joint. If so, cut the hose parallel to the joint connections with a knife or razor. The hose then can be carefully pried loose with a screwdriver.

CAUTION
Excessive force applied to the hose during removal could damage the connecting joint.

4. Examine the connecting joint for cracks or other damage. Repair or replace parts as required. If the joint is in good condition, remove rust with sandpaper.

5. Inspect the hose clamps and replace as necessary.

6. Slide the hose clamps over outside of the hose and install hose to the inlet and outlet connecting joints. Make sure the hose clears all obstructions and is routed properly.

NOTE
If it is difficult to install a hose on a joint, soak the end of the hose in hot water for approximately two minutes. This will soften the hose and ease installation.

7. With the hose positioned correctly on joint, position the clamps back away from the end of the hose slightly. Tighten the clamps securely, but not so much that the hose is damaged.

8. Refill the cooling system as described in Chapter Three. Start the engine and check for leaks. Retighten the hose clamps as necessary.

(27)

10

Table 1 COOLING SYSTEM SPECIFICATIONS

Coolant mixture	50/50 (water/antifreeze)
Cap relief pressure	95-12 kPa (14-18 psi)

Table 2 COOLING SYSTEM TIGHTENING TORQUES

	N•m	in.-lb.	ft.-lb.
Coolant drain screws			
Cylinder block drain screw			
1992	22	–	16
1993	21	–	15
1994-1995	22	–	16
1996-on	8.8	78	–
Water pump drain screw	8.8	78	–
Water pump cover mounting bolts	8.8	78	–
Water pump impeller mounting bolt	6.9	61	–

CHAPTER ELEVEN

WHEELS, TIRES AND DRIVE CHAIN

This chapter describes repair and maintenance for the front and rear wheels, wheel hubs, tires and the drive chain and sprockets.

Tire and wheel specifications are listed in **Table 1**. Drive chain and sprocket specifications are listed in **Table 2**. **Tables 1-3** are at the end of this chapter.

FRONT WHEEL

Removal

1. Support the motorcycle with the front wheel off the ground.

2. Unbolt and remove the disc cover (**Figure 1**, typical).

3. Loosen the right axle clamp nuts (A, **Figure 2**).

4. Loosen and remove the front axle (B, **Figure 2**) from the right side. See **Figure 3**.

5. Remove the front wheel.

6. Remove the left (**Figure 4**) and right (**Figure 5**) side axle spacers and dust caps.

> *NOTE*
> *Insert a plastic or wooden spacer in the caliper in place of the disc. If the brake lever is inadvertently squeezed, the pistons will not be forced out of the caliper. If this happens, you must disassemble the caliper to reseat the pistons.*

7. The axle nut (A, **Figure 6**) can stay in the left fork leg. To remove the axle nut (A, **Figure 6**), loosen the left axle clamp nuts (B) and remove the axle nut.

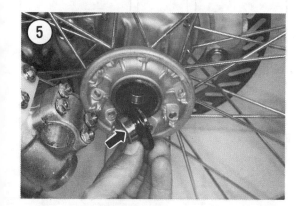

Inspection

1. Inspect the seals (**Figure 7**) for excessive wear, hardness, cracks or other damage. If necessary, replace the seals as described under *Front and Rear Hubs* in this chapter.

2. Turn each bearing inner race (**Figure 8**) by hand. The bearing must turn smoothly. Some axial play (end play) is normal, but radial play (side play) must be negligible. See **Figure 9**. If one bearing is damaged, replace both bearings as a set. Refer to *Front and Rear Hubs* in this chapter.

3. Clean the axle and axle spacers in solvent to remove all grease and dirt. Make sure the axle contact surfaces are clean and free of dirt and old grease.

4. Inspect the dust caps (A, **Figure 10**) and replace if damaged.

5. Assemble the dust caps by inserting their center projection into the axle spacer groove (B, **Figure 10**).

6. Check the axle runout with a set of V-blocks and dial indicator (**Figure 11**). Replace the axle if its runout exceeds the service limit in **Table 1**.

11

7. Check the brake disc bolts for tightness. To service the brake disc, refer to Chapter Fourteen.

8. Check wheel runout and spoke tension as described in this chapter.

Installation

1. Clean the axle bearing surfaces on the fork slider and axle holder.

2. If removed, install the axle holder clamps (**Figure 12**) with their arrow marks facing up. Do not tighten the nuts at this time.

3. If the axle nut was removed, install it as shown in A, **Figure 6**. Tighten the left axle clamp nuts (B, **Figure 6**)—tighten the upper nuts first, then the lower nuts as specified in **Table 3**.

4. Apply a light coat of grease to the axle and oil seal lips (**Figure 7**).

5. Remove the spacer block from between the brake pads.

6. Install the left (**Figure 4**) and right (**Figure 5**) side axle spacers and dust caps.

7. Carefully insert the disc between the brake pads and hold the wheel in position. Install the axle from the right side (**Figure 3**) and thread it into the axle nut.

8. Tighten the front axle (B, **Figure 2**) as specified in **Table 3**.

9. Tighten the right axle clamp nuts (A, **Figure 2**)—tighten the upper nuts first, then the lower nuts as specified in **Table 3**.

10. Install the front brake disc cover (**Figure 1**) and tighten its mounting bolts securely.

11. After the wheel is completely installed, rotate it several times and apply the brake a couple of times to make sure the wheel rotates freely and that the brake is operating correctly.

REAR WHEEL

Removal

1. Support the bike on a workstand with the rear wheel off the ground.

2. On 1992-1994 models, perform the following:
   a. Unbolt and remove the brake caliper cover.
   b. Unbolt and remove the brake caliper (**Figure 13**). Support the brake caliper with a wire hook.

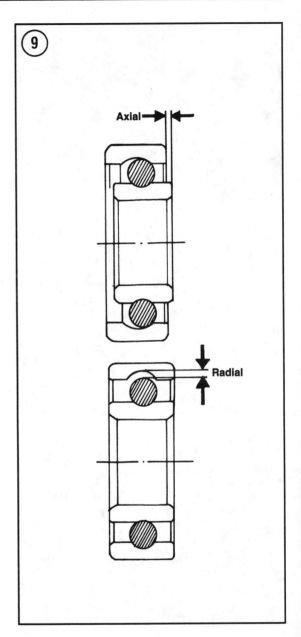

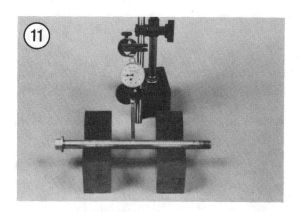

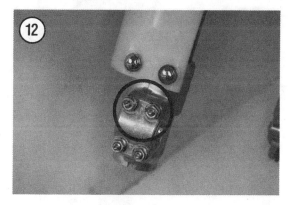

c. Insert a plastic or wooden spacer block in the caliper between the brake pads.

NOTE
The spacer block installed in Step 2 will prevent the piston from being forced out of its cylinder if the brake pedal is operated while the rear brake disc is removed from between the brake pads. If the piston is forced out too far, you will have to disassemble the caliper to reseat the piston.

3. Loosen the axle adjuster locknuts and adjuster (A, **Figure 14**).

4. Remove and discard the cotter pin. Loosen and remove the rear axle nut (B, **Figure 14**) and washer.

5. Push the wheel forward to provide as much chain slack as possible, then slip the drive chain off the sprocket.

6. Remove the axle (**Figure 15**) and rear wheel.

7. Remove the left (**Figure 16**) and right (**Figure 17**) side axle spacers and dust caps.

8. On 1995 and later models, insert a spacer block in the caliper between the brake pads.

11

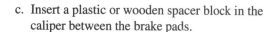

Inspection

1. Inspect the seals (**Figure 18**) for excessive wear, hardness, cracks or other damage. If necessary, replace seals as described under *Front and Rear Hubs* in this chapter.

2. Turn each bearing inner race (**Figure 8**) by hand. The bearing must turn smoothly with no roughness, catching, binding or excessive noise. Some axial play (end play) is normal, but radial play (side play) must be negligible. See **Figure 9**. If one bearing is damaged, replace both bearings as a set. Refer to *Front and Rear Hubs* in this chapter.

3. Clean the axle and axle spacers in solvent to remove all grease and dirt. Make sure all axle contact surfaces are clean and free of dirt and old grease.

4. Inspect the dust caps (A, **Figure 19**) and replace if damaged.

5. Assemble the dust caps by inserting their center projection into the axle spacer groove (B, **Figure 19**).

6. Check the rear axle runout with a set of V-blocks and dial indicator (**Figure 11**). Replace the axle if its runout exceeds the service limit in **Table 1**.

7. Check the brake disc bolts for tightness. To service the brake disc, refer to Chapter Fourteen.

8. Check the driven sprocket nuts for tightness. Tighten the driven sprocket nuts as described under *Sprocket Replacement* in this chapter.

9. Check wheel runout and spoke tension as described in this chapter.

Installation

1. Apply a light coat of grease to the axle and both seal lips (**Figure 18**).

2. If removed, slide the rear brake caliper mounting bracket onto the swing arm slide rail (**Figure 20**).

3. Remove the spacer block from between the brake pads.

4. Install the left (**Figure 16**) and right (**Figure 17**) side axle spacers and dust caps.

5. Position the drive chain over the top of the swing arm and position the rear wheel between the swing arm (**Figure 15**).

6A. Slip the drive chain over the sprocket.

6B. If the drive chain was disconnected, install it around both sprockets and secure it with its master link as described in this chapter.

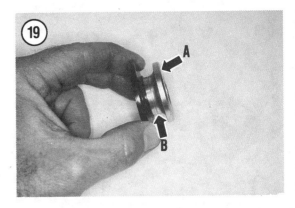

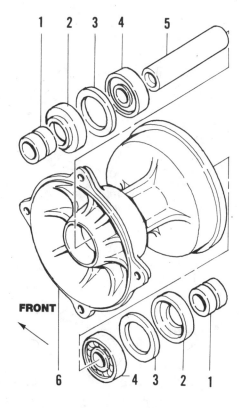

(21)

FRONT HUB

1 2 3 4 5

FRONT

6   4 3 2 1

1. Spacer
2. Dust cap
3. Axle seal
4. Bearing
5. Distance collar
6. Front hub

7. Lift the wheel and install the rear axle (**Figure 15**). On 1995 and later models, carefully insert the disc between the brake pads and hold the wheel in position while you install the axle.

8. Install the washer and axle nut (B, **Figure 14**). Tighten the axle nut finger-tight.

9. On 1992-1994 models, perform the following:

    a. Install the rear brake caliper and tighten its mounting bolts as specified in **Table 3**.

    b. Install the brake caliper cover and tighten its mounting bolts securely.

10. Adjust the drive chain as described in Chapter Three. Tighten rear the axle nut as specified in **Table 3**.

11. After the wheel is completely installed, rotate it several times while applying the rear brake to reposition the rear brake pads and to make sure the wheel rotates freely.

FRONT AND REAR HUBS

The front and rear hubs contain the seals, wheel bearings and distance collar. A brake disc is mounted onto each hub and the driven sprocket is mounted onto the rear hub. Refer to **Figure 21** (front) or **Figure 22** (rear) when servicing the front and rear hubs in this section.

Procedures used to service the front and rear hubs and wheel bearings are basically the same. Where differences occur, they will be pointed out in the service procedure.

Pre-Inspection

Inspect each wheel bearing as follows:

1. Support the bike with the wheel to be checked off the ground. Make sure the axle is tightened securely.

    a. Hold the wheel 180° apart and try to rock it back and forth. If there is any noticeable play at the axle, the wheel bearings are worn or damaged and require replacement. Have an assistant apply the brake while you rock the wheel again. On severely worn bearings, you can detect play at the bearings even though the wheel is locked in position.

> *NOTE*
> *When checking the rear wheel, remove the drive chain before performing substep b.*

11

b. If there is no noticeable play, spin the wheel and listen for excessive wheel bearing noise. A grinding or catching noise indicates worn bearings.

c. To check any questionable bearing, continue with Step 2.

CAUTION
Do not remove the wheel bearings for inspection purposes as they may be damaged during their removal. Remove the wheel bearings only if they are to be replaced.

2. Remove the front or rear wheel as described in this chapter.

CAUTION
When handling the wheel assembly in the following steps, do not lay the wheel down where it is supported by the brake disc as this could damage the disc. Support the wheel on two wooden blocks.

3. Pry the seals out of the hub with a wide-blade screwdriver (**Figure 23**). Support the screwdriver with a rag to avoid damaging the hub or brake disc.

4. Turn each bearing inner race by hand. The bearing must turn smoothly with no roughness, catching, binding or excessive noise. Some axial play (end play) is normal, but radial play (side play) must be negligible (**Figure 9**).

5. Check the bearing's outer seal (**Figure 24**) for buckling or other damage that would allow dirt to enter the bearing.

6. If one bearing is damaged, replace all of the bearings as a set.

Disassembly

This section describes removal of the wheel bearings from the front (**Figure 21**) and rear (**Figure 22**) hubs. If the bearings are intact, one of the removal methods described in this section can be used. To remove a bearing where the inner race assembly has fallen out, refer to *Removing Damaged Bearings* in this section.

CAUTION
When handling the wheel assembly in the following steps, do not lay the wheel down where it is supported by the brake

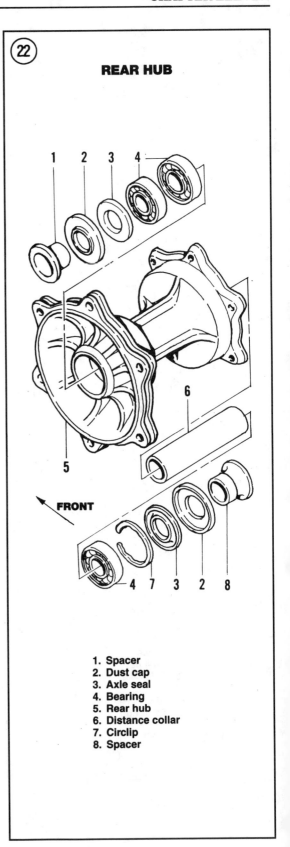

REAR HUB

FRONT

1. Spacer
2. Dust cap
3. Axle seal
4. Bearing
5. Rear hub
6. Distance collar
7. Circlip
8. Spacer

disc as this could damage the disc. Support the wheel on two wooden blocks.

1. Pry the seals out of the hub with a wide-blade screwdriver (**Figure 23**). Support the screwdriver with a rag to avoid damaging the hub or brake disc.

2. Examine the wheel bearings for excessive damage, especially the inner race. If the inner race of one bearing is damaged, remove the other bearing first. If both bearings are damaged, try to remove the bearing with the least amount of damage first. On

rusted and damaged bearings, applying pressure against the inner race may cause the race to pop out, leaving the outer race in the hub.

3A. On 1992 front wheels, remove the circlip from the right side of the wheel.

3B. On rear wheels, remove the circlip (**Figure 25**) from the right side of the wheel.

NOTE
Step 4 describes two methods of removing the wheel bearings. Step 4A requires the use of the Kowa Seiki Wheel Bearing Remover set. Step 4B describes steps on how to remove the bearings with a drift and hammer.

WARNING
Safety glasses must be worn when removing the bearings in the following steps.

4A. To remove the wheel bearings (**Figure 24**) with the Kowa Seiki Wheel Bearing Remover set:

NOTE
*The Kowa Seiki Wheel Bearing Remover set shown in **Figure 26** is available from K & L Supply Co., in Santa Clara, CA. You can order this tool set through a Kawasaki dealership.*

a. Select the correct size remover head tool and insert it into the right side hub bearing (A, **Figure 27**).

b. From the opposite side of the hub, insert the remover shaft into the slot in the backside of the remover head (B, **Figure 27**). Position the hub with the remover head tool resting against a solid surface and strike the remover shaft to force it into the slit in the remover head. This

11

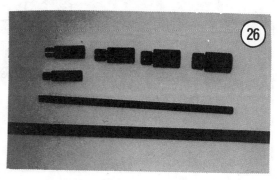

will wedge the remover head tool against the inner bearing race. See **Figure 28**.

c. Position the hub and strike the end of the remover shaft with a hammer to drive the bearing (A, **Figure 29**) out of the hub. Remove the bearing and tool. Release the remover head from the bearing.

d. Remove the distance collar (B, **Figure 29**) from the hub.

e. Remove the left side bearing(s) the same way. On 1997 and later models, two bearings are installed in the left side of the hub (**Figure 22**). On these models, remove the outer bearing first (**Figure 30**), then remove the inner bearing. Do not remove both bearings at the same time (**Figure 31**).

4B. To remove the wheel bearings without special tools:

NOTE
Clean the hub of all chain lube and other chemical residue before heating it with a torch in this procedure.

CAUTION
The hub and bearings will be hot after heating them with a torch. Make sure you wear welding gloves when handling the parts.

a. Heat one side of the hub with a propane torch. Move the torch in a circular motion around the hub, making sure you do not hold the torch in one area. Turn the wheel over and remove the bearing as described in the next step.

b. Using a long drift, tilt the distance collar away from one side of the bearing (**Figure 32**). On 1997 and later models, two bearings are installed in the left side of the rear hub. On these models, remove the outer bearing first (**Figure 31**), then remove the inner bearing. Do not remove both bearings at the same time.

NOTE
Do not damage the distance collar when removing the bearing. You may have to grind a clearance groove in the drift to enable it to grab hold of the bearing while clearing the distance collar.

c. Tap the bearing out of the hub with a hammer, working around the perimeter of the bearing's inner race.

d. Remove the distance collar from the hub.

e. Turn the hub over and heat the opposite side.

f. Drive out the opposite bearing using a large socket or bearing driver.

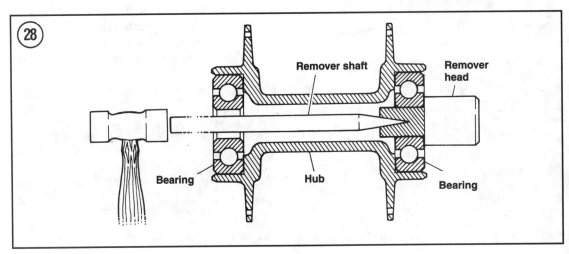

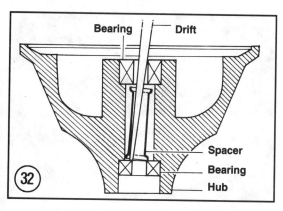

Bearing | Drift

Spacer
Bearing
Hub

g. Inspect the distance collar for burrs created during removal. Remove burrs with a file.

5. Clean and dry the hub (**Figure 33**) and distance collar.

Inspection

1. Check the hub mounting bore for cracks or other damage. If one of the bearings is a loose fit, the mounting bore is damaged and the hub should be replaced.

2. Inspect the distance collar for flared ends. Check the ends for cracks or other damage. Do not try to repair the distance collar by cutting or grinding its end surfaces as this will shorten the distance collar. Replace the distance collar if one or both ends are damaged.

> *NOTE*
> *The distance collar acts as a spacer between the wheel bearings inner races to prevent them from moving inward when the axle is tightened. If a distance collar is too short, or if it is not installed, the inner bearing races will move inward and bind on the axle, causing bearing damage and seizure.*

Assembly

Before installing the new bearings and seals, note the following:

a. The left and right side seals are identical (same part number). See A, **Figure 34**.

b. The left and right side bearings are identical (same part number). See B, **Figure 34**. This

11

includes the three bearings used in the rear hub on 1997 and later models (**Figure 22**).

c. Install both bearings with their closed side facing out. If a bearing is sealed on both sides, install the bearing with its manufacturer's marks facing out.

d. Install both seals with their closed side facing out.

e. When grease is specified in the following steps, use a Lithium based multipurpose grease (NLGI No. 2) or equivalent.

1. Blow any dirt or foreign matter out of the hub (**Figure 33**) before installing the bearings.

2. Pack the open side of each bearing (**Figure 35**) with grease.

3. Place the first bearing (**Figure 36**) squarely against the bore opening with its closed side facing out. Select a driver with an outside diameter just a little smaller than the bearing's outside diameter. Drive the bearing into the bore until it bottoms (**Figure 37**).

4. Install the distance collar (**Figure 38**) and position it against the first bearing's center race.

5. Place the second bearing (**Figure 39**) squarely against the bore opening with its closed side facing out. Using the same driver as before, drive the bearing partway into the bearing bore. Stop and check that the distance collar is centered in the hub. If not, install the axle through the hub to align the distance collar with the bearing. Remove the axle and continue installing the bearing until it bottoms (A, **Figure 40**).

6. When servicing the rear hub on 1997 and later models, repeat Step 5 to install the second left side bearing (B, **Figure 40**). Install the second bearing until it bottoms against the first bearing.

7. Take the axle and insert it though the hub and turn it by hand. Check for any roughness or binding, indicating bearing damage.

NOTE
If the axle will not go in, the distance collar is not aligned correctly with one of the bearings.

8. Install the circlip—flat side facing out—into the right side of the hub, if used (**Figure 25**, typical). Make sure the circlip seats in the groove completely.

9. Pack the lip of each oil seal with grease.

10. Place a seal squarely against one of the bore openings with its closed side facing out. Drive the

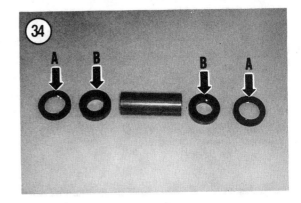

seal in the bore until it is flush with the outside of the bearing bore (**Figure 41**).

11. Repeat Step 10 for the other seal.

Removing Damaged Bearings

When worn and rusted wheel bearings are used too long, a bearing's inner race can break apart and fall out of the bearing, leaving the outer race pressed in the hub. Because the outer race seats against a shoulder inside the hub, its removal is difficult because only a small part of the race is accessible above the hub's shoulder. You have a small and difficult target to drive against. To remove a bearing's outer race under these conditions, first heat the hub evenly with a propane torch. Drive out the outer race with a drift and hammer. You may have to grind a clearance tip on the end of the drift, so you do not damage the hub bore. Check this before heating the hub. When removing the race, apply force at different points around the race to prevent it from binding in the mounting bore once it starts to move. After removing the race, inspect the hub mounting bore carefully for cracks or other damage.

RIM AND SPOKE SERVICE

The wheel assembly consists of a rim, spokes, nipples and hub (containing the bearings, distance collar and seals).

Loose or improperly tightened spokes can cause hub damage. Periodically inspect the wheel assembly for loose, broken or missing spokes, rim damage and runout. Wheel bearing service is described under *Front and Rear Hubs* in this chapter.

Rim Inspection

Inspect the rims for cracks, warpage or dents (**Figure 42**). Check the rim holes where the nipples pass through for cracks, hole enlargement or other damage.

Wheel Truing

When the wheels on your KX were new, they ran true. That is, there was no lateral (side-to-side) or radial (up-and-down) runout and the spokes were tightened to the same tension. However, because of the environment your bike operates in, the wheels take a lot of punishment. When a wheel starts to run with a noticeable wobble, it is out of true. This wobble is usually referred to as wheel runout. Runout is normally caused by loose spokes, but it can also be caused by bent or broken spokes or a damaged rim.

Truing a wheel corrects the lateral and radial runout to bring the wheel back into specification. While truing a wheel is a very standard procedure and can be learned with patience, the condition of the wheel parts will effect its truing. Note the following:

a. Spoke condition. It is very difficult to true a wheel with bent or damaged spokes. Before truing a wheel, visually inspect the spokes. Because bent spokes are hard to straighten, do not try to straighten them by tightening the nipples. This puts an excessive amount of tension on the spoke that will eventually crack the hub or enlarge the rim hole. First replace damaged spokes, then true the wheel.

b. Stuck nipples. The nipples thread into the bottom of the spokes and connect the spokes to the rim. Turning the nipples loosens and tightens the spoke tension. When truing a wheel, the nipples must turn freely. However, when the nipple and spoke threads become corroded, the threads seize. This condition makes it difficult to turn the spokes. When trying to turn a seized spoke, you will round off the nipple head, making further adjustment difficult. Using a pair of locking pliers to turn seized nipples usually crushes and permanently damages the nipples. When faced with this problem, spray a penetrating liquid down on the nipples. Allow sufficient time for the chemical to penetrate, then try to turn the nipple. If the nipples still will not turn, you will have to remove the tire from the rim and then cut the spokes with a wire cutter. Install new spokes and retrue the wheel.

c. Damaged rim. Dings and other damage to the side of a rim will make it run out of true. Flat spots across the outer surface of the rim will cause excessive radial runout. Trying to true these conditions out of the wheel will usually cause hub and rim damage due to overtightened spokes. If the damage is not severe, accept the fact that the wheel will run with some

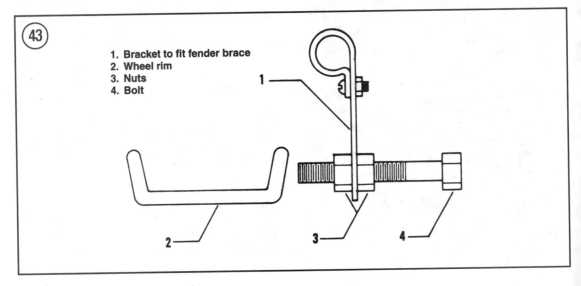

1. Bracket to fit fender brace
2. Wheel rim
3. Nuts
4. Bolt

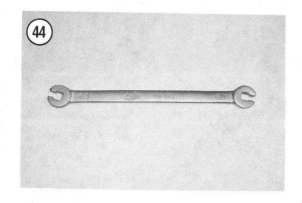

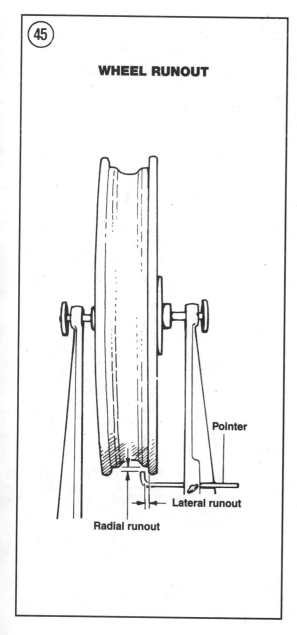

WHEEL RUNOUT

Pointer

Lateral runout

Radial runout

runout. When the damage is excessive, replace the rim, so it does not cause you to lose control.

NOTE
Do not try to true the wheel to a perfect zero reading. When doing so, you usually overtighten the spokes, which puts extreme stress on the spokes, hub and rim. This will eventually cause spoke and hub damage. Adjust the spokes to an even tension while getting it to run true, making sure you take into account the condition of the parts.

When checking runout and truing a wheel, note the following:

a. You can check runout with the wheels on the bike by simply supporting the wheel off the ground and turning the wheel slowly. Mount a pointer against the front fork or swing arm (**Figure 43**).

b. Turning the spoke nipples with an adjustable wrench or an incorrect size spoke wrench will round off the spoke nipple corners, making further adjustment difficult. Always use the correct size spoke wrench (**Figure 44**) when checking and tightening the spoke nipples. The Motion Pro spoke wrench shown in **Figure 44** is designed with square end openings that grip all four nipple corners to prevent them from being rounded off during tightening.

c. Perform major wheel truing with the tire and tube removed from the rim and the wheel placed on a truing stand or mounted in the bike. When truing the wheel with it mounted in the bike, place spacers on each side of the wheel to prevent it from sliding along the axle.

d. Make sure the wheel bearings are in good condition.

e. **Table 1** lists the rim lateral (side-to-side) and radial (up-and-down) runout limits.

f. When using a torque wrench to tighten the spoke nipples, refer to the spoke nipple torque specification in **Table 3**.

1. Position a pointer facing toward the rim as shown in **Figure 45**. Spin the wheel slowly and check the lateral and radial runout. If the rim is out of adjustment, continue with Step 2.

NOTE
If there is a large number of loose spokes, check the hub to make sure it is centered in the rim. You will have to do this visually as there are no hub and rim centering specifications for these models.

2. Lateral runout adjustment: If the side-to-side runout is out of specification, adjust the wheel by using **Figure 46** as an example. To move the rim to the right in **Figure 46**, loosen spoke A and tighten spoke B.

Always loosen and tighten the spokes (**Figure 47**) an equal number of turns.

NOTE
The number of spokes to loosen and tighten in Steps 2 and 3 will depend on how far the runout is out of adjustment. As a minimum, always loosen two or three spokes , then tighten the opposite two or three spokes. If the runout is excessive and affects a greater area along the rim, you will have to loosen and tighten a greater number of spokes.

3. Radial runout adjustment: If the up and down runout is out of specification, the hub is not centered in the rim. Draw the high point of the rim toward the centerline of the wheel by loosening the spokes in the area of the high point, and tightening the spokes on the side opposite the high point (**Figure 48**). Tighten spokes in equal amounts to prevent distortion.

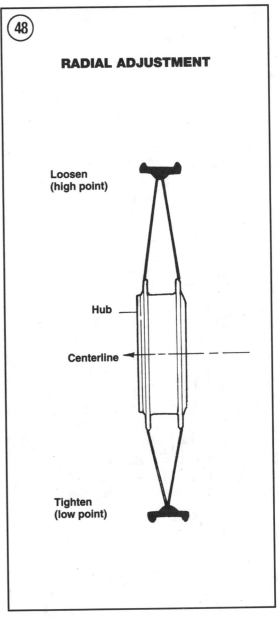

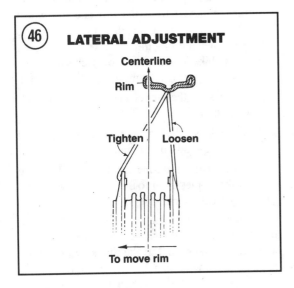

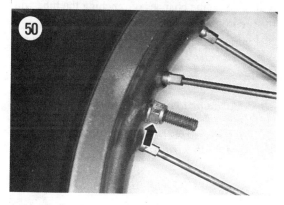

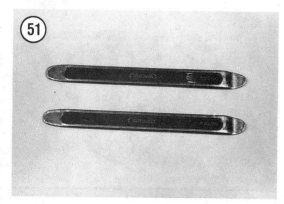

4. After truing the wheel, seat each spoke in the hub by tapping it with a flat nose punch and hammer. Recheck the spoke tension and wheel runout. Readjust if necessary.

5. Check the ends of the spokes where they are threaded in the nipples. Grind off any ends that protrude through the nipples to prevent them from puncturing the tube.

TIRE CHANGING

Removal

1. Remove the valve core (**Figure 49**) and deflate the tire.

2. Loosen the rim lock nuts (**Figure 50**).

3. Press the entire bead on both sides of the tire into the center of the rim.

4. Lubricate the beads with soapy water.

> *NOTE*
> *Use only quality tire irons without sharp edges (**Figure 51**). If necessary, file the ends of the tire irons to remove any rough edges.*

5. Insert the tire iron under the bead next to the valve (**Figure 52**). Force the bead on the opposite side of the tire into the center of the rim and pry the bead over the rim with the tire iron.

6. Insert a second tire iron next to the first to hold the bead over the rim. Work around the tire with the first tire iron, prying the bead over the rim. Be careful not to pinch the inner tube with the tire irons.

7. Reach inside the tire and remove the valve from the hole in the rim. Remove the tube from the tire.

> *NOTE*
> *Steps 8 and 9 are required only if it is necessary to completely remove the tire from the rim.*

8. Remove the nut and washer and remove the rim lock(s) from inside the tire.

9. Stand the tire upright. Insert the tire iron between the second bead and the side of the rim that the first bead was pried over (**Figure 53**). Force the bead on the opposite side from the tire iron into the center of the rim. Pry the second bead off of the rim, working around as with the first.

11

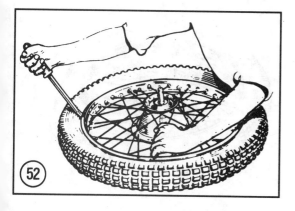

Inspection

1. Carefully check the inside and outside of the tire for any damage.

2. Check the rim locks and replace if damaged (**Figure 54**).

3. Check that the spoke ends do not protrude through the nipples into the center of the rim to puncture the tube. Grind or file off any protruding spoke ends.

> *NOTE*
> *If you are having trouble with water and dirt entering the rim, discard the rubber rim band. Wrap the rim center with two separate revolutions of duct tape. Punch holes through the tape at the rim lock and valve stem holes.*

Installation

> *NOTE*
> *Before installing the tire, place it in a hot place (in the sun or in a hot closed car). The heat will soften the rubber and ease installation.*

1. If you are using the rubber rim band, be sure the band is in place with the rough side toward the rim. Align the holes in the band with the holes in the rim.

2. Liberally sprinkle the inside tire casing with talcum powder. Talcum powder reduces chafing between the tire and tube, and helps to minimize tube damage.

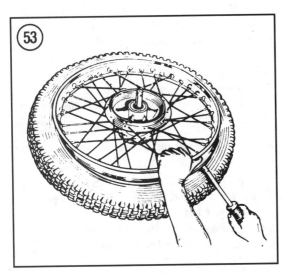

3. If the tire was removed, lubricate one bead with soapy water. Align the tire with the rim and push the tire onto the rim (**Figure 55**). Work around the tire in both directions (**Figure 56**).

4. Install the rim lock(s), lockwasher and nut. Do not tighten the nut at this time. Make sure the rim lock is positioned inside the tire.

5. Install the core into the inner tube valve. Put the tube in the tire, making sure not to twist it. Insert the valve stem through the hole in the rim. Inflate the tube just enough to round it out. Too much air will make installing it in the tire difficult, and too little will increase the chances of pinching the tube with the tire irons.

6. Lubricate the upper tire bead and rim with soapy water.

> *NOTE*
> *Make sure to install the upper tire bead over the rim locks (**Figure 57**) in Step 7. It is easy to overlook the rim locks at this point. If a rim lock is not installed*

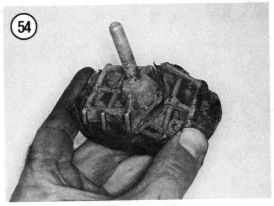

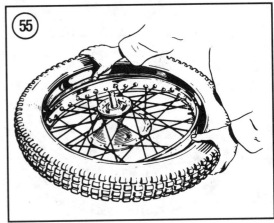

correctly, you will have to pull the side of the tire away from the rim to install it inside the tire. This increases the chances of pinching the tube.

7. Press the upper bead into the rim opposite the valve. Pry the bead into the rim on both sides of the initial point with your hands and work around the rim to the valve. If the tire wants to pull up on one side, either use a tire iron or one of your knees to hold the tire in place. The last few inches are usually the toughest to install; it is also where most pinched tubes occur. If you can, continue to push the tire into the rim with your hands. Relubricate the bead if necessary. If the tire bead wants to pull out from under the rim use both of your knees to hold the tire in place. If necessary, use a tire iron for the last few inches.

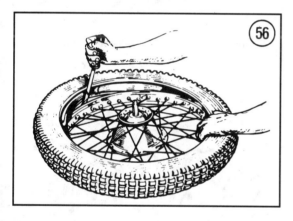

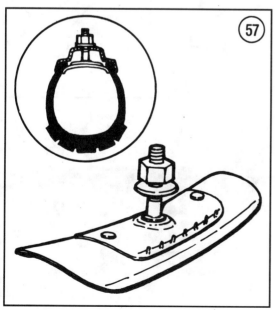

8. Reach inside the tire and wiggle the valve stem to make sure the tube is not trapped under the bead. Set the valve squarely in its hole before screwing on the valve nut.

NOTE
*Make sure the valve stem is not turned sideways in the rim as shown in **Figure 58**.*

9. Check the bead on both sides of the tire for even fit around the rim, then relubricate both sides of the tire. Inflate the tire to approximately 172-207 kPa (25-30 psi) to insure the tire bead is seated properly on the rim. If the tire is hard to seat, release the air from the tube and then reinflate.

WARNING
Do not overinflate the tube when trying to seat the tire onto the rim.

10. Tighten the rim lock nut(s) (**Figure 50**) securely.

11. Bleed the tire pressure back down to 15 psi (100 kPa). Screw on the valve stem nut but do not tighten it against the rim. Instead, tighten it against the air cap. Doing this will prevent the valve stem from pulling away from the tube if the tire slips on the rim.

DRIVE CHAIN

Refer to **Table 2** for drive chain specifications. Refer to *Drive Chain* in Chapter Three for routine drive chain inspection and lubrication procedures.

11

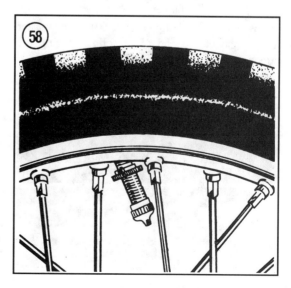

Removal/Installation

1. Support the bike on a workstand with its rear wheel off the ground.

2. Turn the rear wheel and drive chain so the master link is accessible.

NOTE
*If the drive chain is equipped with a press fit master link, remove and install it as described under **Press Fit Master Link** in this section.*

3. Remove the master link spring clip with a pair of pliers (**Figure 59**). Remove the side plate and connecting link and separate the chain. When disconnecting an O-ring chain, remove the 4 O-rings (**Figure 60**, typical).

4. Slowly pull the drive chain off the drive sprocket.

5. Install by reversing the preceding removal steps while noting the following.

6. If you are using an O-ring chain, install the four O-rings following the chain manufacturer's instructions (**Figure 60**, typical) or use the following guideline:

    a. Install an O-ring on each connecting link pin (**Figure 61**).

    b. Insert the connecting link (A, **Figure 62**) through the chain.

    c. Install the remaining two O-rings onto the connecting link pins (B, **Figure 62**).

    d. Install the slide plate (**Figure 63**). If the side plate is a press fit, refer to *Press Fit Master Link* in this chapter.

7. Install the spring clip (**Figure 60**) on the master link so the closed end of the clip is facing the direction of chain travel. See **Figure 64**.

8. Adjust the drive chain as described in Chapter Three.

Press Fit Master Link

Many of the new drive chains use a press fit side plate (**Figure 63**), which helps to keep the chain connected if the spring clip pops off as the bike is being ridden. To remove and install this type of master link, special tools are required. To disconnect the chain, first remove the spring clip (**Figure 59**) from the master link, then use a chain breaker (**Fig-**

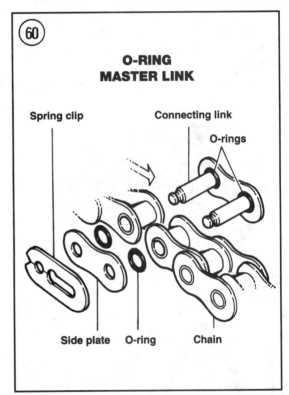

O-RING MASTER LINK

Spring clip   Connecting link

O-rings

Side plate   O-ring   Chain

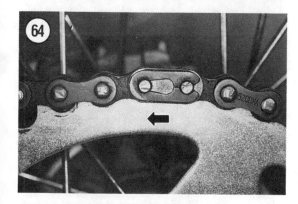

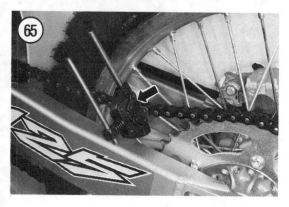

ure 65) to separate the side plate from the master link. To install the side plate, use a press-fit chain tool like the Motion Pro chain press tool (part No. 08-070) shown in **Figure 66**. After pressing the side plate onto the master link, pivot both ends of the chain at the master link. The chain ends must pivot smoothly with no sign of binding. If the chain is too tight or binds at the master link, you pressed the side plate on too far. Usually, the side plate is properly installed when the grooves in the connecting link just show on the outside of the side plate. If the connecting link grooves are partially visible, the spring clip will not seat in the grooves properly. This can cause the spring clip to pop off.

> *CAUTION*
> *Attempting to install a press-fit master link without the proper tools may cause you to damage the master link and drive chain.*

Cutting A Drive Chain To Length

Table 2 lists the correct number of chain links required for stock gearing. If the replacement drive chain is too long, cut it to the desired length as follows.

1. Remove the new chain from its box and stretch it out on your workbench. Set the master link aside for now.

2. If you are installing a new chain onto stock sprockets, refer to **Table 2** for the correct number of links for your chain. If you changed sprocket sizes, install the new chain onto both sprockets (with the rear wheel moved forward) to determine the correct number of links to remove (**Figure 67**). Make a chalk mark on the two chain pins where you want to

11

cut the chain. Count the chain links one more time
or check the chain length to make sure you are
correct.

> *WARNING*
> *Using a hand or bench grinder as*
> *described in Step 3 will cause flying*
> *particles. Do not operate a grinding tool*
> *without proper eye protection.*

3. Grind the head of two pins flush with the face of
the side plate with a grinder or suitable grinding tool.
4. Press the side plate out of the chain with a chain
breaker (**Figure 68**); support the chain carefully
when doing this. If the pins are still tight, grind more
material from the end of the pins and then try again.
5. Remove the side plate and push out the connecting link (**Figure 69**).
6. Install the new drive chain as described in this
chapter.

Service and Inspection

For routine service and inspection of the drive
chain, refer to *Drive Chain* in Chapter Three.

SPROCKET REPLACEMENT

This section describes service procedures for replacing the drive (front) and driven (rear) sprockets.
See **Table 2** for the stock sprocket sizes.

Inspection

Check the drive chain and sprocket wear as described under *Drive Chain* in Chapter Three.

Drive Sprocket
Removal/Installation

Refer to **Figure 70** for this procedure.
1. Unbolt and remove the sprocket cover and the
case saver (**Figure 71**).
2. Remove the circlip (A, **Figure 72**). Pull the drive
sprocket (B) off the countershaft and disconnect it
from the drive chain.

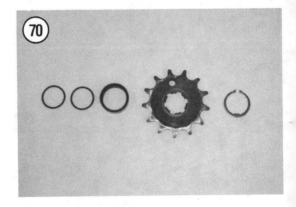

> *NOTE*
> *If you cannot remove the drive sprocket*
> *because the drive chain is too tight,*
> *remove the rear axle nut and loosen the*

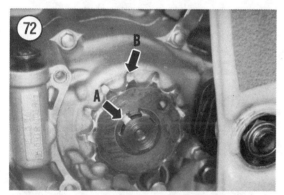

chain adjusters, or if necessary, disconnect the drive chain.

3. Remove the collar (**Figure 73**) and the two O-rings (**Figure 74**).

4. Inspect the sprocket assembly as described in this section.

5. Lubricate the two O-rings with oil and slide them over the countershaft (**Figure 74**).

6. Apply a light coat of grease onto the collar's outside diameter. Install the collar with its shoulder side (**Figure 75**) facing in (toward O-rings). Push the collar all the way in (**Figure 73**), making sure its shoulder engages both O-rings.

7. If the drive chain is installed on the bike, mesh the drive sprocket with the chain, then install the sprocket (B, **Figure 72**) onto the countershaft.

8. Install a new circlip (A, **Figure 72**) into the countershaft groove. Make sure the circlip seats in the groove completely.

9. Install the case saver (**Figure 71**) and the sprocket cover, if used. Tighten the mounting bolts securely.

10. Check the chain adjustment (Chapter Three).

Driven Sprocket
Removal and Installation

NOTE
Allen bolts and nuts secure the driven sprocket to the rear hub. When loosening and tightening these sprocket fasteners, hold the Allen bolts with an Allen wrench or hex socket and turn the nuts. Do not try to hold the nut and turn the Allen bolts as the Allen wrench could slip and round off the hex portion of the bolt, making further removal attempts very difficult.

11

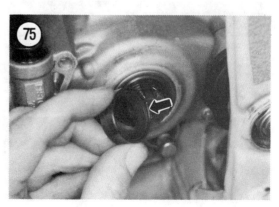

1. Support the bike on a workstand with the rear wheel off the ground.

2. Hold one of the sprocket Allen bolts and loosen its mounting nut with a wrench. Repeat for each Allen bolt, washer and nut.

3. Remove the rear wheel as described in this chapter.

4. Remove the Allen bolts, nuts and driven sprocket from the rear hub.

5. Check the sprocket mounting tabs (**Figure 76**) for cracks or other damage. Replace the hub if any damage is found.

6. Clean and dry the sprocket fasteners. Replace any nut or bolt with damaged threads or hex corners.

7. Install the new sprocket onto the rear hub with its marked or stamped side facing out.

8. Install the Allen bolts, washers and nuts and tighten hand-tight.

9. Install the rear wheel onto the swing arm as described in this chapter.

10. Hold the Allen bolts with a hex socket (A, **Figure 77**), then use a torque adapter (B) and torque wrench to tighten the driven sprocket nuts as specified in **Table 3**. Repeat to tighten all of the nuts.

NOTE
*B, **Figure 73** shows the Motion Pro torque adapter and a torque wrench. For information on using a torque adapter and torque wrench, refer to **Torque Wrench Adapters** in Chapter One. The tool shown in B, **Figure 73** is the same tool used to tighten the cylinder base nuts described in Chapter Four.*

11. Adjust the drive chain as described in Chapter Three.

Drive and Driven Sprocket Inspection

1. Inspect the sprocket teeth (**Figure 78**). If they are visibly worn, replace the sprocket.

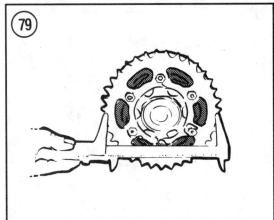

2. Measure the sprocket diameter at the base of the teeth as shown in **Figure 79**. Replace the sprocket if its diameter is out of specification (**Table 2**).

3. Inspect the drive sprocket collar (**Figure 70**) for cracks or other damage. Remove any rust or corrosion from the collar surfaces. Make sure the outer collar surface is smooth. Otherwise, the collar will damage the countershaft seal. If necessary, smooth the outer collar surface with fine grade sandpaper (No. 400 or 600), then clean thoroughly. If necessary, replace the collar.

4. Replace the drive sprocket O-rings if worn or damaged.

5. If either sprocket requires replacement, the drive chain is probably worn also. Refer to *Drive Chain* in Chapter Three.

Table 1 FRONT AND REAR WHEEL SPECIFICATIONS

Front tire	
Size	80/100-21 51M
Make/type	
European model	
1992-1997	Dunlop D752
1998	Dunlop D755
All other models	
1992-1996	Dunlop K490
1997-on	Bridgestone M477
Rear tire	
Size	100/90-19 57M
Make/type	
European model	
1992-1997	Dunlop D752
1998	Dunlop D752
All other models	
1992-1993	Dunlop K695
1994-1996	Dunlop D737
1997-on	Bridgestone M478A
Wheel runout limit	2.0 mm (0.078 in.)
Axle runout limit	0.2 mm (0.008 in.)

11

Table 2 DRIVE CHAIN AND SPROCKET SPECIFICATIONS

Drive chain	
Manufacturer	DAIDO
Type	
1992-1996	DID 520DS
1997-on	DID 520DMA
Number of chain links	
1992-1993	114
1994-1996	112
1997-on	114
Stock sprocket sizes (front/rear)	
1992-1996	14/49
1997	
U.S. models	14/49
All other models	13/49
1998	
U.S. models	14/49
All other models	13/48
	(continued)

Table 2 DRIVE CHAIN AND SPROCKET SPECIFICATIONS (continued)

Drive (front) sprocket diameter	
13 teeth	
Standard	55.48-55.68 mm (2.184-2.192 in.)
Service limit	55.2 mm (2.173 in.)
14 teeth	
Standard	60.99-61.19 mm (2.401-2.410 in.)
Service limit	60.7 mm (2.39 in.)
Driven (rear) sprocket diameter	
48 teeth	
Standard	232.62-233.12 mm (9.158-9.177 in.)
Service limit	232.1 mm (9.138 in.)
49 teeth	
Standard	237.54-238.01 mm (9.352-9.370 in.)
Service limit	237.0 mm (9.331 in.)
50 teeth	
Standard	242.71-243.21 mm (9.555-9.575 in.)
Service limit	242.2 mm (9.535 in.)

Table 3 FRONT AND REAR WHEEL TIGHTENING TORQUES

	N•m	in.-lb.	ft.-lb.
Front axle clamp nuts	9.3	82	–
Front axle			
1992-1993	54	–	40
1994-on	78	–	58
Driven sprocket nuts			
1992-1994	29	–	22
1995-on	34	–	25
Rear axle nut			
1992-1994	98	–	72
1995-on	115	–	87
Spoke nipples	1.5	13	–
Rear brake caliper mounting bolt			
1992-1994	25	–	18

CHAPTER TWELVE

FRONT SUSPENSION AND STEERING

This chapter describes service procedures for the handlebar, steering stem and front forks. **Table 1** lists front suspension and steering specifications. **Tables 1-5** are at the end of this chapter.

HANDLEBAR

NOTE
This section describes service to the stock Kawasaki handlebars. When installing aftermarket handlebars and/or handlebar holder, refer to the manufacturer's instructions for any additional information.

Removal

Refer to **Figure 1** for this procedure.
1. Support the bike on a workstand.
2. Disconnect the number plate strap from the handlebar.
3. Remove the clamp securing the engine stop switch wiring harness to the handlebar.
4. Remove the engine stop switch (A, **Figure 2**).

NOTE
While the engine stop switch is off the handlebar, check its wires for fraying or other damage that could cause the switch to ground against the handlebar and cause a no-spark condition

5. Remove the clutch cable holder (B, **Figure 2**) mounting bolts. Remove the holder and clutch cable from the handlebar.
6. Remove the bolts securing the master cylinder to the handlebar and remove the master cylinder (A, **Figure 3**). Support the master cylinder so it does not hang by its hose.
7. Loosen the throttle housing screws (B, **Figure 3**).
8. Remove the handlebar holder bolts and the upper holder (A, **Figure 4**). Remove the handlebar while sliding the throttle housing off the handlebar.

Inspection

1. Inspect the handlebar for cracks, bending or other damage and replace if necessary.
2. If equipped with an aluminum handlebar, inspect it for scores or cracks, especially at the handlebar clamp and clutch lever perch mounting areas. If any cracks, scores or other damage are found, replace the handlebar. Cracks and scoring of the metal in these areas may cause the handlebar to break.

WARNING
Never attempt to straighten, weld or heat a bent or damaged handlebar. These attempts can weaken the handlebar and may cause it to break while under heavy stress (landing from a jump) or during a crash. Both

12

instances can cause serious personal injury.

3. Inspect the handlebar mounting bolts for bending, thread strippage or other damage. Check the threaded holes in the lower holders for the same conditions. Clean both sets of threads to remove all dirt and grease residue. Replace damaged bolts.

4. Clean the upper and lower handlebar holders and the knurled section on steel handlebars with a stiff

brush and solvent or electrical contact cleaner. If you are using an aluminum handlebar, clean the holder area on the bar with contact cleaner and a soft brush.

5. The lower handlebar holders are rubber mounted onto the upper fork bridge (**Figure 4**). When servicing the lower holders, note the following:

   a. Check the lower holder mounting nuts for tightness. If the nuts are tight, but there is excessive holder play when the handlebar is

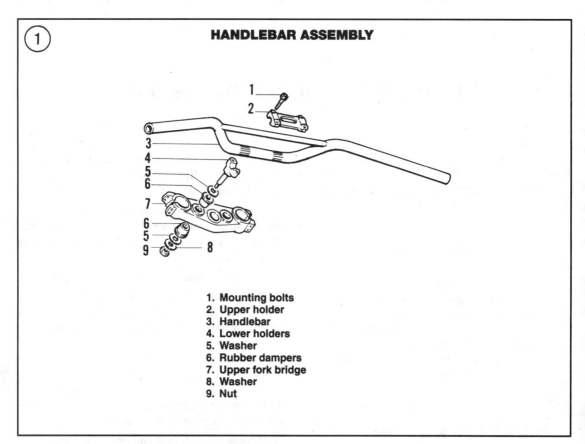

HANDLEBAR ASSEMBLY

1. Mounting bolts
2. Upper holder
3. Handlebar
4. Lower holders
5. Washer
6. Rubber dampers
7. Upper fork bridge
8. Washer
9. Nut

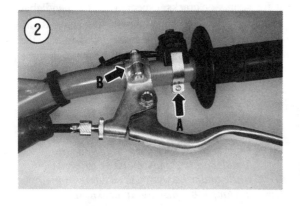

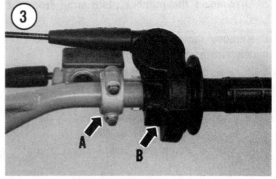

mounted on the bike, the rubber dampers are probably worn or damaged.

b. Remove the nuts and disassemble the holder assembly. Note that two different size washers are used (**Figure 4**). The upper and lower dampers (four total) are identical.

c. Check the dampers for cracks, hardness or other damage. Replace the dampers as a set.

d. Check the damper mounting bores for cracks or other damage. Carefully remove any rubber stuck to the mounting bores with contact cleaner and a rag.

e. Reassemble the holder assembly and tighten the mounting nuts securely.

Installation

Refer to **Figure 1** for this procedure.

1. Slide the throttle housing over the handlebar. Position the handlebar in the lower holders and install the upper holder (**Figure 4**) and the mounting

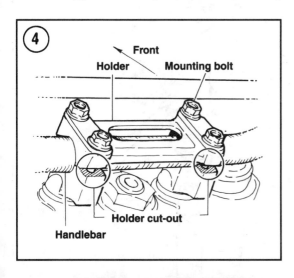

4

Front

Holder   Mounting bolt

Holder cut-out

Handlebar

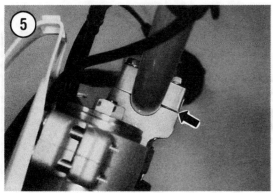

5

bolts. Install the holder so its cut side faces toward the back (**Figure 4**). Tighten the two front mounting bolts hand-tight.

2. Straddle the bike and check the handlebar position. Rotate the handlebar forward or backward until it feels comfortable, then tighten the front and then the rear handlebar mounting bolts as specified in **Table 5**. When the handlebars are correctly installed, the front edges of the clamps will touch, leaving a gap at the back (**Figure 5**).

> *WARNING*
> *Do not ride the bike until the handlebar clamps are mounted and tightened correctly. Improper mounting may cause the bars to slip, resulting in loss of control of the bike.*

3. Position the throttle housing, leaving a small gap between the inside edge of the throttle grip and the end of the handlebar. Tighten its mounting bolts securely. Open and release the throttle grip, making sure it returns smoothly.

4. Install the master cylinder as follows:

a. Install the master cylinder holder with the arrow mark on the holder facing up (A, **Figure 3**).

b. Install and tighten the master cylinder mounting bolts. Tighten the upper bolt, then the lower bolt as specified in **Table 5**.

5. Install the clutch lever perch assembly (B, **Figure 2**) and tighten its bolts securely.

6. Install the engine stop switch (A, **Figure 2**).

7. Secure the number plate strap over the handlebar.

8. Straddle the bike again and recheck the position of the handlebar and its controls.

> *WARNING*
> *Make sure the front brake, clutch cable and throttle cable are operating correctly before riding the bike.*

STEERING HEAD

The steering head (**Figure 6**) is equipped with tapered roller bearings at the top and bottom pivot positions. The tapered roller bearing inner races (mounted in the frame) and the lower bearing (mounted on the steering stem) should not be removed unless they require replacement.

12

⑥

STEERING ASSEMBLY

1. Steering stem nut
2. Washer
3. Upper fork bridge
4. Steering adjust nut
5. Upper bearing
6. Frame neck
7. Lower bearing
8. Steering stem

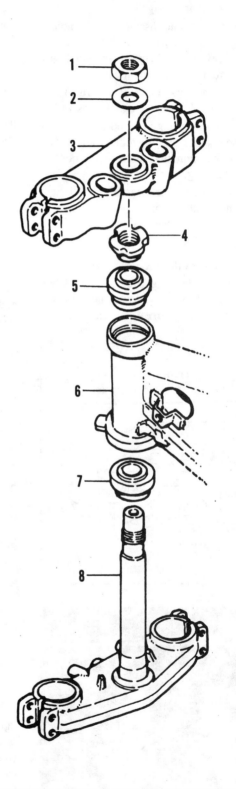

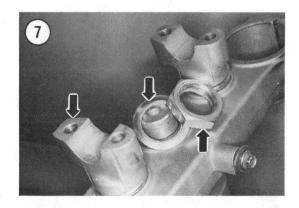

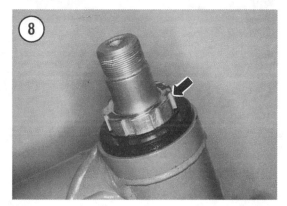

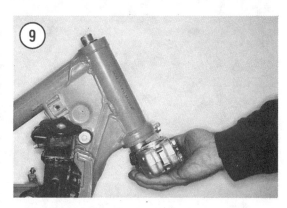

Remove the steering stem and lubricate the bearings at the intervals specified in Chapter Three.

Disassembly

1. Remove the front wheel (Chapter Eleven).
2. Remove the front fender.
3. Remove the handlebar as described in this chapter.
4. Remove the front forks as described in this chapter.
5. Loosen and remove the steering stem nut and flat washer (**Figure 7**).
6. Remove the upper fork bridge (**Figure 7**).
7. Remove the steering adjust nut (**Figure 8**) and steering stem (**Figure 9**).
8. Remove the upper bearing (**Figure 10**).

Inspection

Replace parts that are excessively worn or damaged as described in this section.
1. Clean the bearing races in the steering head, the steering stem races, ball bearings and the tapered roller bearing with solvent.
2. Check the steering head frame welds for cracks and fractures. Refer repair to a qualified frame shop or welding service.
3. Check the steering stem nut and steering adjust nut for damage.
4. Check the steering stem assembly (**Figure 11**) for cracks and damage.
5. Check the bearing races in the frame for pitting, galling and corrosion. Compare the worn bearing race in **Figure 12** with the new race in **Figure 13**. If a race is worn or damaged, replace both races (and bearings) as described in this section.

12

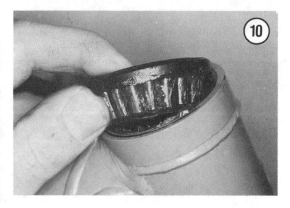

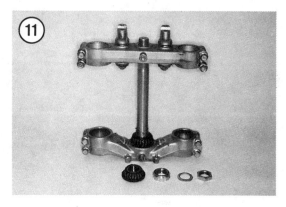

6. Check the tapered roller bearings (**Figure 14**) for pitting, scratches or discoloration that indicate wear or corrosion damage. Compare the worn bearing in **Figure 14** with the new bearing in **Figure 15**.

7. When reusing bearings, clean them thoroughly with a bearing degreaser. After cleaning and drying the bearings, pack them with a waterproof bearing grease.

Outer Bearing Race Replacement

Do not remove the upper and lower (**Figure 12**) outer bearing races unless they are going to be re-

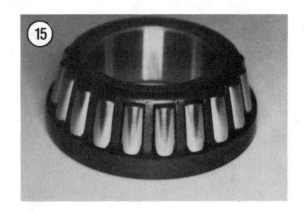

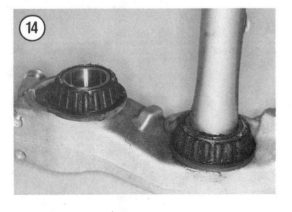

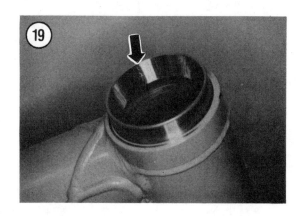

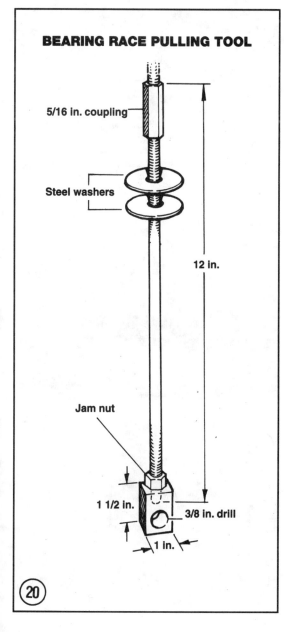

BEARING RACE PULLING TOOL

5/16 in. coupling

Steel washers

12 in.

Jam nut

1 1/2 in.

3/8 in. drill

1 in.

placed. If you replace a bearing race, you must also replace the tapered bearing.

1. Insert an aluminum drift into the frame tube (**Figure 16**) and carefully drive the race out from the inside (**Figure 17**). Strike at different spots around the race to prevent it from binding in the mounting bore. Repeat for the other race.

2. Clean the race bore (**Figure 18**) and check for cracks or other damage.

3. Place the new race squarely into the mounting bore opening with its tapered side facing out (**Figure 19**).

4. To prevent damage to the races or frame mounting bore, install the races as follows:

  a. Assemble the puller tool shown in **Figure 20**. The block mounted at the bottom of the threaded rod is used as a T-handle to hold the rod stationary as you install the race from the opposite end. The hole drilled horizontally through the block must be large enough to accept a suitable rod for the T-handle.

CAUTION
When using the threaded rod or a similar tool to install the bearing races in the following steps, do not allow the rod or tool to contact the face of the bearing race as any contact could damage the bearing.

  b. To install the upper race, insert the puller through the bottom of the frame tube (A, **Figure 21**). Seat the lower washer or plate against the frame as shown in B, **Figure 21**.

  c. At the top of the puller, slide the large washer down and seat it squarely on top of the bearing race (A, **Figure 22**). Install the required wash-

12

ers and coupling nut (B, **Figure 22**) that will work on your puller.

d. Hand tighten the coupling nut (B, **Figure 22**), checking that the washer is centered on the bearing race.

e. Hold the threaded rod to prevent it from turning and tighten the coupling nut with a wrench (**Figure 23**). Continue until the race is drawn into the frame tube and the washer seats against the frame tube. Remove the puller assembly and inspect the bearing race. It must bottom out in the frame tube as shown in **Figure 24**.

f. Repeat to install the bottom race (**Figure 13**).

5. Lubricate the upper and lower bearing races with grease.

Steering Stem Bearing Replacement

Perform the following steps to replace the steering stem bearing (**Figure 25**).

1. Thread the steering stem nut onto the steering stem (**Figure 26**).

> *WARNING*
> *Safety glasses must be worn when removing the steering stem bearing in Step 3.*

2. Remove the steering stem bearing and dust seal with a hammer and chisel as shown in **Figure 26**. Strike at different spots underneath the bearing to prevent it from binding on the steering stem.

3. Clean the steering stem with solvent and dry thoroughly.

4. Inspect the steering stem and replace if damaged.

5. Pack the new bearing with a waterproof bearing grease.

6. Slide the new bearing onto the steering stem until it stops.

7A. To install the new steering stem bearing with a press, perform the following:

a. Install the steering stem and the new bearing in a press and support it with two bearing drivers as shown in **Figure 27**. Make sure the lower bearing driver seats against the inner bearing race and does not contact the bearing rollers.

b. Press the bearing onto the steering stem until it bottoms (**Figure 25**).

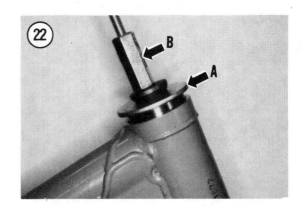

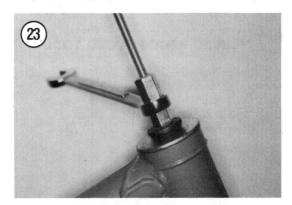

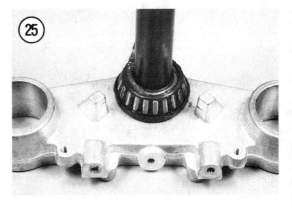

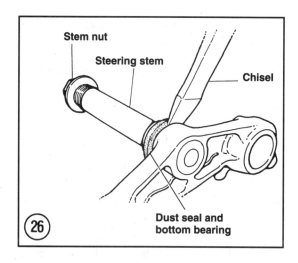

(26)

Stem nut

Steering stem

Chisel

Dust seal and
bottom bearing

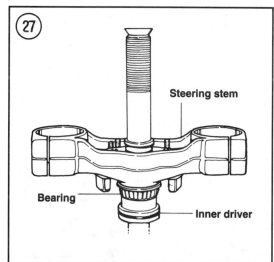

(27)

Steering stem

Bearing

Inner driver

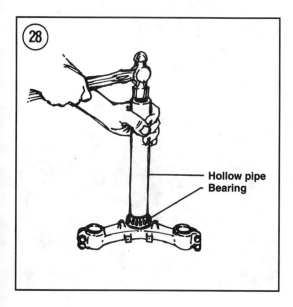

(28)

Hollow pipe
Bearing

7B. To install the new steering stem bearing with a bearing driver, perform the following:

    a. Slide a bearing driver or long hollow pipe over the steering stem until it seats against the bearing's inner race (**Figure 28**).

    b. Drive the bearing onto the steering stem until it bottoms out (**Figure 25**).

Assembly and Steering Adjustment

Refer to **Figure 6** when assembling the steering stem assembly.

1. Make sure the upper (**Figure 24**) and lower (**Figure 13**) bearing races are properly seated in the frame.

2. Lubricate the bearings and races with a waterproof bearing grease.

3. Install the upper bearing (**Figure 29**) and seat it into its race.

4. Install the steering stem through the bottom of the frame and hold it in place.

5. Install the steering adjust nut (**Figure 30**) and tighten finger-tight.

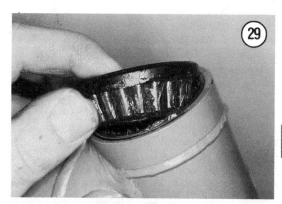

(29)

12

(30)

NOTE

*Kawasaki lists a torque specification to seat and adjust the steering bearings into their races. To do this, you can use a spanner wrench torque adapter like the one shown in **Figure 31**. Before using a torque adapter, refer to the information listed under **Torque Wrench Adapters** in Chapter One, then perform Step 6A. To seat the bearings without special tools, perform Step 6B.*

6A. To seat the bearings using a torque adapter and torque wrench, perform the following:

   a. Tighten the steering adjust nut (**Figure 32**) to the bearing seat torque specification listed in **Table 5**.

   b. Loosen the steering adjust nut, then turn the steering stem from lock-to-lock five times to seat the bearings.

   c. Retighten the steering adjust nut (**Figure 32**) to the final torque specification in **Table 5**.

   d. Check bearing play by turning the steering stem from lock-to-lock. The steering stem must pivot smoothly with no binding or roughness.

NOTE

It is difficult to adjust the steering play to a specific torque specification using a torque wrench and adapter as there are many variables that come into play. If the steering stem is still too loose or tight after performing Step 6A, readjust it as described in Step 6B.

6B. If you do not have the tools described in Step 6A, tighten the steering adjust nut as follows:

   a. Tighten the steering adjust nut (**Figure 30**) to seat the bearings. Loosen the nut completely. Use a spanner wrench or punch and hammer to tighten and loosen the nut.

   b. Tighten the steering adjust nut while checking bearing play. The steering adjust nut must be tight enough to remove play, both horizontal and vertical, yet loose enough so the assembly will turn to both lock positions under its own weight after an assist.

7. Install the upper fork bridge (**Figure 33**).

8. Install the washer and the steering stem nut (**Figure 33**). Tighten the nut finger-tight.

9. Slide both fork tubes into position and tighten the upper and lower fork tube pinch bolts as specified in **Table 5**.

10. Tighten the steering stem nut (**Figure 34**) as specified in **Table 5**.

NOTE

Because tightening the steering stem nut affects the steering bearing preload, it may be necessary to repeat these steps a few times until the steering adjustment is correct.

11. Check bearing play by turning the steering stem from side to side. The steering stem must pivot smoothly. If the steering stem does not turn freely, readjust the bearing play as follows:

   a. Loosen the steering stem nut (**Figure 34**), then slightly loosen the steering adjust nut (**Figure 30**).

   b. Retighten the steering stem nut (**Figure 34**) as specified in **Table 5**.

   c. Recheck bearing play by turning the steering stem from side-to-side. If the play is good, turn the steering stem so the front forks are facing

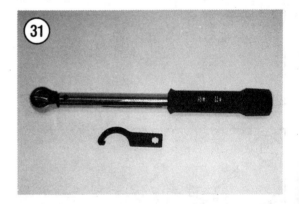

straight ahead. Grasp the fork tubes and try to move them back and forth (front to back). Do this several times while trying to detect any play in the bearings. If there is play and the bearing adjustment feels good, the bearings and races are probably worn and require replacement. It helps to have someone steady the bike when checking steering head play.

12. Install the handlebar as described in this chapter.
13. Install the front fender.
14. Install the front wheel as described in this chapter.
15. After 30 minutes to one hour of riding time, check the steering adjustment. Adjust, if necessary, as described under *Steering Play Check and Adjustment* in this chapter.

Steering Play
Check and Adjustment

Steering adjustment takes up any slack in the steering stem and bearings and allows the steering stem to operate with free rotation. Any excessive play or roughness in the steering stem will make the

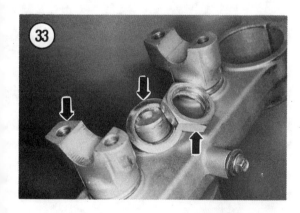

steering imprecise and difficult and cause bearing damage. These conditions are usually caused by improper bearing lubrication or an incorrect steering adjustment (too loose or tight). An incorrectly routed clutch or throttle cable can also affect steering operation.

1. Support the bike with the front wheel off the ground.
2. Turn the handlebar from side to side. The steering stem should move freely and without any binding or roughness.
3. Turn the handlebar so the front wheel points straight ahead. Alternately push (slightly) one end of the handlebar, then the other. The front end must turn to each side from center under its own weight. Note the following:

   a. If the steering stem moved roughly or stopped before hitting the frame stop, check the clutch and throttle cable routing. Reroute the cable(s) if necessary.
   b. If the cable routing is correct and the steering is tight, the steering adjustment is too tight or the bearings require lubrication or replacement.
   c. If the steering stem moved from side to side correctly, perform Step 4 to check for excessive looseness.

NOTE
Have an assistant steady the bike while you check for excessive steering play in Step 4.

4. Grasp the fork tubes firmly (near the axle) and attempt to move the wheel backward-and-forward. Note the following:

   a. If movement can be felt at the steering stem, the steering adjustment is probably loose. Go to Step 5 to adjust the steering.
   b. If there is no excessive movement and the front end turns correctly, as described in Steps 2-4, the steering adjustment is correct.

5. Remove the handlebar (A, **Figure 35**) as described in this chapter.
6. Loosen the lower fork tube pinch bolts (A, **Figure 36**).
7. Loosen the steering stem nut (B, **Figure 35**).
8. Adjust the steering adjust nut (C, **Figure 35**) as follows:

   a. If the steering is too loose, tighten the steering adjust nut.

12

   b. If the steering is too tight, loosen the steering adjust nut.

9. Tighten the steering stem nut (B, **Figure 35**) as specified in **Table 5**.

10. Recheck the steering adjustment as described in this procedure. When the steering adjustment is correct, continue with Step 11.

NOTE
Because tightening the steering stem nut affects the steering bearing preload, it may be necessary to repeat Steps 7-9 a few times until the steering adjustment is correct. If you cannot obtain a correct steering adjustment, the steering bearings may require lubrication or are damaged. Remove the steering stem and inspect the bearings as described in this chapter.

11. Tighten the lower fork tube pinch bolts (A, **Figure 36**) as specified in **Table 5**.

12. Install the handlebar as described in this chapter. Recheck the steering adjustment.

FRONT FORK

Removal

1. Remove the front wheel as described in this chapter.

2. Remove the fork protectors (**Figure 37**).

3. Remove the brake caliper as follows:

   a. Remove the hose clamp bolts and clamp (A, **Figure 38**).

   b. Unbolt (B, **Figure 38**) and remove the brake caliper.

   c. Secure the brake caliper with a wire hook.

NOTE
Insert a spacer block in the caliper in place of the disc. If the brake lever is inadvertently squeezed, the pistons will not be forced out of their caliper bores. If this happens, you must disassemble the caliper to reseat the pistons.

CAUTION
When performing Step 4, release the air pressure gradually. If released too fast, oil may spurt out with the air. Protect your eyes accordingly.

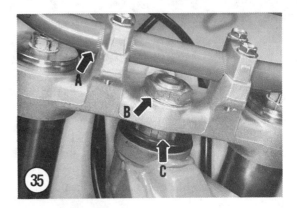

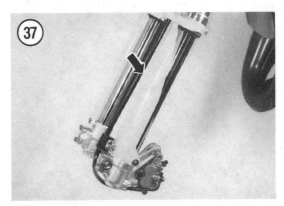

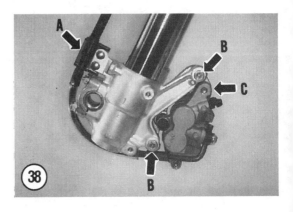

4. Loosen the air release screw in each fork cap (A, **Figure 39**).

5. Loosen the upper fork tube pinch bolts (B, **Figure 36**).

6. If the fork tubes are to be disassembled, loosen, but do not remove, the fork cap (B, **Figure 39**).

7. Loosen the lower (A, **Figure 36**) fork tube pinch bolts. Twist the fork tube and remove it from the steering stem.

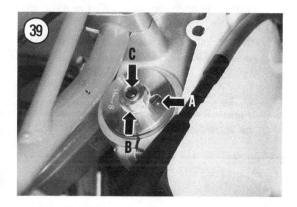

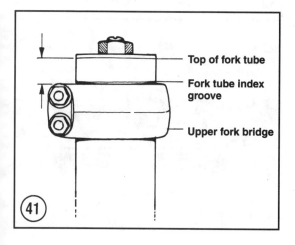

8. Repeat for the opposite fork tube.

9. Clean the fork tubes, upper fork bridge and steering stem clamping surfaces.

10. Remove, clean and inspect the fork tube pinch bolts. Replace damaged bolts.

Installation

CAUTION
Do not overtighten the fork tube pinch bolts in the following steps. Excessive pressure applied against the fork tubes can deform their shape and cause permanent damage.

1. Install one of the fork tubes into the steering stem and tighten the lower pinch bolts (A, **Figure 36**) as specified in **Table 5**. Install the fork tube with the brake caliper mounting bracket on the left side of the bike.

NOTE
If the fork cap was loosened to change the fork oil or overhaul the fork tubes, tighten the fork cap as described in Step 2.

2. Tighten the fork cap (B, **Figure 39**) as specified in **Table 5**. If the handlebar is installed on the bike, use a crowfoot wrench, extension and torque wrench (**Figure 40**) to tighten the fork cap.

NOTE
*For information on using a torque adapter (crowfoot wrench) and torque wrench, refer to **Torque Wrench Adapters** in Chapter One.*

3. Position and tighten the fork tube as follows:
   a. Loosen the lower fork tube pinch bolts and turn the fork tube so the air release screw (A, **Figure 39**) faces forward. Align the groove in the top of the fork tube with the top surface of the upper fork bridge (**Figure 41**). If there is no groove, align the top surface of the fork tube with the top surface of the upper fork bridge (**Figure 42**).
   b. Tighten the lower fork tube pinch bolts (A, **Figure 36**) as specified in **Table 5**.
   c. Tighten the upper fork tube pinch bolts (B, **Figure 36**) as specified in **Table 5**.

4. Repeat Steps 1-3 for the other fork tube.

5. Install the brake caliper as follows:

Top of fork tube

Fork tube index groove

Upper fork bridge

12

a. Position the brake caliper (**Figure 38**) against the left fork tube bracket.

b. Install and tighten the brake caliper mounting bolts (B, **Figure 38**) as specified in **Table 5**.

c. Route the brake hose around the front of the fork tube and secure it with the clamp and mounting bolts (A, **Figure 38**).

6. Install and tighten the fork protector.

7. Remove the spacer block from between the brake pads.

8. Install the front wheel as described in this chapter. Turn the front wheel and squeeze the front brake lever a few times to reposition the pistons and brake pads in the caliper. If the brake lever feels spongy, bleed the front brake (Chapter Fourteen).

9. If necessary, adjust the front fork compression and rebound adjusters as described in this chapter.

FRONT FORK SERVICE

Fork Tools

The following tools are required to disassemble and reassemble the fork tubes:

a. Split fork seal driver (A, **Figure 43**).

NOTE
Before purchasing a split fork seal driver, measure the outside diameter of the fork slider with a vernier caliper. Split fork seal drivers are available in different sizes: 41, 43, 45 and 46/47 mm.

b. Damper rod fork tool: B, **Figure 43** (Motion Pro part No. 08-117 or equivalent).

NOTE
*The Motion Pro tool shown in B, **Figure 43** will work on most all KYB and Showa inverted forks.*

c. 14 mm hex socket (C, **Figure 43**).

The following tools are required to bleed the fork tubes and set the fork oil level:

a. Fork oil level gauge: A, **Figure 44** (Motion Pro part No. 08-121 or equivalent).

b. Fork piston rod puller: B, **Figure 44** (Kawasaki part No. 57001-1289 or equivalent).

NOTE
You can make an acceptable fork piston rod puller from a length of stiff wire cut

*from a coat hanger or welding rod as shown in C, **Figure 44**.*

Disassembly

Refer to **Figure 45** when servicing the front fork.

1. Clean the fork tubes and the bottom of the compression bolt before disassembling the fork tube.

2. Loosen the fork cap air screw (A, **Figure 39**) to release air from the fork tube.

3. Turn the rebound adjuster (C, **Figure 39**) counterclockwise to its softest setting.

4. Turn the compression adjuster (**Figure 46**) counterclockwise to its softest setting.

NOTE
*If you did not loosen the fork cap (B, **Figure 39**) while the fork tube was mounted on the bike, do so now.*

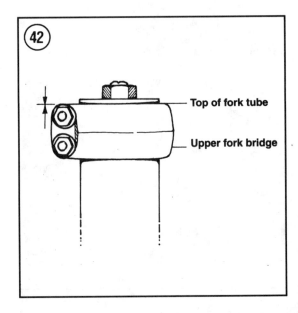

Top of fork tube

Upper fork bridge

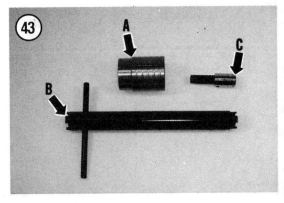

5. Hold the fork tube and unscrew the fork cap. Slowly lower the fork tube into the slider until it stops.

6. Pull the fork spring down with one hand and install a 17 mm wrench onto the piston rod locknut (**Figure 47**). Hold the wrench and loosen the fork cap (**Figure 47**) with a socket or wrench.

7. Remove the fork cap, spring seat and fork spring (**Figure 48**).

8. Hold the fork tube over a drain pan and pump the piston rod to drain oil from the fork tube and cartridge. When doing so, remove the adjuster rod (A, **Figure 49**) and distance collar (B, **Figure 49**) from inside the piston rod.

NOTE
*If you are only servicing the fork tube to change the fork oil and set the oil level, stop at this point and go to the **Fork Oil Refilling** procedure in this section. If you are going to disassemble the front fork, continue with Step 9A or 9B.*

9A. On 1992-1996 models, remove the following parts in order:
   a. Locknut (A, **Figure 50**).
   b. Spring collar (B).
   c. Spring guide (C).
   d. O-ring (**Figure 51**).

9B. On 1997-on models, remove the following parts in order:
   a. Locknut (A, **Figure 52**).
   b. Spring collar (B).
   c. Spring guide (C).
   d. O-ring (D).
   e. Spacer (E).

10. To remove the compression bolt, do the following:

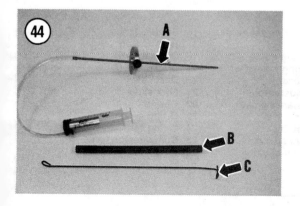

   a. Bottom out the fork tubes, then clamp the axle holder on the bottom of the fork slider in a vise with soft jaws. Do not clamp against the side of the fork tube or fork slider.
   b. Slowly push the piston rod into the cartridge until it stops.
   c. Insert the damper rod holder into the fork tube and lock it into the top of the cartridge housing (**Figure 53**).

NOTE
Figure 54 shows how the damper rod holder (A) locks into the top of the cartridge housing (B) with the cartridge removed for clarity.

   d. Hold the damper rod holder and loosen the compression bolt with the 14 mm hex socket (**Figure 55**).
   e. Remove the compression bolt (**Figure 56**) and its washer from the slider.
   f. Remove the damper rod holder from the fork tube.
   g. Remove the fork slider from the vise.

11. Turn the fork over and remove the cartridge assembly (**Figure 57**).

12. Hold the fork over the drain pan and pump the fork tube to help empty any remaining oil from the fork assembly.

13. Carefully pry the dust seal (A, **Figure 58**) out of the fork tube.

14. Pry the stop ring (B, **Figure 58**) out of the groove in the fork tube.

15. Hold the fork tube and slowly move the fork slider up and down. The fork slider must move smoothly. If there is any noticeable binding or roughness, check the fork tube for dents or other damage.

16. There is an interference fit between the slider and guide bushings. To separate the fork tube from the fork slider, hold the fork tube and pull hard on the slider using quick in and out strokes (**Figure 59**). This action withdraws the guide bushing, backup ring and oil seal from the fork tube. See **Figure 60**.

17. Carefully pry open the end of the slider bushing (A, **Figure 61**) and slide it off the fork slider. Do not pry the opening more than necessary or you may damage the bushing.

18. Remove the following parts from the slider:
   a. Guide bushing (B, **Figure 61**).
   b. Backup ring (C, **Figure 61**).

12

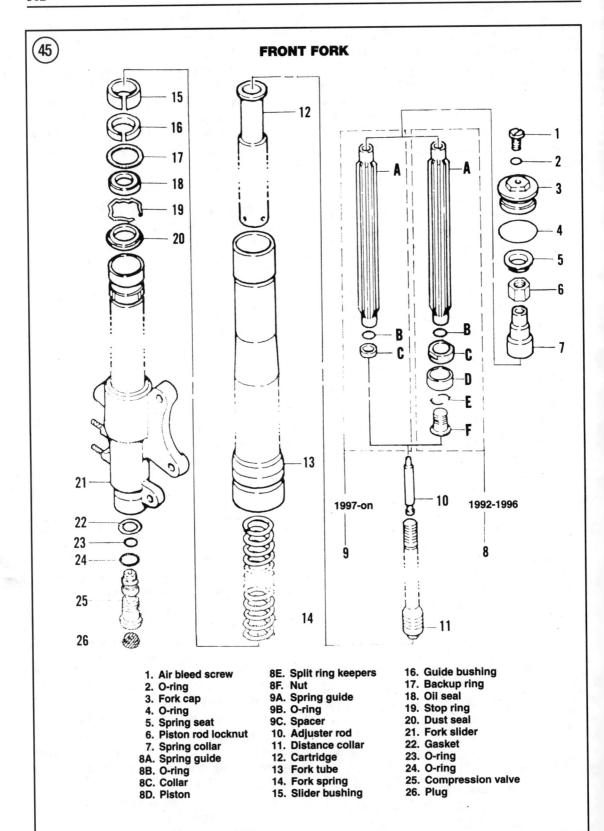

FRONT FORK

1. Air bleed screw
2. O-ring
3. Fork cap
4. O-ring
5. Spring seat
6. Piston rod locknut
7. Spring collar
8A. Spring guide
8B. O-ring
8C. Collar
8D. Piston

8E. Split ring keepers
8F. Nut
9A. Spring guide
9B. O-ring
9C. Spacer
10. Adjuster rod
11. Distance collar
12. Cartridge
13. Fork tube
14. Fork spring
15. Slider bushing

16. Guide bushing
17. Backup ring
18. Oil seal
19. Stop ring
20. Dust seal
21. Fork slider
22. Gasket
23. O-ring
24. O-ring
25. Compression valve
26. Plug

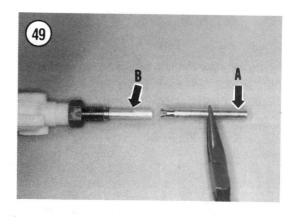

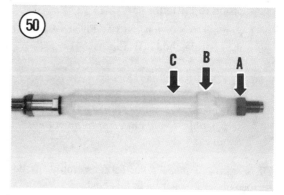

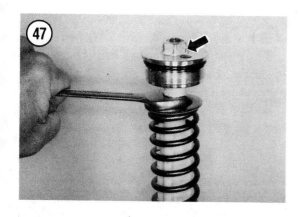

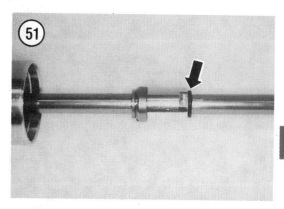

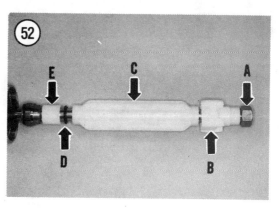

12

c. Oil seal (D, **Figure 61**).

d. Stop ring (E, **Figure 61**).

e. Dust seal (F, **Figure 61**).

19. On 1992-1996 models, disassemble and remove the oil lock piston assembly (**Figure 62**) as follows:

a. Hold the nut (A, **Figure 62**) and loosen the collar (B, **Figure 62**). Separate the collar and nut.

b. Remove the split ring keepers from the groove in the piston rod.

c. Remove the collar, piston and nut from the piston rod (**Figure 63**).

d. Remove the piston rod (A, **Figure 64**) from the cartridge body (B, **Figure 64**).

NOTE
*On 1997 and later fork tubes, the oil lock piston assembly (**Figure 65**) is not serviceable. Do not attempt to open or remove it.*

20. Clean and inspect the fork assembly, as described under *Inspection* in this chapter.

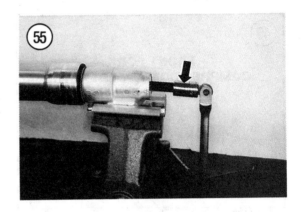

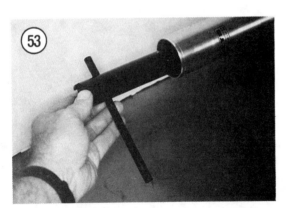

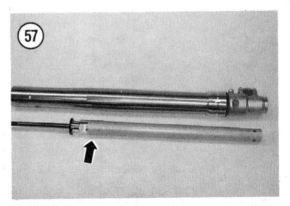

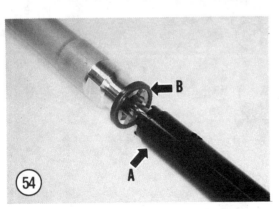

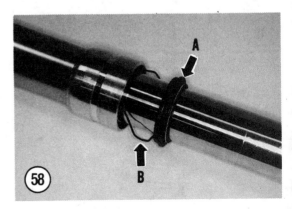

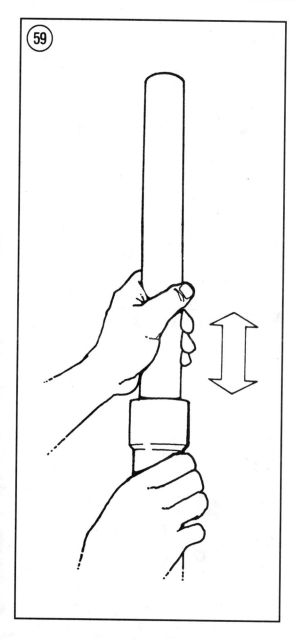

Inspection

> *NOTE*
> *Handle the fork bushings (**Figure 66**)*
> *carefully when cleaning them in Step 1.*
> *Harsh cleaning can remove or damage*
> *their coating material.*

1. Initially clean all of the fork parts in solvent, first making sure that the solvent will not damage the fork bushings or rubber parts. Clean with soap and water and rinse with plain water. Remove all threadlock residue from the compression bolt and cartridge threads. Dry with compressed air.

2. Check the fork slider (A, **Figure 67**) for nicks, rust, chrome flaking or creasing; these conditions will damage the dust and oil seals. Repair minor roughness with 600 grit sandpaper and solvent. Replace the slider if necessary.

> *CAUTION*
> *Kawasaki does not list a runout limit for*
> *the slider, but specifies to replace it if it*
> *is badly bent or creased. Do not*
> *straighten a bent slider. Any attempt to*

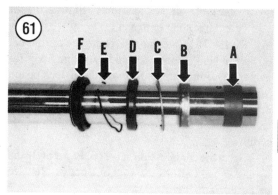

12

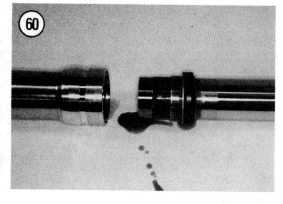

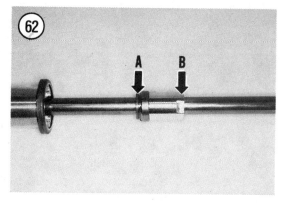

do so may weaken the tube and cause it to fail while under use.

4. Check the axle holder bore inner diameter (**Figure 68**) for dents or burrs that could damage the compression valve O-rings when removing and installing the valve. Remove burrs carefully with a fine grit sandpaper or a fine-cut file.

5. Check the fork tube (B, **Figure 67**) for:

    a. Outer tube damage.

    b. Damaged fork cap threads.

    c. Damaged oil seal bore.

    d. Damaged stop ring groove.

6A. On 1992-1996 models, perform the following:

    a. Check the rebound piston ring (A, **Figure 69**) for excessive wear or damage.

CAUTION
Do not disassemble the rebound piston assembly (A, Figure 69). If further service or adjustment is required, refer service to a qualified suspension specialist.

    b. Check the piston rod, oil lock piston assembly and the cartridge body for damage.

    c. Check the oil lock assembly (**Figure 70**) for excessive wear or damage.

6B. On 1997 and later models, check the piston rod, oil lock piston (**Figure 65**) and cartridge body for damage. Do not attempt to remove the oil lock piston assembly. Hold the cartridge body and operate the piston rod. Check for smooth operation. If there is any roughness or binding, replace the cartridge assembly.

7. Inspect the compression valve (B, **Figure 69**) and its gasket and O-rings for wear or damage. Replace damaged parts (**Figure 71**).

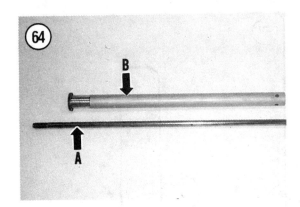

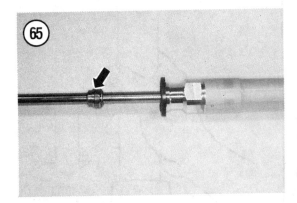

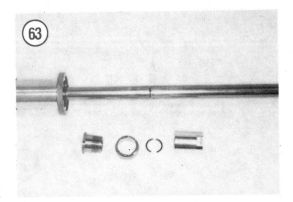

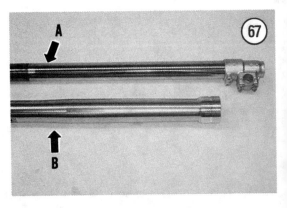

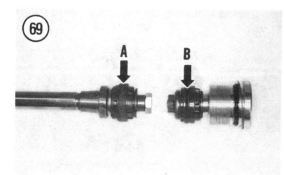

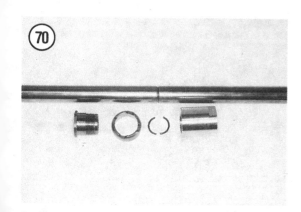

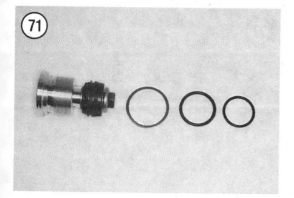

CAUTION
*Do not disassemble the compression valve (B, **Figure 69**). If further service or adjustment is required, refer service to a qualified suspension specialist.*

8. Check the slider and guide bushings (**Figure 66**) for scoring, scratches or excessive wear. Check for discoloration and material coating damage. If you can see any metal showing through the coating material, the bushing is excessively worn. Replace both bushings as a set.

9. Measure the fork spring free length with a tape measure (**Figure 72**). Replace the spring if it is too short (**Table 1**). Replace both the left and right side springs if they are unequal in length.

10. Inspect the fork cap O-ring and replace if leaking or damaged.

Front Fork Assembly

Unless otherwise specified, lubricate the fork tube components with the same fork oil that will be used when refilling the fork. See **Table 1** for a list of fork oils that can be used in the stock KYB fork tubes.

1. Before assembly, make sure you have repaired or replaced all worn or defective parts. Clean all parts before assembly.

2. On 1992-1996 models, install the oil lock piston assembly and assemble the cartridge as follows:

    a. Lubricate the rebound piston assembly (A, **Figure 73**) mounted onto the bottom of the piston rod with fork oil.

    b. Slide the piston rod (B, **Figure 73**) through the cartridge body in the direction shown in **Figure 74**.

12

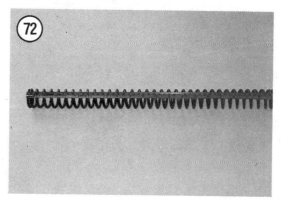

c. Slide the nut (A), piston (B) and collar (C) onto the piston rod as shown in **Figure 75**.

d. Install the split ring keepers (D, **Figure 75**) into the piston rod groove and hold them in place with your fingers (**Figure 76**).

e. Slide the piston onto the nut, then thread the collar (B, **Figure 77**) onto the nut (A, **Figure 77**).

f. Hold the nut and tighten the piston rod collar as specified in **Table 5**. Make sure the split ring keepers stay in the piston rod groove when tightening the nut and collar.

g. Set the cartridge body and piston rod assembly aside for now.

NOTE
On 1997 and later fork tubes, the oil lock piston assembly is not serviceable and should not have been disassembled.

3. Mount the axle holder (located on the bottom of the fork slider) in a vise with soft jaws.

4. Lubricate the oil seal and dust seal lips with SF-3 grease (**Figure 78**) or equivalent.

NOTE
*The grease recommended in Step 4 reduces static and sliding friction on metal-to-rubber applications. It is an ideal grease to use on fork seals. This grease resists wash-off by water and is designed to withstand temperatures up to 300° F (149° C). The SF-3 grease shown in **Figure 78** is packaged under the Simons and Noleens brand names. White Brothers Suspension Lube is a similar type of grease and can be used on the seals.*

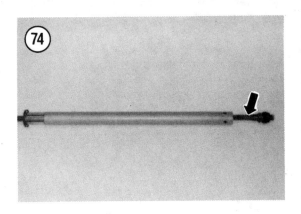

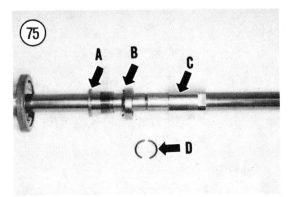

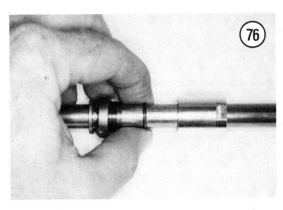

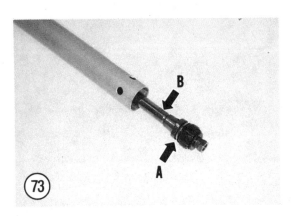

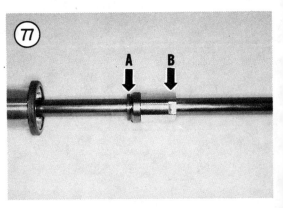

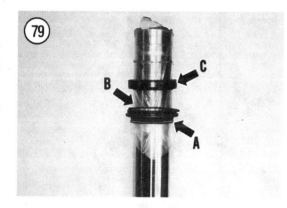

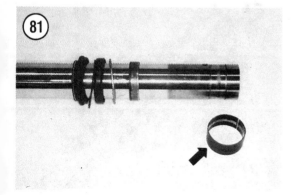

5. Cover the end of the fork slider with a thin plastic bag. Lubricate the bag with SF-3 grease.

NOTE
Covering the slider as described in Step 5 will prevent it from tearing the dust and oil seals when you install them in Step 6.

6. Install the dust seal (closed side facing down) onto the slider (A, **Figure 79**).

7. Install the stop ring (B, **Figure 79**).

8. Install the oil seal (closed side facing down) onto the slider (C, **Figure 79**).

9. Remove the plastic bag from the slider.

10. Install the backup ring (A, **Figure 80**) and guide bushing (B, **Figure 80**) onto the fork slider.

11. Install the slider bushing (**Figure 81**) into the groove in the end of the slider (A, **Figure 82**).

12. Lubricate both bushings with fork oil, then slide the slider bushing (A, **Figure 82**) and fork slider (B) into the fork tube.

NOTE
*Do not try to install the guide bushing (C, **Figure 82**), backup ring (D) or oil seal (E) at this time. These parts must be driven into the fork tube as described in Step 14 and Step 15.*

13. Support the fork with the fork tube facing up.

NOTE
Make sure you use the correct size fork seal driver. Otherwise, you can damage the new oil seal and may damage the fork tube. Refer to Fork Tools in this section.

12

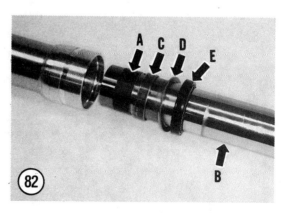

14. Install the guide bushing and backup ring as follows:

    a. Slide the guide bushing down the fork slider until it stops and seats between the fork tube and fork slider. Slide the backup ring down until it seats on top of the guide bushing. See **Figure 83**.

    b. Use the fork seal driver like a slide hammer (**Figure 84**) and drive the back-up ring and guide bushing into the fork tube. Continue until the guide bushing bottoms.

15. Install the oil seal as follows:

    a. Slide the oil seal down the fork slider until it starts to enter the fork tube. Make sure the oil seal is seating squarely against the fork tube bore.

    b. Use the fork seal driver like a slide hammer and drive the oil seal (**Figure 85**) into the fork tube. Install the oil seal until the stop ring groove in the fork tube is visible above the oil seal (**Figure 86**).

16. Install the stop ring (**Figure 87**) into the fork tube groove. Make sure the stop ring seats completely in the groove.

17. Slide the dust seal down the fork slider and seat it into the top of the fork tube (**Figure 88**).

18. Install a new washer (A, **Figure 89**) onto the compression bolt.

19. Apply fork oil onto the compression bolt O-rings (B and C, **Figure 89**), then install the O-rings (**Figure 90**) onto the compression bolt. Note that two different size O-rings are used.

20. To install the cartridge (**Figure 91**) and compression bolt assembly, do the following:

    a. Clamp the axle holder in a vise with soft jaws, then bottom out the fork tube against the fork slider.

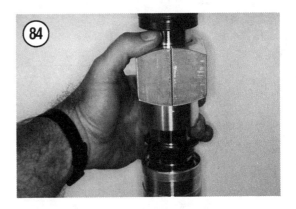

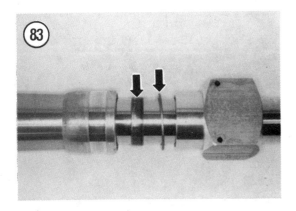

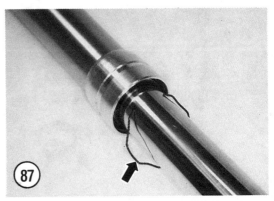

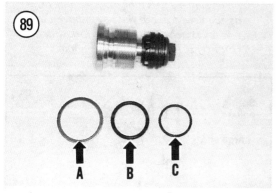

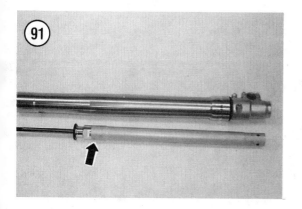

b. Install the cartridge assembly into the fork slider (**Figure 92**), then seat the lower end of the cartridge into the bore in the bottom of the fork slider.

c. Insert the damper rod holder into the fork tube and lock it into the top of the cartridge body (**Figure 53**). Check that the lower end of the cartridge still seats into the fork slider bore.

d. Apply a medium strength threadlock onto the compression bolt threads.

CAUTION
Do not allow the threadlocking compound to contact the O-rings, shim pack, or the piston assembly.

e. Hold the damper rod holder to prevent the cartridge from moving. Install the compression bolt (**Figure 93**) through the fork slider and thread it into the bottom of the cartridge.

f. Hold the cartridge body with the special tool (**Figure 53**) and tighten the compression bolt with the 14 mm hex socket and torque wrench as specified in **Table 5**.

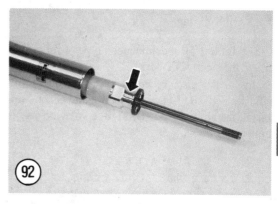

12

g. Remove the damper rod holder from the fork tube.

21A. On 1992-1996 models, install the following parts over the piston rod in order:

a. O-ring (**Figure 94**).

b. Spring guide with its longer end facing down (**Figure 95**).

c. Spring collar with its larger end facing down (**Figure 95**).

21B. On 1997-on models, install the following parts onto the piston rod in order:

a. Spacer (A, **Figure 96**).

b. O-ring (B).

c. Spring guide (C).

d. Spring collar (D) with its larger end facing down.

22. Install the piston rod locknut (E, **Figure 96**) with its chamfered side facing down (**Figure 97**). Tighten the locknut so it is 18.5 mm (0.728 in.) from the top of the piston rod as shown in **Figure 97**.

23. Complete fork assembly and set the correct oil level as described under *Fork Oil Refilling* in this section.

Fork Oil Refilling

See **Table 1** for recommended type of fork oil to use in the stock KYB forks.

1. Install the distance collar (A, **Figure 98**) and adjuster rod (B, **Figure 98**) into the piston rod. Install the adjuster rod (B, **Figure 98**) with its oil hole facing down.

NOTE
*See **Fork Tools** in this section for a description of the tools used in Step 2.*

2. Thread the Kawasaki piston rod puller (**Figure 99**) onto the end of the piston rod or hook a piece of stiff wire onto the piston rod locknut (**Figure 100**). Either tool will allow you to retrieve the piston rod if it slides into the fork tube.

3. Bottom the fork tube against the axle holder.

4. Fill the fork tube to the top with a fork oil specified in **Table 1**. See **Table 2** for fork oil capacity specifications.

NOTE
*When bleeding the fork tube, check the oil level in the fork tube often, adding oil as required to keep the level above the two holes near the top of the fork slider (**Figure 101**). Do not worry about the*

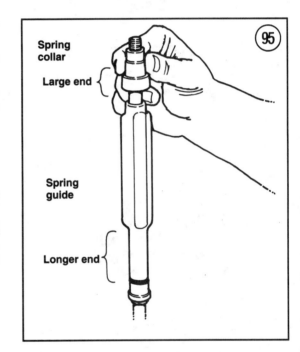

Spring collar

Large end {

Spring guide

Longer end {

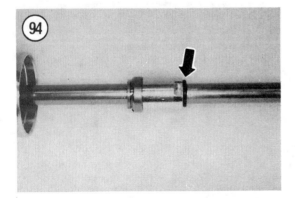

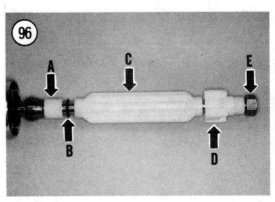

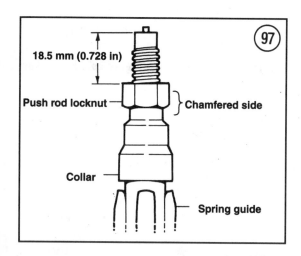

18.5 mm (0.728 in)

Push rod locknut — Chamfered side

Collar

Spring guide

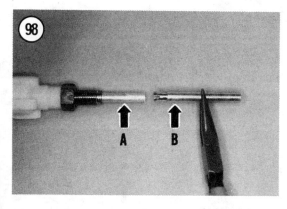

A   B

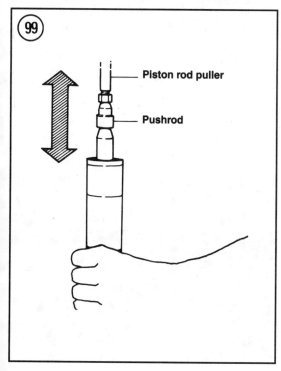

Piston rod puller

Pushrod

*oil capacity or oil level at this point.
Your final step will be to adjust the oil
level, which is a more accurate reading
than the actual oil capacity.*

5. To bleed air from the fork tube, do the following:
   a. Slowly pump the piston rod one time. When doing so, the adjuster rod and distance collar will move up and out of the piston rod. If you are using a piston rod puller, the puller will prevent these parts from falling out. If you are using a piece of stiff wire, pump the piston rod slowly to prevent them from falling out and also to prevent fork oil from squirting out of the piston rod and onto the floor. The oil level will also fall quite rapidly as the oil circulates and fills the cartridge. Refill the fork with oil to maintain its level above the two holes shown in **Figure 101**—see the previous NOTE.
   b. Repeat substep a four more times. After doing so, the piston rod should move under equal tension throughout its entire stroke, indicating that the cartridge is bled of all air. If the piston rod moves under tension and then releases and moves smoothly, air is still trapped in the cartridge and the bleeding procedure must be continued. After bleeding the cartridge of all air, continue with substep c.
   c. Hold the fork slider and pump the fork tube up and down (**Figure 102**) to purge air from between the two tubes.
6. To set the oil level, do the following:
   a. Bottom the fork tube against the axle holder and place it in a vertical position.
   b. Using an oil level gauge (**Figure 103**), set the oil level to the specification listed in **Table 3** (**Figure 104**). If you are not sure what distance

12

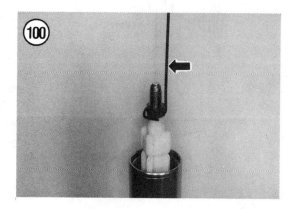

to set the oil level, set it to the standard level. If you are adjusting the oil level, maintain it within the minimum and maximum specifications in **Table 3**.

NOTE

If no oil is drawn out when setting the oil level, there is not enough oil in the fork tube. Add more oil, then reset the level.

   c. Remove the oil level gauge.

7. Unscrew the rebound damping adjuster (A, **Figure 105**) completely. Lubricate the fork cap threads and O-ring (B, **Figure 105**) with fork oil. Set the fork cap aside so you can reach it after installing the fork spring.

8. Install the fork spring (**Figure 106**) over the piston rod puller or wire and into the fork assembly.

9. Slowly pull the piston rod up, then unscrew the piston rod puller or remove the wire tool. Push the fork spring hard against the spring guide on the piston rod to prevent the piston rod from falling into the fork tube.

10. Install the spring seat (A, **Figure 107**) with its shoulder facing down.

11. Thread the fork cap (A, **Figure 107**) all the way onto the end of the piston rod.

12. Hold the locknut with a wrench (**Figure 108**), then tighten the fork cap against the locknut to the torque specification in **Table 5**.

13. Check that the spring seat is positioned correctly against the fork cap and spring.

14. Pull the fork tube up and thread the fork cap into the fork tube. Tighten the fork cap hand-tight.

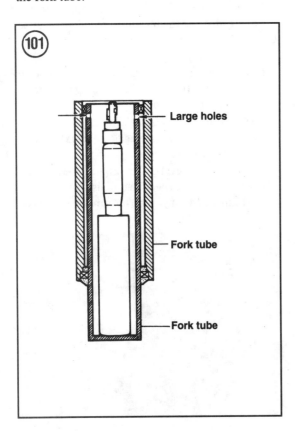

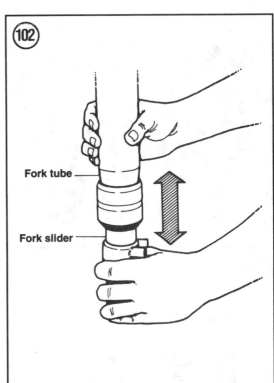

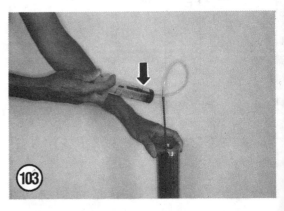

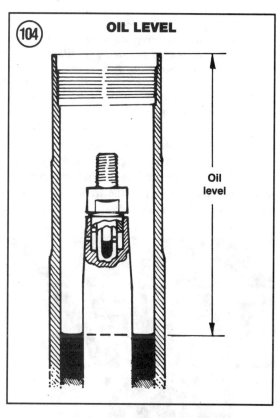

OIL LEVEL

Oil
level

15. Install the fork tube and tighten the fork cap as described under *Fork Tube Installation* in this chapter.

16. Adjust the front fork compression and rebound adjusters as described in this chapter.

FRONT FORK ADJUSTMENT

Air Pressure

These forks are designed to operate without air pressure being added to them. Before riding the bike, bleed the air out of the fork tubes as follows:

1. Support the bike with the front wheel off the ground.

2. Loosen the air screw (A, **Figure 109**) in the fork cap to release air pressure built-up in the fork. Tighten the screw. Repeat for the other fork tube.

Compression Damping Adjustment

The compression damping adjuster is mounted in the center of the compression bolt installed in the bottom of the fork tube (**Figure 110**). The compres-

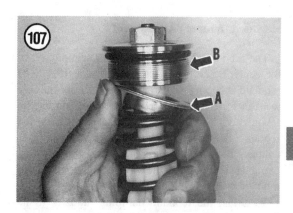

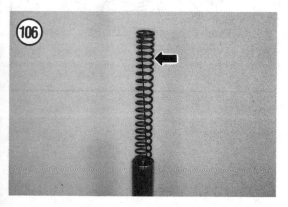

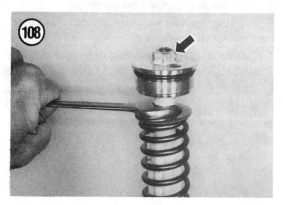

12

sion damping adjustment affects how quickly the front fork compresses. Turning the compression adjuster clockwise increases (stiffens) the compression damping; turning the compression adjuster counterclockwise decreases (softens) the compression damping. **Table 4** lists the standard compression damping positions.

To adjust the compression damping adjuster to its standard position, perform the following:

1. Remove the plug from the bottom of each fork tube.

2. Turn the compression damping adjuster *clockwise* until it stops (**Figure 110**).

3. Turn the compression damping adjuster *counterclockwise* the standard number of turns listed in **Table 4** for your model.

4. Set both fork tubes to the same damping position.

> *NOTE*
> *Make sure the compression adjuster screw is located in one of the detent positions and not in between any two settings.*

5. Install the plug into the bottom of each fork tube.

Rebound Damping Adjustment

The rebound damping adjusters are mounted in the center of each fork cap (B, **Figure 109**). The rebound damping adjustment affects how quickly the front fork extends after compression. Turning the rebound adjuster clockwise increases (stiffens) the rebound damping; turning the rebound adjuster counterclockwise decreases (softens) the rebound damping. **Table 4** lists the standard rebound damping adjustment position.

To adjust the rebound damping adjuster to its standard position, perform the following:

1. Turn the rebound damping adjuster *clockwise* until it stops (B, **Figure 109**).

2. Turn the rebound damping adjuster *counterclockwise* the standard number of turns listed in **Table 4**.

3. Set both fork tubes to the same damping setting.

> *NOTE*
> *Make sure the rebound adjuster screw is located in one of the detent positions and not in between any two settings.*

Front Fork Oil Change and Oil Level Adjustment

The front forks must be removed from the bike and partially disassembled to change the fork oil and to check and adjust the oil level. When this type of service is required, refer to the front fork service procedures in this chapter.

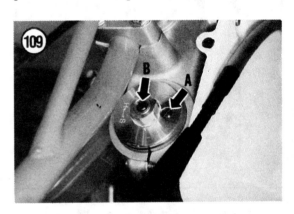

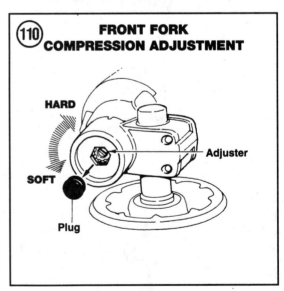

FRONT FORK COMPRESSION ADJUSTMENT

HARD

SOFT

Adjuster

Plug

Table 1 STEERING AND FRONT SUSPENSION SPECIFICATIONS

Steering	
Steering angle	45 degrees
Caster (rake angle)	26 degrees
Trail	109 mm (4.29 in.)
Front wheel travel	310 mm (12.20 in.)
Rear wheel travel	330 mm (13.00 in.)
Fork fluid viscosity*	Kayaba O1
	Bel-Ray HVI 5wt Racing Suspension Fluid
	Honda HP 5W fork oil
	Maxima 5wt Zero Drag
	PJ1 Cartridge Pro Fork Fluid
Fork spring free length	
1992	
New	514 mm (20.24 in.)
Service limit	504 mm (19.84 in.)
1996-on	
New	470 mm (18.50 in.)
Service limit	460 mm (18.11 in.)

*The fork fluid listed in this table can be used to replace the standard KYB 01 fork fluid. For increased dampening, use a 7, 10 or 15 weight fork oil designed for use in inverted forks.

Table 2 FRONT FORK OIL CAPACITY

	ml	U.S. oz.	Imp. oz.
1992	521-529	17.6-17.9	14.7-14.9
1993	506-514	17.1-17.4	14.2-14.5
1994	489-497	16.5-16.8	13.8-14.0
1995	504-512	17.0-17.3	14.1-14.4
1996	604-612	20.4-20.7	17.0-17.2
1997	610-618	20.6-20.9	17.2-17.4
1998	615-623	20.8-21.1	17.3-17.5

Table 3 FRONT FORK OIL LEVEL

	mm	in.
1992		
Standard	113-117	4.44-4.60
Minimum	100	3.93
Maximum	150	5.90
1993		
Standard	118-122	4.64-4.80
Minimum	105	4.13
Maximum	155	6.10
1994		
Standard	128-132	5.04-5.20
Minimum	90	3.54
Maximum	150	5.90
1995		
Standard	118-122	4.64-4.80
Minimum	105	4.13
Maximum	140	5.51
(continued)		

12

Table 3 FRONT FORK OIL LEVEL (continued)

	mm	in.
1996		
Standard	113-117	4.44-4.60
Minimum	105	4.13
Maximum	140	5.51
1997		
Standard	108-112	4.25-4.40
Minimum	105	4.13
Maximum	140	5.51
1998		
Standard	108-112	4.25-4.40
Minimum	105	4.13
Maximum	140	5.51

Table 4 FRONT FORK COMPRESSION AND REBOUND ADJUSTMENT

	Total adjustment positions	Standard adjuster position
Compression damping adjustment		
1992		
U.S. models	16	9
All other models	16	11
1993	16	12
1994	16	8
1995	18	8
1996	18	10
1997	18	12
1998	18	10
Rebound damping adjustment		
1992	16	9
1993	16	12
1994	16	12
1995	18	10
1996	18	10
1997	18	12
1998	18	11

Table 5 TORQUE SPECIFICATIONS

	N•m	in.-lb.	ft.-lb.
Front fork			
Compression bolt	54	–	40
Fork cap	29	–	22
Pinch bolts (@ steering stem)			
Upper	22	–	16.3
Lower	20	–	14.5
Piston rod collar			
1992-1996	27	–	20
1997-on	–		
Piston rod locknut			
1992-1993	15	–	11
1994-on	28	–	21
Front brake caliper mounting bolts	25	–	18
	(continued)		

Table 5 TORQUE SPECIFICATIONS (continued)

	N•m	in.-lb.	ft.-lb.
Front master cylinder mounting bolts	8.8	78	–
Handlebar mounting bolts	25	–	18
Steering adjust nut*			
Bearing seat torque	39	–	29
Final torque	3.9	35	–
Steering stem nut	78	–	58

*See text for adjustment procedure

12

REAR SUSPENSION

This chapter describes service procedures for the rear shock absorber, swing arm, and linkage assembly. **Table 1** lists rear suspension specifications. **Tables 1-5** are at the end of this chapter.

UNI-TRAK REAR SUSPENSION SYSTEM

The single shock absorber and linkage of the Kawasaki Uni-Trak suspension system are attached to the swing arm, just behind the swing arm pivot point, and to the lower rear portion of the frame (**Figure 1**). The linkage consists of the rocker arm, tie rods, pivot bolts and bearings.

The rocker arm and tie rods work together with the shock absorber matched spring rate and damping rates to achieve a "progressive rising rate" rear suspension. This system provides the rider with the best of both worlds—greater rider control and better transfer of power to the ground over rough terrain.

As bumps move the rear suspension upward, movement of the rocker arm compresses the shock absorber.

As rear suspension travel increases, the portion of the rocker arm where the shock absorber is attached rises above the swing arm, thus increasing shock absorber travel (compression). This provides a progressive rate in which the shock eventually moves at a faster rate than the wheel. At about halfway through the wheel travel the shock begins to move at a faster rate than it did at the beginning.

SHOCK ABSORBER

The single shock absorber is a spring-loaded, hydraulically-damped unit with an integral oil/nitrogen reservoir.

Adjustment

To adjust the rear shock absorber (spring pre-load, rebound damping and compression damping), refer to *Rear Suspension Adjustment* in this chapter.

Shock Absorber
Removal/Installation

1. Support the bike with the rear bike off the ground.

2. Remove the seat and side panels (Chapter Fifteen).

3. On 1998 models, disconnect the IC Igniter electrical connectors (**Figure 2**). Remove the wiring harness from around the subframe.

4. Loosen the rear carburetor hose clamp.

5. Unbolt and remove the silencer (A, **Figure 3**).

6. Unbolt and remove the subframe assembly (B, **Figure 3**).

7. Cover the carburetor and air boot openings to prevent dirt from entering.

8. Loosen the front and rear tie rod mounting nuts (**Figure 4**). Remove the front nut and pivot bolt and allow the tie rods to hang down (**Figure 5**). Remove the shims installed between the tie rods and rocker arm.

9. Remove the lower shock absorber mounting bolt (**Figure 5**).

10. Remove the upper shock absorber mounting bolt (A, **Figure 6**) and the shock absorber (B). Check the two upper seals (**Figure 7**) mounted on the shock absorber to make sure they did not fall off.

11. Clean and service the seals, collar and bearing as described in this section.

12. Install the shock absorber by reversing the preceding steps, plus the following:

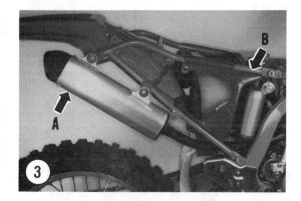

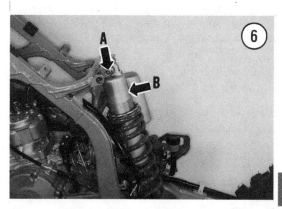

13

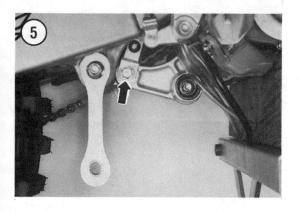

a. Lubricate the shock absorber mounting bolts with grease.

b. Install the shock absorber with its reservoir on the right side.

c. Install the shock absorber upper mounting bolt (A, **Figure 6**) from the left side.

d. Install the lower shock absorber mounting bolt (**Figure 5**) from the left side.

e. Tighten the shock absorber upper and lower mounting bolts as specified in **Table 5**.

f. Tighten the tie rod pivot bolt nuts (**Figure 4**) as specified in **Table 5**.

g. Tighten the subframe mounting bolts (B, **Figure 3**) as described in **Table 5**.

Shock Inspection

1. Inspect the shock absorber (**Figure 7**) for gas or oil leaks.

2. Check the damper rod for bending, rust or other damage.

3. Check the reservoir for dents or other damage.

4. Remove and inspect the spring as described in this section.

5. If the shock is leaking, or if it is time to replace the shock oil, refer all service to a Kawasaki dealership or suspension specialist.

Seal and Bearing Inspection and Replacement

1. Remove the seals and collar (**Figure 8**) from the bearing bore.

2. Clean and dry the seals, collar and needle bearing.

3. Inspect the seals for cracks or other damage.

4. Inspect the collar for cracks, scoring or severe wear.

5. Inspect the needle bearing (**Figure 9**) for excessive wear or damage. Check for loose or missing bearing needles or other visible damage. Lubricate the collar with grease, install it into the bearing and turn it with your fingers. The collar should turn smoothly. If there is any roughness or damage, replace the needle bearing as described in Step 6. If the bearing is okay, go to Step 7.

6. Replace the needle bearing (**Figure 9**) as follows:

a. Support the shock in a press and remove the needle bearing.

b. Clean and inspect the mounting bore.

c. Center the bearing squarely in its mounting bore and install it with a press or bearing driver. Center the bearing in its mounting bore.

7. Lubricate the bearing and collar with a waterproof grease.

8. Install the collar into the bearing. Install the seals (**Figure 10**).

Spring Removal/Installation

1. Remove the shock absorber as described in this chapter.

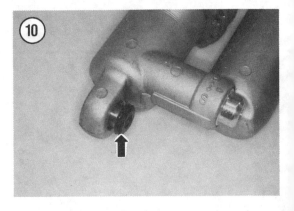

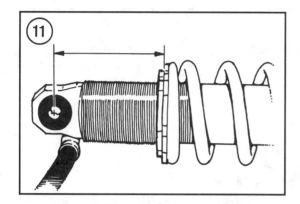

2. Measure the spring's preload length with a tape measure (**Figure 11**) and record the length for installation.

3. Clean the shock threads (**Figure 12**) with contact cleaner.

4. Mount the upper shock mount in a vise with soft jaws.

5. Loosen the locknut (**Figure 13**) with a spanner wrench and turn it all the way down. Do the same for the adjust nut to remove all preload from the spring.

6. Remove the spring retainer, spring seat and spring (**Figure 14**) from the shock.

7. Measure the spring free length with a tape measure. Replace the spring if it is too short (**Table 2**).

8. Install the spring and set the spring preload by reversing the preceding steps, while noting the following:

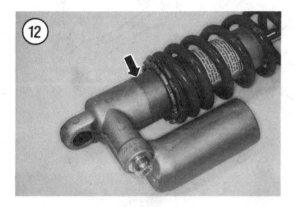

   a. Install the spring, spring guide and spring retainer. Check that the spring guide and spring retainer seat flush against the spring as shown in **Figure 14**.

   b. Adjust the spring preload to the dimension recorded in Step 2, or set it within the minimum and maximum length dimensions listed in **Table 3**. Hold the adjust nut and tighten the locknut (**Figure 13**) securely.

CAUTION
*The spring preload must be maintained within the minimum and maximum specifications listed in **Table 3**. If the minimum specification is exceeded, the spring may coil bind when the shock comes near full compression. This will also overload the spring and cause it to weaken. Setting the preload beyond the maximum limit may allow the spring locknut and adjust nut to loosen on the shock body and remove all preload from the spring.*

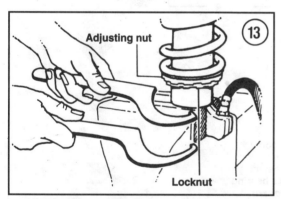

Adjusting nut

Locknut

SHOCK LINKAGE

The shock linkage consists of the rocker arm, tie rods, pivot bolts, seals and bearings. Because the shock linkage bearings operate in a harsh environment of dirt, mud and sand, the assembly must be removed, cleaned and lubricated at the intervals listed in Chapter Three (**Table 1**).

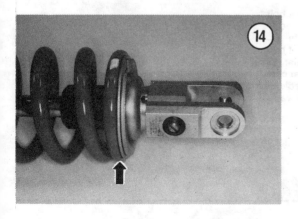

13

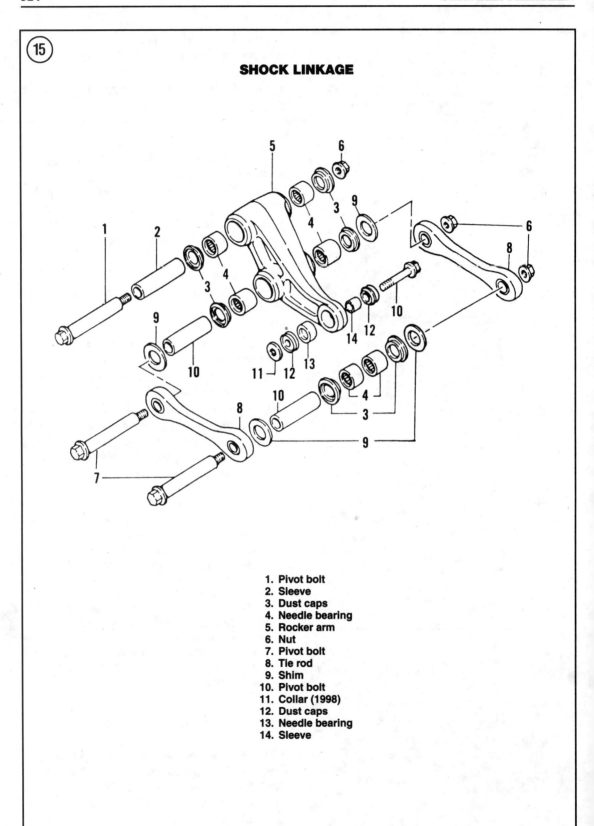

SHOCK LINKAGE

1. Pivot bolt
2. Sleeve
3. Dust caps
4. Needle bearing
5. Rocker arm
6. Nut
7. Pivot bolt
8. Tie rod
9. Shim
10. Pivot bolt
11. Collar (1998)
12. Dust caps
13. Needle bearing
14. Sleeve

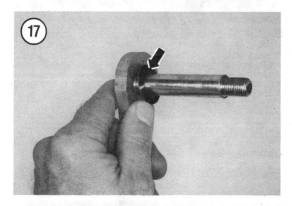

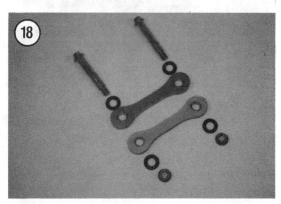

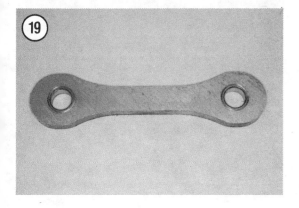

Refer to **Figure 15** when servicing the shock linkage assembly.

Tie Rod
Removal/Installation

The tie rods connect between the swing arm and rocker arm and are secured in place with pivot bolts and nuts.

1. Support the bike with its rear wheel off the ground.

2. Loosen the swing arm pivot bolt nut (**Figure 16**).

3. If the rear wheel is mounted on the bike, support the tire with wooden blocks to remove tension from the shock linkage pivot bolts.

4. Loosen and remove the tie rod pivot bolt nuts (**Figure 4**).

5. Remove the pivot bolts and tie rods (**Figure 4**). Shims (**Figure 17**) installed between the tie rods and rocker arm will fall out as the pivot bolts are removed (2 shims per bolt). Retrieve each shim.

6. Clean and inspect the tie rods and pivot bolts as described in this section.

7. Install the tie rods by reversing the preceding removal steps, plus the following:

    a. Lubricate the pivot bolts with a waterproof grease.

    b. The two tie rods are identical (same part number).

    c. Install the four shims between the tie rods and rocker arms as shown in **Figure 15**.

    d. Install the pivot bolts from the left side.

    e. Tighten the tie rod pivot bolt nuts (**Figure 4**) as specified in **Table 5**.

    f. Tighten the swing arm pivot bolt nut (**Figure 16**) as specified in **Table 5**.

13

Tie Rod
Cleaning and Inspection

Replace parts that are out of specification or show damage as described in this section.

1. Clean and dry all parts (**Figure 18**).

2. Inspect the tie rods for cracks or other damage. Check the tie rod bushings (**Figure 19**) for hole elongation, excessive wear or other damage.

NOTE
The tie rod bushings should not be removed as they are not available

separately. Replace the tie rod if a bushing is excessively worn or damaged.

3. Inspect the pivot bolts for cracks, scoring or other damage.

4. Measure the runout of each pivot bolt with a dial indicator and V-block (**Figure 20**). Replace any bolt where its runout exceeds the service limit in **Table 2**. If you do not have these special tools, roll the pivot bolts (shoulder) on a flat surface to detect any visual runout damage. Replace bent or damaged pivot bolts.

> *NOTE*
> *When you find a bent pivot bolt, check the mating tie rod bushings and tie rod ends for cracks or other damage.*

Rocker Arm
Removal/Installation

The rocker arm is connected to the frame and rear shock absorber. The rocker arm can be removed with the swing arm mounted on the bike.

1. Support the bike with the rear wheel off the ground.

2. Loosen the swing arm pivot bolt nut (**Figure 16**).

3. If the rear wheel is mounted on the bike, support the tire with wooden blocks to remove tension from the shock linkage pivot bolts.

4. Loosen the front and rear tie rod mounting nuts (**Figure 4**). Remove the front nut and pivot bolt and allow the tie rods to hang down (**Figure 5**). Remove the shims installed between the tie rods and rocker arm.

5. Remove the lower shock absorber mounting bolt (**Figure 5**).

> *NOTE*
> ***Figure 21*** *shows the rocker arm with the rear swing arm removed for clarity.*

6. Remove the nut and pivot bolt securing the rocker arm to the frame and remove the rocker arm (**Figure 21**).

7. Clean and inspect the rocker arm, bearings and pivot bolts as described in this section.

8. Install the rocker arm by reversing the preceding removal steps, plus the following:

    a. Lubricate the pivot bolts with a waterproof grease.

b. Install the pivot bolts from the left side.

c. Tighten the rocker arm pivot bolt nut (at the frame) as specified in **Table 5**.

d. Tighten the lower rear shock absorber mounting bolt (**Figure 5**) as specified in **Table 5**.

e. Tighten the tie rod pivot bolt nuts (**Figure 4**) as specified in **Table 5**.

f. Tighten the swing arm pivot bolt nut (**Figure 16**) as specified in **Table 5**.

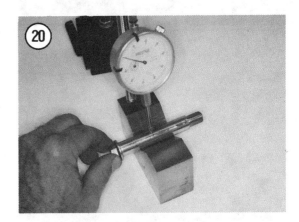

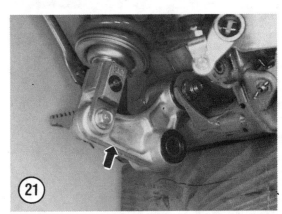

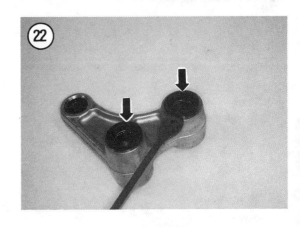

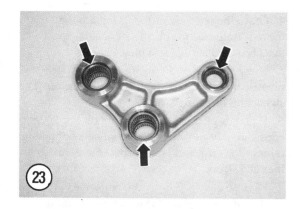

(23)

(24)

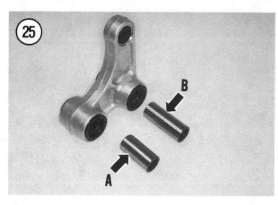

(25)

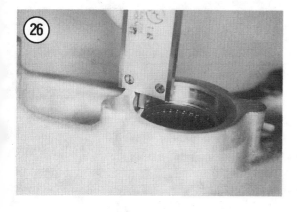

(26)

Rocker Arm
Cleaning and Inspection

When measuring the rocker arm components, compare the actual measurements to the specifications in **Table 2**. Replace the part if its measurement is out of specification or shows damage as described in this section.

NOTE
Use a waterproof bearing grease when grease is called for in the following steps.

1. Remove the sleeves from the rocker arm.

NOTE
The dust caps can be reused if they have not been damaged during use or if they are not damaged during removal. Remove them carefully in Step 2.

2. Using a thin wide-blade screwdriver or similar tool, remove the dust caps (**Figure 22**) from the rocker arm.

3. Remove the loose bearing needles (**Figure 23**) from their outer cage, making sure you do not intermix them with the needles from the other bearings; all of the loose bearing needles must remain with their original bearing assembly. Do not remove a bearing cage unless the bearing requires replacement.

4. Clean and dry all parts (**Figure 24**).

5. Inspect the dust caps for cracks, excessive wear or other damage.

6. Inspect the short and long sleeves (**Figure 25**) for cracks, scoring, rust or other damage. If there no visual damage, measure the outside diameter of the short sleeve (A, **Figure 25**) with a micrometer and compare to **Table 2**. Replace the sleeve if it is too small. Repeat for the long sleeve (B, **Figure 25**).

7. Inspect the loose needle bearings for cracks, flat spots, rust or color change. Bluing indicates that the bearing has overheated. Inspect the separate bearing cages for cracks, rust or other damage. If a bearing is damaged, replace it as described in Step 8.

8. To replace a needle bearing, do the following:
   a. At the point where two individual bearings are used in the same bore, measure the depth of the installed bearings (**Figure 26**). Measure from the outside of each bearing.
   b. Lubricate the new bearings with grease.

13

NOTE
*Install the bearing with the individual
bearing needles installed in their cage.*

c. Press in the new bearings to the same depth
recorded before removal.

9. Inspect the pivot bolts for cracks, scoring or other
damage.

10. Measure the runout of each pivot bolt with a dial
indicator and V-block (**Figure 20**). Replace the bolt
if the runout exceeds the service limit in **Table 2**. If
you do not have these special tools, roll the pivot
bolts (shoulder) on a flat surface to detect any visual
runout damage. Replace bent or damaged pivot
bolts.

NOTE
*In the case of a bent pivot bolt, check the
mating rocker arm sleeves and needle
bearings for damage.*

11. If reusing the original needle bearings, lubricate
the separate bearing needles with grease and install
them into their correct bearing cage.

12. Lubricate the sleeves with grease and install
them into their correct position in the rocker arm
(**Figure 25**). The sleeves will fit flush with their
mounting bores when properly installed.

13. Lubricate the dust caps with grease and install
them into the rocker arm mounting bores.

REAR SWING ARM

Swing Arm Bearing Inspection

Periodically inspect the swing arm needle bearings and bushings for excessive play, roughness or
damage.

1. Remove the rear wheel (Chapter Eleven).

2. Loosen the front and rear tie rod nuts, then remove the rear nut and pivot bolt (**Figure 27**) securing
the tie rods to the swing arm. Remove the shim from
each tie rod.

3. Loosen the swing arm pivot bolt nut (**Figure 28**),
then retighten it to the torque specification in **Table
5**.

NOTE
*Have an assistant steady the bike while
you perform Step 4.*

4. Grasp the rear end of the swing arm and try to
move it from side to side in a horizontal arc. There
must be no noticeable side play.

5. Grasp the rear of the swing arm once again and
pivot it up and down through its full travel. The
swing arm must pivot smoothly.

6. If play is evident and the pivot bolt nut is tightened correctly, or there is any roughness or binding,
remove the swing arm and inspect the needle bearings and sleeves for excessive wear or damage.

7. Reverse Steps 1-3 if you are not going to remove
the swing arm. Tighten the tie rod pivot bolt nuts as
specified in **Table 5**.

Removal/Installation

1. Remove the rear wheel (Chapter Ten).

NOTE
*Unless you are going to service the rear
brake caliper, do not disconnect it from
its brake hose when performing Step 2.*

2. Slide the rear brake caliper off the swing arm.
Remove the brake hose from between the hose

guides on the swing arm and move the caliper out of the way.

3. If necessary, remove the rear brake pedal (Chapter Fourteen).

4. Loosen the front and rear tie rod nuts. Remove the rear nut and pivot bolt (**Figure 27**) securing the tie rods to the swing arm. Remove the shims from the tie rods.

5. Loosen and remove the swing arm pivot bolt nut (**Figure 28**).

6. Remove the pivot bolt and the rear swing arm from the frame.

7. Clean, inspect and lubricate the swing arm bearings as described in the following sections.

8. Install the swing arm by reversing the preceding removal steps, plus the following:

a. Lubricate the pivot bolts with grease prior to installation.

b. Tighten the swing arm pivot bolt nut (**Figure 28**) as specified in **Table 5**.

c. Tighten the tie rod pivot bolt nuts as specified in **Table 5**.

d. Adjust the drive chain as described in Chapter Three.

e. Check that the rear brake pedal and rear brake work properly.

Swing Arm Disassembly

Store the left- and right-side bearing assemblies in separate containers so they can be installed in their original locations. Refer to **Figure 29** (1992-1995) or **Figure 30** (1996-on).

1A. On 1992-1995 models, remove the seals and sleeves (**Figure 31**) from each side of the swing arm.

1B. On 1996 and later models, remove the following parts in order:

a. Sleeve (**Figure 32**).

b. Collar (**Figure 33**).

c. Outer seal (**Figure 34**).

d. Thrust bearing assembly (**Figure 35**).

e. Inner seal (**Figure 36**).

f. Repeat for the other side.

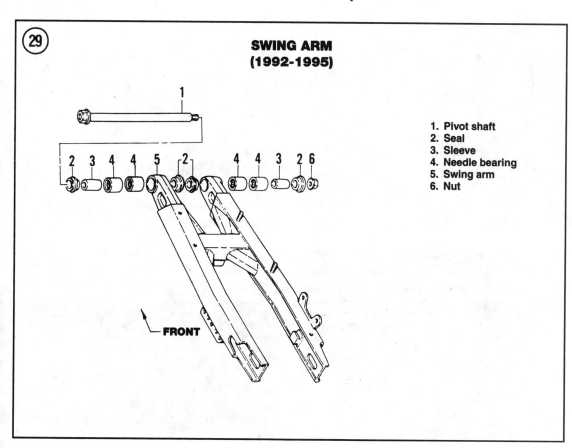

(29)

**SWING ARM
(1992-1995)**

1. Pivot shaft
2. Seal
3. Sleeve
4. Needle bearing
5. Swing arm
6. Nut

FRONT

13

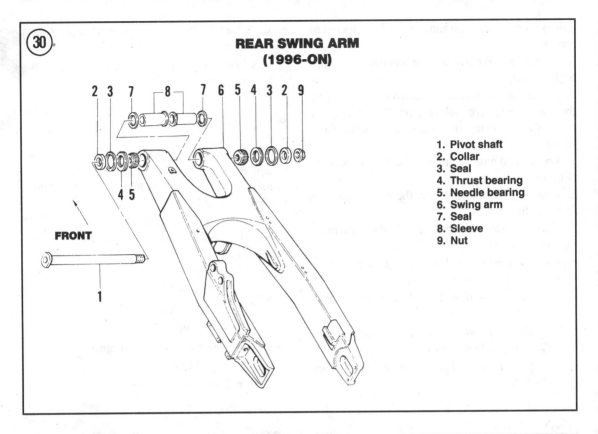

**REAR SWING ARM
(1996-ON)**

1. Pivot shaft
2. Collar
3. Seal
4. Thrust bearing
5. Needle bearing
6. Swing arm
7. Seal
8. Sleeve
9. Nut

FRONT

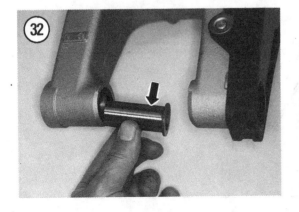

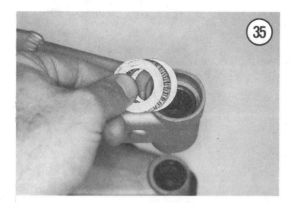

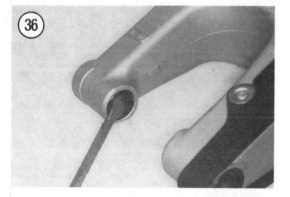

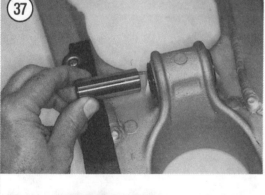

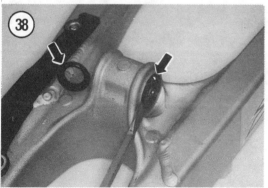

2. Remove the tie rod sleeve (**Figure 37**) and two seals (**Figure 38**) from the bottom of the swing arm.

Swing Arm Inspection

Replace parts that show excessive wear or damage as described in this section.

1. Clean and dry the swing arm and its components.

2A. On 1992-1995 models, inspect the sleeves (**Figure 31**) for scoring, excessive wear, rust or other damage.

2B. On 1996 and later models, inspect the sleeves, collars and thrust bearings (**Figure 39**). Replace those parts which are scored, excessively worn or show any type of visible damage.

NOTE
In the case of an excessively worn or damaged sleeve, its mating needle bearing(s) is probably worn also and must be replaced. Inspect the bearings carefully in Step 3.

3. Inspect the needle bearings (**Figure 40**) for cracks, flat spots, rust or other damage. If there is no

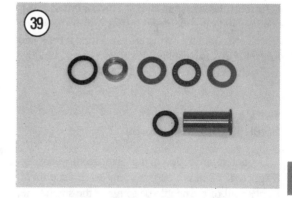

13

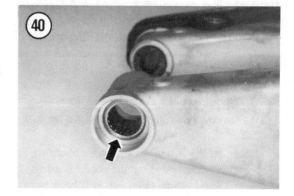

visible damage, lubricate the sleeve with grease and install it into the swing arm. Turn the sleeve and check the bearing for any roughness, excessive play or other damage. To replace the bearings, refer to *Swing Arm Needle Bearing Replacement* in this chapter.

4. Check the swing arm for cracks, bending or other damage. Check the bearing mounting bore for cracks (**Figure 41**) and other damage. Repair or replace the swing arm if damaged.

> *NOTE*
> *Refer swing arm repair to a competent welder/machinist. **Figure 42** shows the same swing arm with the damage repaired.*

5. Inspect the chain slider (**Figure 43**) for excessive wear or missing fasteners.

> *NOTE*
> *The chain slider protects the swing arm from chain contact damage. Replace the chain slider before the chain wears completely through and damages the swing arm.*

6. Inspect the swing arm pivot bolt for cracks, rust, bending and other damage. Install one of the swing arm sleeves onto the swing arm and slide it back and forth (**Figure 44**) by hand. There must be no binding or roughness.

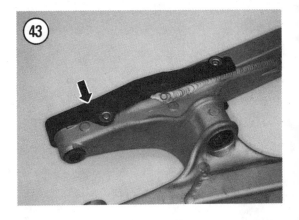

Swing Arm
Needle Bearing Replacement

Do not remove the swing arm needle bearings (**Figure 42**) unless you are going to replace them. Replace all of the needle bearings at the same time. The needle bearings can be removed with a press or they can be removed with a bearing driver.

1. On 1992-1995 models, measure the depth of each installed bearing with a vernier caliper and record the dimensions for reassembly. On 1996 and later models, the needle bearings are aligned with the mounting bore shoulder as shown in **Figure 40**.

2A. To remove the needle bearings with a press, do the following:

    a. Support the swing arm in a press as shown in **Figure 45** and press out the needle bearing(s). On 1992-1995 models, you will be pressing

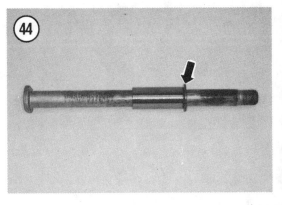

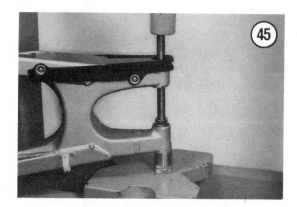

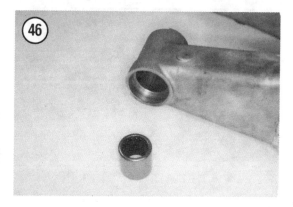

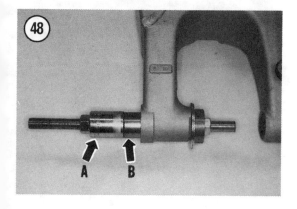

out both needle bearings at the same time (**Figure 29**).

   b. Repeat to remove the needle bearings from the opposite side.

2B. To remove the needle bearings with a bearing driver and hammer, do the following:

   a. Support the swing arm so force can be applied to the bearings.

   b. Remove the chain slider (**Figure 43**) from the swing arm.

   c. Soak the bearings with a penetrating oil. Wait to allow the oil to penetrate between the bearing and mounting bore.

   d. Heat the swing arm with a propane torch. Do not overheat the swing arm, just apply enough heat to allow expansion of the swing arm.

   e. Drive the bearings out of the swing arm with a bearing driver and suitable adapter.

CAUTION
If you can't get the bearings to move, stop and take the swing arm to a dealership or machine shop. Do not continue to apply excessive heat or force, as this will damage the swing arm.

3. Clean and dry the bearing mounting bores (**Figure 46**). Check each bore for cracks or other damage.

4. Lubricate the new needle bearing rollers with grease. Use your fingers to force grease between the bearing rollers.

5A. To install the needle bearings with a press, perform the following:

   a. Install both bearings with their manufacturer's name and size code marks facing out.

   b. Support the swing arm in a press as shown in **Figure 47**.

   c. On 1992-1995 models, press in both needle bearings to the depth measurements recorded in Step 1. Repeat for the other side.

   d. On 1996 and later models, install the bearing so that it is flush with the inside mounting bore shoulder (**Figure 40**). Repeat for the other side.

5B. To install the needle bearings with a threaded rod and bearing driver set:

   a. Assemble the fine-threaded rod tool shown in **Figure 48**. Use a socket or bearing driver (A, **Figure 48**) placed on the outer needle bearing diameter.

13

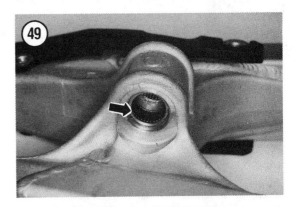

NOTE

*When you set up the puller, check that the socket or bearing driver (A, **Figure 48**) is of sufficient diameter to seat squarely against the needle bearing, but is small enough to slide through the swing arm's bearing mounting bore.*

b. Hold the inner nut and turn the outer nut to pull the bearing into the swing arm. On 1992-1995 models, install the inner bearing first, then the outer bearing (**Figure 29**).

c. On 1992-1995 models, install both needle bearings to the depth measurements recorded in Step 1. Repeat for the other side.

d. On 1996 and later models, install the bearing so that it is flush with the inside mounting bore shoulder (**Figure 40**). Repeat for the other side.

Tie Rod Bearing Replacement

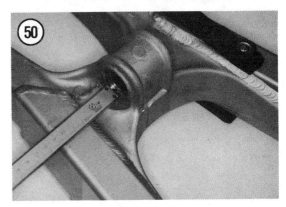

To replace the tie rod needle bearings (**Figure 49**) mounted in the bottom of the swing arm, do the following:

1. Measure the installed depth of each bearing (**Figure 50**). Both bearings must be installed correctly, so the seals can be properly installed.

2. Remove the needle bearings as follows:

a. Support the swing arm so that force can be applied to the bearings.

b. Drive the bearings out of the swing arm with a bearing driver and suitable adapter (**Figure 51**).

3. Clean and dry the mounting bore.

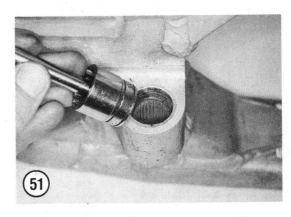

4. Lubricate the new needle bearing rollers with grease. Use your fingers to force grease between the bearing rollers.

5. Install the needle bearings with a threaded rod and bearing driver set as follows:

a. Assemble the fine-threaded rod tool shown in **Figure 52**.

NOTE

*When you set up the puller, check that the socket or bearing driver (A, **Figure 48**) is of sufficient diameter to seat squarely against the needle bearing, but is small enough to slide through the swing arm's bearing mounting bore.*

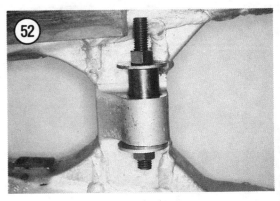
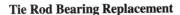

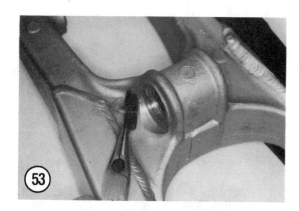

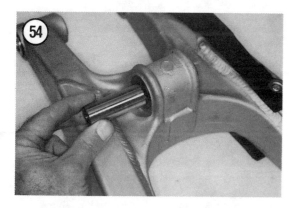

b. Hold the inner nut and turn the outer nut to pull the first bearing into the swing arm. Repeat to install the second bearing.

c. Install both needle bearings to the depth measurements recorded in Step 1.

Swing Arm Assembly

NOTE
Use a waterproof bearing grease when grease is called for in the following steps.

1. If removed, install the chain slider (**Figure 43**).

2. Lubricate the needle bearings with grease. Use your fingers to force grease between the bearing rollers.

3. Install the tie rod dust caps and sleeve as follows:

a. Install the two dust caps into the mounting bore (**Figure 53**).

b. Lubricate the sleeve with grease and install it through the dust caps and bearings (**Figure 54**). Center the sleeve in the swing arm.

4A. On 1992-1995 models, perform the following:

a. Install the two seals into the mounting bore (**Figure 55**). Install the seals with their closed side facing out.

b. Lubricate the sleeve with grease and install it through the seals and bearings (**Figure 56**). Center the sleeve in the swing arm.

c. Repeat for the opposite side.

4B. On 1996 and later models, perform the following:

a. Pack the lip of each swing arm seal with grease.

b. Install the inner seal—closed side facing out—into the bore opening as shown in **Figure 57**.

c. Lubricate the thrust bearing assembly (**Figure 58**) with grease.

d. Assemble the thrust bearing assembly with the bearing rollers on the inside (**Figure 58**), then install the bearing assembly into the outer bore opening and seat it against the shoulder inside the swing arm (**Figure 59**)

e. Install the outer seal—closed side facing out—into the bore opening as shown in A, **Figure 60**. Install the seal until it seats against the thrust bearing assembly.

13

f. Lubricate the collar (B, **Figure 60**) outside diameter with grease, then install it into the outer seal and seat it against the thrust bearing assembly.

g. Lubricate the sleeve (**Figure 61**) with grease, then install it through the bearing from the inside of the swing arm (**Figure 61**).

h. Repeat for the opposite side.

5. Install the swing arm as described in this chapter.

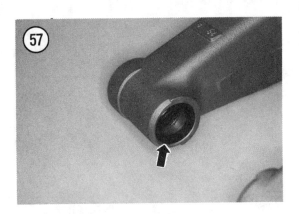

REAR SUSPENSION ADJUSTMENT

Shock Spring Preload Adjustment

The spring preload adjustment can be performed with the shock mounted on the bike.

1. Support the bike on a workstand with the rear wheel off the ground.

2. Remove the subframe as described in Chapter Fifteen.

3. Clean the threads at the top of the shock absorber (**Figure 62**).

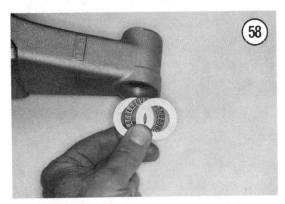

> *NOTE*
> *Shock preload is adjusted by changing the position of the adjust nut on the shock absorber.*

4. Measure the existing spring preload length (**Figure 63**) with a tape measure.

> *NOTE*
> *Use the spanner wrench provided in your owner's tool kit or a similar tool to turn the locknut and adjust nut on the shock absorber.*

5. To adjust, loosen the locknut (**Figure 63**) and turn the adjust nut (**Figure 63**) in the desired direction, making sure you maintain the spring preload length within the dimensions listed in **Table 3**. Tightening the adjust nut increases spring preload and loosening it decreases preload.

> *CAUTION*
> *The spring preload must be maintained within the minimum and maximum specifications listed in **Table 3**. If the minimum specification is exceeded, the spring may coil bind when the shock approaches full compression. This will also overload the spring and cause it to weaken. Setting the preload beyond the*

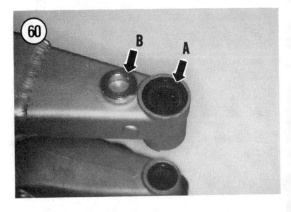

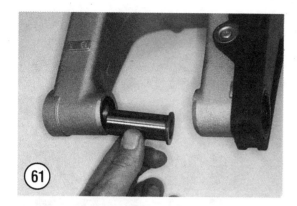

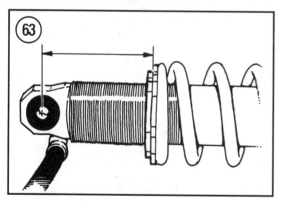

maximum limit may allow the spring locknut and adjust nut to loosen on the shock body and remove all preload from the spring.

6. After the desired spring preload is achieved, tighten the locknut (**Figure 63**) securely.

Rebound Damping Adjustment

Rebound damping affects the rate of speed at which the shock absorber is able to return to the fully extended position after compression. This adjustment will not affect the action of the shock absorber on compression. If the rebound is too slow, the rear wheel may bottom on subsequent bumps.

Rebound damping can be adjusted to the number of the settings specified in **Table 4**. The adjuster screw is located at the bottom of the shock absorber (**Figure 64**). A clicker adjuster is used; each click of the adjuster screw represents one adjustment change.

For the standard setting, turn the adjuster screw clockwise until it stops, then turn it counterclockwise the number of clicks (standard) listed in **Table 4**. When the standard setting is set, the two index marks on the adjuster will align.

To increase the rebound damping, turn the adjuster screw toward the "H" mark on the adjuster.

To decrease the rebound damping, turn the adjuster screw toward the "S" mark on the adjuster.

Make sure the adjuster wheel is located in one of the detent positions and not in between any two settings.

Compression Damping Adjustment

Compression damping affects the rate of speed that the shock compresses when the rear wheel hits a bump. This adjustment will not affect the action of the shock absorber on rebound.

Compression damping can be adjusted to the number of the settings specified in **Table 4**. The adjuster screw is located at the top of the shock absorber reservoir (**Figure 65**). A clicker adjuster is used; each click of the adjuster screw represents one adjustment change.

For the standard setting, turn the adjuster screw clockwise until it stops, then turn it counterclockwise the number of clicks (standard) listed in **Table 4**. When the standard setting is set, the two index marks will align.

13

For the maximum setting, turn the adjuster screw clockwise until it stops.

To increase the rebound damping, turn the adjuster screw clockwise.

To decrease the rebound damping, turn the adjuster screw counterclockwise.

Make sure the adjuster wheel is located in one of the detent positions and not in between any two settings.

Nitrogen Pressure Adjustment

Refer all nitrogen pressure adjustment to a Kawasaki dealer or suspension specialist.

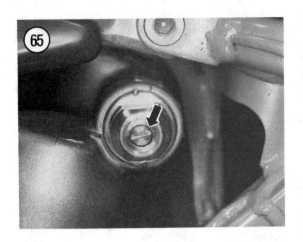

Table 1 REAR SUSPENSION SPECIFICATIONS

Rear suspension type	Swing arm/Uni-Trak
Rear shock gas pressure	980 kPa (142 psi)
Rear wheel travel	330 mm (13.0 in.)

Table 2 REAR SUSPENSION SERVICE SPECIFICATIONS

	New mm (in.)	Service limit mm (in.)
Pivot bolt runout	0-0.1 (0-0.0039)	0.2 (0.0078)
Rocker arm sleeve outside diameter		
Short sleeve	15.989-16.000 (0.6295-0.6299)	15.85 (0.624)
Long sleeve	21.987-22.000 (0.8656-0.8661)	21.85 (0.860)
Shock spring free length		
1992-1997	275.0 (10.83)	270.0 (10.63)
1998	280.0 (11.02)	270.0 (10.63)

Table 3 REAR SHOCK ABSORBER SPRING PRELOAD LENGTH

	mm	in.
1992		
Standard		
U.S. models	136.5	5.37
All other models	134.5	5.29
Minimum	118	4.64
Maximum	143	5.63
1993		
Standard	132.5	5.22
Minimum	118	4.64
Maximum	137	5.39
(continued)		

Table 3 REAR SHOCK ABSORBER SPRING PRELOAD LENGTH (continued)

	mm	in.
1994		
Standard	118	4.64
Minimum	108	4.25
Maximum	127	4.99
1995		
Standard	121.5	4.78
Minimum	108	4.25
Maximum	127	4.99
1996		
Standard	121.5	4.78
Minimum	111.5	4.38
Maximum	131	5.16
1997		
Standard	118.5	4.66
Minimum	108	4.25
Maximum	131	5.16
1998		
Standard	111	4.37
Minimum	99.5	3.91
Maximum	118	4.64

Table 4 REAR SHOCK ABSORBER COMPRESSION AND REBOUND ADJUSTMENT

	Total adjustment postions	Standard adjustment position
Compression damping adjustment		
1992		
Europe	16	15
All other	16	13
1993	16	12
1994	16	12
1995-1996	20	12
1997	18	12
1998	18	12
Rebound damping adjustment		
1992-1993	16	12
1994	16	14
1995	20	10
1996	20	12
1997	18	12
1998	18	11

13

Table 5 TORQUE SPECIFICATIONS

	N•m	ft.-lb.
Rear shock absorber mounting bolts	39	29
Rocker arm pivot bolt nuts		
1992-1997	81	60
1998	88	65
Tie rod pivot bolt nuts		
1992-1997	81	60
1998	88	60
Subframe mounting bolts		
1992-1993	26	19.5
1994-on	29	22
Swing arm pivot bolt nut	98	72

CHAPTER FOURTEEN

BRAKES

This chapter describes service procedures for the front and rear disc brakes.

Table 1 and **Table 2** lists front and rear brake specifications. **Table 1** and **Table 2** are at the end of this chapter.

BRAKE FLUID SELECTION

Use DOT 3 or DOT 4 brake fluid from a sealed container.

DISC BRAKE

The front and rear disc brakes are actuated by hydraulic fluid and controlled by a hand lever or foot pedal on the master cylinder. As the brake pads wear, the brake fluid level drops in the reservoir and automatically adjusts for wear.

When working on the brake system, the work area and all tools must be absolutely clean.

Consider the following when servicing the disc brakes.

1. Do not allow disc brake fluid to contact any plastic parts or painted surfaces as damage will result.

2. Always keep the master cylinder reservoir and spare cans of brake fluid closed to prevent dust or moisture from entering and contaminating the brake fluid.

3. Use new disc brake fluid to wash and lubricate internal parts of the brake system. Never clean any internal brake components with solvent or any other petroleum-base cleaners. These will cause the rubber parts in the system to swell, permanently damaging them.

4. Whenever you loosen any brake hose banjo bolt, the brake system is considered opened. You must bleed the system to remove air bubbles. Also, if the brake feels spongy, this usually means there are air bubbles in the system. Bleed the brakes as described under *Brake Bleeding* in this chapter

> *CAUTION*
> *Do not reuse brake fluid. Contaminated brake fluid can cause brake failure. Dispose of brake fluid properly.*

FRONT BRAKE PADS

Pad wear depends greatly on riding habits and conditions. Replace the brake pads when excessively worn, damaged or when contaminated with oil or other chemicals.

To maintain even brake pressure on the front disc, replace both brake pads as a set.

Replacement
1992-1993

Refer to **Figure 1**.

① **FRONT BRAKE CALIPER
(1992-1993)**

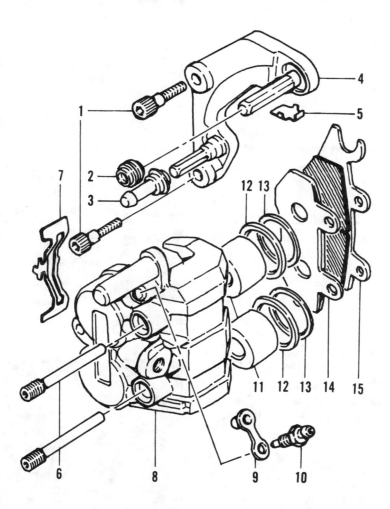

1. Caliper mounting bolts
2. Friction boot
3. Friction boot
4. Brake caliper mounting bracket
5. Pad retainer
6. Brake pad mounting bolts
7. Pad spring
8. Housing
9. Cover
10. Bleed valve
11. Pistons
12. Piston seals
13. Dust seals
14. Outer brake pad
15. Inner brake pad

14

1. Read the information listed under *Disc Brake* in this chapter.

2. Remove the brake disc cover, if used.

CAUTION
Do not allow the master cylinder reservoir to overflow when performing Step 3. Brake fluid will damage most surfaces it contacts.

3. Hold the caliper body (from the outside) and push it toward the brake disc. This will push the pistons into the caliper to make room for the new brake pads.

4. Loosen the brake pad mounting bolts (A, **Figure 2**).

5. Remove the brake caliper mounting bolts (B, **Figure 2**) and lift the caliper off the brake disc.

6. Remove the two brake pad mounting bolts (**Figure 3**).

NOTE
If the pads are to be reused, handle them carefully to prevent grease contamination.

7. Remove the outer (**Figure 4**) and inner (**Figure 5**) brake pads.

8. Inspect the brake pads (**Figure 6**) for uneven wear, damage or contamination. Replace both brake pads as a set.

NOTE
Both brake pads should show approximately the same amount of wear. If the pads are wearing unevenly, the support bracket is probably not sliding correctly on the caliper.

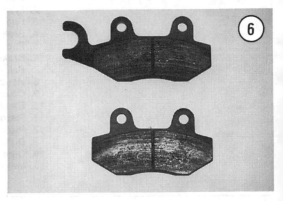

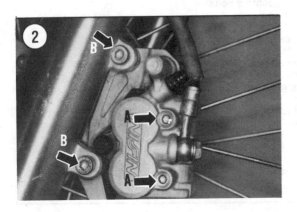

NOTE

The front brake pads can be contaminated by a leaking left side fork oil seal. If this seal is damaged and oil has leaked onto the caliper, inspect the brake pads for oil contamination.

9. Measure the lining thickness (**Figure 7**) of each brake pad (do not include the metal backing plate

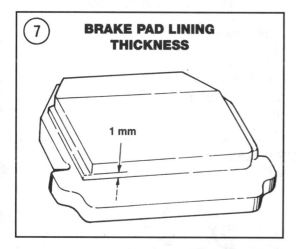

7 **BRAKE PAD LINING THICKNESS**

1 mm

8

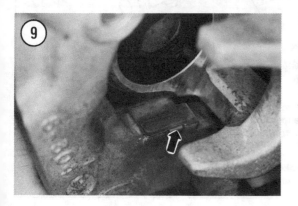

9

thickness). Replace the brake pads if their thickness is less than the service limit in **Table 1**.

10. Check both pistons for fluid leakage. If brake fluid is leaking from the caliper bores, remove and overhaul the brake caliper as described in this chapter.

11. Remove rust and corrosion from the brake pad mounting bolts.

12. Replace the pad spring (**Figure 8**) and pad retainer (**Figure 9**) if corroded or damaged.

13. Check the brake disc for wear as described in this chapter.

14. Install the pad retainer clips (**Figure 9**), if removed. Replace the pad retainer if its own spring tension does not hold it in place.

15. If removed, install the pad spring as shown in **Figure 8**. Replace the pad spring if its own spring tension does not hold it in place.

16. Install the inner brake pad as shown in **Figure 5**.

17. Hook the outer brake pad onto the bracket pin (**Figure 4**) and pivot it into the caliper. Push both pads against the pad spring (**Figure 10**) and install the two brake pad mounting bolts (**Figure 3**). Install the bolts through the brake pads and thread them into the caliper housing. Tighten the bolts finger-tight.

NOTE

Make sure both brake pad mounting bolts were installed through both brake pads.

18. Carefully install the brake caliper over the brake disc, then install the brake caliper mounting bolts (B, **Figure 2**).

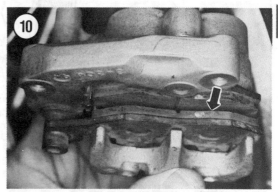

10

NOTE
*If there is not enough room for the brake
pads to slide over the brake disc, you did
not push the pistons far enough into the
caliper as described in Step 3. Take a
clean long flat tool or piece of metal
(like a tire iron) and slide it between the
brake pads. Hold the caliper and then
push the metal tool against the pad that
rests against the caliper pistons to move
the pistons into their bores.*

19. Tighten the brake caliper mounting bolts (B,
Figure 2) as specified in **Table 2**.

20. Tighten the brake pad mounting bolts (A, **Figure 2**) as specified in **Table 2**.

21. Operate the brake lever a few times to seat the
pads against the brake disc, then check the brake

fluid level in the reservoir. If necessary, add new
brake fluid. See *Brake Fluid Selection* in this chapter.

WARNING
*Do not ride the bike until you are sure
that the front brake is operating
correctly with full hydraulic advantage.
If necessary, bleed the front brake as
described in this chapter.*

22. Install the brake disc cover, if used.

**Replacement
(1994-On)**

Refer to **Figure 11**.

1. Read the information listed under *Disc Brake* in
this chapter.

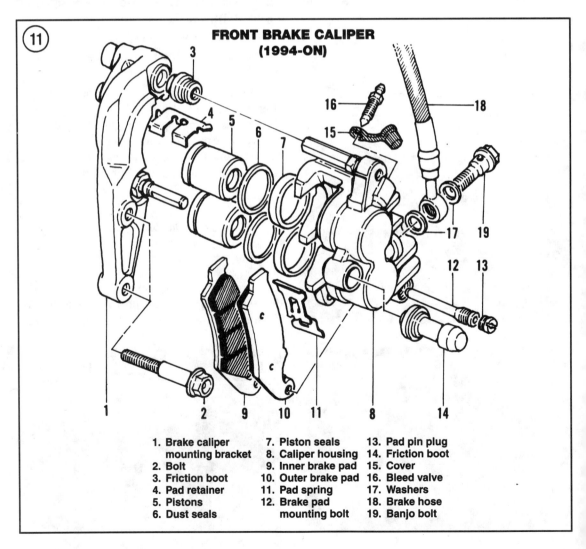

**FRONT BRAKE CALIPER
(1994-ON)**

1. Brake caliper mounting bracket	7. Piston seals	13. Pad pin plug
2. Bolt	8. Caliper housing	14. Friction boot
3. Friction boot	9. Inner brake pad	15. Cover
4. Pad retainer	10. Outer brake pad	16. Bleed valve
5. Pistons	11. Pad spring	17. Washers
6. Dust seals	12. Brake pad mounting bolt	18. Brake hose
		19. Banjo bolt

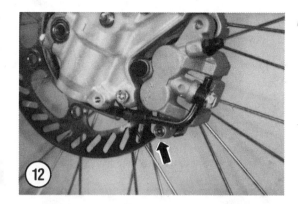

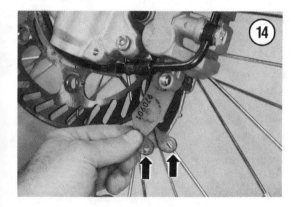

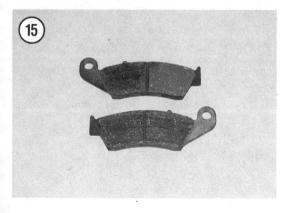

2. Remove the brake disc cover.

3. Remove the pad pin plug (**Figure 12**).

CAUTION
Do not allow the master cylinder reservoir to overflow when performing Step 4. Brake fluid will damage most surfaces it contacts.

4. Hold the caliper body (from the outside) and push it toward the brake disc. This will push the pistons into the caliper to make room for the new brake pads.

5. Loosen and remove the brake pad mounting bolt (**Figure 13**).

NOTE
If the pads are to be reused, handle them carefully to prevent grease contamination.

6. Remove the two brake pads (**Figure 14**).

7. Inspect the brake pads (**Figure 15**) for uneven wear, damage or contamination. Replace both brake pads as a set.

NOTE
Both brake pads should show approximately the same amount of wear. If the pads are wearing unevenly, the support bracket is probably not sliding correctly on the caliper.

NOTE
The front brake pads can be contaminated by a leaking left side fork oil seal. If this seal is damaged and oil has leaked onto the caliper, inspect the brake pads for oil contamination.

8. Measure the lining thickness (**Figure 7**) of each brake pad (do not include the metal backing plate thickness). Replace the brake pads if their thickness is less than the service limit in **Table 1**.

9. Check both pistons for fluid leakage. If brake fluid is leaking from the caliper bores, overhaul the brake caliper as described in this chapter.

10. Clean the pad mounting bolt and plug. Inspect both parts and replace if damaged.

11. Check the brake disc for wear as described in this chapter.

12. Check that the pad spring is installed in the caliper as shown in **Figure 16**.

13. Install the inner and outer brake pads as shown in **Figure 14**. Push them in place so that the upper

14

end of each pad seats in the retainer at the top of the caliper.

14. Push both pads against the pad spring (**Figure 17**). Install the brake pad mounting bolt (**Figure 17**) into the caliper and through the hole in the bottom of each brake pad.

15. Tighten the brake pad mounting bolt (**Figure 13**) as specified in **Table 2**.

16. Install and tighten the pad pin plug (**Figure 12**) securely.

17. Operate the brake lever a few times to seat the pads against the brake disc, then check the brake fluid level in the reservoir. If necessary, add new brake fluid. See *Brake Fluid Selection* in this chapter.

WARNING
Do not ride the bike until you are sure that the front brake is operating correctly with full hydraulic advantage. If necessary, bleed the front brake as described in this chapter.

18. Install the brake disc cover.

BRAKE CALIPER

Refer to **Figure 1** (1992-1993) or **Figure 2** (1994-on) when servicing the brake caliper in this section.

Brake Caliper
Removal/Installation
(Caliper Will Not Be Disassembled)

To remove the caliper without disassembling it, perform this procedure. To disassemble the caliper, refer to *Caliper Removal/Piston Removal* in this chapter.

1A. To remove the caliper from the bike, perform the following:

    a. Loosen the brake hose banjo bolt (A, **Figure 18**) at the caliper.

    b. Remove the bolts (B, **Figure 18**) holding the brake caliper mounting bracket to the fork tube. Lift the caliper off the brake disc.

    c. Remove the banjo bolt, the two washers and the brake caliper. Seal the hose so that brake fluid cannot leak out.

1B. To remove the brake caliper without disconnecting the brake hose, perform the following:

    a. Remove the bolts (B, **Figure 18**) holding the brake caliper mounting bracket to the fork tube. Lift the caliper off the brake disc.

    b. Insert a spacer block between the brake pads.

NOTE
The spacer block will prevent the pistons from being forced out of the caliper if the front brake lever is applied with the brake caliper removed.

    c. Support the caliper with a wire hook.

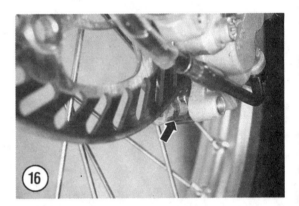

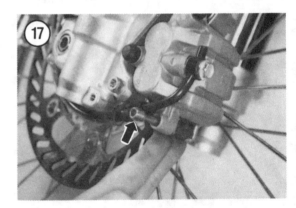

3. Install the caliper by reversing the preceding steps, while noting the following.

4A. If you removed the caliper from the bike, perform the following:

   a. Check that the brake pads were not contaminated with brake fluid.

   b. Route the brake hose against the bottom of the brake caliper (**Figure 19**).

   c. Place a new washer on each side of the brake hose. Install the banjo bolt and tighten finger-tight.

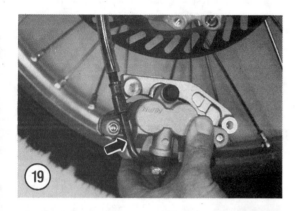

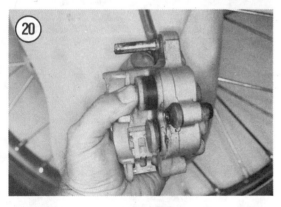

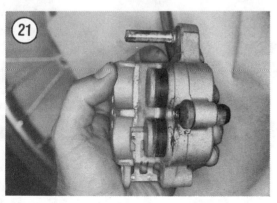

   d. Carefully install the caliper assembly over the brake disc. Be careful not to damage the leading edge of the pads during installation.

   e. Install the two brake caliper mounting bolts (B, **Figure 18**) and tighten as specified in **Table 2**.

   f. Tighten the brake hose banjo bolt (A, **Figure 18**) as specified in **Table 2**.

   g. Refill the master cylinder and bleed the front brake as described in this chapter.

4B. If you did not remove the caliper from the bike, perform the following:

   a. Remove the spacer block from between the brake pads.

   b. Install the caliper over the brake disc. Be careful not to damage the leading edge of the pads during installation.

   c. Install the two brake caliper mounting bolts (B, **Figure 18**) and tighten as specified in **Table 2**.

   d. Operate the brake lever to seat the pads against the brake disc.

5. Operate the brake lever a few times to seat the pads against the brake disc.

> *WARNING*
> *Do not ride the bike until the front brake operates with full hydraulic advantage.*

Caliper Removal/Piston Removal (Caliper Will Be Disassembled)

Force is required to remove the pistons from the caliper. This procedure describes how to remove the pistons with the caliper connected to its brake hose.

1. Remove the brake pads as described in this chapter.

2. Remove the two brake caliper mounting bolts (B, **Figure 18**) and the brake caliper.

3. Wrap a large cloth around the brake caliper.

4. Operate the front brake lever to force the pistons partway out of the caliper bores. If one piston is stuck, block the other piston with your thumb (**Figure 20**). Continue to operate the brake lever to force both pistons evenly out of their bore (**Figure 21**). However, do not completely remove the pistons until after you take the caliper to your workbench for disassembly. By leaving the pistons partially in their bores, they help to prevent brake fluid from spilling out.

14

NOTE
*If the pistons will not come out, remove them as described under **Disassembly** in this chapter.*

6. Remove the caliper banjo bolt (A, **Figure 18**) and both washers. Seal the brake hose to prevent brake fluid from dripping out.

7. Take the caliper to your workbench for disassembly.

Disassembly

Refer to **Figure 1** (1992-1993) or **Figure 11** (1994-on) for this procedure.

1. Remove the brake caliper as described in this chapter.

2. Slide the caliper mounting bracket out of the caliper.

3. Tighten the bleed valve to prevent air from escaping through it when removing the pistons in Step 4.

WARNING
Compressed air will force the pistons out of the caliper under considerable force. Do not block or cushion the pistons with your fingers, as injury will result.

4. Cushion the caliper pistons with a shop rag, making sure to keep your hand away from the pistons. Then apply compressed air through the brake hose port (**Figure 22**) and remove the pistons. If only one piston is blown out, remove it completely, then block its bore opening with a piece of thick rubber (old inner tube) or a rubber ball. Apply compressed air through the caliper once again (**Figure 23**) and remove the remaining piston. See A, **Figure 24**.

5A. On 1992-1993 models, remove the friction boots (**Figure 25**) from the caliper body.

5B. On 1994 and later models, remove the friction boot from the caliper body (B, **Figure 24**) and mounting bracket (**Figure 26**).

6. Remove the dust and piston seals (C, **Figure 24**) from the cylinder bore grooves.

7. Remove the bleed valve and its cover from the caliper.

8. Remove the pad spring from the caliper housing. See 7, **Figure 1** (1992-1993) or 11, **Figure 11** (1994-on).

9. Remove the pad retainer from the caliper mounting bracket. See 5, **Figure 1** (1992-1993) or 4, **Figure 11** (1994-on).

Inspection

Replace parts that show excessive wear or damage as described in this section.

CAUTION
Do not get any oil or grease onto any of the brake caliper components. These

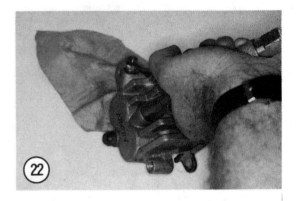

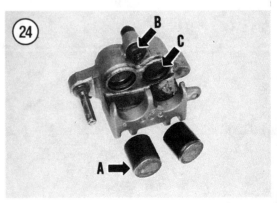

chemicals will cause the rubber parts in the brake system to swell, permanently damaging them.

1. Clean and dry the caliper housing and the other metal parts. Scrape the seal grooves with a wooden or plastic tip tool.

NOTE
The caliper bore and seal grooves can be difficult to clean, especially if brake fluid was leaking past the seals. Clean

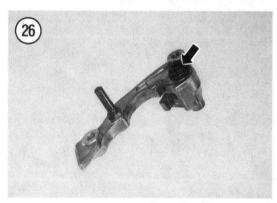

the caliper carefully to avoid damaging the seal grooves and bore surface.

2. Discard the dust and piston seals.
3. Inspect the caliper shaft assembly as follows:

NOTE
A floating caliper is used on all models. Fixed shafts mounted on the brake caliper and mounting bracket allow the brake caliper to slide or float during piston movement. Friction boots installed around each shaft help to control caliper movement by preventing excessive shaft vibration and play. The boots also prevent dirt from damaging the shaft operating surfaces. If the shafts are excessively worn or damaged, the caliper cannot slide smoothly. This condition will cause one pad to wear more than the other, resulting in brake drag and overheating of the brake disc and brake fluid. The shafts and friction boots are an important part of the brake caliper and must be maintained to provide proper brake operation.

a. Inspect the friction boots for cracks, tearing, weakness or other damage.
b. Inspect the caliper shafts for excessive wear, uneven wear (steps) or other damage.

4. Check each cylinder bore (**Figure 27**) for corrosion, pitting, deep scratches or other wear. Do not hone the cylinder bores.
5. Check the pistons for wear marks, cracks or other damage.
6. Check the bleed valve and cap for wear or damage.
7. Check the banjo bolt for wear or damage. Discard the washers.
8. Inspect the caliper mounting bracket for cracks or other damage. Check the sliding shafts for wear grooves, pitting and other damage.

14

NOTE
On 1992-1993 models, one of the sliding shafts is mounted on the brake caliper.

9. Remove any rust and corrosion from the pad retainer and pad spring with a wire brush. Check for cracks and other damage.
10. Inspect the brake pads as follows:

a. Inspect the brake pads for uneven wear, damage or contamination.

b. Measure the thickness of each brake pad (**Figure 7**). Replace the brake pads if the thickness of any one pad is out of specification (**Table 1**).

c. Replace both brake pads as a set.

11. Replace the pad mounting bolts and plug (1994-on) if damaged.

Assembly

NOTE
*Use new brake fluid when lubricating the parts in the following steps. Refer to **Brake Fluid Selection** in this chapter.*

1. Install the bleed valve and its cover into the caliper.

2. Soak the piston and dust seals in brake fluid (**Figure 28**) for approximately five minutes.

3. Lubricate the cylinder bores with brake fluid.

NOTE
*The piston seals (A, **Figure 29**) are thicker than the dust seals (B, **Figure 29**).*

4. Install a new piston seal into each rear bore groove (A, **Figure 30**).

5. Install a new dust seal into each front bore groove (B, **Figure 30**).

NOTE
Check that each seal fits squarely inside its cylinder bore groove.

6. Lubricate the pistons with brake fluid.

NOTE
The pistons can be difficult to install because they must compress the dust and piston seals in order to slide past them. When installing the pistons in Step 7, turn them into their bore. Do not try to push them straight in. Once a piston is installed past both seals, you can then push it all the way into its bore.

7A. On 1992-1993 models, install each piston into its cylinder bore with its cupped side facing out (**Figure 31**). Push both pistons in all the way.

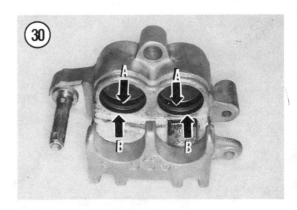
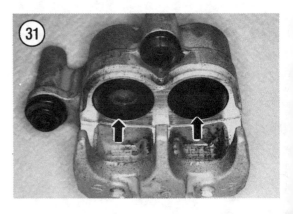

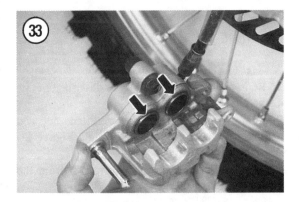

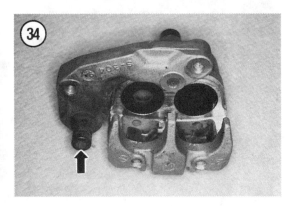

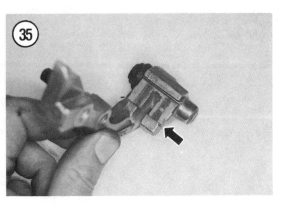

7B. On 1994 and later models, install each piston into its cylinder bore with its metal (**Figure 32**) or open (**Figure 33**) side facing out. Push both pistons in all the way.

> *CAUTION*
> *Silicone brake grease is not the same type of lubricant as a silicone sealant (RTV) used on engine gaskets. Silicone brake grease is a high temperature, water-resistant grease. Make sure the lubricant used in Step 8 is a silicone grease specified for brake use. For example, Permatex Ultra Disc Brake Caliper Lube (part No. 20356).*

8A. On 1992-1993 models, perform the following:
   a. Install the pad retainer (5, **Figure 1**) onto the mounting bracket.
   b. Install the pad spring (7, **Figure 1**) into the caliper.
   c. Install the two friction boots (**Figure 25**) into the caliper housing.
   d. Lubricate the mounting bracket pins (4, **Figure 1**) and the inside of each friction boot with silicone brake grease.
   e. Slide the mounting bracket into the caliper (**Figure 34**).

8B. On 1994 and later models, perform the following:
   a. Install the pad retainer (**Figure 35**) onto the mounting bracket.
   b. Install the pad spring (**Figure 36**) into the caliper housing.
   c. Install the large friction boot (A, **Figure 37**) into the caliper housing.
   d. Install the small friction boot (B, **Figure 37**) into the mounting bracket.

14

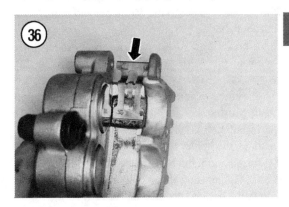

e. Lubricate the caliper and bracket pins (C, **Figure 37**) and the inside of each friction boot with silicone brake grease.

f. Slide the mounting bracket into the caliper (**Figure 38**).

9. Install the brake caliper assembly and brake pads as described in this chapter.

FRONT MASTER CYLINDER

Read the information listed under *Disc Brake* in this chapter before servicing the front master cylinder.

Refer to **Figure 39** (1992-1996) or **Figure 40** (1997-on) when servicing the front master cylinder in this section.

Removal/Installation

1. Support the bike on a workstand.

2. Cover the area under the master cylinder to prevent brake fluid from damaging any component that it might contact.

CAUTION
Wipe up any spilled brake fluid immediately as it will stain or destroy the finish of most plastic and metal surfaces. Use soapy water and rinse thoroughly.

3. Drain the front brake system as described under *Draining Brake Fluid* in this chapter.

4. Remove the banjo bolt (**Figure 41**) and washers securing the brake hose to the master cylinder. Seal the brake hose to prevent brake fluid from dripping out.

5. Remove the bolts and clamp (**Figure 42**) holding the master cylinder to the handlebar and remove the master cylinder.

6. If brake fluid is leaking from the cylinder bore, overhaul the master cylinder as described in this chapter.

7. Clean the handlebar, master cylinder and clamp mating surfaces.

8. Install the master cylinder holder with the "UP" mark on the holder facing up (**Figure 42**).

9. Install and tighten the master cylinder mounting bolts. Tighten the upper bolt first, then the lower mounting bolt as specified in **Table 2**.

10. Secure the brake hose to the master cylinder with the banjo bolt (**Figure 41**) and two new washers. Install a washer on each side of the brake hose. Center the brake hose between the arms on the master cylinder (**Figure 41**). Tighten the banjo bolt as specified in **Table 2**.

11. Bleed the front brake as described under *Brake Bleeding* in this chapter.

WARNING
Do not ride the bike until the front brake works properly.

Disassembly (1992-1996)

Refer to **Figure 39** for this procedure.

1. Remove the master cylinder as described in this chapter.

2. Remove the brake lever pivot bolt and nut, and then remove the brake lever and spring (**Figure 43**) from the master cylinder.

3. Remove the dust cover (**Figure 44**) from the groove in the end of the piston.

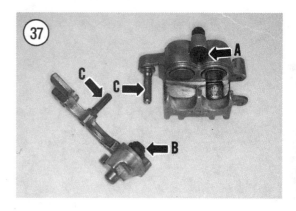

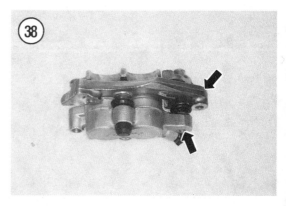

**FRONT MASTER CYLINDER
(1992-1996)**

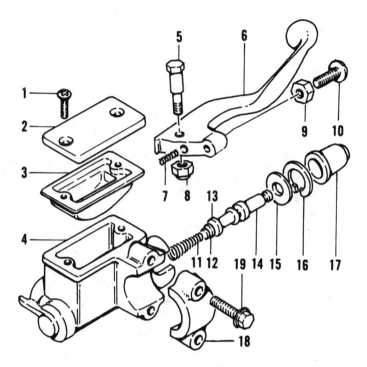

1. Screw
2. Cover
3. Diaphragm
4. Housing
5. Pivot bolt
6. Brake lever
7. Spring
8. Nut
9. Locknut
10. Adjust bolt

11. Spring
12. Primary cup
13. Secondary cup (O-ring)
14. Piston
15. Washer
16. Circlip
17. Dust cover
18. Clamp
19. Bolt

14

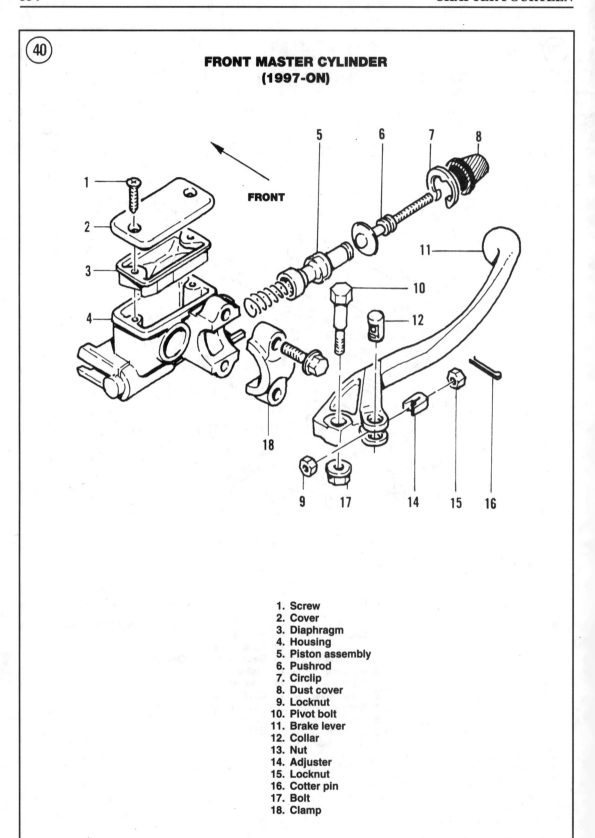

**FRONT MASTER CYLINDER
(1997-ON)**

FRONT

1. Screw
2. Cover
3. Diaphragm
4. Housing
5. Piston assembly
6. Pushrod
7. Circlip
8. Dust cover
9. Locknut
10. Pivot bolt
11. Brake lever
12. Collar
13. Nut
14. Adjuster
15. Locknut
16. Cotter pin
17. Bolt
18. Clamp

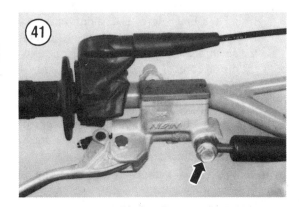

NOTE
*Use a bolt and nut as shown in **Figure 45** to help hold the master cylinder in a vise when removing and installing the piston circlip.*

4. Compress the piston, then remove the circlip (**Figure 46**) from the groove in the master cylinder with a pair of circlip pliers.

5. Remove the circlip, washer and piston assembly (**Figure 47**) from the master cylinder bore.

6. Perform the *Inspection* procedure to clean and inspect the parts.

Assembly
(1992-1996)

Refer to **Figure 39** for this procedure.

CAUTION
Do not get any oil or grease onto any of the master cylinder components. These chemicals will cause the rubber parts in the brake system to swell, causing brake drag and other problems.

14

1. Make sure all of the components are clean before reassembly.

2. If you are installing a new piston assembly, assemble it as described under *Inspection* in this section.

3. Lubricate the piston assembly and cylinder bore with brake fluid.

4. Install the spring—small end first—onto the piston as shown in A, **Figure 48**.

> *CAUTION*
> *Do not allow the piston cups to tear or turn inside out when installing the piston into the master cylinder bore. Both cups are larger than the bore. To ease installation, lubricate the cups and piston with brake fluid*

5. Insert the piston assembly—spring end first—into the master cylinder bore (**Figure 47**).

> *NOTE*
> *Before installing the washer and circlip, mount the master cylinder in a vise (**Figure 45**) as described under **Disassembly**.*

6. Compress the piston assembly and install the washer and circlip (**Figure 47**). Note the following:

   a. Install the washer (**Figure 47**) with its flat side facing up.

   b. Install the circlip (**Figure 47**) with its flat side facing up. See **Figure 46**. Push and release the piston a few times to make sure it moves smoothly and that the circlip does not pop out.

> *NOTE*
> *The circlip must seat in the groove completely (**Figure 46**).*

7. Slide the dust cover over the piston with its large end facing toward the piston. Seat the large end into the cylinder bore and the small end into the groove in the end of the piston (**Figure 44**).

8. Install the diaphragm, master cylinder cover and screws.

9. Assemble the brake lever as follows:

   a. Install the spring (**Figure 43**) into the hole in the brake lever.

   b. Apply a dab of silicone brake grease onto the end of the brake lever adjust bolt where it contacts the piston.

   c. Install the brake lever and spring onto the master cylinder. The end of the spring fits into the small hole in the master cylinder next to the piston bore.

   d. Install the brake lever pivot bolt and nut. Tighten the bolt and then check that the brake lever moves freely. Hold the bolt and tighten the nut securely. Check again that the brake lever moves freely.

10. Install the master cylinder as described in this chapter.

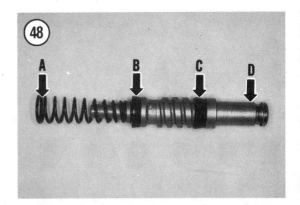

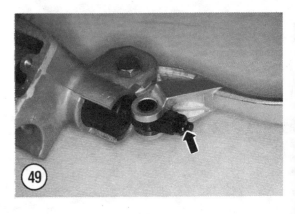

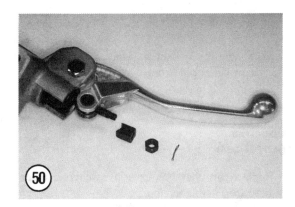

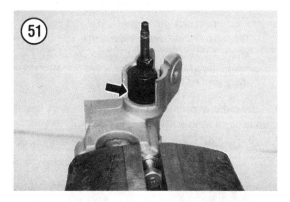

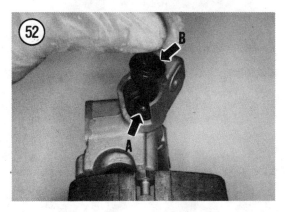

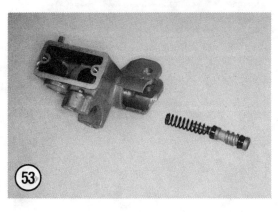

Disassembly
(1997-on)

Refer to **Figure 40** for this procedure.

1. Remove the master cylinder as described in this chapter.

2. Remove the cotter pin (**Figure 49**), locknut and brake adjuster assembly. See **Figure 50**.

3. Remove the brake lever pivot bolt, nut and brake lever (**Figure 50**). Remove the collar from the hole in the brake lever.

NOTE
*Use a bolt and nut as shown in **Figure** 45 to help hold the master cylinder in a vise when removing and installing the piston circlip.*

4. Pull the dust cover (**Figure 51**) out of the master cylinder bore to uncover the circlip.

5. Compress the piston, then remove the circlip (**Figure 52**) with circlip pliers and remove the pushrod assembly.

6. Remove the piston assembly (**Figure 53**) from the master cylinder bore.

7. Perform the *Inspection* procedure to clean and inspect the parts.

Assembly
(1997-on)

Refer to **Figure 40** for this procedure.

CAUTION
Do not get any oil or grease onto any of the master cylinder components. These chemicals will cause the rubber parts in the brake system to swell, causing brake drag and other problems.

1. Make sure all of the components are clean before reassembly.

2. If you are installing a new piston assembly, assemble it as described under *Inspection* in this section.

3. Lubricate the piston assembly and cylinder bore with brake fluid.

4. Install the spring—small end first—onto the piston as shown in A, **Figure 54**.

CAUTION
Do not allow the piston cups to tear or turn inside out when installing the

14

piston into the master cylinder bore. Both cups are larger than the bore. To ease installation, lubricate the cups and piston with brake fluid.

5. Insert the piston assembly—spring end first—into the master cylinder bore (**Figure 53**).

> *NOTE*
> *Before installing the pushrod and circlip, mount the master cylinder in a vise (**Figure 45**) as described under* **Disassembly**.

6. Install the pushrod assembly and circlip as follows:
   a. Install the boot over the pushrod, then seat its small end into the pushrod shoulder. Pull the large end of the boot back toward the end of the pushrod to make room when installing the circlip. See **Figure 55**.
   b. Install the circlip over the pushrod with its flat side facing up.
   c. Place the curved part of the pushrod against the piston (B, **Figure 52**). Compress the piston assembly and install the circlip (A, **Figure 52**) into the master cylinder groove. Push and release the piston a few times to make sure it moves smoothly and that the circlip does not pop out.

> *NOTE*
> *The circlip must seat in the groove completely (A, **Figure 52**).*

7. Slide the dust cover over the piston. Seat the dust cover's large end into the cylinder bore next to the circlip (**Figure 51**). Make sure the small end stays centered between the pushrod shoulder.
8. Install the diaphragm, master cylinder cover and screws.
9. Assemble the brake lever assembly as follows:
   a. Install the collar (**Figure 56**) into the hole in the brake lever, then slide the collar onto the pushrod.
   b. Install the brake lever pivot bolt and nut. Tighten the bolt and check that the brake lever moves freely. Then hold the bolt and tighten the nut securely. Recheck the brake lever to make sure it moves freely.
   c. Slide the brake adjuster (A, **Figure 57**) over the pushrod so its curved edge fits against the

collar, then install the locknut (B) and tighten securely.
   d. Secure the locknut and brake adjuster with a new cotter pin (**Figure 49**).
10. Install the master cylinder as described in this chapter.

**Inspection
(All Models)**

Replace parts that show excessive wear or damage as described in this section.

> *CAUTION*
> *Do not get any oil or grease onto any of the master cylinder components. These chemicals will cause the rubber parts in the brake system to swell, causing brake drag and other problems.*

1. Clean the master cylinder parts with new brake fluid or with rubbing (isopropyl) alcohol.
2A. **Figure 48** identifies the piston assembly used on 1992-1996 models:
   a. Spring.
   b. Primary cup.

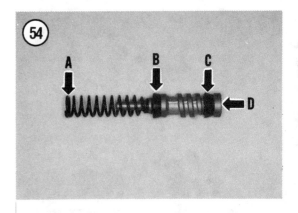

c. Secondary cup.

d. Piston.

2B. **Figure 54** identifies the piston assembly used on 1997 and later models:

a. Spring.

b. Primary cup.

c. Secondary cup.

d. Piston.

CAUTION
Do not remove the primary and secondary cups from the piston

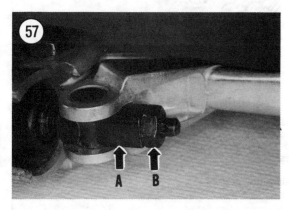

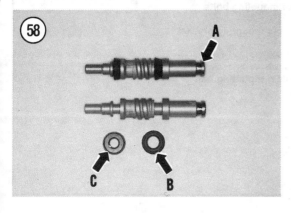

assembly. If the cups are damaged, you must replace the piston assembly.

3. Check the piston assembly (**Figure 48** or **Figure 54**) for the following defects:

a. Broken, distorted or collapsed piston return spring.

b. Worn, cracked, damaged or swollen primary and secondary cups.

c. Scratched, scored or damaged piston.

d. On 1992-1996 models, corroded or damaged washer.

e. On 1997 and later models, corroded or damaged pushrod assembly (**Figure 55**).

f. Excessively worn or damaged dust cover.

If any of these parts are excessively worn or damaged, replace the piston assembly.

4. To assemble a new piston assembly, perform the following:

NOTE
*A new piston assembly consists of the piston, primary cup, secondary cup and spring. Because these parts come unassembled, you must install the new primary and secondary cups onto the piston. See **Figure 58**, typical. Use the original piston and pistons cups (A, **Figure 58**) as a reference when assembling the new piston assembly.*

a. Place the new cups in a container filled with new brake fluid and allow to soak for 15 minutes. This will soften them and ease installation. Clean the new piston in brake fluid and place it on a clean lint-free cloth.

b. Install the secondary (B, **Figure 58**) and then the primary (C, **Figure 58**) cups onto the piston.

5. Inspect the master cylinder bore for corrosion, pitting or excessive wear. Do not hone the master cylinder bore to remove scratches or other damage.

6. Check for plugged supply and relief ports in the master cylinder. Clean with compressed air.

7. Inspect the reservoir cover and diaphragm for cracks and other damage. Inspect the small Phillips screws for damage.

8. Inspect the brake lever assembly for:

a. Damaged brake lever.

b. Excessively worn or elongated brake lever hole.

c. Excessively worn brake lever pivot bolt.

14

REAR BRAKE CALIPER
(1992-1994)

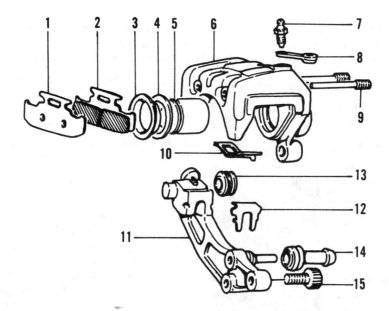

1. Brake pad
2. Brake pad
3. Dust seal
4. Piston seal
5. Piston
6. Brake caliper housing
7. Bleed valve
8. Rubber cap
9. Brake pad mounting bolts
10. Pad spring
11. Brake caliper mounting bracket
12. Pad retainer
13. Friction boot
14. Friction boot
15. Brake caliper mounting bolt

BRAKES

361

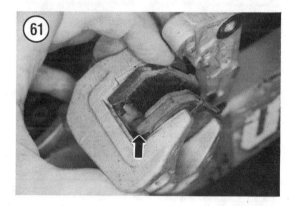

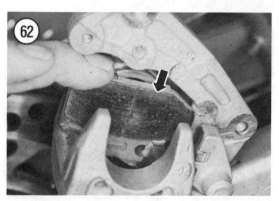

d. Damaged brake lever spring (1992-1996).

e. Damaged pushrod and brake adjuster assembly (1997-on).

REAR BRAKE PADS

Pad wear depends greatly on riding habits and conditions. Replace the brake pads when excessively worn, damaged or when contaminated with oil or other chemicals.

To maintain even brake pressure on the rear disc, replace both brake pads as a set.

Replacement
1992-1994

Refer to **Figure 59**.

1. Read the information listed under *Disc Brake* in this chapter.

2. Place the bike on a workstand with the rear wheel off the ground.

3. Unbolt and remove the brake caliper cover.

CAUTION
Do not allow the master cylinder reservoir to overflow when performing Step 4. Brake fluid will damage most surfaces.

4. Hold of the caliper body (from the outside) and push it toward the brake disc. This will push the piston into the caliper to make room for the new brake pads.

5. Loosen the brake pad mounting bolts (A, **Figure 60**).

6. Remove the brake caliper mounting bolt (B, **Figure 60**) and lift the brake caliper off the brake disc.

7. Remove the two brake pad mounting bolts (A, **Figure 60**).

NOTE
If the pads are to be reused, handle them carefully to prevent grease contamination.

8. Remove the inner (**Figure 61**) and outer (**Figure 62**) brake pads.

NOTE
*Each pad is equipped with a silencer shim (**Figure 63**). These shims hook onto the back of the pads and should not fall off.*

14

9. Inspect the brake pads (**Figure 64**) for uneven wear, damage or contamination. Replace both brake pads as a set.

> *NOTE*
> *Both brake pads should show approximately the same amount of wear. If the pads are wearing unevenly, the support bracket is probably not sliding correctly on the caliper.*

10. Measure the thickness (**Figure 65**) of each brake pad (do not include the metal plate backing plate thickness). Replace the brake pads if their thickness is less than the service limit in **Table 1**.

11. Check the end of the piston for fluid leakage. If the caliper is leaking, overhaul the brake caliper as described in this chapter.

12. Remove rust and corrosion from the brake pad mounting bolts. Check the shoulder on each bolt for wear grooves, nicks and other damage. Replace the bolts if the damage cannot be repaired.

13. Check that the pad spring is positioned inside the caliper (**Figure 66**) and is held in place by its own spring tension. Replace the pad spring if it is excessively corroded or if it falls out.

14. Check that the pad retainer (12, **Figure 59**) is hooked onto the caliper mounting bracket.

15. Check the brake disc for wear as described in this chapter.

16. If removed, install the silencer shim (**Figure 63**) on the backside of each brake pad. Make sure each silencer shim hooks onto the back of its pad and does not fall off.

17. Install the outer (**Figure 62**) and inner (**Figure 61**) brake pads.

18. Push both pads against the pad spring (**Figure 67**). Install the brake pad mounting bolts (A, **Figure 60**) into the caliper and through the hole in each brake pad. Tighten each bolt finger-tight.

19. Check that the pad retainer is hooked onto the caliper mounting bracket and is positioned between the bracket and caliper as shown in **Figure 68**.

20. Install the brake caliper over the brake disc, making sure you do not damage the leading edge of the brake pads.

21. Install the brake caliper mounting bolt (B, **Figure 60**) and tighten as specified in **Table 2**.

22. Tighten the brake pad mounting bolts (A, **Figure 60**) as specified in **Table 2**.

23. Install the brake caliper cover.

24. Operate the brake pedal a few times to seat the pads against the brake disc, then check the brake fluid level in the reservoir. If necessary, add new brake fluid. See *Brake Fluid Selection* in this chapter.

> *WARNING*
> *Do not ride the bike until you are sure that the rear brake is operating correctly with full hydraulic advantage.*

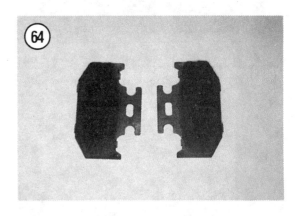

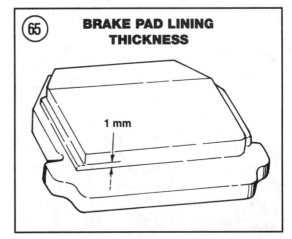

BRAKE PAD LINING THICKNESS

1 mm

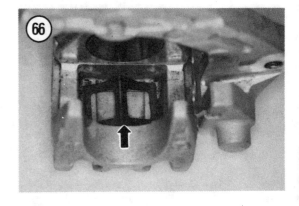

If necessary, bleed the rear brake as described in this chapter.

Replacement
1995-on

Refer to **Figure 69**.

1. Read the information listed under *Disc Brake* in this chapter.
2. Unbolt and remove the brake caliper cover.
3. Remove the mounting bolt plug (**Figure 70**).

CAUTION
Do not allow the master cylinder reservoir to overflow when performing Step 4. Brake fluid will damage most surfaces it contacts.

4. Hold the caliper body (from the outside) and push it toward the brake disc (**Figure 71**). This will push the piston into the caliper to make room for the new brake pads.
5. Loosen and remove the brake pad mounting bolt (A, **Figure 72**).
6. Remove the outer and inner brake pads (B, **Figure 72**).

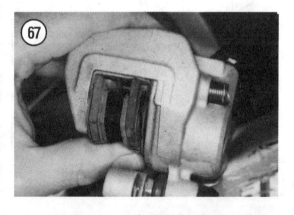

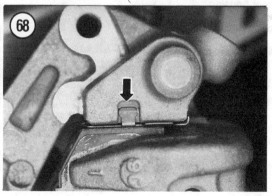

NOTE
*Each pad is equipped with a silencer shim (**Figure 73**). These shims hook onto the back of the pads and should not fall off.*

7. Inspect the brake pads (**Figure 74**) for uneven wear, damage or contamination. Replace both brake pads as a set.

NOTE
Both brake pads should show approximately the same amount of wear. If the pads are wearing unevenly, the support bracket is probably not sliding correctly on the caliper.

8. Measure the thickness of each brake pad (**Figure 65**). Replace the brake pads if their thickness is less than the service limit listed in **Table 1**.
9. Check the end of the piston for fluid leakage. If the caliper is leaking brake fluid, overhaul the brake caliper as described in this chapter.
10. Clean the brake pad mounting bolt and plug. Remove all rust and corrosion from the mounting bolt shoulder. Replace if damaged.
11. Check the brake disc for wear as described in this chapter.
12. Check that the pad spring is installed in the caliper as shown in **Figure 75**.
13. If removed, install the silencer shim on the backside of each brake pad (**Figure 73**). Make sure each silencer shim hooks onto the back of its pad and does not fall off.
14. Install the inner and outer brake pads (**Figure 72**). Push them in place so the front end of each pad seats into the pad retainer mounted on the caliper mounting bracket.

NOTE
Figure 76 *(removed for clarity) shows how the front part of each brake pad seats into the pad retainer.*

15. Push both pads against the pad spring, then install the brake pad mounting bolt into the caliper and through the hole in each brake pad (**Figure 77**).
16. Tighten the brake pad mounting bolt (**Figure 78**) as specified in **Table 2**.
17. Install and tighten the mounting bolt plug (**Figure 70**) securely.
18. Operate the brake pedal a few times to seat the pads against the brake disc, then check the brake

14

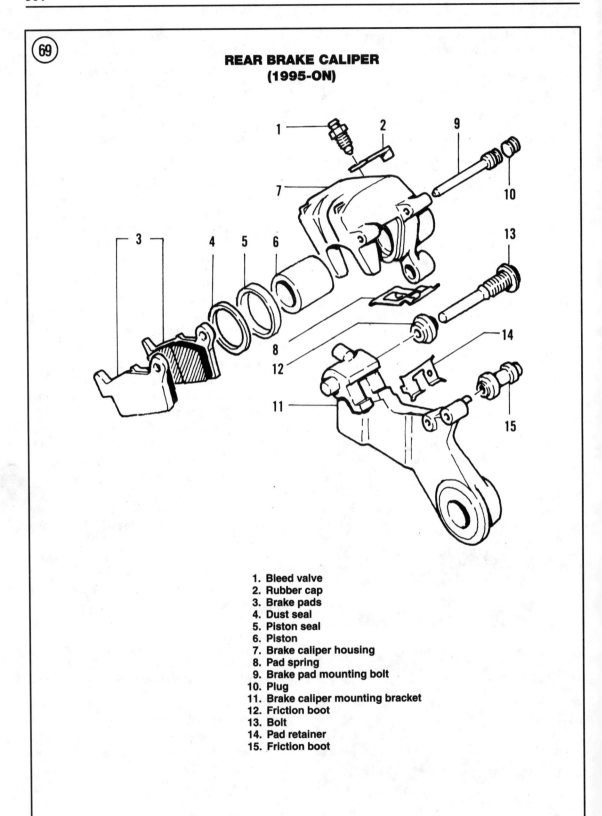

**REAR BRAKE CALIPER
(1995-ON)**

1. Bleed valve
2. Rubber cap
3. Brake pads
4. Dust seal
5. Piston seal
6. Piston
7. Brake caliper housing
8. Pad spring
9. Brake pad mounting bolt
10. Plug
11. Brake caliper mounting bracket
12. Friction boot
13. Bolt
14. Pad retainer
15. Friction boot

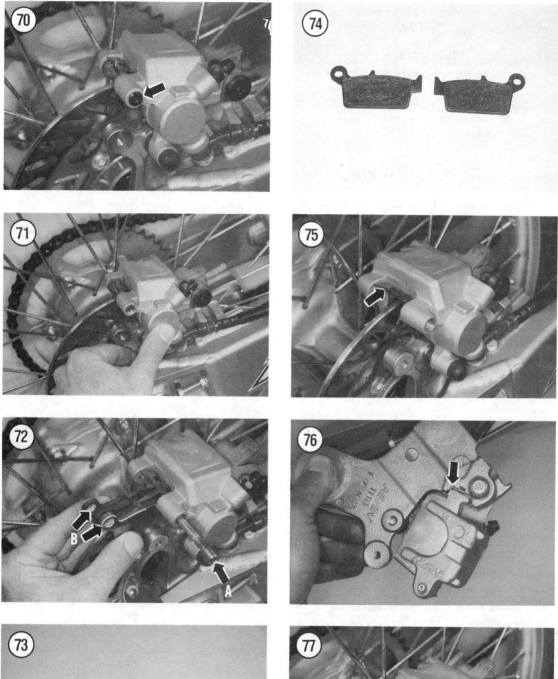

fluid level in the reservoir. If necessary, add new brake fluid. See *Brake Fluid Selection* in this chapter.

WARNING
Do not ride the bike until you are sure that the rear brake is operating correctly with full hydraulic advantage. If necessary, bleed the rear brake as described in this chapter.

REAR BRAKE CALIPER

Refer to **Figure 59** (1992-1994) or **Figure 69** (1995-on) when servicing the rear brake caliper in this section.

Rear Brake Caliper Removal/Installation (Caliper Will Not Be Disassembled)

To remove the caliper without disassembling it, perform this procedure. To remove and disassemble the caliper, refer to *Caliper Removal/Piston Removal* in this chapter.

1. Remove the brake caliper cover (A, **Figure 79**).

NOTE
If you are not going to remove the brake caliper from the bike, do not drain the brake fluid or disconnect the brake hose (B, Figure 79) from the caliper.

2A. On 1992-1994 models, remove the brake caliper as follows:

  a. Loosen the brake hose banjo bolt at the caliper, then retighten it hand-tight so that no brake fluid can leak out.

  b. Remove the brake caliper mounting bolt (B, **Figure 60**) and lift the brake caliper off the brake disc.

  c. Slide the brake caliper mounting bracket back and off the swing arm stay.

  d. Remove the banjo bolt and the two washers and remove the brake caliper. Seal the hose so brake fluid does not leak out.

2B. On 1995-on models, remove the brake caliper as follows:

  a. Remove the rear wheel (Chapter Eleven).

  b. Loosen the brake hose banjo bolt (B, **Figure 79**) at the caliper, then retighten it hand-tight so no brake fluid can leak out.

  c. Slide the brake caliper mounting bracket (**Figure 80**) off the swing arm stay.

  d. Remove the banjo bolt and the 2 washers and remove the brake caliper. Seal the hose so brake fluid does not leak out.

3. If you are not going to remove the brake caliper from the bike, insert a spacer block between the brake pads.

NOTE
The spacer block will prevent the piston from being forced out of the caliper if

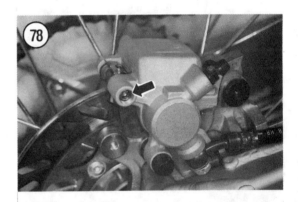

the rear brake pedal is applied with the brake caliper removed from around the disc.

4. Install the brake caliper by reversing these steps, while noting the following:

   a. If you did not disconnect the brake hose, remove the spacer block from between the brake pads.

   b. Check that the brake pads were not contaminated with brake fluid.

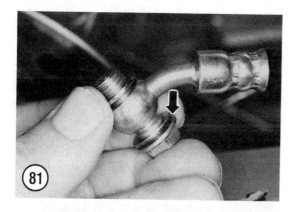

c. Place a new washer on each side of the brake hose. Install the banjo bolt and tighten finger-tight. See **Figure 81**, typical.

d. Hold the brake caliper mounting bracket with a large adjustable wrench (**Figure 82**), then tighten the brake hose banjo bolt as specified in **Table 2**.

e. On 1995 and later models, slide the brake caliper mounting bracket over the swing arm stay (**Figure 80**). Install the rear wheel as described in Chapter Eleven.

f. If you disconnected the brake hose at the caliper, refill the master cylinder and bleed the rear brake as described in this chapter.

g. On all models, press and release the rear brake pedal to seat the pads against the brake disc.

> *WARNING*
> *Do not ride the bike until the rear brake operates with full hydraulic advantage.*

Caliper Removal/Piston Removal (Caliper Will Be Disassembled)

Force is required to remove the piston from the caliper. This procedure describes how to remove the piston with the caliper connected to its brake hose.

1. Remove the brake pads as described in this chapter.

2. Remove the brake caliper as described in this chapter.

3. Wrap a large cloth around the brake caliper.

4. Hold the caliper so your hand and fingers are placed away from the piston.

5. Operate the rear brake pedal to force the piston (**Figure 83**) partway out of the caliper bore.

> *NOTE*
> *You do not have to completely remove the piston in Step 5. When the piston extends far enough out of its bore so you can grab hold of it with your fingers, you can remove it later at your workbench. This way, you are less likely to spill brake fluid all over your hands and bike.*

> *NOTE*
> *If the piston will not come out, remove it as described under* **Disassembly** *in this chapter.*

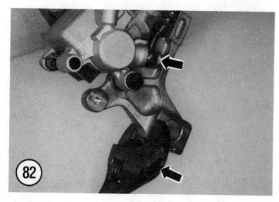

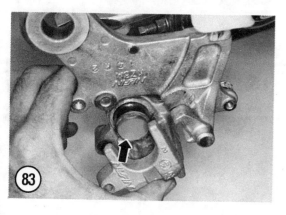

6. Hold the brake caliper mounting bracket with a large adjustable wrench, then loosen and remove the

brake hose banjo bolt (**Figure 82**) and both washers. Seal the brake hose to prevent brake fluid from leaking out.

7. Take the caliper to your workbench for disassembly.

Disassembly

Refer to **Figure 59** (1992-1994) or **Figure 69** (1995-on) in this section.

1. Remove the brake caliper as described in this chapter.

2. Slide the brake caliper off its mounting bracket. See **Figure 84** (1992-1994) or **Figure 85** (1995-on).

3. Tighten the bleed valve to prevent air from escaping through it when removing the piston in Step 4.

WARNING
Compressed air will force the piston out of the caliper under considerable force. Do not block or cushion the piston with your fingers, as injury will result.

4. Cushion the caliper piston with a shop rag, making sure you keep your hand away from the piston area. Apply compressed air through the brake hose port (**Figure 86**) and remove the piston (**Figure 87**).

5. Remove the dust and piston seals (**Figure 87**) from the caliper bore grooves.

6. Remove the friction boot from the caliper body.

7. Remove the friction boot from the caliper mounting bracket.

8. Remove the bleed valve and its cover from the caliper.

9. Remove the pad spring from the caliper housing.

10. Remove the pad retainer from the caliper mounting bracket.

Inspection

Replace parts that show excessive wear or damage as described in this section.

CAUTION
Do not get any oil or grease onto any of the brake caliper components. These chemicals will cause the rubber parts in the brake system to swell, causing brake drag and other problems.

1. Clean and dry the caliper housing and the other metal parts. Clean parts with new brake fluid, then place on a clean lint-free cloth until reassembly.

Clean the seal grooves with a plastic or wooden tip tool.

NOTE
The caliper bore and seal grooves can be difficult to clean, especially if brake fluid was leaking past the seals. Clean the caliper carefully to avoid damaging the seal grooves and bore surface.

2. Discard the dust and piston seals.

3. Inspect the caliper shaft assembly as follows:

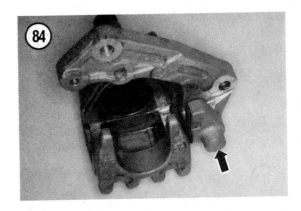

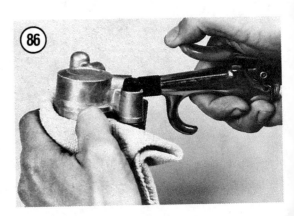

NOTE

A floating caliper is used on all models. Fixed shafts mounted on the brake caliper and mounting bracket allow the brake caliper to slide or float during piston movement. Friction boots installed around each shaft help to control caliper movement by preventing excessive shaft vibration and play and to prevent dirt from damaging the shaft operating surfaces. If the shafts are excessively worn or damaged, the caliper cannot slide smoothly. This condition will cause one pad to wear more than the other, resulting in brake drag and overheating of the brake disc and brake fluid. The shafts and friction boots are an important part of the brake caliper and must be maintained to provide proper brake operation.

a. Inspect the friction boots for cracks, tearing, weakness or other damage. See A and B, **Figure 88**, typical.

b. Inspect the caliper shafts for excessive wear, uneven wear (steps) or other damage. See C, **Figure 88**, typical.

4. Check the cylinder bore for corrosion, deep scratches or other wear. Do not hone the cylinder bore to clean or repair it. A rough or damaged bore surface will damage the piston seal and increase its wear, causing brake fluid leakage.

5. Inspect the piston for excessive wear, cracks or other damage. Remove any rust or corrosion from steel pistons.

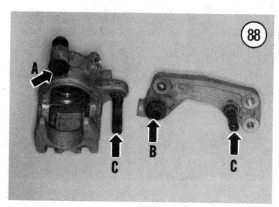

6. Clean the bleed valve with compressed air. Check the valve threads for damage. Replace the dust cap if missing or damaged.

7. Clean the banjo bolt with compressed air. Discard the washers.

8. Inspect the pad spring (A, **Figure 89**) and pad retainer (B) for weakness, corrosion, rust or other damage. Replace if they cannot be cleaned thoroughly or if their individual spring tension is insufficient to hold them in place when installed inside the caliper (pad spring) or on the caliper mounting bracket (pad retainer).

9. Inspect the brake pads as follows:

a. Inspect the brake pads (C, **Figure 89**) for uneven wear, damage or contamination.

b. Measure the thickness of each brake pad. Replace the brake pads if the thickness on any one pad is less than the service limit in **Table 1**.

c. Replace both brake pads as a set.

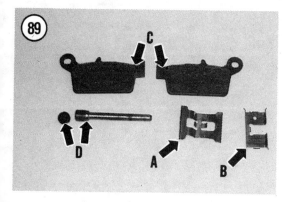

10. Inspect the brake pad mounting bolt(s) (D, **Figure 89**) for excessive wear, uneven wear or other damage.

14

Assembly

> *NOTE*
> *Use new brake fluid when lubricating the parts in the following steps. Refer to **Brake Fluid Selection** in this chapter.*

1. Install the bleed valve and its cover into the caliper.
2. Soak the piston and dust seals in brake fluid for approximately five minutes.
3. Lubricate the cylinder bore with brake fluid.

> *NOTE*
> *The piston seal (A, **Figure 90**) is thicker than the dust seal (B, **Figure 90**).*

4. Install a new piston seal into the rear bore groove (A, **Figure 91**).
5. Install a new dust seal into the front bore groove (B, **Figure 91**).

> *NOTE*
> *Check that each seal fits squarely in its cylinder bore groove.*

6. Lubricate the piston with brake fluid.

> *NOTE*
> *The piston can be difficult to install because it must compress the dust and piston seals in order to slide past them. When installing the piston in Step 7, turn it into the bore. Do not try to push the piston straight in. Once the piston is installed past both seals, push it all the way into its bore.*

7. Install the piston into the cylinder bore with its metal or open side facing out. Push the piston in all the way. See **Figure 92** (1992-1994) or **Figure 93** (1995-on).

> *CAUTION*
> *Silicone brake grease is not the same type of lubricant as a silicone sealant (RTV) used on engine gaskets. Silicone brake grease is a high temperature, water-resistant grease. Make sure the lubricant used in Step 8 is specified for brake use. For example, Permatex Ultra Disc Brake Caliper Lube (part No. 20356).*

8. Install the large friction boot into the caliper housing. See A, **Figure 88**, typical.
9. Install the small friction boot into the caliper mounting bracket. See B, **Figure 88**, typical.
10. Lubricate the inside of each friction boot and mating caliper and bracket shafts with silicone brake grease. See C, **Figure 88**, typical.
11. Install the caliper housing onto the caliper support bracket. See **Figure 84** (1992-1994) or **Figure 85** (1994-on).
12. Install the pad retainer onto the caliper support bracket.
13. Install the pad spring onto the caliper housing.
14. Install the brake caliper assembly and brake pads as described in this chapter.

REAR MASTER CYLINDER

Read the information listed under *Disc Brake* in this chapter before servicing the rear master cylinder.

Refer to **Figure 94** when servicing the rear master cylinder in this section.

Removal/Installation

1. Support the bike on a workstand.

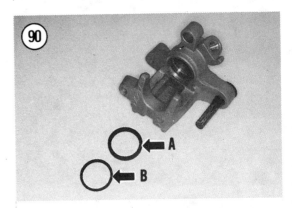

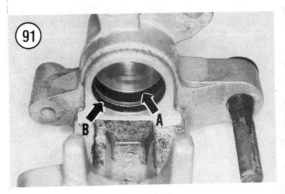

CAUTION
Wipe up any spilled brake fluid immediately, as it will stain or destroy the finish of most plastic and metal surfaces. Use soapy water and rinse thoroughly.

2. Drain the rear master cylinder reservoir as described in this chapter.

3. Unbolt and remove the master cylinder cover .

4. Remove the rear master cylinder reservoir mounting bolt (A, **Figure 95**).

5. Remove the rear brake pedal (B, **Figure 95**) mounting or pivot bolt, then disconnect the brake pedal return spring.

6. Remove the cotter pin, washer and clevis pin that connects the master cylinder to the rear brake pedal (**Figure 94**). Discard the cotter pin.

7. Remove the banjo bolt (C, **Figure 95**) and both washers. Seal the brake hose to prevent brake fluid from dripping out.

8. Remove the master cylinder mounting screws (D, **Figure 95**), then remove the master cylinder and reservoir from the frame. See **Figure 96**.

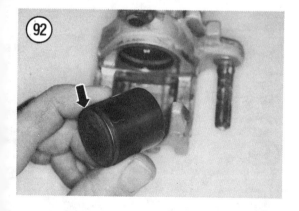

9. If brake fluid is leaking from the cylinder bore or if other service is necessary, overhaul the master cylinder as described in this chapter.

10. Install the master cylinder onto the frame while routing the reservoir beside the frame. Install the master cylinder and reservoir mounting bolts finger-tight.

11. Tighten the rear master cylinder mounting bolts (D, **Figure 95**) securely.

12. Tighten the reservoir mounting bolt (A, **Figure 95**) securely.

13. Secure the brake hose to the master cylinder with the banjo bolt and two new washers. Install a washer on each side of the brake hose (C, **Figure 95**). Route the end of the hose so it sits against the raised tab on top of the master cylinder, then tighten the banjo bolt as specified in **Table 2**.

CAUTION
Make sure the brake hose does not contact the rear shock absorber or any other moving suspension parts.

14. Connect the brake pedal to the master cylinder pushrod with the clevis pin, washer and a *new* cotter pin. Install the clevis pin from the outside. Spread the cotter pin ends to lock it.

15. Refill the master cylinder with brake fluid and bleed the brake as described in this chapter.

16. Check the rear brake pedal adjustment (Chapter Three).

WARNING
Do not ride the bike until the rear brake is working properly.

Disassembly

Refer to **Figure 94** for this procedure.

1. Remove the master cylinder as described in this chapter.

2. Remove the reservoir from the master cylinder (**Figure 96**) as follows:

   a. Remove the circlip (**Figure 97**) and pull the hose out of the master cylinder.

   b. Remove the O-ring (**Figure 98**) from the master cylinder.

3. Loosen the locknut (A, **Figure 99**), then remove the clevis (B, **Figure 99**) and locknut from the pushrod.

14

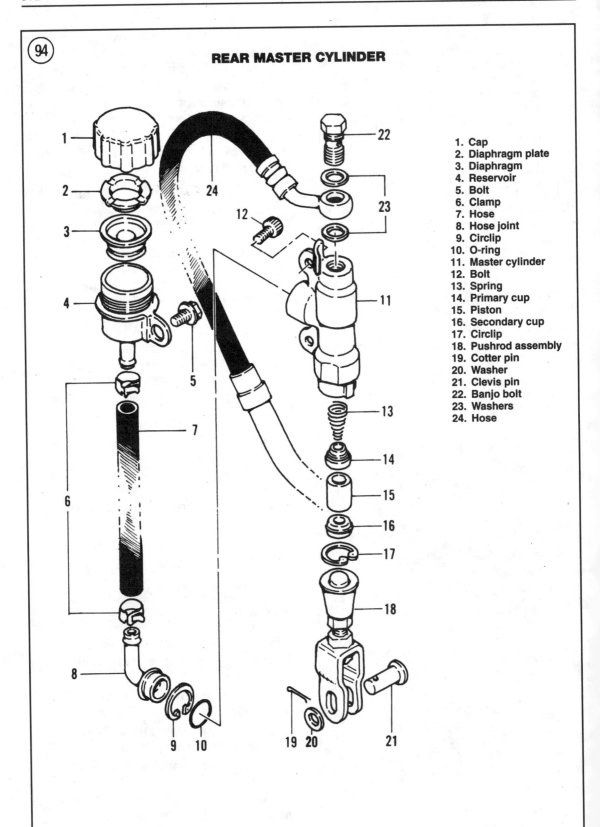

REAR MASTER CYLINDER

1. Cap
2. Diaphragm plate
3. Diaphragm
4. Reservoir
5. Bolt
6. Clamp
7. Hose
8. Hose joint
9. Circlip
10. O-ring
11. Master cylinder
12. Bolt
13. Spring
14. Primary cup
15. Piston
16. Secondary cup
17. Circlip
18. Pushrod assembly
19. Cotter pin
20. Washer
21. Clevis pin
22. Banjo bolt
23. Washers
24. Hose

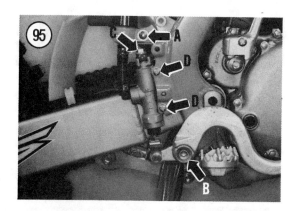

NOTE

*Secure the master cylinder in a vise using a bolt and nut as shown in **Figure 100**. Position the master cylinder so the piston bore faces up.*

4. Remove the dust cover (**Figure 101**) from the master cylinder.

5. Compress the piston, then remove the circlip (**Figure 102**) from the groove in the master cylinder. Use circlip pliers to remove the circlip.

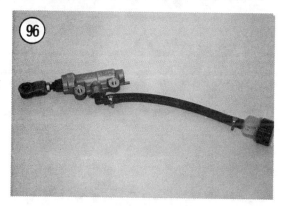

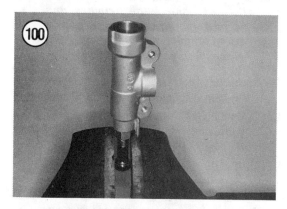

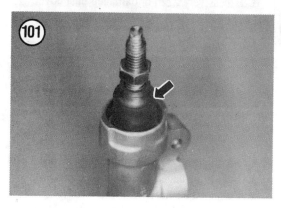

14

6. Remove the pushrod (**Figure 103**) and piston assembly (**Figure 104**) from the master cylinder bore.

Inspection

Replace parts that show excessive wear or damage as described in this section.

> *CAUTION*
> *Do not get any oil or grease onto any of the master cylinder components. These chemicals will cause the rubber parts in the brake system to swell, causing brake drag and other problems.*

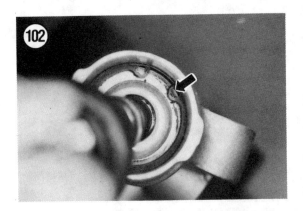

1. Clean and dry the master cylinder housing and the other metal parts. Clean parts with new brake fluid, then place on a clean lint-free cloth until reassembly.

2. **Figure 105** identifies the piston assembly:
   a. Spring.
   b. Primary cup.
   c. Secondary cup.
   d. Piston.

> *CAUTION*
> *Do not remove the primary and secondary cups from the piston assembly. If the cups are damaged, you must replace the piston assembly.*

3. Check the piston assembly (**Figure 105**) for:
   a. Broken, distorted or collapsed piston return spring (A, **Figure 105**).
   b. Worn, cracked, damaged or swollen primary (B, **Figure 105**) and secondary cups (C, **Figure 105**).
   c. Scratched, scored or damaged piston (D, **Figure 105**).
   d. Excessively worn or damaged dust cover.

If any of these parts are worn or damaged, replace the piston assembly.

> *NOTE*
> *If the master cylinder was leaking brake fluid, the pushrod assembly (**Figure 106**) may be excessively corroded. If this is the case, inspect the pushrod and all of its metal parts carefully.*

4. Check the pushrod assembly (**Figure 106**) for:
   a. Bent or damaged clevis (A, **Figure 106**).
   b. Damaged pushrod (B, **Figure 106**).

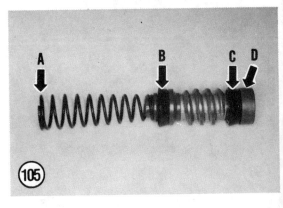

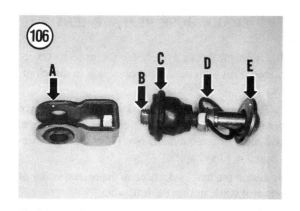

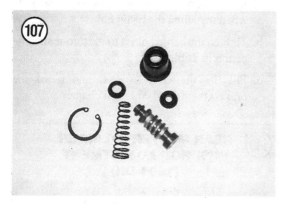

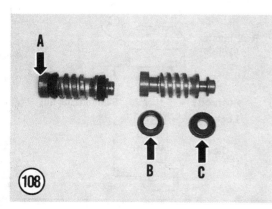

c. Cracked or swollen dust cover (C, **Figure 106**).

d. Corroded, bent or damaged circlip (D, **Figure 106**).

e. Damaged washer (E, **Figure 106**).

> *NOTE*
> *A factory piston kit will include the piston, both cups and spring. The circlip and dust cover must be purchased separately. See **Figure 107**.*

5. To assemble a new piston assembly, perform the following:

    a. When you replace the piston, you must install the new primary and secondary cups (**Figure 108**) onto the piston.

    b. Use the original piston assembly (A, **Figure 108**) as a reference when installing the new cups onto the piston.

    c. Before installing the new piston cups, soak them in brake fluid for approximately 15 minutes. This will soften them and ease installation. Clean the new piston in brake fluid.

    d. Install the secondary (B, **Figure 108**) and then the primary (C, **Figure 108**) cups onto the piston. See **Figure 109**.

6. Inspect the master cylinder bore. Replace the master cylinder if the bore is corroded, scored or damaged in any way. Do not hone the master cylinder bore to remove scratches or other damage.

7. Check for plugged supply and relief ports in the master cylinder. Clean with compressed air.

8. Flush the master cylinder and its reservoir hose with new brake fluid. Set aside until reassembly.

9. Replace the reservoir hose O-ring if it is excessively worn, deteriorated or damaged.

10. Check the reservoir cap and diaphragm for damage.

14

Assembly

1. Clean all of the components before reassembly.

2. If you are installing a new piston assembly, assemble it as described under *Inspection* in this section.

3. Lubricate the piston assembly and cylinder bore with brake fluid.

4. Install the spring (small end first) onto the piston as shown in A, **Figure 105**.

CAUTION

Do not allow the piston cups to tear or turn inside out when you install the piston into the master cylinder bore. Both cups are larger than the bore. To ease installation, lubricate the cups and piston with brake fluid

5. Insert the piston assembly (spring end first) into the master cylinder bore (**Figure 104**).

6. Compress the piston assembly and install the pushrod, washer and circlip (**Figure 103**). Install the circlip with its flat side facing out. See **Figure 102**.

NOTE

The circlip must seat in the groove completely (Figure 102). Push and release the pushrod a few times to make sure it moves smoothly and that the circlip does not pop out.

7. Slide the dust cover over the pushrod and seat it against the circlip (**Figure 101**).

8. Install the locknut (A, **Figure 99**) and clevis (B, **Figure 99**) onto the pushrod. Note the following:

   a. On 1992-1993 models, tighten the locknut. Adjust the rear brake after installing the rear master cylinder onto the bike. Refer to Chapter Three.

   b. On 1994 and later models, adjust the position of the clevis to the dimension shown in **Figure 110**. Tighten the locknut securely.

9. Connect the reservoir hose to the master cylinder as follows:

   a. Lubricate the brake hose O-ring with brake fluid, then install it into the master cylinder (**Figure 98**).

   b. Install the brake hose into the master cylinder, then turn it so its upper end faces toward the top of the master cylinder (**Figure 96**).

   c. Install the circlip (flat edge facing up) into the groove in the master cylinder (**Figure 97**). Make sure the circlip seats in the groove completely.

10. Install the master cylinder as described in this chapter.

11. Adjust the rear brake as described in Chapter Three.

BRAKE HOSE REPLACEMENT

1. Drain the brake system for the hose to be replaced. Refer to *Draining Brake Fluid* in this chapter.

2. Remove the banjo bolts and washers for the brake hose to be replaced. To replace the rear brake hose, you must first remove the rear brake caliper as described in this chapter.

3. Install the new brake hose in the reverse order of removal while noting the following.

   a. Install new sealing washers (**Figure 111**) when installing the banjo bolt(s).

   b. Tighten the banjo bolt(s) to the torque specification in **Table 2**.

   c. Fill the master cylinder(s) and bleed the brake(s) as described in this chapter.

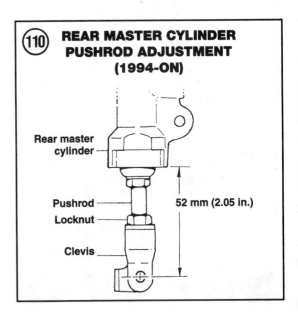

(110) **REAR MASTER CYLINDER PUSHROD ADJUSTMENT (1994-ON)**

Rear master cylinder

Pushrod

Locknut

Clevis

52 mm (2.05 in.)

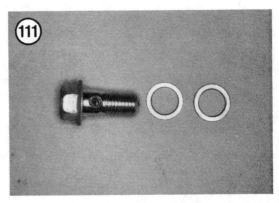

(111)

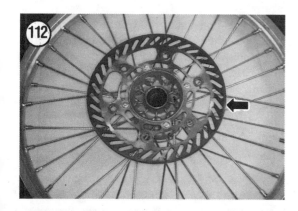

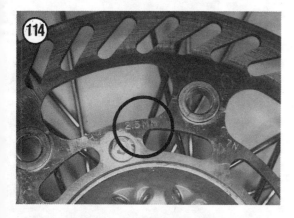

d. Operate the brake lever or brake pedal while observing the brake hose connections. Check for a loose connection or other damage.

> *WARNING*
> *Do not ride the bike until you are sure that both brakes are operating properly.*

BRAKE DISC

The brake discs are separate from the wheel hubs and can be removed once the wheel is removed from the bike. See **Figure 112** (front) and **Figure 113** (rear).

Inspection

You can inspect the brake disc with it mounted on the bike. Small marks on the disc are not important, but radial scratches deep enough to snag a fingernail can reduce braking effectiveness and increase brake pad wear. If these grooves are evident, and the brake pads are wearing rapidly, replace the brake disc.

See **Table 1** for standard and service limit specifications for the brake discs. Kawasaki also stamps the minimum thickness dimension on the outside of each disc (**Figure 114**).

When servicing the brake discs, do not grind a disc to compensate for warpage. The discs are thin and grinding will reduce their thickness, causing them to warp quite rapidly. A warped disc will cause the brake pads to drag and overheat the disc.

1. Support the bike on a workstand.

2. Measure the thickness around the disc at several locations with a micrometer (**Figure 115**). Replace the disc if its thickness at any point is less than the service limit in **Table 1**, or less than the dimension stamped on the disc (**Figure 114**).

3. Clean the disc of any rust or corrosion and wipe clean with lacquer thinner. Never use an oil-based solvent that may leave an oil residue on the disc.

14

Removal/Installation

1. Remove the wheel as described in Chapter Eleven.

2. Remove the nuts and bolts securing the brake disc to the wheel hub. Remove the brake disc.

3. Inspect the brake disc flanges on the hub for cracks or other damage. Replace the hub if damage of this type is found.

4. Install the brake disc onto the hub with the side of the disc marked DRIVE facing out.

5. Tighten the brake disc mounting bolts to the torque specification in **Table 2**.

6. Install the wheel as described in Chapter Ten.

DRAINING BRAKE FLUID

Before loosening a banjo bolt to service the brake system, drain as much brake fluid from the system as possible. This will help you service the brake system without having to deal with a large amount of leaking brake fluid.

To drain the front or rear brake system, you will need an empty bottle, a length of clear hose that fits tightly onto the caliper bleed screw and an 8 mm wrench (**Figure 116**). You can also use a vacuum pump like the Mityvac (**Figure 117**).

1A. Connect the hose onto the brake caliper's bleed screw (**Figure 118**). Insert the other end of the hose into a clean bottle. Pour some new brake fluid into the bottle until it covers the end of the hose.

1B. When using a vacuum pump, assemble it and then mount it onto the caliper's bleed screw (**Figure 119**).

2A. Loosen the bleed screw with a wrench (**Figure 120**) and pump the brake lever or brake pedal to drain the brake system. Continue until the brake fluid stops flowing out of the caliper.

2B. Operate the vacuum pump handle to create a vacuum, then open the bleed screw with a wrench to drain the system.

3. Close the bleed screw and remove the hose or vacuum pump.

4. Discard the brake fluid captured in the bottom or vacuum pump reservoir.

BRAKE BLEEDING

Whenever air enters the brake system, you must bleed the system to remove the air. Air can enter the system when the brake fluid level drops too low, after flushing the system or when a banjo bolt or brake hose is loosened or removed. Air in the brake system will increase lever or pedal travel while causing it to feel spongy and less responsive. Under excessive conditions, it can cause complete loss of the brake.

You can bleed the brakes manually or with the use of a vacuum pump. Both methods are described in this section.

When adding brake fluid during the bleeding process, use the DOT (Department of Transportation) approved brake fluid as listed under *Brake Fluid Selection* in this chapter. Do not reuse brake fluid drained from the system or use a silicone based brake fluid. Brake fluid is very harmful to most surfaces, so wipe up any spills immediately with soap and water.

NOTE
When bleeding the brakes, check the fluid level in the master cylinder

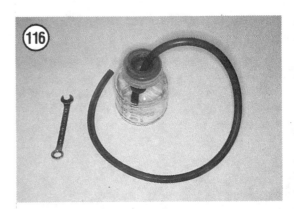

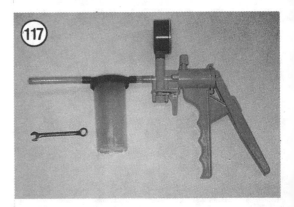

frequently. If the reservoir runs dry, air will enter the system and you must start over.

Manual Bleeding

This procedure describes how to bleed the brake system with an empty bottle, length of clear hose that fits tightly onto the caliper bleed screw and an 8 mm wrench (**Figure 116**).

1. Check that both brake system banjo bolts are tight.

2. Flip off the dust cap from the brake bleed valve and clean the valve and its opening of all dirt and other debris. If a dust cap was not used, use a thin screwdriver or similar tool and compressed air to remove all dirt from inside the bleed valve opening.

> *CAUTION*
> *Dirt left inside the bleed valve opening can be sucked into the brake system. This could plug the brake hose and contaminate the brake fluid. Dirt that makes its way into the caliper can cause wear to the caliper piston, bore and seals.*

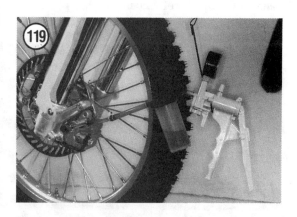

3. Connect the clear hose to the bleeder valve on the caliper (**Figure 120**). Place the other end of the hose into a clean container. Fill the container with enough new brake fluid to keep the end submerged. Loop the hose higher than the bleeder valve to prevent air from being drawn into the caliper during bleeding (**Figure 118**).

> *CAUTION*
> *Cover all parts which could become contaminated by the accidental spilling of brake fluid. Wash any spilled brake fluid from any surface immediately, as it will destroy the finish. Use soapy water and rinse completely.*

4. Clean the top of the front master cylinder or the rear reservoir cap of all dirt and foreign matter. Remove the cap and diaphragm. Fill the reservoir to about 10 mm (3/8 in.) from the top.

5. Apply the brake lever or brake pedal, then open the bleeder valve. This will force air and brake fluid from the brake system. Close the bleeder valve before the brake lever or pedal reaches its maximum limit or before brake fluid stops flowing from the bleeder screw. Do not release the brake lever or pedal while the bleeder valve is open.

> *NOTE*
> *As the brake fluid enters the system, the level will drop in the master cylinder reservoir. Maintain the level at 10 mm (3/8 in.) from the top of the reservoir to prevent air from being drawn into the system.*

6. Repeat Step 5 until the brake fluid exiting the system is clear, with no air bubbles. If the system is difficult to bleed, tap the master cylinder and caliper housing with a soft faced mallet to release air bubbles trapped in the system.

> *NOTE*
> *If the brake lever or pedal feel firm, indicating that air has been bled from the system, but there are still air bubbles visible in the hose connected to the bleed valve, air is probably entering the hose from its connection around the bleed valve.*

7. The system is bled when the brake lever or pedal feels firm, and there are no air bubbles exiting the system. Make sure the bleeder screw is tight and

14

remove the bleed hose. If the lever or pedal feels spongy, air is still trapped in the system and you must continue the bleeding procedure.

8. If necessary, add brake fluid to correct the level in the master cylinder reservoir. It must be above the level line.

> *WARNING*
> *Before riding the bike, make sure both brakes are working properly.*

Pressure Bleeding

This procedure describes how to bleed the brake system with a vacuum pump like the Mityvac pump shown in **Figure 117**.

1. Check that both brake system banjo bolts are tight.

2. Flip off the dust cap from the brake bleed valve and clean the valve and its opening of all dirt and other debris. If a dust cap was not used, use a thin screwdriver or similar tool and compressed air to remove all dirt from inside the bleed valve opening.

> *CAUTION*
> *Dirt left inside the bleed valve opening can be sucked into the brake system. This could plug the brake hose and contaminate the brake fluid. Dirt that makes its way into the caliper can cause wear to the caliper piston, bore and seals.*

> *CAUTION*
> *Cover all parts which could become contaminated by the accidental spilling of brake fluid. Wash any spilled brake fluid from any surface immediately, as it will destroy the finish. Use soapy water and rinse completely.*

3. Clean the top of the front master cylinder or the rear reservoir cap of all dirt and foreign matter. Remove the cap and diaphragm. Fill the reservoir to about 10 mm (3/8 in.) from the top.

4. Assemble the vacuum tool by following the manufacturer's instructions.

5. Attach the vacuum pump's hose to the bleeder valve (**Figure 119**).

> *NOTE*
> *When bleeding the front brake, suspend the vacuum pump with a piece of wire (**Figure 119**). This will allow you to*

release the pump (without it disconnecting from the bleed valve) when checking and adding brake fluid to the master cylinder reservoir.

> *NOTE*
> *When using a vacuum pump in the following steps, the brake fluid level in the master cylinder will drop quite rapidly. This is especially true for the rear reservoir because it does not hold as much brake fluid as the front reservoir. Stop often and check the brake fluid level. Maintain the level at 10 mm (3.8 in.) from the top of the reservoir to prevent air from being drawn into the system.*

6. Operate the pump handle a few times to create a vacuum, then open the bleeder valve with a wrench (**Figure 120**). Doing so forces air and brake fluid from the system. Close the bleeder valve before the brake fluid stops flowing from the bleeder or before the master cylinder reservoir runs empty. If the vacuum pump is equipped with a vacuum gauge, close the bleeder valve before the vacuum reading on the gauge reaches 0 HG of vacuum.

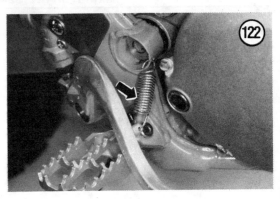

7. Repeat Step 6 until the brake fluid exiting the system is clear, with no air bubbles. If the system is difficult to bleed, tap the master cylinder and caliper housing with a soft-faced mallet to release air bubbles trapped in the system.

8. The system is bled when the brake lever or pedal feels firm and there are no air bubbles exiting the system. Make sure the bleeder screw is tight and remove the hose. If the lever or pedal feels spongy, air is still trapped in the system and you must continue the bleeding procedure.

9. If necessary, add fluid to correct the level in the master cylinder reservoir. It must be above the level line.

WARNING
Before riding the bike, make sure both brakes are working properly.

REAR BRAKE PEDAL

Removal/Installation

1. Remove the rear brake pedal mounting bolt (1992-1997) or pivot bolt (1998). See A, **Figure 121**, typical.

2. Disconnect the return spring (**Figure 122**) at the brake pedal.

3. Remove the cotter pin, washer and clevis pin (A, **Figure 121**), then remove the rear brake pedal.

4. Clean and dry the brake pedal parts.

5. On 1995 and later models, replace the brake pedal O-rings if damaged.

6. Inspect the brake pedal and replace if damaged.

7. On 1998 models, inspect the pivot bolt and replace if damaged.

8. Reverse the preceding steps to install the brake pedal, plus the following.

9. Lubricate the O-rings (1995-on) and the pivot shaft or bolt with a waterproof grease.

10. Install a new cotter pin. Bend over the ends of the cotter pin to lock it.

11. Tighten the rear brake pedal mounting bolt (A, **Figure 121**) as specified in **Table 2**. Operate the rear brake pedal, making sure it pivots and returns correctly.

Table 1 BRAKE SERVICE SPECIFICATIONS

	New mm (in.)	Service limit mm (in.)
Brake disc thickness		
Front	2.85-3.15 (0.11-0.12)	2.5 (0.09)
Rear	4.35-4.65 (0.17-0.18)	3.8 (0.14)
Brake pad thickness		
Front	4.2 (0.16)	1.0 (0.039)
Rear	4.7 (0.18)	1.0 (0.039)

14

Table 2 BRAKE TIGHTENING TORQUES

	N•m	in.-lb.	ft.-lb.
Banjo bolts	25	–	18
Brake disc mounting bolts			
Front and rear	9.8	87	–
Front brake caliper			
Brake caliper mounting bolts	25	–	18
Brake pad mounting bolt(s)	18	–	13
Front master cylinder			
Clamp bolts (at handlebar)	8.8	78	–
Rear brake caliper			
Brake pad mounting bolt(s)	18	–	13
Brake caliper mounting bolt			
1992-1994	25	–	18
1995-on	*		
Mounting bracket pivot bolt			
1992-1994	**		
1995-on	27	–	20
Rear brake pedal			
1992-1997	8.8	78	–
1998	25	–	19

*Not used on these models
**Pivot bolt is not removeable on these models

CHAPTER FIFTEEN

BODY

This chapter describes service procedures for the seat, side panels and subframe.

Table 1 is at the end of the chapter.

SEAT

Removal/Installation

1. Remove the two seat bolts and remove the seat (A, **Figure 1**).

2. To install the seat, align the hook on the seat with the fuel tank mounting screw while aligning the seat prongs with the subframe tabs.

3. Lift up on the front of the seat (A, **Figure 1**) to make sure it is locked in place.

4. Install the seat bolts and tighten securely.

SIDE COVERS

Removal/Installation

1. Remove the seat as described in this chapter.

2. Remove the side cover mounting bolts and remove the side cover (B, **Figure 1**).

3. Reverse the preceding steps to install the side covers.

RADIATOR COVERS

Removal/Installation

1. Remove the seat.

2. Remove the radiator cover mounting bolts and remove the covers (**Figure 2**).

3. Reverse the preceding steps to install the radiator covers.

SUBFRAME

Removal/Installation

1. Support the bike on a workstand so the rear wheel clears the ground.

2. Remove the seat and side panels as described in this chapter.

3. On 1998 models, disconnect the igniter electrical connectors (**Figure 3**). Remove the wiring harness from around the subframe.

4. Loosen the rear carburetor hose clamp (**Figure 4**).

5. Unbolt and remove the silencer (A, **Figure 5**).

6. Unbolt and remove the subframe assembly (B, **Figure 5**).

7. Reverse the preceding steps to install the subframe, plus the following.

8. Install and tighten the subframe bolts finger-tight.

9. Recheck the silencer-to-exhaust pipe and air boot-to-carburetor connections.

10. Tighten the subframe mounting bolts as specified in **Table 1**.

11. Tighten the air boot hose clamp securely.

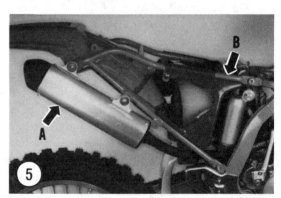

Table 1 TIGHTENING TORQUES

	N•m	ft.-lb.
Subframe mounting bolts		
1992-1993	26	19.5
1994-on	29	22

INDEX

16

16

16

KX250 (1992-1994)

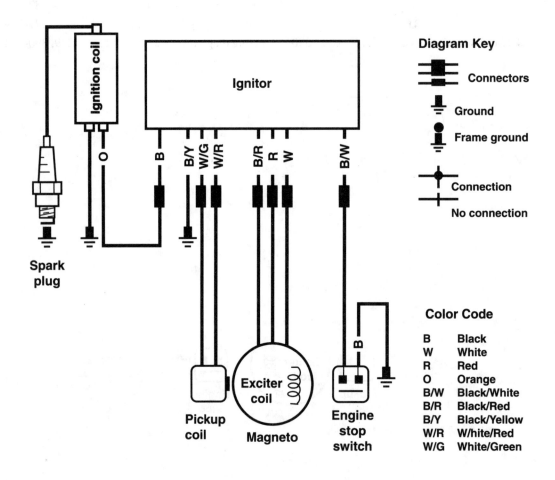

KX250 (1995-1997)

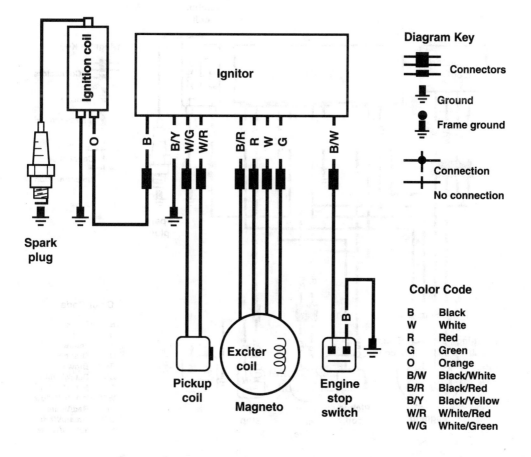

Diagram Key

Connectors

Ground

Frame ground

Connection

No connection

Spark plug

Pickup coil

Exciter coil

Magneto

Engine stop switch

Color Code

B	Black
W	White
R	Red
G	Green
O	Orange
B/W	Black/White
B/R	Black/Red
B/Y	Black/Yellow
W/R	W/hite/Red
W/G	White/Green

KX250 (1998)

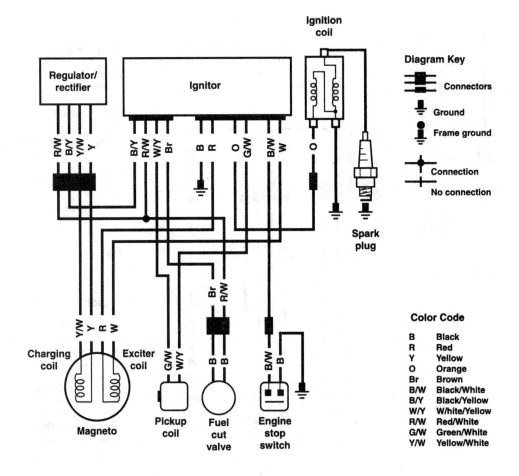

NOTES

NOTES

NOTES

NOTES

NOTES

MAINTENANCE LOG

Service Performed	Mileage Reading				
Oil change (example)	2,836	5,782	8,601		